CRIME AND JUSTICE AT THE MILLENNIUM
Essays by and in Honor of Marvin E. Wolfgang

CRIME AND JUSTICE AT THE MILLENNIUM
Essays by and in Honor of Marvin E. Wolfgang

edited by

Robert A. Silverman
Queen's University, Canada

Terence P. Thornberry
University at Albany, U.S.A.

Bernard Cohen
Queens College, U.S.A.

Barry Krisberg
San Francisco, U.S.A.

KLUWER ACADEMIC PUBLISHERS
Boston / Dordrecht / London

Distributors for North, Central and South America:
Kluwer Academic Publishers
101 Philip Drive
Assinippi Park
Norwell, Massachusetts 02061 USA
Telephone (781) 871-6600
Fax (781) 681-9045
E-Mail <kluwer@wkap.com>

Distributors for all other countries:
Kluwer Academic Publishers Group
Distribution Centre
Post Office Box 322
3300 AH Dordrecht, THE NETHERLANDS
Telephone 31 78 6392 392
Fax 31 78 6546 474
E-Mail <services@wkap.nl>

 Electronic Services <http://www.wkap.nl>

Library of Congress Cataloging-in-Publication Data

Crime and justice at the millennium: essays by and in honor of Marvin E. Wolfgang/
edited by Robert A. Silverman ... [et al.].
   p. cm.
  Includes bibliographical references and index.
  ISBN 0-7923-7592-0 (alk. paper)
  1. Wolfgang, Marvin E., 1924- 2. Crime. 3. Criminology. 4. Criminal justice,
Administration of. I. Wolfgang, Marvin E., 1924- II Silverman, Robert A., 1943-

HV6025. C69 2001
364—dc21

                                       2001050334

Printed on acid-free paper.   Printed in the United States of America

Crime and Justice at the Millennium: Essays by and in Honor of Marvin E. Wolfgang

I. Introduction

II. Crime and Justice at the Millennium

A. The Criminal in Society

1. Patterns of Violent Behavior

C.   The Criminal Under Restraint

1. Prisons

III.   In His Own Voice: Selected Essays by Marvin E. Wolfgang

INTRODUCTION

Ira Lipman

Marvin Wolfgang was the greatest criminologist in the United States of America in the last half of the 20th century, if not the entire century. We first met on March 3, 1977, in Philadelphia. I sought him out after his work with Edwin Newman's *NBC Reports: Violence in America.*

He was a tender, loving, caring individual who loved excellence—whether it be an intellectual challenge, the arts or any other pursuit. It is a great privilege to take part in honoring Marvin Wolfgang, a great American.

Our approaches to the subject of crime came from different perspectives—one as a researcher and the other as the founder of one of the world's largest security services companies. We both wanted to understand the causes of crime, and our discussions began a more than 21-year friendship, based on mutual respect and shared values.

Dr. Wolfgang's scholarship aimed for the goal of promoting a safer, more prosperous society, one in which economic opportunity replaced criminal enterprise. He never saw crime in isolation but as part of a complex web of social relations. Only by understanding the causes and patterns of crime can society find ways to prevent it. Only through scholarship can the criminal justice community influence policy makers.

To encourage the innovative scholarship that marked Marvin's career, Guardsmark established the Lipman Criminology Library at the University of Pennsylvania, at his request, and created a national criminology award in his name, the Wolfgang Award for Distinguished Achievement in Criminology. This honor is awarded at the annual American Society of Criminology convention, and, as Wolfgang imagined, it has become known as the "Nobel Prize of Criminology."

The Wolfgang Award recognizes the person whose work most clearly upholds the standards set by Marvin during his outstanding career. In 1993, we presented the first Wolfgang Award to its namesake. In the months before his death in 1998, Marvin chose a committee to recommend his successors for the award. Since then, we have presented this award to criminologists who exemplify the qualities of scholarship and intellect that Marvin possessed.

His celebrity was not limited to the United States. He was a visiting professor at Hebrew University in Jerusalem and the University of Cambridge in England, and he also practiced his profession in Buenos Aires, Paris, Belgrade, Rome, Stockholm and Oslo. In addition, Dr. Wolfgang advised many governments, including those of England, Israel, Italy and China.

Marvin also exerted a worldwide influence through his academic contributions. In 1994, the British *Journal of Criminology* named him "the most influential criminologist in the English-speaking world." During nearly 50 years at the University of Pennsylvania, where he earned his doctorate, Dr. Wolfgang introduced and developed a method of analyzing great amounts of crime data over several years—such as arrest records for a cohort of individuals. These "longitudinal studies" found patterns that helped predict criminal behavior.

Before Marvin Wolfgang, criminology focused on criminal psychology and anecdotal material. Wolfgang's 1958 study, *Patterns of Criminal Homicide,* changed that focus. By analyzing nearly 600 murders in Philadelphia, his research found that more than a quarter of the victims had instigated the violence. *Delinquency in a Birth Cohort,* published in 1972, was his greatest work. This study of 10,000 Philadelphia boys demonstrated that a relatively small number of repeat offenders were responsible for a large percentage of crime—a finding that has influenced legislative bodies and policy makers around the world. As one writer put it, "Much of what everybody really knows about crime came from [Marvin Wolfgang's] research."

At the University of Pennsylvania, Dr. Wolfgang was a professor of criminology and law and director of the Sellin Center for Studies in Criminology and Criminal Law, named for his mentor, Penn criminologist Dr. Thorsten Sellin. Under Marvin's guidance, Penn became the center of criminology studies. More than 100 doctoral students, many of whom are now professors at universities around the world, thrived from his mentoring, which produced a new generation in criminology. Studying with him bestowed a prized credential. An extraordinary teacher, his lessons coupled the substance of his scholarship and high expectations. Students responded with top-level performance.

It is impossible in a limited space to do justice to Dr. Marvin Wolfgang's career and his impact on public policy. He served as president of the American Academy of Political and Social Science and the American Society of Criminology, as a leader of the National Council on Crime and Delinquency for twenty-five years, and as the editor of *The Journal of Criminology and Criminal Law* and *Annals of the American Academy of Political and Social Science.*

Dr. Wolfgang served on several presidential commissions as research director for such topics as Law Enforcement and the Administration of Justice (Johnson administration); Causes and Prevention of Violence (Johnson and Nixon administrations) and Pornography (Nixon administration). His many honors included the Guggenheim Fellowship and the Fulbright Prize; the Dennis Carrol Prize, presented by the International Society for Criminology; the American Society of Criminology's August Vollmer Research Award; and the Roscoe Pound Award, presented by the National Council on Crime and Delinquency for distinguished contributions to the field of criminal justice.

Dr. Wolfgang's interests were varied; his intellectual curiosity ranged across many disciplines, giving a breadth and depth to his scholarship. His research on crime was always grounded in the context of human society and history, in the way people actually lived. Before Dr. Wolfgang, the science of criminology was not widely known. By pioneering interdisciplinary partnerships between sociologists, psychologists, medical professionals, economists, political scientists and statisticians, he elevated criminology into the center of social studies. He was a historian of Renaissance Italy, a giant of American sociology, a philosopher and a public policy analyst.

In addition to his intellectual strengths, Marvin Wolfgang was a charismatic and remarkable presence to those who came in contact with him. Despite the fame, influence and honors, the growth of his beloved students was always foremost. His home and heart were always open to students, present and former. To those of us fortunate enough to know him, he was a man of the highest standards of personal and professional behavior.

Marvin was a gentle, discerning, elegant man, whom we miss terribly. Although most of his life was spent studying violence and crime, Marvin Wolfgang was the quintessential man of peace. While others played to fears about crime, his writings conveyed the need for unity and calm. He exemplified the Gandhian ideal that nonviolent action was the most powerful force for social change.

Perhaps because Marvin had studied society so thoroughly, including its worst elements, he was able to understand human behavior. Instead of producing anger and despair, this understanding of his fellow human beings engendered tolerance, compassion and hope.

The chapters of this publication testify to the greatness of Marvin's legacy through examples of his writing and assessments from those who knew him. It is a tremendous honor to participate in this important project. We hope that readers will gain an insight into what made Marvin Wolfgang such a significant scholar, such a towering intellect and such a warm and endearing friend. His work lives forever.

ESSAYS IN HONOR OF MARVIN E. WOLFGANG: AN OVERVIEW

Terence P. Thornberry
School of Criminal Justice, University at Albany

Bernard E. Cohen
Queens College and the Graduate Center, City University of New York

Robert A. Silverman
Faculty of Arts and Science, Queen's University

Introduction

Marvin E. Wolfgang was an amazingly catholic scholar with a criminological imagination that knew no bounds. He was equally interested in theory development and in detailed empirical investigation. He was as at home with crime in Renaissance Florence as he was with crime in 20th century Philadelphia or China, and he studied both with equal élan. He was concerned with scientific objectivity, but also with informing and influencing public policy on the basis of his science. His scholarly life was animated by an abiding desire to understand what makes offenders tick so as to prevent their criminal behavior. It was equally animated by a concern for victims and a yearning to reduce their suffering. He was interested in all things criminological and refused to let his imagination be channeled into narrow topics.

Given the broad canvas on which he painted, perhaps the most surprising characteristic of his scholarship was its combined novelty and quality. Over a career that spanned the second half of the 20th century, he continuously ventured down new pathways of criminological investigation – patterns of criminal offending, the subculture of violence, the measurement of delinquency, and the study of birth cohorts, to recall a few – and in all of these areas the quality of his work was first rate. Not only did he introduce new areas of inquiry, new theories, and new methodological approaches to criminology, he did so in works that instantly became, and still remain, classics. Amazing!

Like his mentor Thorsten Sellin, Marvin was always "very curious" about new topics. And, like his mentor, he addressed them in the most rigorous and valid scientific ways. Whether he was struggling with a basic research question – how to measure the seriousness of crime – or a highly charged political issue – racial discrimination in the application of the death penalty – his high criteria for scholarship never wavered. He would amass the data, analyze them fully and carefully, and finally, offer only those interpretations strictly consistent with the data.

As Marvin acquired many of these traits from his mentor, so too did he pass them on to a new generation of scholars. Marvin himself was a marvelous mentor to hundreds of students and colleagues. He encouraged all of us to have – and to improve upon – the same standards he demanded of himself. To have insatiable curiosity about one's subject matter. To read and study broadly. To have an historical and comparative outlook so as to put contemporary issues in proper perspective. To engage policy without ever loosening the reins of scientific rigor. To search for new theories and methods. To take teaching seriously and to mentor young scholars. And, above all, to keep in mind that the common purpose of our enterprise is to rehabilitate offenders and assist victims alike in order to create a more just and equitable society. A tall order indeed.

It is not surprising, therefore, that Marvin succeeded at it far better than we – his students and colleagues. But we have tried to follow his lead, however inadequately. And we think it most appropriate to honor his life-long commitment to scholarship and his vast contributions to criminology with a volume of essays by some of his students and colleagues. The resulting Festschrift is divided into two major sections. The first, Crime and Justice at the Millennium, contains essays by Marvin's students and colleagues. The second, In His Own Voice, reprints several of Marvin's own essays to remind us all of what a strong, resonant voice it was, and is. This chapter introduces the first section; a later one by Barry Krisberg introduces the second.

Crime and Justice at the Millennium

In organizing this Festschrift, we simply could not invite all of Marvin's students and colleagues to contribute to it. His reach was so broad that it would have led to a multi-volume publication that was unrealistic and impractical. We therefore asked a smaller group of scholars to contribute to this undertaking. We apologize to those not included here and hope that they understand the dilemma faced by the editors of this volume.

In inviting contributors, we selected scholars working in a diverse set of areas that is reflective of the topics that Marvin dealt with in his own scholarship. We also confess to a slight generational or cohort bias. The editors were Marvin's students during the late 1960s and the list of contributors somewhat overrepresents our classmates and colleagues.

As you will see, the Festschrift does not have a single theme. The essays cover a range of topics from basic theory construction, to patterns of crime, to prison adjustment. This is hardly surprising. Just as Marvin followed his own criminological imagination, he always encouraged his students to follow their own intellectual pathways, not his. Clearly his scholarship and sage counsel were tremendously influential in guiding what we did and how we did it. So, many of these essays are in areas to which Marvin contributed, like studies of homicide and research based on longitudinal designs. Others are in areas in which Marvin had a more passing interest, such as policing or prison adjustment, although many of these studies reflect concepts and tools that he developed. But this is as he would have wanted it.

This section is divided into three major parts: The Criminal in Society, The Criminal in the Arms of the Law, and The Criminal Under Restraint. Many of you will recognize these as the subtitles of his massive three-volume reader in criminology, *Crime and Justice*, co-edited with Sir Leon Radzinowicz. What better way to organize these contributions than by using the same taxonomic principles that Radzinowicz and Wolfgang developed in 1971? They hold up remarkably well.

The Criminal in Society

Patterns of Violent Behavior

We begin our examination of the criminal in society with a section on patterns of violence. A strong theme that runs through and unites Wolfgang's scholarship is a concern with understanding and preventing violent behavior. Violence was never narrowly conceived or defined in his work, however; it ranged from individual acts of criminal violence to riots and collective violence. It was concerned with contemporary and historical violence, with American and comparative violence. The breadth of this concern is reflected in the essays in this section.

In 1967 Marvin Wolfgang, the sociologist, published with his long-time friend and colleague, Franco Ferracuti, the Italian psychiatrist, *The Subculture of Violence*. That book presented a general theory of violent crime that was one of the first systematic efforts to develop an integrated theory of crime. Their theory combined aspects of culture conflict, social disorganization, social learning, and psychiatric approaches to studying crime and violence. In "Subcultures of Violence and Beyond: Theory Integration in Criminology" Charles Wellford and David Soulé assess Wolfgang and Ferracuti's approach to theoretical integration, especially what they called "theoretical fusion." Wellford and Soulé place that approach within the context of current models of theoretical integration. They first distinguish between within-discipline strategies and interdisciplinary strategies and then review several current theories that are exemplars of each approach. In their discussion and conclusion, they point to the continuing vitality of "fusion" as a model for theoretical integration.

In "Political Violence: Patterns and Trends," Austin Turk offers a general theoretical model of the social conditions that lead some political disputes to escalate into political violence and others to de-escalate before violence erupts. Understanding these processes is fundamentally related to an understanding of the interplay between political and social power, on the one hand, and legal power and the enforcement of laws, on the other. Turk's fine-grained model distinguishes among types of political violence – coercive, injurious, and destructive violence – and examines the conditions that lead to them, as well as the consequences that flow from them. Throughout his discussion, Turk grounds his discussion in examples of contemporary political conflicts.

Interest in intimate partner violence is a relatively recent phenomenon in criminological research. It is rare to find Wolfgang's name associated with this stream of research or theory. In his chapter, "Intimate Partner Violence: The Legacy of Marvin Wolfgang's Thinking", Albert Cardarelli shows that Wolfgang's interests were sufficiently broad to incorporate most areas of research on family and intimate partner violence, however. Wolfgang's early interest in victim-offender relationships, which is first seen in *Patterns in Criminal Homicide*, is embedded in most of the subsequent work involving intimate violence. Certainly, there has been a culture shift since Wolfgang's 1958 work, and, of course, there have been a myriad of policy changes regarding intimate violence, but the basic concepts (and many of the original findings) presented in those early works are still valid for contemporary research and theory in this area.

Patterns in Criminal Homicide has served as a model for much research on violence in general and homicide in particular. Landau used it when he first explored "Ethnic Patterns of Homicide in Israel" with I. Drapkin. In his chapter included here "Social Stress and Violence in Israel: A Macro Level Analysis", Simha Landau examines the relationship between social stress and violence in Israel. Given its size and brief history, Israel has proven to be a natural laboratory for sociologists and criminologists. In this case, added to normal society stresses, Israel is consumed by its continuous concern for security. Using data on robbery and homicide, Landau examines a stress-support model that he generated in an earlier work. Stress and support are seen as two parts of the same theoretical model, a model that proves to be quite useful in examining stress and violence in Israeli society.

Elmar Weitekamp and Kerstin Reich combine the themes of some of the earlier chapters by examining involvement in violence from a comparative perspective and by using the subculture of violence theory as the guiding conceptual model. Their essay "Violence among Russian-Germans in the Context of the Subculture of Violence Theory" focuses on the formation of violent subcultures in contemporary Germany, especially among the "Aussiedler", recent immigrants from Russia whose families originally came from Germany. Their analysis traces the history of this group, describes their current status in German society, and examines how traditional cultures and current government policy can shape the behavior of these youth. Their cogent analysis reminds us of the continuing relevance of Sellin's culture conflict theory and Wolfgang and Ferracuti's subculture of violence thesis. Their chapter also raises profound questions about the criminological consequences of globalization and the proper role of government immigration policy.

Criminal Homicide

Wolfgang's doctoral dissertation, conducted under the guidance of Thorsten Sellin, focused on a detailed empirical description of 588 homicide cases in Philadelphia. His dissertation was subsequently published, in 1958, as *Patterns in Criminal Homicide*. That study began Wolfgang's life-long interest in homicide, an interest that influenced many of his students and colleagues, as reflected in the essays by Marc Riedel and by Satyanshu Mukherjee.

When *Patterns in Criminal Homicide* was published in 1958 the clearance rate for homicide in the United States was about 92%. That is, very few homicides were "unsolved". As we enter the 21st century, the clearance rate is less than 70% and it was as low as 65% in the mid-1990s. It is no wonder that Wolfgang devoted a scant 10 pages to the topic of homicide clearance while some of his students have made it a major research focus. Marc Riedel is one of those and in this volume presents a thorough analysis of homicide arrest clearance rates for Los Angeles. In "Arrest Clearances for Homicide: A Study of Los Angeles" Riedel presents both the literature and his findings on the relationship between a number of variables (e.g., gender, race, age, gun use, the presence of another felony, stranger involvement) and the clearance of a homicide event. Lagging the dependent variable for up to three months, Riedel is able to confirm some findings from previous research while challenging others. Finally, he decries certain policies that thwart greater precision in clearance analysis.

One of the hallmarks of Marvin Wolfgang's research was a focus on a detailed empirical description of the phenomenon under investigation. That same care and respect for the data are seen in Satyanshu Mukherjee's chapter "Trends and Patterns of Homicide in Australia." Mukherjee's chapter covers two major issues. The first is a comparative trend study of Australian homicide in which he both traces levels of homicide over the better part of the 20th century and compares Australian rates to those of the U.S., Canada, and England and Wales.   These data place homicide in comparative perspective and, especially for an American audience, highlight the devastating role that guns play in lethal assaults. The second section focuses on a more detailed portrayal of patterns in Australian homicide over a ten-year period, 1989-1999. Mukjerhee describes both offenders and victims, paying particular attention to the role of gender and of race in understanding the crime of homicide.

Longitudinal Studies

Marvin Wolfgang is probably best known for his pioneering longitudinal research project on the Philadelphia birth cohort of 1945. The first phase of that project was published in 1972 in *Delinquency in a Birth Cohort*, with Thorsten Sellin and Robert Figlio, and the second phase in 1987 in *From Boy to Man--From Delinquency to Crime*, with Terence Thornberry and Robert Figlio. This study, especially *Delinquency in a Birth Cohort*, is arguably the most influential criminological investigation ever undertaken. It opened the way to increased reliance on longitudinal research and contemporary panel studies of delinquency, to the criminal career paradigm, to developmental and life-course theories of crime, and to revised policies to fight crime. Since then, longitudinal studies have become the design of choice for etiological investigations and for understanding the course and development of antisocial careers. Two chapters represent this style of research.

Alex Piquero and Stephen Buka, in "Investigating Race and Gender Differences in Specialization in Violence," focus on the issue of offense specialization, especially with respect to violent crime. One of the most basic findings of the Philadelphia cohort study was the absence of offense specialization. Juvenile offenders turned out to be quite versatile in their delinquent behavior, an observation that challenged both theories and common observations of the day. That finding has been replicated several times and Piquero and Buka re-examine it using data from the Providence cohort of the National Collaborative Perinatal Project. Tracing the official criminal careers of the nearly 4,000 members of this cohort allows for a detailed investigation of this issue. Piquero and Buka found no discernable tendency for offenders to specialize in violence. Noting the paucity of studies that examined this issue within race and gender groups, the authors next examined this issue for males and females, for whites and non-whites, and for the four race-by-gender groups. Again, they found no evidence of violent specialization in the Providence data. Piquero and Buka end by discussing the implications of these findings for current developmental theories of delinquency and crime.

In their chapter "Carrying Guns and Involvement in Crime" Alan Lizotte, Trudy Bonsell, David McDowall, Marvin Krohn, and Terence Thornberry use data from the Rochester Youth Development Study to examine the relationship between hidden gun carrying and the rate and types of crime committed by adolescent males. By tracing the pattern of gun carrying over time with repeated interviews, the authors investigated whether involvement in self-reported delinquency increases during those time periods when the adolescent also reports carrying a gun. Doing so combines two issues that characterized Wolfgang's own scholarship – longitudinal investigations and a concern for the impact of firearms on crime, especially violent crime. Briefly, these authors found that during time periods when young males carry guns, their involvement in violent crime and selling drugs, but not property crimes, escalates. The chapter closes by discussing several policy implications of these findings.

Victims of Crime

Throughout his life Marvin Wolfgang was concerned with victims, both with their role in the criminal event as seen in his seminal study on victim-precipitated homicide, and in the broader study of victimization and victimology.

When he introduced the concept that a victim could contribute to his or her own victimization, Marvin Wolfgang set the stage for a new area of research concern. There had been few scholars before him who showed any interest at all in the role of the victim (von Hentig being a notable exception). Most readers will know that serious scholarly interest in victimization really did not flourish until the late 1960s. The first International Conference on Victimization took place in 1973 in Jerusalem but Wolfgang's initial contribution to the area predates the conference by almost two decades.

Simon Singer co-authored "Victim Categories of Crime" with Marvin Wolfgang in the late 1970s. Here he revisits that issue and re-examines the major categories, illustrating Wolfgang's insightful and precise work. In his discussion of victims who precipitate crime, Singer convincingly places Wolfgang within an interactionist framework – a theory with which Wolfgang is rarely associated. Later he shows how victims played a role in the generation of Wolfgang's subculture of violence thesis, efforts to measure the seriousness of delinquency, and the birth cohort studies. In effect, Singer shows that many aspects of Wolfgang's contribution to the discipline emanate from or were influenced by an interest in victims of crime. Clearly, taking victims into account enhances our understanding of the criminal event. Wolfgang was among the first contemporary criminologists to appreciate and capitalize on that fact.

The Criminal in the Arms of the Law

This section moves us away from a focus on the causes and patterns of offending to a focus on how the criminal and juvenile justice systems react to offenders. There are three chapters, two on policing and one on the juvenile court.

Policing

According to most criminal justice practitioners and scholars, an initial step in learning how to control police misconduct is to measure various forms of police corruption. "Wrong", assert Carl Klockars, Maria Haberfeld, Sanja Ivkovich, and Aaron Uydess, in their chapter "A Minimum Requirement for Police Corruption." They discuss the problems of measuring police corruption, arguing that it is difficult to examine this abstract concept utilizing quantitative techniques. Instead, the research team examined its conceptual antithesis, police integrity, a concept more manageable and amenable to empirical analysis. Drawing on a sample of 3,235 police officers from thirty different U.S. police agencies, they develop a set of measures characteristic of police integrity, based upon carefully constructed sketches of police misbehavior, reminiscent of the crime scenarios developed by Marvin Wolfgang and Thorsten Sellin in their study on the measurement of delinquency. The system for estimating police integrity by Klockars et al. is extremely flexible and permits comparative ranking of police agencies on a continuum of police honesty. The study also administered the same measure to a sample of 375 university students and compared their scores to those of police officers. The findings lead to conclusions that are both informative and run counter to common sense notions derived from previous research on police corruption. Readers will find this chapter highly evocative and challenging as they emerge with fresh perspectives and insights on how to conduct research on police deviance.

Andre Normandeau's chapter "Community Policing in Canada: An Evaluation for Montreal" adds a comparative perspective on one of the most important contemporary questions in policing: Is community policing an effective law enforcement strategy? Is this approach more potent than traditional methods of policing? According to Normandeau, that depends somewhat on who is queried. He provides a list of "best sellers" on community policing in the United States and Canada from 1975-2000, as well as a concise summary of the main components of community policing in Canada (which includes problem-oriented policing). Normandeau developed a highly innovative questionnaire consisting of some 60 items in 1990 and applied it thereafter, with ongoing revision over a ten-year period, to neighborhoods with community policing and areas with traditional policing strategies. This allows him to determine the extent to which community policing succeeded in Montreal. Among the interesting findings is a comparative analysis of the way police managers, police officers, and civilians working for law enforcement agencies viewed the shift towards community policing. The varying levels of satisfaction towards community policing of these different groups, especially between police managers and line-officers, serve as a guide and perhaps a caution to agencies seeking to introduce this style of policing. Normandeau does not hesitate to offer his final opinion on community policing which should provide insight and direction for police agencies willing to experiment with this relatively recent police stratagem.

Should society abolish the juvenile court and try juveniles as adults? Should the criminal justice system's adjudication and sentencing procedures distinguish juvenile from adult offenders? Barry Krisberg, in his imaginative, informative, and concise chapter "Should the Juvenile Court Survive?" debates this issue as he examines the history of the juvenile court as it was transformed over the decades. He discusses several relevant U. S. Supreme Court decisions and evaluates arguments for and against the juvenile court's retention. He points out that the National Council on Crime and Delinquency, of which he serves as President, was established in 1907 as an advocate for standards for this court, and that Wolfgang, as a long-time board member, was a strong advocate in the Council's ardent campaign against the movement to prosecute juveniles in adult courts. In a perceptive re-analysis of Wolfgang's three major criticisms of current juvenile court procedures, operations, and policies, and a re-evaluation of a two-decades old alert by Wolfgang sounding the alarm for radical reform of the juvenile court, Krisberg argues that, had Wolfgang been alive today, he most certainly would have vigorously opposed the current political firestorm to *eradicate* altogether rather than *reform* the "children's court." Krisberg's thoughtful and tightly-argued retort to Wolfgang's major argument, based upon his classic cohort studies – that a relatively small group of chronic offenders who accounted for the majority of serious crimes were inadequately processed by juvenile court – must be read by everyone interested in the effectiveness, equity, and social justice of current sentencing systems for serious juvenile and adult offenders.

The Criminal Under Restraint

The final section of Part II brings us to essays that address the two most severe forms of punishment in the American criminal justice system – imprisonment and the death penalty.

Prisons

Although very different in research methods and in their conclusions, the two essays on prisons use as their starting point one of Wolfgang's earlier and lesser known articles "Quantitative Analysis of Adjustment to the Prison Community." In the first essay "The Life of Lifers: Wolfgang's Inquiry into the Prison Adjustment of Homicide Offenders", Hans Toch re-examines the topic of prison adjustment with a particular focus on inmates serving life sentences. A better understanding of this group is especially important in contemporary corrections given the shift in recent years to longer and longer sentences. Toch's treatment of the prison adjustment of long-term inmates is sensitive to the various settings or environments offered by different prisons, the harshness of "maxi-maxi" prisons generated by current policies, and the interactional processes that emerge between guards and the guarded. Consistent with his humanistic approach to the study of prisons, Toch argues for a more reasoned and reasonable response to aid the "adjustment" of inmates, especially those who are likely to spend their entire adulthood in confinement.

In "Truth in Sentencing and Prison Infractions" James Collins, Donna Spencer, George Dunteman, and Peter Siegel examine the interplay between two of the major changes in criminal justice during the latter part of the 20th century. One is the shift to mandatory or determinate sentences and the other is the increasing length of prison sentences. In particular they examine the impact that North Carolina's new structured sentencing law had on the corrections process in North Carolina. The study compares the overall involvement in infractions of inmates sentenced under the previous law and those sentenced under structured sentencing. The authors show that both male and female inmates sentenced under structured sentencing had a higher total infraction rate than those sentenced before structured sentencing. The chapter concludes with a discussion of some of the policy implications of the findings and offers several possibilities for correctional administrators to modify their practices in order to affect inmates' behavior while incarcerated.

Capital Punishment

Marvin Wolfgang abhorred the death penalty and was philosophically opposed to the State taking a human life. He spent considerable time investigating the death penalty scientifically to see if such goals of capital punishment as deterrence, fairness, and equity were consistent with the data. Time and again he found capital punishment wanting: there was no evidence that it deterred crime and there was ample evidence that it was applied in a discriminatory fashion. Wolfgang's research in this area formed the empirical infrastructure for a moratorium on the death penalty in the United States imposed, for a period, by the U.S. Supreme Court.

In the final essay in Part II, "The Wolfgang Legacy on the Intersection of Race and the Death Penalty," Ruth-Ellen Grimes traces the history of Wolfgang's pioneering research on race and the death penalty. In collaboration with Anthony Amsterdam of the University of Pennsylvania Law School, Wolfgang undertook one of the most exhaustive investigations of this topic ever conducted. Under the auspices of the National Association for the Advancement of Colored People's Legal Defense Fund, these two scholars used social science data to challenge the constitutionality of the death penalty. Grimes succinctly summarizes the research, its conceptual underpinnings, and its use in various court cases. She also brings this chapter in Wolfgang's intellectual history up to date, indicating how Wolfgang's original research continues to shape the debate on capital punishment and current court cases about it.

The chapter that follows this overview begins this Festschrift with excerpts from an interview that Freda Adler conducted with Marvin as part of the oral history program of the American Society of Criminology. Many readers, while familiar with the scholarship of Marvin Wolfgang, may not know him as an individual. What were his private thoughts, those not directly related to criminological research? What were the personal and professional influences that shaped the work of this brilliant scholar? Adler's contribution, "Reflections on a Scholarly Career: An Interview with Marvin E. Wolfgang", conducted only a few months prior to his death, offers clear and informative insights into these questions. The candid, straightforward, and often anecdotal style in which Marvin describes his most significant academic, professional, and personal experiences captures concisely the essence of Marvin's perspective, philosophy, and shifts in thinking over time. For the first time, we learn that it was not Thorsten Sellin, but another professor who influenced Marvin to delve into homicide and to complete his initial classic, *Patterns in Criminal Homicide,* as well as the influences that inspired him to conduct other classic projects. Marvin also discusses the precise contributions that he and his long-time colleague, Franco Ferracuti, made to *The Subculture of Violence,* the theoretical opus of which Marvin was most proud. In this interview, he discusses his candid opinions and feelings toward his students and the substantial way they influenced him. Near the end of the interview Marvin discusses his last research project, the cohort studies in Wuhan, China, as well as his positions on policy research, theory, cross-cultural global studies, and the future prospects for criminology.

ACKNOWLEDGEMENTS

The completion of a project of this scope acquires many debts along the way. Several people helped the editors in developing this project, working with the contributors, and copy editing and preparing the manuscript for publication. In particular, we would like to express our deep appreciation to Barbara Cohen and Ahuva Jacobs; Lynda Macdonald, Diane Reid, and Victoria McGraw of Queen's University, Pamela K. Porter, Michele Carlton, and Patricia Lambrecht of the University at Albany; Sandi English, Carolyn Haynes, and Lila Booth of the National Council on Crime and Delinquency. Without their constant assistance and professionalism throughout this process, it would not have been successful.

REFLECTIONS ON A SCHOLARLY CAREER:
AN INTERVIEW WITH MARVIN E. WOLFGANG

Freda Adler

Rutgers University, School of Criminal Justice

This interview was conducted as part of the Criminological Oral History Project, co-sponsored by the American Society of Criminology and the Academy of Criminal Justice Sciences

FA: I am Freda Adler. It is November 14, 1997, and I am interviewing Professor Marvin Wolfgang at the University of Pennsylvania. It is a delight to be interviewing Professor Wolfgang. We met about 45 years ago when I was an undergraduate and Professor Wolfgang was an instructor, and then we met again when I returned to graduate school and Professor Wolfgang was my mentor who saw me through and chaired my dissertation. I am honored for you to meet Dr. Wolfgang.

MW: Thank you.

FA: Can we start by my asking you how you became interested enough in criminology to devote your entire career to it?

MW: I've been asked that question on more than a few occasions and I have a consistent answer. When I came to the University of Pennsylvania to do graduate work, I was a young arrogant man, carrying my Phi Beta Kappa, and thought that all the professors that I had were inferior except one, and that one was a gentleman and a scholar. His name was Thorsten Sellin. And I decided after taking one course with him that whatever he is teaching I wanted to teach as well.

FA: I know that those of us who were fortunate enough to be in Professor Sellin's class agree wholeheartedly with you. Your first book was *Patterns in Criminal Homicide*, and of course we know it has become a classic. How did you engage in the research on that topic?

MW: I contacted the head of the homicide squad in Philadelphia. The idea for doing the study of criminal homicides came not from Thorsten but from a former professor, and he suggested that more systematic empirical work was needed. I contacted the homicide squad and obtained access to their files for a five-year period, and read the elaborate files on 588 homicides. It took me several years to do that, because I was teaching full time as an instructor. In those days you were teaching anywhere from 10-12 hours a week which is twice what we teach now. So most of my reading and data collection occurred in the evenings anywhere from 8 o'clock until 2 a.m. More than that, though, I wanted to get an observable impression of the homicide squad and the work that they did. So for three years I rode around with them, not every week but commonly on Friday and Saturday evenings, the period of highest homicide rates. I got to know their work, I came to appreciate them very much. I respected them. They didn't function in an efficient way just because I was present, because I became a part of the woodwork and they forgot all about my being there. And so I respected the way they handled things. Even in those early days, I didn't see one instance of police brutality. At that time there were only 28 members of the homicide squad. It is nearly double that now, I think. I became close to all of them, and when I finished my work I had a little party for them. All 28 of them came, and we had champagne and celebrated.

FA: I am curious: How did they feel about you as they went about their jobs? How did they feel about you being in potentially a very dangerous situation?

MW: They didn't think it was dangerous, nor did I. When I was working with the homicide squad, it was before the days of the high degree of institutional sensitivity to danger. These days I am sure I'd have to sign a waiver of some sort indicating that if anything happened to me the police department would not be held responsible or liable. I never was in any dangerous situation. Even when they made arrests and I was right at their elbow, there was no danger. That's particularly the case, I think, Freda, you know as well as I, with homicide offenders. We are not talking about armed robbers. In those days a higher proportion of homicide offenders were family members, getting into arguments and killing their wives and friends and neighbors. That proportion is lower now. On more than a few occasions an offender would come in the office while I was working, going over files at midnight, and say: I'm giving myself up, I just killed my wife. That is an indication that they were not a dangerous population.

FA: Yes. Although we do hear that those spousal situations can be quite volatile.

MW: Yes, I think more so now than 25, 30 years ago. They are much more volatile.

FA: Well, you continued your work in the area of violence. You conducted empirical and theoretical work in that area. You talked about youth and violence, collective violence, riots, victim compensation in crimes of violence. So we come now to another classic, and that is *The Subculture of Violence*, the book that you did with our dear friend Franco Ferracuti, the medically trained psychologist. Could you tell us about the relationship and the book and how the two of you decided to get together on the project?

MW: Well, Franco Ferracuti and I had been doing research together in Puerto Rico. He had a second home there, as a matter of fact he bought a condominium. Over a 20-year period that we were working together, we did some work on homicide in Puerto Rico. We have altogether collaborated on at least three books. It was my idea, however, and I am going to say this immodestly, to write *The Subculture of Violence.*

The Patterns of Criminal Homicide was a quantitative descriptive study, and there was hardly any theory involved. As I came toward the end of the book I speculated about the high proportion of homicides within certain groups of people, and so I decided to engage in some theory, and that is how Subculture of Violence was born. I came to believe that any of the people who engage in physical violence and that become criminal, do so out of a system of values where the ready resort to use of violence and physical aggression is a common phenomenon. Many grow up with it. The children, as infants and children, are given physical discipline more than psychological deprivation of love or anything of that sort. The child sees the husband and wife or the persons who are their biological reasons for being alive, fighting. They go out into the schools and there's violence, into the street and there's violence, and violence becomes a way of life. There is no sense of guilt about using physical violence. They often engage in aggression and get into arguments which many people in the middle class culture view as trivial reasons for getting into an argument. The fights are mostly with people who also are part of the subculture of violence.

In addition to writing about that theoretically, I set out in the book to explore the development of criminology as well. Ferracuti made a contribution to one chapter and that was on biological aspects of violence. All the other chapters I wrote, and if he were here today I'd be saying the same thing because he knows it. But that was a major contribution from him, because as an MD and as a trained psychologist, and coming from the clinical criminology in the University of Rome, he was much more aware of the literature and the research dealing with the biological aspects of aggression. For that chapter I owe him a great debt.

FA: Well, the book is still used by students of criminology and it certainly remains a classic, and we are all grateful that you wrote that book.

MW: Thank you.

FA: Let us turn to another of your books, and a very interesting project on your part and on Professor Sellin's part. In the 1960s, you began your work with Thorsten on constructing an index of delinquency – the *Sellin-Wolfgang Index*. It is so well-explained in your book *The Measurement of Delinquency*. Can you tell us a bit about how the index was developed and the original way in which it was used?

MW: Originally, Thorsten and I wanted to do something about criminal statistics. Thorsten Sellin had been writing about criminal statistics even at the time shortly after the FBI was formed and the *Uniform Crime Reports* were initiated. So he was deeply involved in that from the beginning, and he taught me. We applied to the Ford Foundation for funds. The Ford Foundation's criminal section at that time was directed by Jackson Toby, a colleague of yours. He was interested in supporting us, but we had to get the word delinquency in somewhere. So the book is called The Measurement of Delinquency but there is very little concern with delinquency as such. It is the measurement of crime. Thorsten and I were both aware and I tried to tell my students the same thing: The way the FBI now counts crime means every crime is given a score of one and they're all treated the same, whereas, particularly in the case of robbery, there is simple robbery and maybe armed robbery, but that is about it. Yet we all know a person can be threatened without any injury, or he can be seriously injured and sent to the hospital. A whole variety of amounts of money can be taken, from ten dollars to thousands; and sometimes robbery is intimidation with a weapon and sometimes not. These are differences in degree of seriousness, and that is what we wanted to capture, and that is why we went to the public first: Approximately a thousand people in Philadelphia, including 300 police officers. Later, after the publication of that, the federal government became interested in our doing a national representative sampling for which we interviewed nearly 60,000 people.

FA: I remember having my students add up the amount of injury, theft and damage to get to that event score. It seems to me that the new system that the FBI has been using is kind of an offshoot of that work.

MW: Well, yes, it is an offshoot but I have yet to convince the FBI to use the psycho-physical scaling, as we call it, in the enumeration of factors to capture the varying degrees of seriousness of the criminal offense. They have always been receptive but they move very slowly. I haven't talked to the current director Freeh about it yet.

FA: Let us talk about something that is kind of near and dear to me. As a former student in the 1960s I remember well the work of the Criminology Center, now the Sellin Center, on the birth cohort study. It was really the very beginning of criminal career research. I wonder whether you realized then how highly significant the study of delinquency in a birth cohort would become to criminal justice policy?

MW: No, no, I didn't, nor did Thorsten Sellin. At that point in my career, I shared Sellin's perspective that criminology is a scientific study of crime, and criminals, and society's reaction to both. We were in academia. We were not in public policy, nor did we think anything we did would necessarily have any practical payoffs in the administration of justice. We were in a mode of knowledge for knowledge's sake. However, *Delinquency in a Birth Cohort* was published in 1972 and after that, when newspaper reports summarized the study of those 10,000 boys born in 1945, both state and federal legislators in Harrisburg and in Washington, got word of it. They asked me to testify on more than a few occasions. And they concentrated a great deal on what we called the chronic offenders.

FA: The "six percent."

MW: Yes, that "six percent," out of the total birth cohort of some 10,000 boys, who were responsible for so many crimes including all but one of the homicides and three quarters of the rapes and robberies. So 627 of the boys out of 10,000 had committed over 50 percent of all the offenses. With that kind of emphasis in my testimonies before the Senate and House Judiciary Committees, eventually some legislation was passed and appropriations for developing criminal career programs around the country were made. I remember that the first money was appropriated to 100 district attorneys around the country to concentrate on criminal careers, and those who were chronic offenders, in terms of investigation and prosecution. The district attorney here in Philadelphia at that time told me that because they got funds from Washington the conviction rate jumped from about 65 percent to over 90 percent.

FA: And of course you followed that research with the 1958 birth cohort. I am curious: were the crimes more serious in the 1958 cohort?

MW: Yes. Here are two cohorts of males 13 years apart. In 1958 we had slightly over 13,000 boys and in order to satisfy some of our critics who said we ignored females, we included 14,000 females born in 1958. As you know, Freda, the proportion that was arrested at least once was about the same for males in both cohorts, about 33-35 percent. As for the chronic offenders, those arrested more than five times, the percent remained about the same also, between 6 and 7 percent. Those figures were fairly constant. They have been found in other cohort studies that have been done in Racine, WI, and in David Farrington's work in London. But, to answer your question, yes, the 1958 cohort was three times more violent than the 1945 cohort. That was one of the major differences. Paul Tracy and Bob Figlio and Terry Thornberry were all involved in the research center at the time.

We speculated about the reasons, and we still do. The 1945 birth cohort was born at a time, and had their teenage years, during a period of relative quiescence, and there was virtually no social unrest. Those were the Eisenhower years, and we were just moving along bountifully economically, whereas the 1958 birth cohort in their adolescence passed through the period of social unrest, race riots, urban riots, protest against Vietnam, campus riots, increasing drug abuse. In the first birth cohort out of 10,000 arrests, that is 3,500 boys were arrested 10,000 times, we had only one recorded drug offense. In the '58 birth cohort, by the time they were in the mid60s, late 60s, we had a couple thousand.

FA: You are a real pioneer. Even today the debate goes on about career criminals and the need for longitudinal studies. I think you have demonstrated that we do need longitudinal studies again. We have benefited so much from your pioneering work.

MW: Well, I'm glad to say that there are three major longitudinal studies going on now. Our studies were retrospective, that is, we waited until the children were 18, then looked back on their careers. Later we took a sample of the cohorts, and interviewed them when they were 25 or 26.

FA: Was that the boy to man work?

MW: That's the book called *From Boy to Man, From Delinquency to Crime*. We were still primarily retrospective, whereas in Denver, Pittsburgh and Rochester, there are now prospective studies.

FA: Yes, and I know Terry Thornberry is handling the Rochester study, continuing on with what he learned working with you on your career criminal studies. I have known you for many years, but as I was preparing for this discussion of ours today, I realized just how many topics you've pioneered, and how much you have taught to a generation of students. During all those years as your student, you were doing so many things I couldn't keep up with your work. Your criminological interests extended well beyond the US (before any of us thought about extending our interests abroad) to Italy, Puerto Rico, the former USSR, Africa and now, to China. Would you comment on your current interest?

MW: I would be glad to. Before I do, let me elaborate on what you just said about the students. Yes, I was very active in research while teaching full time, but I was able to do these things because of the enthusiasm and encouragement of my students. I feel very privileged that I have been able to have some of the most intelligent, capable graduate students you could find at any university anywhere in the country, and that has kept me going.

My current activity since 1986 has been in the People's Republic of China. It happened because in 1986 our National

Academy of Social Science and the Chinese Academy of Sciences had joint programs of exchanging professors and lecturers. So I was invited by the Chinese Academy of Social Science in Beijing to come and lecture, and they were my host. I lectured in five different cities for over a month and became fascinated with China itself. I, not unlike a lot of Americans, knew very little about China or Chinese history. But I quickly began to learn. Two years later there was a conference on juvenile delinquency. They called it "Re-educating Delinquents", in Shanghai, and I was one of the few out of a half-dozen foreigners invited to give a paper. When I did, I renewed my contacts with some of my Chinese colleagues. There was no one teaching criminology yet. They were teaching criminal law. They wanted to become involved in the scientific behavioral study of crime and criminals, and so I was honored to know that they had translated *From Boy to Man – From Delinquency to Crime* into Chinese, and they wanted to do a longitudinal study. Even though juvenile delinquency in China is relatively low, very low compared to the United States, nonetheless it was and still is a growing phenomenon. That is one reason they were interested. The other is that they wanted to become a part of the international community. Just as from an economic point of view (Under Deng Xiaoping), China opened up to investments from abroad and wanted to become known internationally in the trade industry. People concerned with criminology wanted to be known internationally. And that is why at the last several annual meetings of the American Society of Criminology they send delegations of a dozen people. I don't think we get a dozen from any other country. It's amazing.

Consequently, I have been involved in advising and consulting. This is not my research. It's their research. I've helped them raise the money both provincially and outside of China, because as you know longitudinal research can become expensive. Up until this year, I have been going to China twice a year, for a period of about three weeks, working with them. The research, at the suggestion of several professors in Beijing, is being done in Wuhan, which is the capital city of Hubei province, in China. Hubei Province is one of the smaller ones. It has a population the size of Germany. Wuhan is a city of about 5-6 million and the police records there are very good. There is one little anecdote I'd like to tell you. Initially, if you do research like this in some other culture you have to make adjustments of one sort or another, so it took us two years to get through the bureaucracy, to get permission and so on. On one of my trips to Wuhan, I said, "Well, now we're ready to collect data," and they said, "Yes, and we would like you to meet the research assistants, give them a kind of pep talk about standardized collection of data and so forth." I said, certainly. Now as you know, Freda, for our birth cohort studies here in Philadelphia, we got money from Washington; we were lucky if I could put four or five research assistants on the payroll. So they took me into a room where I was supposed to talk to the research assistants, the new ones who were going to work on this study, and low and behold there were 75 assigned to this particular research.

Then I said that I wanted to see the police reports. And they got their heads together and said, "Well, we're very sorry but no foreigner has ever been allowed to see police reports, at least since the revolution in '49. We're very sorry." Although I wasn't as blunt as this, in effect I said, "If I can't see the police reports, I'm not going to be an advisor on this research any more." They broke down, and they showed them to me. I had consistent and very good interpreters who read them off to me in English, and I was very impressed, because the amount of data that they collect is as good as or sometimes better than in Philadelphia.

FA: And you think you did not get a biased sample?

MW: They showed me not only records that had been filled out. I wanted to see what the form looked like even before it was filled out. And then I had the courage to ask for blank copies in Chinese, and they gave them to me. I had five Chinese graduate students translate for me. So they yielded, and they said that I was the first foreigner to see these records, and I said, "I hope I am not the last."

FA: And the project goes on.

MW: Project goes on. I expect that we'll be ready to do our analysis in another year or two.

FA: Were these 75 assistants university students?

MW: Yes.

FA: In a graduate type of program? All of them?

MW: No, some of them were undergraduates, and some in police work too.

FA: Men and women?

MW: Yes.

FA: I am looking forward to following that project.

We have been covering many of the topics that you have spent your life studying. Several of your books, *Patterns in Criminal Homicide, Measurement of Delinquency, Subculture of Violence*, were reprinted well over a decade after they came out in the original publication. This might be a difficult question for you, but what single book, of all those you've written, would you consider most important?

MW: It is a difficult question. I think have a different perspective from my colleagues, and from persons who write textbooks. The book that is most frequently quoted and referred to as, I hesitate to say it, a classic, is *Patterns of Criminal Homicide*. I have been amazed at the endurance of that book. It is still referred to in most books, including your textbook, but to answer you more directly, from my own point of view, I think *Subculture of Violence* is the one I feel most strongly about.

FA: I do not know whether you have kept track, but about how many dissertations have you supervised, and can you tell us something about your former students. I know you stay in contact with many of them, and I know we all feel comfortable coming to you, still dependent on your expertise and your help. Tell us about what mentoring means, and how you have managed to do it so well.

MW: Well, thank you. I do not know whether I have done as well as my students have done. You ask about dissertations. My former student at Queens College, Bernard Cohen, recently did a rough count, and he came up with 100 dissertations that I have supervised, or am still supervising. As I have indicated before, I have been very proud of my students and felt privileged to have such good ones. Yes, many of us do keep in touch. And more than a few, I hesitate to name names but I'll name a few, who have become very prominent in the field of criminology. There is a woman named Freda Adler, for example, whose prominence was recognized by the American Society of Criminology and whose members elected you president. There are others, Charles Wellford at the University of Maryland, who succeeded you. He was a wonderful student. Terry Thornberry became dean of the School of Criminal Justice at Albany, and we keep in touch. Paul Tracy is at the University of Texas and we keep in touch by telephone and sometimes he comes up to visit me. We're working on research proposals together. There is Bob Figlio who was with us for a long time and who is now at the University of Riverside in California. We keep in touch. There are just so many, many other ones, including Bob Silverman who is a dean at the University of Ontario. Then there is Mukherjee from India. After getting his PhD, he worked in Australia and became a criminologist there.

FA: I think you created an atmosphere in which we as students were a very close group, and as each cohort of students came in we accepted them and we took them under our wings. You continue doing that because we know that at least once a year you will meet with us and we have our special little discussions and our dinners and we stay in very close contact.

MW: But now I feel another source of pride and interest. Professor Laufer here at the University of Pennsylvania was not a student of mine, but he was a student of yours, and now he is an associate professor and we are working together so there's a kind of a generation continuance.

FA: How would you describe the changes that have occurred in criminology since you entered the field? If you sit back and you look at the years since you were the director of the Center for Studies in Criminology and Criminal Law?

MW: First of all, when I was a graduate student, when I was instructing you as an instructor, I read every criminology textbook that was published. I had them all, and any new book in criminology I immediately obtained and digested, and it was very easy to keep up with everything. Over the years the number of books, the number of textbooks, the number of people coming into the field, greatly increased, so it has become impossible for any one person today to keep up with all the writings, even with the benefit of computerization of bibliographies. Next, criminology has become increasingly sophisticated in its research methods. There had been a long debate in the field on the extent to which we should take on the attributes of the physical sciences in terms of hypothesis formation and data collection, etc. I think we are beyond that now. We are indeed a behavioral science, and we are not just philosophizing about crime or speculating. We are doing very sophisticated research. That sophistication has increased with the sophistication of our quantitative methods and statistics. One place where I think criminology is still in a stammering, stuttering and turtle-like advance is in theory. I think if you were to ask me what I think criminology should be doing more intensively than it has been is trying to develop a broader theoretical perspective. not necessarily a unified theory of crime, but more intense and precise and testable theories.

FA: Yes, for many years, one of the problems was that most of the journals wanted empirical research for publication, and of course young professors were trying to publish and it was very difficult to have a theoretical piece published. That is one of the reasons why, as you know, about 10 years ago we developed an annual series, *Advances in Criminological Theory*. I strongly agree with you on the need for more theoretical concentration. But we have definitely begun to increase our theoretical dialogue with revisiting of traditional theories, new and integrated theories.

MW: I have been meaning to applaud you for several years now about your starting the advanced theory work. When you first told me you were going to have this annual review, I thought at that time, well, there was not enough work being done in the area to have an annual review. But your having such a solid publication each year has stimulated more thinking, theoretically, than I think we would have had otherwise and so, I consider that a real advance.

FA: You remind me of the time that Bill Laufer, whom you mentioned before, and I, went to see Irving Horowitz, the publisher of *Transaction*. We said that we had an idea for an annual in criminological theory. He looked at us and he said, "In what? Is there any?!" And so we talked him into two small volumes. He was reluctant. I know that at this point with volume ten on the drawing board, he has changed his mind. But it has not been easy. You know well the time and thought that goes into writing a first-rate theoretical piece.

By the way, I guess that I am not letting cats out of any bags, but the next volume, of *Advances in Criminological Theory*, which is entitled *The Criminology of the Criminal Law*, will be dedicated to you.

MW: That's wonderful.

FA: Can you tell us what you think the future prospects of criminology as an academic discipline are? Where are we going from here?

MW: I think one of the areas that criminology and criminal justice disciplines, which used to be quite different but are now very much the same, should go into more deeply is international comparisons. I have become keenly aware of making these comparisons not just because I've spent some time in Israel, and Italy and England, but primarily now because of my exposure with China. Nearly a dozen years convinces me that there is so much that we do not know, not only about China as a culture and also history, but about our own special field of criminology. There is so much that we can learn from international comparisons. That is one area that I would like to see stressed. Criminology and criminal justice programs have blossomed all over this country as you know, and the American Society of Criminology now has what, over 2000 persons who attend? When I was president we were lucky to get 200. As criminology grows, we should expand our horizons.

Again, I would stress international comparisons, for example, crime in South Africa, Russian organized crime and so forth.

FA: I think we're going in that direction, as the world turns into a global village. The UN now has a new focus, namely transnational crime. I think we are headed more toward the international and comparative stage of criminology. We have so much to learn. I'm sure you know a whole lot more, for example, about conflict negotiation in China now that you have done research there. I agree with you that we have a lot to learn from foreign countries.

MW: We do. One of my current Chinese students is ready to do her dissertation on mediation committees in China, and the extent to which mediation committees help to resolve problems between criminals and, between offenders and victims. These save the courts a lot of trouble and time. There's an old saying in China, "When you die, don't go to hell, and when you get in trouble, don't go to court."

FA: Well, I take it from all that you have said that you feel there is a definite role for the criminologist in social policy making.

MW: Yes, I do indeed. I encourage my current students to get involved and to think about possible dissertation topics that involve criminal justice policy. This, as I indicated earlier, is a different perspective than I had 25 years ago.

FA: Marvin, you have had so many honors that it would be difficult to count them. They include an award in your name, the Wolfgang Award for Distinguished Achievement in Criminology, the American Society of Criminology's Edwin Sutherland Award, the Hans von Hentig award from the World Society of Victimology, and the Roscoe Pound Award. You have had many major grants from the federal government. You have mentored and served as role model for criminology students around the world. You have written many classics in our field. Dare I ask, what next?

MW: Well, on the horizon now is the analysis and writing of the birth cohort, the 1973 birth cohort in the People's Republic of China. That is my most immediate goal. The one after that, or almost simultaneous with it, is the development of a small book on crime and punishment in Renaissance Florence. I have always had a considerable interest in the history of penology. One of my arguments is that the prison that was opened in 1300 in Florence (Florence being in the vanguard of the Renaissance) was one of the first prisons, in western society at least, to incarcerate people as a punishment without corporal punishment, without any other kinds of punishment, just the sheer deprivation of liberty. This type of punishment antedated the Eastern State Penitentiary here in Philadelphia by about five centuries. So those two things are what I'm looking forward to.

FA: When we met at the University of Pennsylvania 45 years ago you were an instructor, a very busy instructor, and here we are, sitting in the same institution, 45 years later, and you're just as busy, if not busier, than you were in those days. Each time I talk with you I feel energized, and I think of what a good future criminology has. I can tell you as a former student that we are indebted to you for the major role you played in building our discipline. We can only repay you with our mentoring the next generation of students and with the continuance of our research and writing.

MW: That is what pleases me most.

FA: I appreciate very much having been able to conduct this interview.

SUBCULTURES OF VIOLENCE AND BEYOND: THEORY INTEGRATION IN CRIMINOLOGY

Charles F. Wellford, David A. Soulé
University of Maryland

Introduction

At the core of every discipline are issues addressing conceptualization, measurement, description, and theory. Developing precise concepts, organizing ways to operationalize those concepts, and describing the critical variables related to those concepts are essential to the development of any scientific discipline. In at least one tradition of theory development, these are necessary precursors to the development of scientific theories. In any review of scientific disciplines, those individuals who contributed significantly to these topics are given special prominence. It is for that reason that Marvin Wolfgang has achieved such a special place of recognition in the field of Criminology. Throughout this book and in other reviews of Marvin Wolfgang's work, one can clearly see his contributions in many of these areas.

Marvin Wolfgang is consistently recognized as one of the most important criminologists of this century, primarily because of his contributions in conceptualization, measurement and description. His works (with others) defining delinquency and developing quantitative ways to assess the seriousness of that central element in our field (Sellin & Wolfgang, 1964) have had a profound impact on not only criminologists, but those who use the output of our research. Marvin's first work, *Patterns in Criminal Homicide* (1958), was a careful description of a specific type of crime. Probably best known are Marvin's (collaborating with his mentor and students) series of monumental contributions to describing the patterns of delinquent and criminal careers (1972, 1987). Having contributed in this way to two of the three central elements of the development of a scientific discipline, it would be obvious that Marvin Wolfgang would have special prominence in our field.

Less noted are Marvin's contributions in the area of theory. Perhaps because his works in conceptualization, measurement and description had such profound impacts, his less developed contributions in theory, while often noted, have not been appreciated for the importance they held for Criminology. In this Chapter we discuss Marvin Wolfgang's major theoretical work, place it in the context of similar efforts in our field, and then close by discussing ways in which Wolfgang's work could be extended with great benefit to the current state of criminological theory.

The Subculture of Violence

We take as our starting point the work *Subculture of Violence: Towards an Integrated Theory in Criminology* (1967), by Marvin Wolfgang and his close friend and associate, Franco Ferracuti. This work, first published in 1966 in its Italian version, was published in English in 1967. Significantly, the book was dedicated to the mentors of these two prominent criminologists: Thorsten Sellin and Benigno DiTullio – themselves leaders of very different criminological foundations. This work was described in the introduction to the English version by Hermann Mannheim, as "The most constructive attempt so far made to end the wasteful struggle between the adherents of Sutherland and those of the multi-factor theory" (p. xvi). Wolfgang and Ferracuti, while recognizing the importance of multi-factor approaches to the understanding of criminal behavior, also recognized that such approaches were at best, atheoretical. Therefore, they saw the need to move beyond traditional sociological (e.g., Sutherland) approaches by finding a way to take advantage of the strengths of multi-factor approaches while not being atheoretical. Their work was a demonstration of the difficulties of doing this, and to its importance for criminological theory.

To frame their approach to theory, Wolfgang and Ferracuti (1967:10) described various ways individuals and models from different disciplines could be coordinated to address behaviors that cannot be adequately explained by any single discipline. These were described as follows:

1. *Fusion.* In this approach, 'disciplinary loyalties are discarded and all researchers subscribe to an over-all theoretical system within which an attempt is made to handle all problems that are undertaken'.
2. *Multivariate Approach* – with a common focus. Members of a research team 'work together on the same central problem but use their own methods and stay essentially within their own theoretical framework'.
3. *Formal Integration* – within which the separateness of disciplines is maintained.
4. *Division of problem* – into subinquiries with inter-disciplinary collaboration.
5. *Collation.* This is the loosest kind of collaboration, 'a type of

inter-disciplinary research in which members of different disciplines, each with different theories, work in the same general problem area without any specific provisions for integration. They exchange information and data, but essentially each uses his own techniques to work on his own part of the research'.

Wolfgang and Ferracuti unabashedly admit their commitment to fusion as the model for theory development. Without repeating all the arguments in their book, let us summarize why fusion should be the model for theory development.

First, the object of criminological study is criminal behavior. Criminal behavior is not defined by the field of criminology. It is defined by a broader set of social and historical factors that establish for a particular time and location, those behaviors that are considered crimes. To the contrary, in some disciplines, it is possible for the discipline to define the object of study itself. That is, the discipline, using its own theory, creates a dependent variable that is unique to that discipline. This has been the case in Economics, Sociology and Psychology, the social sciences closest to the field of Criminology. By creating their own dependent variable, these disciplines are able to explain that variable using strategies, concepts and organizing principles that are specific to that discipline. In those fields discipline reduction is by definition the most appropriate approach to theory development. Wolfgang and Ferracuti recognized that criminal behavior could not so be defined. It was a form of behavior that fortunately or unfortunately required a variety of intellectual approaches and disciplines to explain it in its various forms. For this reason, multi-factor approaches had emerged as the best way empirically to explain the variation in crime. Yet Wolfgang and Ferracuti also recognized those approaches as atheoretical and urged Criminology to move beyond multi-factor to fusion.

Second, as researchers Wolfgang and Ferracuti represented a very interesting combination of approaches. Wolfgang was the classic, empirical criminologist—dedicated to careful description, measurement and subsequent conceptualization. Franco Ferracuti was a clinician, interested in the case study, and understanding the meanings and interpretations of behaviors. In their collaboration, they considered the classical issue of clinical vs. statistical prediction. They concluded, as did most other scholars of that time, that these approaches were not a matter of choice, but of collaboration. If research methods were to be joined, then they concluded the theories that guide the research would also need to be integrated.

Finally, Wolfgang and Ferracuti saw little use for the distinction between pure and applied criminology. This recognition of the interaction between pure research and its applications also called upon them to move beyond disciplinary boundaries in their research and theory because they concluded the application of knowledge required a much broader set of understandings than could be derived from any particular discipline.

For these reasons and others, Wolfgang and Ferracuti sought to create an integrated discipline for criminology. Unfortunately this task proved too daunting for them at the time. Their approach, best summarized in the phrase subcultural violence, failed to achieve their own goals of an integrated theory (i.e., fusion). Essentially it established subcultural theory as the overarching explanation for violent crime. They then attempted to, within that general framework, note the secondary importance of other approaches, for example, biological, and psychoanalytic. Finally, by focusing on violent crime, they raised the possibility that other theoretical models would be required to explain other forms of criminal behavior. Therefore, as ambitious as Wolfgang and Ferracuti were in their goals for criminological theory, their own contribution more closely resembled other contemporary theoretical approaches [for example, Cloward and Ohlin (1960) and Cohen (1955)] than it did a breakthrough in theory development.

Still, we contend that Wolfgang and Ferracuti's work deserves a much more prominent place in the development of criminology than it has had, because it so carefully and clearly articulated what had to be achieved-- the goal we should be striving for in order to move criminological theory forward.

In more contemporary criminology this issue has been discussed under the title of theoretical integration. Today, for the most part, criminologists have recognized the importance of multidisciplinary components in the explanation of criminal behavior even if we have failed to adequately develop criminological research or theories that contain such elements. In fact, some of the leading criminological theorists have argued against theory integration in the broad form anticipated by Wolfgang and Ferracuti because it is too difficult, too complex and too challenging. Most noted among these, of course, is Travis Hirschi (1979), who suggested various forms of integration, none of which would have approximated the notion of fusion in the work of Wolfgang and Ferracuti. It was not until the work of Messner, Krohn and Liska (1989) and their acknowledgement that integration could be across levels did we see in the criminological literature a more contemporary version of Wolfgang and Ferracuti's idea of fusion. In this approach, articulated by one of us in an article in the Messner, et al. work, the goal is to find a theoretical schema that allows for the independence of different theoretical models from different disciplines, but also accounts for the ways in which they can influence each other. This cross- level or grand theory integration represents the goal that Wolfgang and Ferracuti articulated. The importance of their vision has not been refuted even as we struggle to achieve it.

In the contemporary integration literature, more modest efforts have followed several different strategies. The following divides these integration efforts into two groups: within-discipline and interdisciplinary integrations, and reviews examples of contemporary efforts in each form of integration.

Within Disciplines Integration

Elliott et al.'s Integrated Theory

Based on the idea that previously established criminological theories share some basic assumptions, Delbert Elliott and his colleagues (1979; 1985) proposed a "conceptual framework in which strain, social learning, and social control perspectives are integrated into a single explanatory paradigm" (1979:4). Together, the integration of these three sociological theories led to the development of two primary pathways to delinquency. The first pathway includes the integration of traditional social control theory and social learning theory. The authors suggest that early socialization influences a child's social bond or social control. Those individuals with weak bonds to conventional restraints become vulnerable to strong relationships and commitments to delinquent peer groups, which in turn increases the likelihood of engaging in delinquent behavior.

The second pathway integrates social learning and control theories with a traditional strain perspective. Individuals who follow this path development may have strong social bonds, but these bonds may also be attenuated by certain modifying variables including limited opportunities to achieve conventional goals (strain), negative labeling experiences, and finally the effects of social disorganization in the home (e.g., parental divorce, parental death) and/or in the community (e.g., disadvantaged neighborhoods, high mobility rates, high unemployment rates). The weakening of a commitment to conventional restraints may lead to an increased risk for delinquent behavior by itself, while it may also lead to the development of strong bonds with delinquent peers.

In sum, individuals with initially weak social bonds are susceptible to sustained patterns of delinquency if they become committed to delinquent peers, while at the same time those individuals with weak social bonds may avoid continued delinquent behavior patterns if they are able to escape the influence of delinquent peers. On the other hand, individuals with initially strong bonds to a conventional society are likely to evade delinquency all together unless their bonds are weakened by the previously mentioned modifying variables.

Elliott and his associates (1985) tested a slightly modified version of their model using longitudinal data from the National Youth Survey. In general, their findings supported their integrated model. Association with delinquent peers was a strong predictor of delinquent behavior. Additionally, they concluded that weak social bonds to conventional restraints increased the likelihood of association with delinquent peer groups and these social bonds moderated the effects of delinquent peers in that the association between delinquent peers and delinquent behavior was strongest when social control was low. Finally, strain increased the probability that an individual would have weak conventional bonds. However, neither strain nor low social control directly impacted subsequent delinquent behavior as predicted in the model.

While Elliott et al.'s theory continues to be a popular contemporary example of theoretical integration; their model is not without limitations. First, Hirschi (1989) criticizes their integration for ignoring critical differences in the underlying assumptions of social control, social learning, and strain theories. In addition, Tittle (1995:96) points out several shortcomings to this integrated theory including its lack of attention to an offender's ability and opportunity, imprecise development as to how and why an individual precedes through a developmental sequence, and its lack of depth. Finally, in keeping with the theme of this chapter, it is important to note that Elliott and his colleagues have advanced a purely sociological model that ignores Wolfgang and Ferracuti's (1967) call for "fusion" – incorporating ideas and theories from multiple disciplines.

Thornberry's Interactional Theory

Similar to Elliott et al.'s integrated theory, Thornberry's (1987) interactional theory suggests that weakened social bonds lead to delinquent behavior by increasing the likelihood that an individual will interact with delinquent peers. Thornberry maintains that his model differs from previous theoretical attempts by addressing three specific shortcomings of previous theories. First, Thornberry (1987; 1996) suggests most contemporary theories of delinquency are overwhelmingly reliant on unidirectional rather than reciprocal causal effects. Second, previous theories tend not to allow for dynamic processes throughout the life-course and were inclined to focus on a narrow age range. Finally, Thornberry (1987) suggests that contemporary theories are likely to assume uniform causal effects throughout the social structure.

Thornberry's interactional theory focuses on the dynamic and non-recursive aspects of criminological thought by integrating ideas from social control theory (Hirschi, 1969), social learning theory (Akers, 1977), Elliott et al.'s integrated theory (1979; 1985), and social structure variables. Interactional theory assumes that human behavior develops over time in an interactive environment where delinquency is learned and reinforced. The central contention of interactional theory is that delinquent behavior is the result of a weakening of bonds to conventional society. While weakened bonds are necessary criteria for delinquency, Thornberry (1987) and his colleagues (1991) suggest that associations with delinquent peers provide the primary mechanism for persistent and serious delinquency. Variations in the strength of social bonds and exposure to delinquent peers are systematically related to social structure variables such as one's community, social class, race and gender. Most importantly, Thornberry emphasizes the reciprocal effects of many of the variables included in the model. For instance, while an association with delinquent peers increases the likelihood of delinquency, Thornberry also suggests that delinquency fosters an increased association with delinquent peers. Finally, Thornberry argues the variables included in his model can change in importance for many individuals over the life course and this explains why some people desist from crime while others continue their delinquent behavior well into adulthood.

Evaluations of Thornberry's interactional theory have provided mostly supportive evidence for many of the theory's aspects. Using data from the Rochester Youth Development Study, Thornberry and his associates (1991) found no support for the hypothesized reciprocal relationship between parental attachment and school commitment, yet they did find a weak relationship for the reciprocal effect of delinquency on attachment and commitments. In his own review of empirical support for interactional theory, Thornberry (1996) concluded that while there is substantial support for the theory's main assertion that delinquent behavior is rooted in a network of mutually reinforcing causal effects, additional research is needed to adequately assess the utility of the interactional theory specifically with regards to the dynamic aspects of the theory. To this extent, Jang's (1999) multilevel, longitudinal analysis supported many of the theory's developmental hypotheses about the age-varying causal importance of the family, school, and peer influence.

Both Elliott et al.'s integrated theory and Thornberry's interactional theory are traditional sociological integrations, yet each can be viewed as a stepping stone in the direction of multiple discipline integrations because they expanded the scope of previous theoretical attempts. Each stresses the need to focus on the normative orientations of groups (a central element of Wolfgang and Ferracuti's subcultural theory), including how bonds to conventional groups may be attenuated and ultimately facilitate or sustain delinquent behavior through an association with delinquent peers. In the sense that both groups were among the first contemporary theorists to integrate multiple concepts from differing theoretical paradigms, their models can be perceived as preliminary steps towards the interdisciplinary scheme envisioned by Wolfgang and Ferracuti. In fact, Thornberry and his colleague, Marvin Krohn (forthcoming) discuss a revised version of interactional theory which incorporates a life course perspective toward understanding antisocial behaviors across the full life cycle and brings interactional theory closer to Wolfgang's notion of "fusion."

Transition to Interdisciplinary Integrations

When Wolfgang and Ferracuti published *The Subculture of Violence* (1967), they noted that criminological development could be traced across traditional lines of biology, sociology and psychology, yet without much overlapping or integration of any of these approaches. For example, they suggest that while the Gluecks' (1950) celebrated work was multi-dimensional, it was not interdisciplinary. The Gluecks use of inductive reasoning allowed each discipline to contribute to the accumulation of facts, but did so with a separate perspective and independent conclusions, without reference to other disciplines. Wolfgang and Ferracuti called for a unified criminology that incorporates constructs, theory and research designs/ standards from multiple disciplines. The failure of previous attempts at interdisciplinary integration proves that such a task is difficult, but Wolfgang and Ferracuti suggested theory development without exclusive dominance from a particular field must be attempted or our field will continue to be separated from a large body of potentially useful knowledge (1967:75).

Since Wolfgang and Ferracuti, other contemporary researchers have called for criminology to recognize the important contributions that additional fields of study could add to traditionally sociologically based explanations of crime. In 1989, one of us suggested that Criminology needed to end the useless debate between various systemic positions, develop a language for understanding the requirements of interdisciplinary theory, recognize and encourage our students to recognize the importance of psychological and biophysical approaches as essential elements in explanations of criminal behavior, and finally begin to identify some of the correlates of interdisciplinary theory (Wellford 1989). In his summation of the future directions for criminality research, Adrian Raine (1993) echoed this idea. Raine suggested that current criminal behavior researchers have a tendency to pursue independent specialties, ignore relevant research in other disciplines, and closely defend their own work. He further suggests this is unfortunate because "it is likely that biologically-oriented research can contribute much to socially-oriented research, and vice-versa" (1993:317). Unfortunately, for various reasons, attempts at interdisciplinary integration have been limited. The next section provides a brief review of three contemporary theories that seek the "fusion" suggested by Wolfgang and Ferracuti.

Wilson and Herrnstein

Wilson and Herrnstein's *Crime and Human Nature* (1985) presents a complex learning theory that merges classical school ideas with biosocial and personality factors. They suggest that the reinforcement of certain behaviors are linked to constitutional factors like low IQ, impulsivity and other personality traits that are present at birth or soon after birth, appear during early child development, and are manifested in the family, friends and in society. Social influences (such as parenting and schooling) determine whether or not these traits are expressed through criminal behavior. In this sense, one's constitutional predisposition will only lead to criminality under certain psychological and social conditions. Furthermore, low IQ and failure in school of individuals with constitutional factors may make the rewards of non-crime less important. As a result of this interaction, poorly socialized impulsive individuals are less able to perceive the costs and benefits of crime versus non-crime and therefore are less deterred by punishment. In sum, they argue that human nature is developed in intimate settings out of a complex interaction of constitutional and social factors. This complex interaction thus effects how people choose between crime and non-crime.

The weaknesses of Wilson and Herrnstein's theory or perspective have been outlined in numerous critiques of their work. In his review, Jack Gibbs (1985) suggests that most of the theory's claims about links between low intelligence, impulsivity, hereditary factors, the effects of the media, and many other variables are merely observational and overall the theory lacks clearly defined and/or testable concepts. Additionally, Wilson and Herrnstein appear to conduct a subjective review of the criminological literature in support of their theory. By being selective with the research literature, many of the studies they cited were plagued by weak research designs and inadequate statistical analysis and measurement techniques. Finally, the empirical validity of their theory is questionable since few studies have successfully tested any of the theory's propositions.

Despite numerous critiques of Wilson and Herrnstein's theory, the strengths of their perspective lie in its interdisciplinary contribution to the field of criminology. By challenging the "status quo" of criminological thought and providing a lengthy review of existing literature on crime and criminal behavior, Wilson and Herrnstein provided a preliminary example of an interdisciplinary approach which approaches the unified criminology that Wolfgang and Ferracuti visualized in 1967 and future criminologists should consider as we proceed into the 21st century. While the overall scholarship of Wilson and Herrnstein's multi-disciplinary theory may not be overwhelming, their work demonstrates the need to further examine multiple disciplines and paths to criminal behavior.

Moffitt's Dual Taxonomy

Terrie Moffitt's (1993) theory incorporates concepts from the fields of biology, sociology and developmental psychology and suggests offenders can be divided into two distinct groups. Those offenders who begin offending early in life and continue offending into adulthood (life course persistors) and those offenders who start offending later in their teenage years and generally desist from crime during the early adult years (adolescence limited). Moffitt (1993) contends that the etiological chain for these two groups of offenders will differ. The adolescence limited offender learns antisocial behavior by mimicking adult-like behaviors (e.g., money from theft, early sexual activity, and drinking alcohol) to feel more mature. Consequently, this group will engage mostly in instrumental crimes (minor property crimes) to gain an adult status. Because their social bonds have not been attenuated, adolescent limited offenders will desist from crime as they gain more "stakes in conformity" (Toby, 1957) such as getting a job or going to college.

The life course persistent offender's causal sequence begins with factors that produce individual differences in the neuropsychological functions in the infant nervous system. The factors that produce these individual differences are a host of biosocial factors that occur prior to birth or shortly thereafter (e.g. exposure to lead and other toxins, maternal drug use, parental abuse, pre/perinatal complications). The resulting neuropsychological damages have behavioral consequences, which result in a breakdown of the socialization process. Additionally, Moffitt incorporates macro level variables into her theory by suggesting that the socialization process for the life course persistent offender is inhibited by an interaction between a child's neuropsychological vulnerabilities and a criminogenic or disadvantaged environment (1993:679). This "double hazard" of perinatal risk and social disadvantage increases the risk for deviant behavior (Brennan and Mednick, 1997:272). Her interactional hypothesis emphasizes the joint influence, rather than independent effect of each of these factors and is consistent with recent findings that show support for the combination of biological, psychological, and sociological factors in predicting offending patterns in offending behavior (see Tibbetts and Piquero, 1999).

Typological models like Moffitt's have received some empirical support. Many studies have concluded there are at least two pathways to crime (e.g., Caspi et al., 1994; Simons et al., 1994; Nagin and Land, 1993) and possibly more (Nagin et al., 1995). While the argument over typological versus general theories of crime continues to be widely debated (see Paternoster and Brame, 1997 for review), Moffitt's contributions remain essential because her review of the existing research forces the field to "acknowledge that personality and behavior are shaped in large measure by the interaction between the person and the environment" (1993:682). By adopting an interdisciplinary and multi-level approach to studying anti-social behavior, Moffitt's work can be viewed as a significant extension of Wolfgang and Ferracuti's integrated conceptualization.

Vila's General Paradigm

Based on Cohen and Machalek's (1988) evolutionary ecological approach for understanding expropriative crime, Bryan Vila's (1994) general paradigm focuses on how individuals develop over their life course. Vila attempts to explain how one acquires criminality, a predisposition that favors criminal behavior, when and why people express this predisposition as crime, and how individuals or groups respond to these crimes. In a complex set of thoughts and ideas, Vila (1994:312) suggests that the evolutionary ecological approach allows theorists to integrate ecological factors that determine what opportunities for crime exist, micro-level factors that influence an individual's propensity to commit a criminal act at a particular point in time, and macro-level factors that influence the development of individuals in society over time.

Vila (1994) first suggests that people acquire attributes such as knowledge, skills, and beliefs over the course of their lives through an interaction of biological (e.g., physical size, swiftness, strength and the excitability/reactivity of the nervous system), sociocultural (e.g., traditional social learning, social control, and strain variables) and developmental factors. At the same time, Vila (1997:19) suggests that a child's development is particularly susceptible to poor family socialization practices that arise from stressors like poverty, marital conflict and lack of education. Each of these attributes influences a person's ability to obtain resources and how they value these same resources. Vila further suggests that an individual's motivation to commit a crime is influenced by both these factors and a "tempting" opportunity. Finally, the general paradigm stresses that responses from other individuals and groups may modify an individual's motivation for crime or alter a particular opportunity.

Vila's general paradigm is a broad, comprehensive coordination of a substantial body of existing knowledge. He does not suggest that his general paradigm is a better explanation than other traditional theoretical models in criminology, but rather he suggests it provides a framework for integrating findings from multiple disciplines and serves as a guide for thinking from a more holistic and systematic view of social problems. Yet, because of the general paradigm's complex nature, no empirical evaluations have been able to test the theory in its entirety. At the very least, Vila's paradigm (similar to Moffitt's work) is an asset to the field of criminology because it organizes a significant quantity of literature from multiple disciplines and recognizes the contributions each has to offer. Finally, by predicting that nuturant social programs will improve the development of human and social capital and thus have a considerable impact on future crime rates for generations to come, Vila (1994; 1997) outlines specific policy implications that have already stimulated much debate (see volume 16 of *Politics and the Life Sciences* for an extensive commentary on Vila's plea for nuturant strategies).

Conclusion

Marvin Wolfgang, in his work with Ferracuti and especially in his teaching, recognized that theories of criminal behavior had to draw upon all social and behavioral disciplines. His involvement in detailed empirical, descriptive research reinforced this recognition. The complexity of human behavior was evident in homicide and delinquency patterns and measurement. This singularly important insight should have moved criminological theory towards "fusion" but the counter forces have been too strong.

As we have noted above, contemporary criminological theory, while showing some signs of movement, is still dominated by discipline specific theories. In fact, many (e.g., Hirschi 1979, 1989; Sweigert, 1989) continue to argue against fusion models essentially for reasons of convenience (e.g., too complex, requires combining theories with different assumptions, etc.). While theory can develop in a variety of ways (crime specific, discipline specific and even time specific), without an understanding of the need for an overarching "grand" theory these efforts will explain little and continue meaningless controversies over which is "better".

The tradition we take from Wolfgang's scholarly work and teaching is that it is time for our field to integrate, rather than just compete for theoretical dominance. In an earlier effort one of us outlined in a very rudimentary way an integrating framework (Wellford, 1989). Drawn from Parsons (1961), Reiff (1961) and Edel (1959) this approach seeks theory integration within and across disciplines. As Wolfgang and Ferracuti prescribed, this approach should recognize that any explanation of behavior (including criminal behavior) must include cultural, social, psychological and behavioral components. Understanding these components and how to integrate them is the challenge facing Criminology today as it was when "fusion" was offered to us as the model for theory development. This framework offers a way to achieve fusion or at a minimum, organize the noise that's contemporary theory into a (simple) melody. Marvin Wolfgang would have urged us to fuse our voices.

REFERENCES

Akers, Ronald L., Marvin D. Krohn, Lonn Lanza-Kaduce, and Marcia Radosevich. (1979). "Social Learning and Deviant Behavior: a Specific Test of a General Theory." *American Sociological Review*, 44:635-55.

Brennan, Patricia A. and Sarnoff A. Mednick. (1997). "Medical Histories of Antisocial Individuals." In D.M. Stoff, J. Breiling, and J.D. Maser (eds.), *Handbook of Antisocial Behavior*. New York: John Wiley and Sons, Inc.

Caspi, Avshalom, Terrie E. Moffitt, Phil A. Silva, Magda Stouthhamer-Loeber, Robert Krueger, and Pamela Schmutte. (1994). "Are Some People Crime Prone? Replications of the Personality-Crime Relationships across Countries, Genders, Races and Methods." *Criminology*, 32:163-196.

Cloward, Richard A. and Lloyd Ohlin. (1960). *Delinquency and Opportunity*. New York: Free Press.

Cohen, Albert. (1955). *Delinquent Boys*. New York: Free Press.

Cohen, Lawrence E. and Richard Machalek. (1988). "A General Theory of Expropriative Crime." *American Journal of Sociology*, 94:465-501.

Edel, Abraham. (1959). "The Concept of Levels in Social Theory." In Llewllyn Gross (ed.), *Symposium on Sociological Theory*. Evanston, IL: Row, Peterson, and Co.

Elliott, Delbert S., Suzanne S. Ageton, and Rachelle J. Canger. (1979). "An Integrated Theoretical Perspective on Delinquent Behavior." *Criminology*, 16:3-27.

Elliott, Delbert S., David Huizinga, and Suzanne S. Ageton. (1985). *Explaining Delinquency and Drug Use*. Beverly Hills: Sage.

Elliott, Delbert S., David Huizinga, and Scott Menard. (1989). *Multiple Problem Youth*. New York: Springer-Verlag.

Gibbs, Jack P. (1985). "Review Essay." *Criminology*, 23(2):381-388.

Glueck, Sheldon and Eleanor Glueck. (1950). *Unraveling Juvenile Delinquency*. New York: Commonwealth Fund.

Hirschi, Travis. (1989). "Exploring Alternatives to Integrated Theory." In S. F. Messner, M.D. Krohn and A.E. Liska (eds.), *Theoretical Integration in the Study of Deviance and Crime: Problems and Prospects*. Albany: State University of New York Press.

Hirschi, Travis. (1979). "Separate and Unequal is Better." *Journal of Research in Crime and Delinquency*, 16:34-38.

Hirschi, Travis. (1969). *Causes of Delinquency*. Berkeley, CA: University of California Press.

Jang, Sung Joon. (1999). "Age-Varying Effects of Family, School, and Peers on Delinquency: A Multilevel Modeling Test of Interactional Theory." *Criminology*, 37(3):643-686.

Messner, Steven F., Marvin D. Krohn, and Allen E. Liska, eds. (1989). *Theoretical Integration in the Study of Deviance and Crime: Problems and Prospects.* Albany: State University of New York Press.

Moffitt, Terrie E. (1993). "Adolescent-limited and Life-Course Persistent Antisocial Behavior: A Developmental Taxonomy." *Psychological Review*, 100:674-701.

Nagin, Daniel S., David P. Farrington, and Terrie E. Moffitt. (1995). "Life-Course Trajectories of Different Types of Offenders." *Criminology*, 33:111-139.

Nagin, Daniel S. and Kenneth C. Land. (1993). Age, Criminal Careers, and Population Heterogeneity: Specification and Estimation of a Nonparametric, Mixed Poisson Model. *Criminology*, 31:327-362.

Parsons, Talcott. (1961). "Outline of the Social System." In T. Parsons, E. Shils, K.D. Naegele, J.R. Pitts (eds.), *Theories of Society*. New York: Free Press.

Paternoster, Raymond and Robert Brame. (1997). "Multiple routes to delinquency? A Test of Developmental and General Theories of Crime." *Criminology*, 35(1):49-84.

Raine, Adrian. (1993). *The Psychopathology of Crime: Criminal Behavior as a Clinical Disorder.* San Diego: Academic Press.

Rieff, Philip. (1961). *Freud: The Mind of the Moralist.* New York: Doubleday & Co.

Sellin, Thorsten and Marvin E. Wolfgang. (1964). *The Measurement of Delinquency.* New York: Riley.

Simons, Ronald L, C. Wu, Rand D. Conger, and F.O. Lorenz. (1994). "Two Routes to Delinquency: Differences Between Early and Late Starters in the Impact of Parenting and Deviant Peers." *Criminology*, 32:247-276.

Swigert, Victoria L. (1989). "The Discipline as Data: Resolving the Theoretical Crisis in Criminology." In S. F. Messner, M.D. Krohn and A.E. Liska (eds.), *Theoretical Integration in the Study of Deviance and Crime: Problems and Prospects.* Albany: State University of New York Press.

Thornberry, Terence P. (1987). "Toward an Interactional Theory of Delinquency." *Criminology*, 25(4): 863-891.

Thornberry, Terence P. (1996). "Empirical Support for Interactional Theory: A Review of the Literature." In J. David Hawkins (ed.), *Delinquency and Crime: Current Theories.* Cambridge: Cambridge University Press.

Thornberry, Terence P. and Marvin D. Krohn (forthcoming). *The Development of Delinquency: An Interactional Perspective.*

Thornberry, Terence P., Alan J. Lizotte, Marvin D. Krohn, Margaret Farnworth, and Sung Joon Jang (1991). "Testing Interactional Theory: An Examination of Reciprocal Causal Relationships among Family, School, and Delinquency." *Journal of Criminal Law and Criminology,* 82(1):3-35.

Tibbetts, Stephen G. and Alex R. Piquero. (1999). "The Influence of Gender, Low Birth Weight, and Disadvantaged Environment in Predicting Early Onset of Offending: A Test of Moffitt's Interactional Hypothesis." *Criminology*, 37(4):843-878.

Tittle, Charles R. (1995). *Control Balance: Toward a General Theory of Deviance.* Boulder, CO: Westview Press.

Toby, Jackson. (1957). "Social Disorganization and Stake in Conformity: Complementary Factors in the Predatory Behavior of Hoodlums*."* *Journal of Criminal Law, Criminology, and Police Science*, 48:12-17.

Vila, Bryan. (1997). "Human Nature and Crime Control: Improving the Feasibility of Nurturant Strategies." *Politics and the Life Sciences*, 16:3-21.

Vila, Bryan. (1994). "A General Paradigm for Understanding Criminal Behavior: Extending Evolutionary Ecological Theory." *Criminology*, 32(3):311-360.

Wellford, Charles. (1989). "Towards an Integrated Theory of Criminal Behavior." In S. F. Messner, M.D. Krohn and A.E. Liska (eds.), *Theoretical Integration in the Study of Deviance and Crime: Problems and Prospects.* Albany: State University of New York Press.

Wilson, James Q. and Richard J. Herrnstein. (1985). *Crime and Human Nature.* New York: Simon & Schuster.

Wolfgang, Marvin E. (1958). *Patterns in Criminal Homicide.* Philadelphia: University of Pennsylvania Press.

Wolfgang, Marvin E., Terence P. Thornberry, and Robert M. Figlio. (1987). *From Boy to Man: From Delinquency to Crime.* Chicago: University of Chicago Press.

Wolfgang, Marvin E., Robert M. Figlio, and Thorsten Sellin. (1972). *Delinquency in a Birth Cohort.* Chicago: University of Chicago Press.

Wolfgang, Marvin E. and Franco Ferracuti. (1967). *The Subculture of Violence: Towards an Integrated Theory in Criminology.* London: Tavistock.

POLITICAL VIOLENCE: PATTERNS AND TRENDS

Austin T. Turk

University of California, Riverside

A much revised extension of Turk, 1996, this paper was presented at the annual meetings of the American Society of Criminology, San Francisco, November 15, 2000.

Marvin Wolfgang's interest in violence focused mainly on patterns of criminal homicide and traditions of aggression that he called "subcultures of violence" (Wolfgang and Ferracuti, 1967). However, he was anything but indifferent to political violence. Like many criminologists, he sought to understand the civil turmoil of the 1960s—evidenced in his work with the National Commission on the Causes and Prevention of Violence and his collaboration with James F. Short, Jr., in editing an authoritative volume of works on the collective violence of that time (Short and Wolfgang, 1972). And in a seminal study deserving of far more attention than it has received, he provided a fascinating scholarly analysis of the savage political struggle between the Guelph and Ghibelline parties of Florence during the late thirteenth and early fourteenth centuries (Wolfgang, 1954). That study was one of the first to extend criminological inquiry to larger issues of political conflict and violence in specific historical contexts.

Consistent with that approach, it had become evident by the end of the 1980s that "disease and breakdown models" cannot explain collective political violence (Gurr, 1989: 12-13). Instead, empirically grounded theoretical models were being constructed that emphasized the real fears and grievances of groups finding themselves in inescapable and unequal competitions with one another. (For examples and reviews see Gurr, 1980, and Zimmerman, 1983.) Accordingly, the aims of research were to specify the social conditions under which such competitions lead to political violence and under which political violence leads to structural changes.

Studies of political violence since then have generally focussed on differences in social power rather than structural breakdowns or cultural pathologies. Even in terrorism research, political violence is seen increasingly as a reasoned form of political action. The challenge is to understand the reasoning. To do so, it is necessary to identify the conditions that lead toward or away from adopting the violence option. This paper is a step toward formulating a model of the political-legal process through which social conflicts within politically organized societies (polities) escalate or de-escalate. Toward this end, we will consider (a) the linkage between power and legality; (b) the social dynamics of political violence; and (c) trends in contemporary political violence that illustrate factors promoting the escalation of violence and factors associated with its de-escalation.

Power and Legality

Greater social power (Mann, 1986: 1-33) leads to greater law power – the capacity to enlist the forces of the state to define and defend one's interests and demands as "legal" against the "illegal" or "non-justiciable" concerns and demands of competitors. As long as the less powerful acquiesce in their relatively disadvantaged social position, the political-legal order may be described as "legitimate" and its hierarchical form may be held to be a structure of "authority." The facts of political, economic, and cultural inequalities are either dismissed or justified by an ideology defining them as legitimate (at least under present and foreseeable circumstances) and asserting the right of "authorities" to demand compliance from persons "lawfully subject" to their directives.

No ideology is ever fully successful in persuading losers to believe in the legitimacy of inequalities and the claims of authorities. Knowing this, dominant groups use their law power not only to penalize lawbreaking (crime) after the fact but also to deter potential lawbreaking. Short of totalitarian repression, the deterrence effort always falls short of success. There are always some people dissatisfied with the political order, or at least with their place in it. If they are members of readily identifiable groups, they and those with whom they are associated will be seen by dominants (and the authorities) as "the dangerous classes."

As long as groups promote their interests through conventional politics, their actions are unlikely to be seen as threatening. However, even clearly legal acts are likely to be viewed as threatening if they signal potential changes in the distribution of social power. In particular, dominants are threatened by electoral and legislative outcomes favorable to subordinate groups such as workers and minorities. Consequently, dominants typically try to use their law power to dilute or negate such underdog successes as the passage of labor protection and anti-discrimination laws.

Political actions by members of dangerous classes are very likely to be defined in legal terms as political crimes whenever members of dominant classes perceive a significant threat to the authority structure. Whether or not laws explicitly defining political offenses such as treason or sedition are invoked, the policing of political offenders is even less restrained by procedural rules than is regular policing (Turk, 1982: 54-68). The greater the perceived threat, the less restrained is political policing. Violent acts expressing or implying the denial of legitimacy and the rejection of authority are likely to be seen as especially threatening. It follows that police actions to counter violent political challenges will be minimally, if at all, restrained by laws proclaimed as limits on abuses of power.

The essential element in political authority is the power to create and impose defined realities. Specifically, the power to label events and people as "criminal" implies that ostensibly similar actions and actors may be differently labeled, while dissimilarities may be ignored. For instance, when dominants feel seriously threatened, attacks by anti-government demonstrators on government supporters are much more likely to result in criminalization (labeling as criminal) than are assaults by supporters on demonstrators. And the concept of "violence" is more likely to be applied to assaults by than to assaults on demonstrators. This is especially true when demonstrators are assaulted by police or military forces engaged in "riot control' or "restoring order"—which may in fact mean the repression of peaceful and orderly gatherings or processions.

Assuming that incidents or situations are defined as criminal and violent, authorities face the issue of whether the threat is to be explicitly defined as political. There are two tactical options, each with attendant benefits and risks.

First, to treat opponents as mere criminals is to brush aside their political views without having to address them. Potentially embarrassing revelations and arguments can be avoided or muted by denying their relevance in the processing of "ordinary crimes"—though the offenders may still be punished more severely (Smith and Damphousse, 1994). On the other hand, the decision to treat political challengers as ordinary criminals carries with it (at least in democracies) formal and operational limits on the control effort. Insofar as the accused have substantive and procedural legal rights, the criminalization process must at least appear to recognize and safeguard those rights. Otherwise, the authority structure will in time dissolve as the general public is increasingly frightened by the evident absence of restraints on governmental power.

Second, to denounce opponents as political offenders is to classify them as a "dangerous class" requiring special defense measures. Such measures may be formally authorized by laws describing (more or less vaguely) the kinds of political actions deemed illegal. ("Terrorism" is an obvious example.) Or "extraordinary" measures may be authorized by proclamations declaring an emergency necessitating the suspension of legal restraints on the policing of political activities. Less openly, special policing agencies may be established with an on-going mandate to deter and neutralize serious political threats.

Whether authorized by political crime laws, emergency edicts, or special agency mandates, treating opponents as politically dangerous risks drawing public attention to their concerns and attracting support for their cause. The more unrestrained and violent the policing effort, the more likely are sympathy and support to grow—particularly as other groups realize that they may also become targets of political repression.

To counter such fears, authorities have often exaggerated the danger to social order and the general welfare. Isolated acts of violence against police and other officials may be pictured as a coordinated onslaught against civilized society. Protest demonstrations against government policies may be described as threats to patriotism or religion. Labor strikes may be depicted as subversive efforts to bring about economic collapse. It follows that violence by officials and supporters against such "enemies of the people" is likely to be "legal" (i.e., ignored or condoned) while even attempts by the targeted to flee or defend themselves are likely to be considered "illegal" political violence.

Despite millenia of effort, no universal standard for resolving conflicting notions of what is, or ought to be, "legal" has been established (Stone, 1966). Thus, the distinction between legal and illegal political violence is simply to be accepted as itself a political construction reflecting the greater power of authorities, not as an objective product of legal reasoning. The implication for research is that explanation of domestic political violence requires analysis of the conditions under which the line between legal and illegal violence is drawn. This means that variations in the form and level of illegal political violence cannot be explained without also explaining variations in the form and level of legal political violence. Indeed, it is proposed that the two are linked in a reciprocal causal interaction that is the key process in the social dynamics of domestic political violence.

The Social Dynamics of Political Violence

Given that political action is any effort to challenge or defend an authority structure, political violence may be defined as any effort to coerce, injure, or destroy in the course of political action. It is assumed that attacks on property are politically equivalent to attacks on persons, in that the intent is the same: to force opponents to behave so that one's political objectives are achieved.

Because violence causes or threatens physical harm, it might be argued that political violence is intrinsically coercive: the target is constrained by the threat or fact of victimization. However, this view leaves us unable to consider variation in the degree of coercion—i.e., variation in the form and level of political violence. A more useful approach is to narrow the meaning of coercion by treating it not as a defining characteristic but instead as one of three possible goals of political violence. Accordingly, *coercive violence* is intended to persuade opponents to cease or reduce their political actions. *Injurious violence* is aimed at punishment rather than persuasion. *Destructive violence* is the ultimate punishment: the objective is extermination.

Which goal, and thus which form of political violence, has priority will vary according to the perceptions of the party resorting to violence. As perceptions change, so will goals. In any case, coercion, injury, and destruction are not mutually exclusive objectives. Rather, they are likely to be interrelated in an unfolding strategy as the violent actor gains experience in dealing with the opposition. Some targets may be destroyed or injured in order to coerce others. Failure to coerce may lead to an escalation in violence to punish the opponent for not giving up. Persistent opposition may frustrate the violent actor to the point where destruction becomes the overriding aim. Tracing such progressions from one form of violence to another is central to understanding the social dynamics of political violence. That is the research agenda for the future.

The following chart indicates how specific acts of violence by defenders and challengers of authority may be fitted into the three basic forms. As will be evident, the progression from coercive to injurious to destructive violence orders acts in terms of the extent to which they tend to be restrained by legal or moral concerns. Note that any differences in the terms used for particular acts generally reflect conventional usage in the literature on political crime, which has tended to assume that most violent acts by defenders are legal while most acts by challengers are illegal.

Table 1
Levels of Violence: Political Actors and Labels

Levels of Violence	Political Actors	
	Defenders	**Challengers**
Coercive	Restrictions on mobility (e.g. house arrest, passport control, ban on assembly)	Warnings and threats (e.g. phone calls, letters, posters, graffiti)
	Confiscation of property (e.g., fines, levies, seizures, forfeitures)	Theft Robbery
	Destruction of facilities (e.g., microphones, offices, vehicles)	Arson and vandalism
	Detainment and arrest	Kidnapping
Injurious	Riot control (e.g. beating, hosing, gassing demonstrators/rioters)	Rioting (e.g. assaulting police, loyalists, or bystanders; looting)
	Corporal punishment Forceful Interrogation	Beating prisoners Torture

Levels of Violence	Political Actors	
	Defenders	**Challengers**
Destructive	Capital punishment Termination Suppression Pacification Internal war	Murder Assassination Lynching Massacre Terrorism

Coercive Violence

Implicit in the existence of an authority structure is the threat of punitive action in the event that the law power of dominants is challenged. Laws are threats, even though the element of threat may be hidden or minimized, as in the routine invocations of contractual agreements by attorneys negotiating disputes among their clients. However, contrary to the views of anarchists (cf. Bankowski, 1983), the inherent threat of law does not in itself constitute coercive violence. Even very powerful rulers may well be convinced of their own beneficence and legitimacy in the eyes of their subjects, particularly where the comforting doctrines of natural law theorists are taught in justifying to all the obvious disparities of life chances between dominants and subordinates. It is only when "legal socialization" fails to inhibit challenges to authority that its defense must be undertaken: coercive violence is intentional, not structural ("institutional").

Further, passing laws such as anti-terrorism statutes also does not amount to coercive violence. It is what is done in implementing them (or rationalized by claims to be doing so) that is the reality. Although the consequent harm may not be insignificant to those targeted, the least damaging form of violence done to challengers is to limit their ability to travel and communicate. This is not to minimize the harmfulness of such measures, as when the former South African government expelled African university student anti-apartheid protesters and isolated them for years in remote rural places.

Challengers to authority who fail to obtain redress of grievances by peaceful appeals have the minimal option of coercing by warning or threatening unresponsive dominants. In eighteenth-century England growing literacy enabled aggrieved workers to produce and circulate the letters of "Captain Blood" and other dire messages (Hay et al., 1975). A more recent example of minimally coercive action challenging authority is Wei Jingsheng's famous wall poster in Beijing arguing the need for democracy ("the fifth modernization"), with the hardly veiled threat of deteriorating order and lack of progress if the dominants did not change their policies (Butterfield, 1982: 412-414 and passim).

When minimal coercion fails, as it usually does, each side begins to perceive the other as more intransigent than had been believed, or at least hoped, and so each moves to the next level: depriving the other of material resources. Officials typically fine offenders, evict them from housing or offices, confiscate records, freeze bank accounts, and in other ways seek to deprive challengers of the means to carry on their opposition. The American government, for instance, has used the RICO (Racketeer-Influenced and Corrupt Organizations) law, originally aimed at criminal organizations such as the Mafia, to impose crushing financial penalties on "terrorist" right-wing organizations (Smith, 1994: 62, 72, 105).

Having no legal right to deprive their opponents of resources, challengers can only resort to lawbreaking. By definition, their taking of property is theft. If the threat of personal violence is used, the taking is robbery. Whatever their political orientation, every challenging group tends quickly to move to "direct action" when their warnings are unpersuasive. Not only is the appropriation of resources a clear demonstration of resolve, it is also an obvious way of obtaining resources for use – and increasingly necessary to replace resources taken by the authorities. Bank robberies, extortion, and thefts of firearms, explosives, and vehicles are standard tactics.

It is a short step from taking property to destroying it. With or without warrants, authorities may use their powers of "search and seizure" as pretexts for entering and "trashing" the homes and workplaces of opponents. Donner, (1990) has documented myriad instances of such "aggressive surveillance" in the history of political policing in the United States, where labor, student, and minority struggles have commonly been attributed to communist subversion. On the other side, militants have engaged in arson and vandalism, usually rationalized as responding to police outrages. Regardless of who acted first (something always disputed), property destruction marks a significant escalation in political conflicts insofar as it increases the risks of injuries, signals rejection of legal and/or customary restraints, and gives credence to each side's stereotyping of the other as morally defective (Turk, 1982: 71-81).

The limits of coercive violence are reached when individuals are selected for detention. For officials, detention and arrest formally indicate that challengers have crossed the line between legal and illegal political action. At this point, authorities continue to invoke the law as justification for their actions. Procedural rules are followed to a greater or lesser extent; and police actions are formally reviewed by courts, tribunals, or commissions of inquiry.

Having no authority to detain anyone, challengers may detain symbolically important figures (e.g., police officers, government representatives, corporate executives) in the hope of pressuring authorities for concessions. This of course is kidnapping, and is unlikely to achieve more than temporary and relatively minor concessions as hostage-negotiators go about their work. Kidnapping is an extremely risky step, likely to provoke even more repression and to lessen public sympathy. Most importantly, it is virtually impossible to justify kidnapping in moral terms, so that the ideological basis of resistance is eroded – particularly if the target suffers injury or illness while in custody.

Imprisonment is the most extreme form of coercive violence. Beyond imprisonment, political violence loses its coercive rationale: to make the other side come to terms. Increasingly, the implied goal can only be to injure or destroy.

Injurious Violence

Rioting is an indicator of the failure of coercive violence. Again, neither authorities nor challengers can be expected to be objective in their accounts of who is to be blamed. The official view will be that "riot control" was necessary to protect persons and property. Challengers may argue that a "police riot" (Stark, 1972) occurred, in which peaceful demonstrators were attacked. Each side will accuse the other of provoking the clash. Whether the batons, water hoses, or teargas of the police, or the clubs, rocks, or Molotov cocktails of the crowd, the weaponry used in the first stage of injurious violence will not be primarily intended to kill or permanently injure. As many observers have suggested (for examples, see Short and Wolfgang, 1972; Skolnick, 1969) rioting by challengers may well be a last desperate way to communicate grievances. Similarly, excessive as riot police violence predictably will be, it similarly indicates the last vestige of concern for law insofar as the use of deadly force is minimized.

After rioting is suppressed, defenders and challengers are faced with the choice of either seeking a resolution without further violence or adopting tactics clearly aimed at injuring if not destroying opponents. Irrespective of whether it is legal, corporal punishment has no defensible rationale other than to injure. Flogging, for example, is demonstrably counterproductive in that it reinforces instead of deterring alienation and hostility. Beating prisoners implies the desire to injure, not to persuade.

When beating is augmented by other physically and psychologically painful assaults on the senses, the escalation to torture has occurred. The usual rationale is that torture is a regrettable necessity, used to obtain timely vital information (e.g., regarding an imminent assassination, bombing, or other great violence) from persons who would not otherwise provide it (Peters, 1985: 176-187). In reality, only in rare instances can torture be rationalized even in these terms. Instead, it is most commonly used to punish and intimidate individuals who may be targeted merely for demonstration purposes. When either defenders or challengers resort to torture, reciprocity can be anticipated. There is scant hope then of avoiding the transition to destructive violence.

Destructive Violence

Executing prisoners implies that no basis for reconciliation or accommodation exists. Legal no less than illegal execution means the extinction of the target, sending the message that destruction, neither coercion nor injury, is the primary goal. To defenders of authority, capital punishment is likely to be viewed as the appropriate penalty for heinous crimes. To challengers, it is likely to be seen as "judicial murder" confirming the refusal to address their grievances. The most probable response by either side is increased readiness to kill instead of negotiate— generally on the spurious argument that executing prisoners somehow deters the opposition.

On the scale of political violence, assassination ("termination" as authorities often prefer to call their own killings) marks the last point at which a modicum of restraint is found: instead of indiscriminate slaughter, individuals are selectively targeted to maximize the political impact of their dying (Ben-Yehuda, 1993: 46-47). Even though some tactical advantages may result (e. g., from killing an effective leader), assassination is very unlikely to contribute to resolving conflicts because it increases fear, distrust, and hostility.

Lynching is the more or less spontaneous killing of one or a few persons by one or more persons who consider their victims to be representatives of the opposition. As the history of lynching in the United States shows, individual guilt or innocence has little if any bearing on the selection of victims. It has typically occurred where legal authority is weak, and is sometimes depicted as a complement to governmental social control. However, neither legally nor morally can lynching be justified as an alternative form of social control or conflict negotiation. Consequently, though dominants—often with the active or tacit help of law enforcement officers, as in the infamous Neshoba County, Mississippi case (Huie, 1965)—have lynched minorities, dissidents, and deviants, they typically prefer not to use the term "lynching" but rather excuse such killings as acts necessary to suppress or prevent threats to the social order. Regardless of euphemisms, lynching denies the possibility of constructing a society based on anything but terror.

Massacre is the slaughter of whoever happens to be found in a "kill zone," a space in which actual or potential opponents are detected and from which escape is cut off. Government forces describing their own massacres typically use euphemisms such as "pacification" or "reprisals." Even the brutal vestigial order reflected in lynching is absent when defenders or challengers begin indiscriminate killing of targeted categories of people. Dominance through such terror may for awhile be achieved, but at the cost of drastically reducing the chances of building a viable polity. (Armenians do not forget 1917 in Ottoman Turkey; Colombians do not forget *la violencia* between liberals and conservatives.)

The difference between internal war and terrorism lies only in the fact that governments prefer the notion of "low-intensity warfare" for their own actions. Their opponents, of course, prefer appellations such as "guerrillas" or "freedom-fighters" to being called terrorists. Regardless, the escalation to terrorism means that claims to legal or moral authority are belied. War within a polity is the ultimate expression of the zero-sum conception of politics. The conflict can end only in either the annihilation of one party or mutual exhaustion. Either outcome marks a reversal of the process of politically organizing social life. The survivors have to begin anew the effort to create a social order in which there is acceptance of the basic right of any group to survival as long as it does not demonstrably threaten the survival of other groups—or obstruct the quest for a more viable social order.

Trends in Political Violence

The social dynamics of political violence clearly tend to lead to escalation. However, escalation is not inevitable: the process may be halted or reversed. Assuming that political violence ends short of destroying one or both sides, how do the opponents justify stopping short of total victory? The short answer is that each is able to find some loophole in the motivating ideology that permits compromise. Where limited economic or political gains are envisioned, incremental progress can be offered and accepted. Explanations of political violence have often assumed that such material goals are both the causes of, and the means to end, violence: negotiation will eventually find a meeting ground and the conflicting parties, being "reasonable," will be willing to end the violence. It is scarcely imagined that violence is not necessarily an aberration in politics and that accommodation may be impossible.

There is mounting evidence that violent political conflicts are becoming less amenable to negotiation and de-escalation. Although there are a few hopeful developments (e.g., the mutual effort to resolve the internal war between the Mexican government and the Chiapas rebels; the fitful progress in Ireland), the increasing significance of religious beliefs in the ideologies of political violence suggests that conflicts over authority will be increasingly hard to resolve. Juergensmeyer, (2000: 10-12), for instance, has documented that the meaningfulness of their struggle for growing numbers of terrorists derives from religious traditions and innovations that encourage "cultures of violence." Religious ideas provide an explanation of the believer's sense of loss and threat; define in cosmic terms the need to struggle against those responsible; and give the believer's life significance as a holy warrior in a just cause. Drawn from elements in all the major religious traditions, religious justifications for political violence resonate with widely held feelings that the secularism of the modern world order is threatening the nonmaterial values (family, morality, faith, caring, sharing) on which humanity depends. Insofar as either such challengers of authority or its defenders adhere to the notion that they are engaged in a "cosmic war" for survival of Truth against an ungodly enemy, they are very unlikely to be deterred by the other's violence or to be amenable to any notion of compromise.

Those who work for democratic transitions to peaceful social orders will find much to debate in the observations presented here. They are invited to join in the empirical and theoretical work needed to clarify and refine, validate or refute them. The aim is to produce a theoretical model of domestic political violence that is not distorted by the ideological preferences and aversions of either the defenders or the challengers of authority.

REFERENCES

Bankowski, Zenon. (1983). "Anarchism, Marxism and the Critique of Law." In David Sugarman (ed.) *Legality, Ideology, and the State.* New York: Academic Press.

Ben-Yehuda, Nachman. (1993). *Political Assassinations by Jews.* Albany, NY: State University of New York Press.

Butterfield, Fox. (1982). *China: Alive in the Bitter Sea.* New York: Times Books.

Donner, Frank. (1990). *Protectors of Privilege: Red Squads and Police Repression in Urban America.* Berkeley, CA: University of California Press.

Gurr, Ted Robert (ed.) (1980). *Handbook of Political Conflict.* New York: The Free Press.

Gurr, Ted Robert (ed.) (1989). "The History of Protest, Rebellion, and Reform in America: An Overview." In Ted Robert Gurr (ed.), *Violence in America.* Volume 2.

Hay, Douglas, Peter Linebaugh, John G. Rule, E. P. Thompson, and Cal Winslow. (1975). *Albion's Fatal Tree: Crime and Society in Eighteenth-Century England.* New York: Pantheon.

Huie, William Bradford. (1965). *Three Lives For Mississippi.* London: Heinemann.

Juergensmeyer, Mark. (2000). *Terror in the Mind of God: The Global Rise of Religious Violence.* Berkeley, CA: University of California Press.

Mann, Michael. (1986). *The Sources of Social Power.* Volume 1. London: Cambridge University Press.

Peters, Edward. (1985). *Torture.* New York: Basil Blackwell.

Short, James F., Jr. and Marvin E. Wolfgang (eds.) (1972). *Collective Violence*. Chicago: Aldine.

Skolnick, Jerome H. (1969). *The Politics of Protest*. New York: Ballantine.

Smith, Brent L. (1994). *Terrorism in America: Pipe Bombs and Pipe Dreams*. Albany, NY: State University of New York Press.

Smith, Brent L. and Kelly R. Damphousse. (1995). "Punishing Political Offenders: The Effect of Political Motive on Federal Sentencing Decisions." *Criminology* 34: 289-321.

Stark, Rodney. (1972). *Police Riots: Collective Violence and Law Enforcement*. Belmont, CA: Wadsworth.

Stone, Julius. (1966). *Social Dimensions of Law and Justice*. Stanford, CA: Stanford University Press.

Turk, Austin T. (1982). *Political Criminality: The Defiance and Defense of Authority*. Beverly Hills, CA: Sage Publications.

Turk, Austin T. (1996). "La violencia politica desde una perspectiva criminologica." *SISTEMA* 132-133: 41-55.

Wolfgang, Marvin E. (1954). "Political Crimes and Punishments in Renaissance Florence." *Journal of Criminal Law, Criminology, and Police Science* 44: 555-581.

Wolfgang, Marvin E. and Franco Ferracuti. (1967). *The Subculture of Violence*. London: Tavistock.

Zimmermann, Ekkart. (1983). *Political Violence, Crises, and Revolutions: Theories and Research*. Cambridge, MA: Schenkman.

INTIMATE PARTNER VIOLENCE:
THE LEGACY OF MARVIN WOLFGANG'S
THINKING

Albert P. Cardarelli
University of Massachusetts, Boston

Introduction

As we enter the 21st Century, an ever-growing body of research continues to demonstrate an inordinate level of violence among intimate partners throughout American society. Estimates of intimate partner violence involving women as victims indicate that one in four were victimized during their lifetime (Tjaden and Thoennes, 2000). While the prevalence of women who are victimized by violence is no longer a surprise to researchers, policymakers and activists, it is important to note that prior to the 1970's, little research on spousal and intimate partner violence existed. Most research on family violence before that time was concerned with child abuse. Historically, the widespread prevalence of gender inequality meant that the cultural construction of intimate partner violence was defined in male terms and viewed largely as a private matter to be dealt with outside of law enforcement sanctions.

Much of the explanation for the explosion in research on family and intimate partner violence since the 1970's has been attributed to the women's movement and its support of rape crisis centers and shelters for battered women. The growth of shelters from less than 25 in the mid 1970's, to more than 1200 today, is the result of significant advocacy within the public realm by women on the part of women and children victimized by violence and abuse. As a result of this advocacy, major changes in the law and public policy redefined violence between intimate partners as an appropriate area for legal intervention (Koss et al., 1994). Today, nearly every state has specific legislation dealing with violence between intimate partners, including same-sex partners; more than forty states have also enacted mandatory arrest statutes in cases of domestic violence even while such policies remain controversial (Sherman and Smith, 1992; Hirschel, Hutchison and Dean, 1992; Thistlethwarte, Wooldredge and Gibbs, 1998). These legal changes, many of which have not yet been effectively evaluated, have played a major role in the acceptance of the view that private violence is a serious problem that impacts on public life and, therefore, should be subject to the control of the state and the penalties of criminal law. Whether such policies will lead to significant reductions in the levels of intimate violence in the years ahead is difficult to determine, although recent evidence shows that intimate partner homicide continues to decline in the United States, especially among African-Americans (Block and Christakos, 1995; Dugan, Nagin and Rosenfeld, 1999). Further, the rate of intimate partner violence against women decreased 21 percent from 1993 to 1998 (Rennison, 2000).

Prior to this focus on intimate partner violence, articles in the major scholarly journals rarely addressed the phenomena of violence and victimization associated with partner violence. The journal *Criminology*, the official publication of the American Society of Criminology, published only one article in the 1970's dealing with family violence, and only five throughout the 1980's. The establishment after 1985 of more than a dozen new journals focusing on some aspect of family and intimate partner violence, as well as the ever growing numbers of women who were entering academic life and placing greater emphasis on the role of gender in the causes of intimate partner violence, intensified the debate over the patterns, causes and consequences of violence between intimate partners.

In raising the issue of intimate partner violence to the level of public debate, advocates were instrumental in the allocation by the U.S. government of millions of dollars in grants for research, evaluation and demonstration programs for family and domestic violence through the National Institute of Justice and the Violent Crime Control and Law Enforcement Act of 1994. These initiatives have resulted in a greatly expanded body of research on family and intimate partner violence, as well as sweeping policy changes and legal strategies addressing the causes and consequences of this violence for contemporary society.

Marvin Wolfgang's influence in bringing about these changes should not be understated. His research and writings were significantly broad enough in scope to incorporate most areas of research on family and intimate partner violence research undertaken today. To understand the historical linkage of Wolfgang's ideas with current research on intimate partner violence, it is necessary to examine how his early views on partner violence continue to be embodied in today's violence research. A starting point for this undertaking must begin with his analysis of the "victim-offender" relationship in *Patterns in Criminal Homicide*, published in 1958. In so doing, we are aware that significant cultural changes have taken place since its publication, and that these changes influence the ways in which researchers select and interpret behavioral phenomena. Pre-marital sex, for example, once a central topic of texts on social deviance, is hardly likely to raise even an eyebrow among researchers today.

Patterns of Homicide and Intimate Partner Violence

Marvin Wolfgang's *Patterns in Criminal Homicide* (1958) is frequently cited as one of the most important works published in the field of homicide studies over the last 50 years. Using data from the files of the homicide squad of the Philadelphia Police Department, Wolfgang set out to discover and analyze the patterns in 588 cases of criminal homicide involving 621 offenders and 588 victims that took place during the 1948-1952 period. Rich in detail, *Patterns* provided one of the most comprehensive overviews of homicide at the time, and was to be the model upon which researchers studied violent crime in the following decades, even while data collection methods and statistical models continued to improve our understanding of the patterns, causes and consequences of violent behavior, especially that involving intimate partners. In his analysis of the nature of the interpersonal relationship between victim and offender in criminal homicide, three central themes emerged: the nature of the primary relationships in homicide events; the influence of the subculture of violence in supporting the use of violence as an appropriate response in certain situations; and the role of the victim in precipitating the event. Each of these themes is addressed below.

Primary Relationships and Violence

A major focus of Wolfgang's *Patterns* revolved around the character of the interpersonal relationships between victims and offenders. Among 550 known relationships, Wolfgang found that primary contacts (close friend, family member, paramour, and homosexual partner) constituted 65 percent of all victim-offender relationships. Thus, not unlike current research on intimate violence, Wolfgang's data showed that violence takes place not only between spousal partners but between same sex partners and dating couples. The implications of these findings remain critical even today. Approaching intimate partner violence in terms of traditional spousal partners will provide limited understandings as to how violence is incorporated into everyday systems of action, regardless of the marital status or sexual preference of the partners.

Unfortunately, however, during the 25 year period after the publication of *Patterns*, there was little research directed to the study of violence among dating couples, and even less for same sex partners. Prior to 1980, there is little data on the nature and extent of courtship violence; researchers and policy makers alike continued to overlook violence and abuse incidents among dating couples. In a pioneering study of college students, Makepeace (1986) found that one-in-six students had experienced at least one incident of courtship violence. Since then, a large body of research has shown similar levels of violence among dating couples of all ages.

Similar to dating violence, research on the nature and extent of violence among same sex couples was virtually non-existent until the last decade (Hammond, 1989; Lie and Gentlewarrior, 1991; Renzetti, 1992). Wolfgang's *Patterns*, for example, involved only a small number of homosexual homicides and the reasons for the low number are not fully explored. Perhaps, the negative stigma attached to homosexuality at the time of his study reduced the potential for long-term intimate relationships among same sex partners, thus lessening the potential for homicide.

Renzetti (1997) in her analysis of violence among gay and lesbian couples argued that the lack of interest in same sex violence was a result of widespread heterosexism in the social sciences, as well as the belief that battering was basically a male phenomenon. Recent studies demonstrate that partner abuse in same-sex relationships is as extensive and serious as that among heterosexual couples (Dutton, 1994; Renzetti, 1997). Current research on violence among dating and same sex partners provides support for the view that all intimate relationships carry the risk of violence, and that this risk depends in part on the symmetry of power between the partners; the degree of intimacy or mutual responsiveness between partners; and the exposure to, and internalization of, violence throughout one's life span (Cardarelli, 1997).

It has long been recognized that men are not only more violent than women, but that they resort to violence in a wide range of settings. One of the key findings in *Patterns* showed that females in primary relationships were far more at risk of being killed than males, and that 52 percent of the female victims were killed by primary group partners in contrast to 16 percent of the males (Wolfgang, 1958). When race was taken into account, the results were even more pronounced for white females, 65 percent of whom were victims of a primary relationship, compared to 47 percent for black females. When women were the homicide perpetrators, 45 percent killed their husbands in contrast to male offenders who killed their wives in only 12 percent of the homicide cases (Wolfgang, 1958). Recent research continues to show that men are more likely to be involved in felony murder and the killing of friends and acquaintances than women, who are more likely to kill intimate partners (Browne, 1987; Browne and Williams, 1989; Wilson and Daly, 1992; Gauthier and Bankston, 1997).

Even today, women are arrested for criminal violence less often than men. In 1999, for example 83 percent of all arrests for violent crimes in the United States involved males; a pattern that has remained fairly constant over time. In the area of intimate violence, however, the use of violence by women against men remains controversial (Dobash et al., 1992; Straus,

1999). Some studies have concluded that both men and women are equally likely to be victims of partner violence (Straus and Gelles, 1990; Stacey et al., 1994; Straus, 1993), while others argue that women are not only more likely to be victimized by their male partners, but that they suffer greater injury (Browne, 1993; Rennison, 2000). In a national survey of 8000 men and 8000 women conducted in 1995 and 1996, the researchers found that women were more likely than men to report being victimized by an intimate partner in their lifetime, and that the rates of physical assault became greater for men than women as the seriousness of the violence increased (Tjaden and Thoennes, 2000). The survey also reported less violence among lesbian couples living together than women living with a male partner (11 percent v. 30.4 percent); men living with male intimate partners were more likely to be victims of violence than men who lived with female partners (15 percent v. 7.7 percent).

In the same survey, the findings suggest that all racial minorities experience more intimate partner violence than do whites; African-American men and women were also more likely to be victimized by an intimate partner in their lifetime than white men and women (Tjaden and Thoennes, 2000). Why violence continues to vary among partners of different ethnic and racial backgrounds is not the focus of the present chapter. Wolfgang also encountered this challenge without much success in arriving at a definitive explanation of the variance in the prevalence of intimate partner violence among black and white offenders and victims in Philadelphia. Almost fifty years later, race continues to be a controversial variable in violence research, in part, because of the racial disparities associated with law enforcement and the administration of justice during the past century (Block and Christakos, 1995; Hawkins, 1999).

Violence as Normative Behavior

A central concern of Wolfgang's *Patterns* revolves around the normative context in which violence unfolds in everyday life. His research on homicide led him to conclude that "...major patterns of elements involved in criminal homicide suggest that there may exist a subculture of violence within the larger community culture..." and further, that in this subculture violence becomes a part of the normative structure of its members and is often tolerated and encouraged in certain kinds of interpersonal situations (Wolfgang, 1958, pp. 328-329). These early ruminations were, of course, to become the basis for his expanded analysis of the subculture of violence paradigm with Franco Ferracuti in 1967; one that integrated both sociological and psychological perspectives associated with the definition, description and measurement of violence (Wolfgang and Ferracuti, 1967).

In focusing on the normative structure within which violence occurs, Wolfgang demonstrated that many offenders of intimate partner homicide had previous arrest records for criminal violence. In a recent effort to understand the role of gender for both victim and offender in victim precipitated homicide, Felson and Messner (1998) found that male offenders were more likely than female offenders to have prior records for violence, and that this was especially true for males who were killed by their female partners. Individuals with previous histories of violence may come to accept violence against an intimate partner as falling within a repertoire of violence appropriate to the resolution of conflictual situations in which they find themselves. These same individuals may be more likely to use violence in the public realm (Moffitt, et al., 2000).

Although criminologists have long been interested in the relationship between community and criminal behavior, there are few empirical studies concerned with the relationship between community and intimate partner violence. Because of the spatial concentration of violence in neighborhoods with high rates of poverty, social isolation of families, which is known to increase the risk of partner assault, is commonplace. The more pervasive social isolation becomes, the less likely strategies of control will be effective in preventing violent behavior. In these communities, interpersonal violence involving strangers and acquaintances may become routine, thereby, leading many women to downplay the seriousness of violence in their own relationships. Since economic dependence is one of the main factors in keeping women from leaving their abusers, women living in poverty are especially vulnerable to persistent abuse and violence (Brewer and Smith, 1995). Under these conditions, children will also have a high risk of being exposed to violence either as victims or witnesses. This exposure, as research has shown, can potentially increase the risk that children will learn that violence is an appropriate strategy to resolve conflict in intimate relationships (Kalmuss, 1984; O'Leary, 1988). Although violence exists across the economic spectrum, neighborhoods that are socially disorganized will require extraordinary efforts on the part of the police and other municipal and private agencies to prevent and control interpersonal violence, including that involving intimate partners.

While more than three decades have passed since Wolfgang and Ferracuti set out to develop a theory of violence, the need for an integrated theory of violence for understanding the causes and consequences of intimate partner violence remains critical (Williams, 1992; Miller and Wellford, 1997). To move beyond a reactive and ideological address to the violence and abuse between intimate partners, it is essential to understand the factors at both the societal and interpersonal levels that lead to destructive behavior. As Wolfgang and Ferracuti (1967) cautioned in their analysis, focusing exclusively on either violent offenders or victims will result in individually-oriented perspectives that emphasize psychological defects or deficiencies to the exclusion of the socio-cultural imperatives associated with the use and avoidance of violence in interpersonal relationships. Chronic violence, they argued, may result more from the normative frameworks to which individuals are exposed and socialized than from psychological defects or deficiencies. Because violence between intimate partners is in almost all cases the end result of a series of episodes - psychological and otherwise - it must be seen as part of the network of violence that takes place in society, whether the partners are aware of the network or not. Understanding the meanings and motives behind the use of violence between intimate partners is not only essential to the establishment of appropriate measures of deterrence, but even more important, the dissolution or disruption of the network of violence is dependent on this endeavor (Kelly, 1987; Kennedy and Forde, 1999).

Violence and the Role of the Victim

Although all incidents of intimate partner violence are not lethal, Wolfgang's argument that "homicide is a dynamic relationship between two or more persons caught up in a life drama where they operate in a direct interactional relationship. [and where] the relationship the victim bears to the offender plays a role in explaining the reasons for such flagrant violation" (Wolfgang, 1958 p. 203) continues to underlie most research on interpersonal violence. This is especially evident in attempts to understand the role of the victim in the unfolding events that lead to the onset and dissolution of violent behavior between intimate partners (Sobol, 1997; Polk, 1997). What is it about intimate partner violence, for example, that only a small number of violent acts become lethal, even while that potential is possible in many instances? Research dealing with the escalation and desistance of violence between intimate partners remains a critical area of inquiry (Feld and Straus, 1990).

Even less considered is the nature, extent and consequences of abuse and violence between intimate partners in a variety of stages of intimacy and commitment. Thus, violence in dating and courtship relationships needs to be considered in terms of the degree of maturity and levels of resources that individuals bring to the partnership (Makepeace, 1997), as well as the responses of both victims and offenders to the initial and subsequent acts of violence that take place within the parameters of their relationship.

While the need to examine the role of the victim in the onset and dissolution of violence continues to be a central tenet of homicide research, it has not yet been fully developed and explored in research that focuses on intimate partner violence. Much of the research on violence towards women, for example, has until recently been victim driven with emphasis directed to the nature and extent of the violence as well as the barriers that impede victims from leaving abusive relationships. Only recently has there been increased attention directed to the types of individuals who batter their intimate partners (Gondolf, 1987; Dutton, 1988; Saunders, 1992; Johnson, 1995; Holtzworth-Munroe, 1999). Intimate partner violence, like all forms of violence and deviance in general, may be a one-time event, an episodic activity, or a chronic pattern of violence resistant to formal intervention. The establishment of batterer typologies would begin to provide a more precise picture of recidivist batterers and the potential effectiveness of graduated sanctions for those individuals responsible for chronic abuse and violence of their intimate partners (Miller and Wellford, 1997). Further, the identification of those offenders who resort to violence in both the private and public realm would be a major accomplishment in violence research.

Conclusions

The above discussion is not intended to provide a comprehensive overview of intimate partner violence; such analyses are available elsewhere (Jasinski and Williams, 1998; Browne, Williams and Dutton, 1999). The focus rather, is on the ways in which Wolfgang's ideas about the interactive dynamics of violence continue to resonate in today's research more than 40 years after the publication of his *Patterns in Homicide*, even though major social changes have taken place in American society.

The "subculture of violence" theme, for example, raised in *Patterns* and elaborated upon more fully in Wolfgang and Ferracuti's *The Subculture of Violence* (1967), while given perfunctory address in most criminology textbooks, is rarely the organizing framework around which research on violence is conducted today. This is not to deny the richness of ideas associated with the debates over the utility of the "subculture" theme to explain violence, but rather to illustrate that ideas and issues rise and fall from the level of public debate, thus influencing the manner in which public resources are allocated to address the causes and consequences of violent behavior. Throughout the 1990's, for example, much attention was directed to youth violence in the United States with millions of dollars allocated by Congress to delinquency prevention and control measures.

Unlike the current address to youth violence and drug use, Wolfgang's finding that women in primary relationships were far more at risk of being killed than men was largely ignored and absent from debate in the public realm until women took up the cause in the 1970's. One reason for the failure of researchers and policy makers to raise the issue of partner violence to a level of importance may stem form the overwhelming focus by researchers on youth gangs and delinquency, the fascination with organized crime, corruption and the reification of prison "societies and cultures";

themes that dominated the criminological enterprise throughout the 1970's and 1980's.

In addition, much research was no doubt influenced by the turmoil of the times. In 1968 the United States saw the political assassinations of Martin Luther King Jr. and Robert Kennedy, the excessive use of force and violence by the Chicago Police Department at the 1968 Democratic Convention, and major destruction of property as a result of riots in black neighborhoods throughout the country. The over-riding focus on criminal and collective violence is clearly evident in the volumes released in 1969 by the National Commission on the Causes and Prevention of Violence. In 13 separate volumes dealing with violence in America; only one chapter was devoted to violence between intimate partners. Given that little was known at this time about the scope of violence in the family, it is not difficult to understand why such behavior garnered little debate or concern in American society. The growing protest movement against the Vietnam War on college campuses, the killing of students at Kent State in 1970, the Watergate scandal and the government crisis associated with the resignation of President Nixon further delayed any address to the prevalence of family and intimate partner violence in American society.

In an early publication, Wolfgang wrote of Cesare Lombroso as a major pioneer in Criminology. More than four decades later, it is not unreasonable to bestow this same accolade on Wolfgang. His seminal thinking on violence continues to manifest itself in our own endeavors to understand the causes and consequences of interpersonal violence in the 21st century.

REFERENCES

Block, C.R. and Christakos, A. (1995). "Intimate Partner Homicide in Chicago over 29 Years." *Crime and Delinquency* 41 (4) 496-526.

Brewer, V. and Smith, M.D. (1995). "Gender Inequality and Rates of Female Homicide Victimization across U.S. Cities." *Journal of Research in Crime and Delinquency* 32 (2) 175-190.

Browne, Angela. (1987). *When Battered Women Kill*. New York: Macmillan/Free Press.

Browne, Angela. (1993). "Violence against Women by Male Partners: Prevalence, Outcomes, and Policy Implications". *American Psychologist* 48:1077-1087.

Browne, Angela. (1997). "Violence in Marriage: Until Death Do Us Part?" In Albert P. Cardarelli (Ed.) *Violence Between Intimate Partners: Patterns, Causes, and Effects* (48-69) Boston: Allyn and Bacon.

Browne, A. and Williams, K.R. (1989). "Gender, Intimacy and Lethal Violence: Trends from 1976 through 1987." *Gender & Society* 7 (1) 78-98.

Browne, A., Williams, K.R. and Dutton, D. G. (1999). "Homicide between Intimate Partners: A 20-year Review." In *Homicide: A Sourcebook of Social Research.* M. Dwayne Smith and Margaret A. Zahn (Eds.) Thousand Oaks, CA: Sage.

Cardarelli, Albert, P. (1997). "Violence and Intimacy: An Overview". In Albert P. Cardarelli (Ed.) *Violence Between Intimate Partners: Patterns, Causes and Effects.* (1-9) Boston: Allyn and Bacon.

Dobash, R.P. et al. (1992). "The Myth of the Symmetrical Nature of Domestic Violence." *Social Problems* 39:71-91.

Dugan, L., Nagin, D.S. and Rosenfeld, R. (1999). "Explaining the Decline in Intimate Partner Homicide: The Effects of Changing Domesticity, Women's Status, and Domestic Violence Resources." *Homicide Studies,* 3 (3) 187-214.

Dutton, D.G. (1988). "Profiling of Wife Assaulters: Preliminary Evidence for a Trimodal Analysis." *Violence and Victims* 3:3-30.

Dutton, D.G. (1994). "Patriarchy and Wife Assault: The Ecological Fallacy." *Violence and Victims* 9:167-182.

Feld, S.L. and Straus, M.A. (1990). "Escalation and Desistance from Wife Assault in Marriage." In *Physical Violence in American Families: Risk Factors and Adaptations To Violence in 8,145 Families* M.A. Straus and R.J. Gelles (Eds.) New Brunswick, NJ: Transaction Publisher.

Felson, R.B. and Messner, S.F. (1998). "Disentangling the Effects of Gender and Intimacy on Victim Precipitation in Homicide". *Criminology* 36 (2) 405-423.

Gauthier, D.K. and Bankston, W.B. (1997). "Gender Equality and the Sex Ratio of Intimate Killing.". *Criminology* 35 (4) 577-600.

Gondolf, E.W. (1987). "Who are These Guys? Toward a Behavioral Typology of Batterers." *Violence and Victims* 3:187-201.

Hammond, N. (1989). "Lesbian Victims of Relationship Violence." *Women and Therapy* 8:89-105.

Hawkins, Darnell, F. (1999). "What Can We Learn from Data Disaggregation. The Case of Homicide and African Americans." In *Homicide: A Sourcebook of Social Research.* M. Dwayne Smith and Margaret A. Zahn (Eds.) Thousand Oaks, CA: Sage.

Hirschel, J.D., Hutchison, I.W. and Dean, C.W. (1992). "The Failure of Arrest to Deter Spousal Abuse." *Journal of Research in Crime and Delinquency* 29 (1) 7-33.

Holtzworth-Munore, Amy et al. (1999). "A Typology of Male Batterers: An Initial Examination." In X.B. Arriaga and S. Oskamp (Eds.) *Violence in Intimate Relationships* (45-72) Thousand Oaks, CA: Sage.

Jasinski, J.L. and Williams, L.M. (Eds.). (1998*). Partner Violence: A Comprehensive Review of 20 Years of Research.* Thousand Oaks, CA: Sage.

Johnson, M.P. (1995). "Patriarchal Terrorism and Common Couple Violence: Two Forms of Violence against Women." *Journal of Marriage and the Family* 57:283-294.

Kalmus, D. (1984). "The Intergenerational Transmission of Marital Aggression." *Journal of Marriage and the Family* 44:277-286.

Kelly, Liz. (1987). "How Women Define their Experiences of Violence" In K Yllo and M. Bograd (Eds.) *Feminist Perspectives On Wife Abuse* (114-132) Newbury Park, CA: Sage.

Kennedy, Leslie W. and Forde, David R. (1999). *When Push Comes to Shove: A Routine Conflict Approach to Violence.* Albany, NY: State University of New York Press.

Koss, M.P., et al. (1994). *No Safe Haven: Male Violence Against Women At Home, At Work, And In The Community.* Washington, DC: American Psychological Association.

Lie, G.Y., and Gentlewarrior, S. (1991). "Intimate Violence in Lesbian Relationships: Discussion of Survey Findings and Practice Implications." *Journal of Social Service Research* 15:41-59.

Makepeace, James M. (1999). "Courtship Violence as Process: A Developmental Theory." In Albert P. Cardarelli (Ed.) *Violence Between Intimate Partners: Patterns, Causes, and Effects* (29-47) Boston: Allyn and Bacon.

Miller, S.L. and Wellford, C.F. (1997). "Patterns and Correlates of Intimate Partner Violence." In Albert P. Cardarelli *Violence Between Intimate Partners: Patterns, Causes, and Effects* (16-28) Boston: Allyn and Bacon.

Moffitt, T.E., Krueger, R.F., Caspi, A. and Fagan, J. (2000). "Partner Abuse and General Crime: How are they the Same? How are They Different?" *Criminology* 38 (1) 199-231.

O'Leary, K.D. (1988). "Physical Aggression between Spouses: A Social Learning Perspective." In V. B. Van Hasselt, R. L. Morrison, A. S. Bellack and M. Hersen (Eds.) *Handbook of Family Violence* (31-55) New York: Plenum.

Polk, Kenneth. (1997). "A Reexamination of the Concept of Victim Precipitated Homicide.". *Homicide Studies* 1 (2) 141-168.

Rennison, C.M. and Welchans, S. (2000). *Intimate Partner Violence Special Report, Bureau of Justice Statistics.* Washington, DC: U. S. Department of Justice.

Renzetti, Claire, M. (1992). *Violent Betrayal: Partner Abuse In Lesbian Relationships.* Newbury Park, CA: Sage.

Renzetti, Claire, M. (1997). "Violence and Abuse among Same-Sex Couples." In Albert P. Cardarelli (Ed.) *Violence Between Intimate Partners: Patterns, Causes, and Effects* (70-89) Boston: Allyn and Bacon.

Rosenfeld, Richard. (1997). "Changing Relationships between Men and Women: A Note on the Decline of Intimate Partner Homicide." *Homicide Studies* 1 (1) 72-83.

Saunders, D.G. (1992). "A Typology of Men Who Batter: Three Types Derived from Cluster Analysis." *American Journal of Orthopsychiatry* 62 (2) 264-275.

Sherman, L. and Smith, D. (1992). "Crime, Punishment and State in Conformity: Legal and Extralegal Control of Domestic Violence." *American Sociological Review* 58 (3) 680-690.

Sobol, J.J. (1997). "Behavioral Characteristics and Level of Involvement for Victims of Homicide." *Homicide Studies* 1 (4) 359-376.

Stacey, W.A., L.R. Hazlewood and Shupe, Anson . (1994). *The Violent Couple*. Westport, CT: Praeger.

Straus, Murray A. and Gelles, Richard J. (1990). *Physical Violence in American Families: Risk Factors and Adaptations to Violence in 8, 145 Families*. New Brunswick, NJ: Transaction Publishers.

Straus, Murray A. (1999). "The Controversy over Domestic Violence by Women: A Methodological, Theoretical, and Sociology of Science Analysis." In X.B. Arriaga and S. Oskamp (Eds.) *Violence In Intimate Relationships* (17-44) Thousand Oaks: Sage.

Straus, Murray A. (1993). "Physical Assault by Wives: A Major Social Problem." In R.J. Gelles and D.R. Loseke (Eds.) *Current Controversies on Family Violence* (67-87) Newbury Park, CA: Sage.

Thistlethwaite, A. Wookdredge and Gibbs, D. (1998). "Severity of Dispositions and Domestic Violence Recidivism." *Crime and Delinquency* 44 (3) 388-398.

Tjaden, P. and Thoennes, N. (2000). Extent, Nature, And Consequences Of Intimate Partner Homicide: Findings From *The National Violence Against Women Survey*. Washington, DC: U.S. Department of Justice.

Williams, K.R. (1992). "Social Sources of Marital Violence and Deterrence: Testing an Integrated Theory of Assaults between Partners." *Journal of Marriage and the Family* 554 (3) 620-628.

Wilson, M.I. and Daly, M. (1992). "Who Kills Whom in Spouse Killings? On the Exceptional Sex Ratio of Spousal Homicides in the United States." *Criminology*, 30 (2) 189-215.

Wolfgang, Marvin E. (1958). *Patterns in Criminal Homicide*. New York: John Wiley & Sons, Inc.

Wolfgang, Marvin E. and Ferracuti, Franco. (1967). *The Subculture Of Violence: Towards An Integrated Theory In Criminology*. Tavistock Publications Limited.

SOCIAL STRESS AND VIOLENCE IN ISRAEL: A MACRO LEVEL ANALYSIS

Simha F. Landau
The Hebrew University of Jerusalem

Introduction

My first large-scale study in criminology, conducted with the cooperation of Israel Drapkin, was on "Ethnic Patterns of Homicide in Israel" (Landau and Drapkin, 1968; Landau, Drapkin and Arad, 1974; Landau, 1975a). Needless to say, Marvin Wolfgang's pioneering work on "Patterns in Criminal Homicide" (Wolfgang, 1958) was a major inspiration for this study and, in practice, served as its main blueprint. His careful analysis of personal, situational, and interactional variables laid the foundation for the phenomenological approach to the analysis of crime. This approach was later adopted by many other researchers, including Israeli criminologist Menachem Amir in his study on forcible rape (Amir, 1971).

Since that early study, homicide and other types of violence in Israeli society have become the main foci of my research activity. My endeavor to arrive at a better understanding of patterns of violence in society, especially Israeli society, has generally been based on empirical research on the macro social level, with Israeli society as the main unit of analysis, and the search, development and confirmation of appropriate explanatory models.

In this paper, I will attempt to provide a concise account of research findings regarding violence in Israel. My basic thesis is that patterns of violent crime in Israel are closely related to various stress factors in society. I begin with an outline of general trends in violent crime in Israel over time. I then enumerate some of the most prominent stress factors experienced by Israelis. This is followed by a brief descriptive account of trends in violent crime on the background of significant events in Israel's short history. I then introduce and discuss a number of conceptual models relating stress and violence, including my own stress-support model (Landau and Beit-Hallahmi, 1983; Landau, 1997b). Empirical evidence in support of these models is then provided, together with a brief account of some unique measures of stress developed by me in the course of my research (objective/subjective indicators of stress and social support). I then provide a brief outline of the differential contribution of various social groups to violence in Israel. The paper concludes with some comments regarding implications of the Israeli findings for criminological theory and methodology in general.

General Trends of Violent Crime in Israel

The two main sources of information about the extent of criminal behavior, including violent crime, are criminal statistics and victim surveys. Victim surveys in Israel have, to date been very few and far between (Landau and Sebba, 1998). Therefore, the present analysis on trends in crimes of violence in Israel will be based mainly on reported criminal statistics.

"Violent crime" is a general label covering a variety of unlawful behaviors. Quite a number of these crimes are notoriously underrepresented in criminal statistics. Among these are rape (and other forms of sexual assault), assaults against family members (spouses, children), and violence within certain social groups. The present analysis will focus mainly on homicide (including attempted homicide) and robbery. Homicide is universally considered to be the most severe of violent crimes, whereas robbery combines personal violence with threat to property. The seriousness of these two crimes of violence, coupled with their high visibility, make them the most reliable reported crimes, and thus they can be used as relatively accurate indicators of the level of violence in society.

The data cover a period of fifty years, from 1949 (the first year for which annual statistics are available) to 1999. They were collected from the Israeli Central Bureau of Statistics (Central Bureau of Statistics, 1949-1999).

Figure 1 presents the annual rates of homicide (including attempted homicide). As can be seen, several distinct trends in homicide rates are observed during this period. The first years after the establishment of the state of Israel (in 1948) witnessed a sharp increase in homicide, peaking in 1952 and 1953. This was followed by a consistent decline lasting sixteen years, down to 1.9 in 1969. During the 1970s, homicide rates rose again, reaching 6.3 in 1979. The gradual decrease from 1980 onwards was interrupted by a relatively sharp upward trend in 1989 and 1990 (5.6 and 6.4, respectively). Since 1994, these rates have been quite stable (around 4 per 100,000 population).

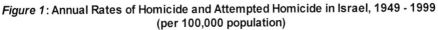

Figure 1: Annual Rates of Homicide and Attempted Homicide in Israel, 1949 - 1999 (per 100,000 population)

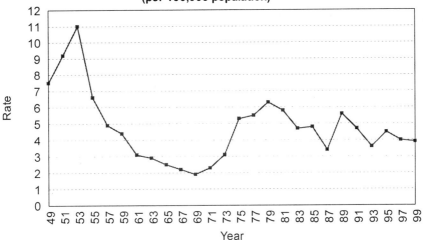

The annual rates of robbery, presented in Figure 2, reveal that the general trend of this violent crime between 1949 and 1995 is very similar to that of homicide. The overall pattern of robbery rates is given by a U-shaped curve during the years 1949-1980, followed by a smaller J-shaped curve during the years 1980-1999. The larger U-shaped curve starts at 18.5 in 1949, followed by a fairly consistent decline, reaching a low of 1.8 in 1965. From 1966, a fairly stable upward trend is observed, reaching its highest point (15.3) in 1980. The slight decrease in robbery between 1980 and 1987 (to 11.7) was followed by a consistent increase (with the exception of 1991) to the all time high of 29.5 in 1999.

Figure 2: Annual Rates of Robbery in Israel, 1949 - 1999 (per 100,000 population)

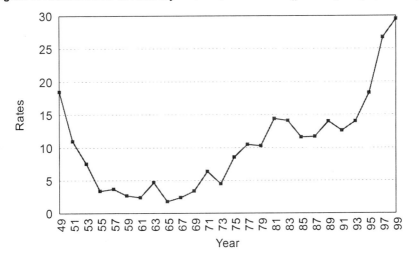

It should be mentioned that the above trends in violent crime are
quite different from the trend of all offenses (mainly offenses against
property), which show a constant (almost linear) increase over the years,
from 16.0 per 100,000 population in 1949, to 62.5 in 1999 (Central Bureau of
Statistics, 1949-1999).

The trends in violent crime call for an explanation. Any given act of
violence (like any other human behavior) has its immediate causes or
explanations on the individual level. The present analysis, however, focuses
on the aggregate level, and I will attempt to analyze and explain the above
patterns of violence from a wider social perspective. My basic thesis is that
the above patterns of violent crime in Israel are closely related to various
stress factors experienced by Israelis.

Stress Factors in Israeli Society

Israeli society can justifiably be described as an ideal natural
laboratory for the study of the effects of stress on human beings. In addition
to the usual types of stress experienced in all modern societies, Israelis are
exposed to a number of additional stressors which, in their particular
combination, are quite unique.

The foremost of these stressors is the continuous concern of Israelis
with security, both on the national and on the individual level. Since its
establishment in 1948, Israel has been involved in five major wars and in
endless hostilities with its neighboring Arab countries as well as with the
Palestinian inhabitants of the occupied territories. The need to take
precautions and to be on guard keeps men, women and children aware of the
constant threat to their daily routines. The permanence of the threat of war
for so many years, and the lifetime commitment of Israeli men to national
service in the military, have had a considerable effect on Israeli society. It
would not be an overstatement to say that belligerence has been the most
stable aspect of the history of the state of Israel, and that Israel has come to
regard itself as a society at war, if not a society of warriors. Periodic national
surveys have indeed shown that the fear of war and related issues (fear of
terrorism, prolonged army service) became the most salient concern of
Israelis from 1968 onwards (Katz, 1982a, 1982b; Mayseless, 1989; Stone,
1982).

A number of Israeli studies have investigated the effects of wars (as
well as more prolonged security-related stress situations) on a wide range of
topics, from its direct effects on soldiers on the frontlines, to more
generalized effects on public morale, on children, on the level of
psychopathology, on change in gender roles, and on emigration from Israel
(see, Landau, 1998b). It should be noted that the number of casualties
caused by wars, terrorist acts and the like, in Israel's history, far exceeds the
number of casualties caused by "regular" crimes of violence.

Economic hardship (recession, unemployment, and high rates of inflation) is another important source of stress in Israel. Over the last three decades, Israel's economy has witnessed times of prosperity and development during which the standard of living rose to unprecedented heights, as well as times of economic hardship and recession, high inflation rates and increased unemployment. The economic uncertainty caused by inflation has tremendous psychological implications and constitutes an additional stressful burden on everyday life, particularly for those in the lower income brackets (Epstein and Babad, 1982; Mimon, 1983). The detrimental effects of economic stress factors have been widely discussed in the literature. In a number of studies conducted in the United States (Brenner, 1977; Brenner and Swank, 1986), it was found that economic stress such as unemployment, inflation, and per capita income have a substantial bearing on physical health, mental health, and criminal aggression. In a cross-cultural study on fourteen different countries, Landau (1984) reported that in most countries increased inflation rates were accompanied by parallel increase in homicide, robbery and general criminal activity.

A third, more general, stress-related factor has to do with the extreme social and demographic changes that have taken place in Israel over a relatively short period. Israel is basically a society of immigrants with the majority of its members either born elsewhere or born to immigrant parents. The Jewish population in the country grew more than sevenfold, from 650,000 in 1948, to 4,785,100 in 1998 (Central Bureau of Statistics, 1999). During the years 1948-1998, an impressive number of 2,611,000 immigrants were absorbed (Central Bureau of Statistics, 1999) and, according to recent estimates, about one million immigrants arrived from the former Soviet Union during the 1990s.

Another important social-demographic change, closely related to the security situation, is the inclusion of a sizable Arab population under Israeli rule in the territories occupied by Israel during the 1967 War: the West Bank, the Gaza Strip, and the Golan Heights.

The description of the above mentioned stress factors provide the background for my research into criminal violence in Israel. This will be done on two levels: (1) the descriptive-historical level, trying to relate trends in violent crime to major stressful events and processes of national significance; and (2) the analytical level, reviewing major Israeli scientific research on this topic within the framework of several theoretical models.

Violent Crime and Significant Events in Israel's History

Unfortunately, the most salient landmarks in Israel's history are the major wars in which the country has been involved. The first war, the War of Independence, broke out even before the official declaration of the establishment of the state of Israel on May 15, 1948. This was the most crucial and the bloodiest war of all, with casualties amounting to about 1 percent of the total Jewish population (more than 6,000 killed out of 650,000). The first few years of Israel's existence were undoubtedly the most turbulent in the country's history. The immediate period following independence was characterized by an enormous influx of Jewish immigrants from Europe (survivors of the Holocaust) as well as from Arab and other countries. Within a period of about three years (1948-1951), the Jewish population more than doubled, absorbing 688,000 immigrants (Smooha, 1994). Inevitably, during these years Israelis experienced serious economic hardship due to the national priority given to immigrant absorption.

As can be seen in Figures 1 and 2, these highly stressful early years have very high rates of both homicide and robbery. Thereafter, a steady decline in violent crime is observed, except for 1956, the year of the Sinai Campaign, during which there was an increase in the homicide rate.

The decade between 1957 and 1967 (between the Sinai Campaign and the Six Day War) can be described as the most peaceful period in Israel's history. Military clashes with neighboring countries were at a very low level, the state of the economy improved, and immigration slowed down considerably. Note also that the level of violent crime during this decade was, on the whole, very low. However, robbery started to increase in 1966, a year of severe economic recession, and especially after 1967, following the Six Day War. The increase in homicide started a little later, between 1967 and the 1973 (Yom Kippur) war.

As mentioned before, following the occupation of Arab territories in the 1967 war, security-related stress (terrorist attacks and the like) became a matter of daily concern to Israelis. There was a sharp increase in both homicide and robbery during the 1970s, particularly after the 1973 (Yom Kippur) war. This war and its heavy casualties, proved to be a major turning point in Israel's history. It was followed by severe political, economic and social upheavals. According to the approach presented here, the sharp increase in violent crime is an indicator of the high level of stress experienced by Israelis during those years.

The late 1970s witnessed the historical peace agreement between Israel and its strongest enemy, Egypt (in 1979). As can be seen in Figures 1 and 2, during most of the 1980s, there was a consistent decline in homicide and robbery. During this period (in 1982), Israel was involved in the controversial Lebanese War. However, the most significant turning point in the 1980s was the outbreak of the Palestinian uprising (Intifada) in December

1987. As can be seen in the two figures, the years following the outbreak of
the Intifada saw a considerable increase in both homicide and robbery. The
decrease in these crimes in 1991 could well be related to Israel's involvement
in the Persian Gulf War. This war differed in many respects from all the
previous wars in which Israel was involved. On the one hand, the population
was under serious threat from Iraqi missiles and, on the other hand, for the
first time in its history, Israel was forced to take a totally passive role.
Moreover, despite the numerous missiles landing in residential areas, the
number of casualties was negligible. In addition, for the duration of this war,
there was a lull in the Intifada due to the curfews imposed on the occupied
territories coupled with the fact that the Palestinian population also felt
threatened by the Iraqi missiles.

The year 1993 saw a political breakthrough in the Israeli-Arab
conflict with the signing of the Declaration of Principles between Israel and
the Palestinian Liberation Organization (PLO) in Oslo, Norway.
Consequently the Palestinian Authority (PA) was established, and extensive
parts of the Israeli occupied territories were gradually transferred to the PA's
control. The existence of Palestinian autonomous areas over which the
Israeli authorities have no control adjacent to densely populated Israeli areas
has been shown to be related to the steady and salient increase in robbery and
motor vehicle theft, particularly during the second half of the 1990s (Herzog,
2000).

Although the above overview of the most significant events in
Israel's history is somewhat selective, it most certainly provides clues
towards understanding the general trends of violent crime in Israel.
However, what it does not do is to establish a relationship between violent
crime and the various stress factors. For such a relationship to be
established, research has to demonstrate that these stress factors have a
measurable effect on violent crime. However, before presenting such data,
let us provide a conceptual analysis of the relationship between stress and
crime.

Stress and Violence: Some Conceptual Models

In this section, two major conceptual frameworks will be presented:
one that specifically relates violence to warfare, and the other, relating
violence to stress in general.

Warfare and Violent Crime

Two opposing hypotheses may be posited regarding the effect of war
and security-related stress on violent crime: the cohesion hypothesis versus
the legitimation-habituation hypothesis. The cohesion hypothesis (based on
Coser, 1956; and Simmel, 1955) suggests that outside pressures and threats

serve to unify and strengthen the community and to reduce internal conflict, including in-group violence. According to this model, when the external threat is over, the level of in-group violence returns to its pre-emergency level.

The prediction of the legitimation-habituation hypothesis (put forward by Archer and Gartner, 1984) is entirely different. According to this model, the authorized and sanctioned killing that takes place during war has a depreciating effect on human life and provides legitimation to acts of aggression and to the perception of violence as a habitual way of behavior. According to this hypothesis, one should expect an increase in homicide after war. In their cross-national study (of eighty nations), Archer and Gartner (1984) confirmed the above hypothesis by showing that combatant nations were more likely to experience substantially higher homicide rates in the postwar period than in the prewar period. No such parallel increase was found for noncombatant nations. Postwar increase in homicide rates were most frequent in nations with a high death toll in combat.

Yet another departure from the cohesion hypothesis is expressed in the positive relationship between internal conflict and external conflict found by Ross (1985) in his study of ninety pre-industrial societies. He interpreted this finding through the psychological mechanisms of generalization and habituation: Societies with a tendency to violence will express this violence both internally and externally; teaching citizens to fight external enemies will have the effect of increasing "internal warfare" (violence within society).

Stress, Support and Violence

Landau and Beit-Hallahmi's (1983) stress-support model for the explanation of violent crime extends the frustration-aggression hypothesis (Dollard, Doob, Miller, Mowrer, and Sears, 1939; Henry and Short, 1954; Hovland and Sears, 1940) from the level of the individual to the level of populations. This model postulates that the prevalence of violent crime in society will be positively related to the intensity of stress factors and negatively related to the intensity of social support systems. At a later stage, Landau (1997b) adopted an even wider perspective, accommodating non-violent as well as violent crime.

In line with recent theoretical and empirical studies, this model conceives stress in terms of negative affect (for reviews of the relevant literature, see among others Agnew, 1992; Agnew and White, 1992; Berkowitz, 1993). The model incorporates two important elements (instead of one) for the explanation of violence and aggression: social stressors and social support systems.

The relationship between stress and aggression was noted by Halleck (1967) who argued that aggression is a response to stress which, in turn, can arise from a variety of sources (both external and internal to the individual).

This relationship is widely reported in the literature on family violence (see, among others, Farrington, 1986; MacEwen and Barling, 1988). Berkowitz (1993) conceives negative affect as a major intervening variable between external stressors and aggression: "It is not the external stressor in itself but rather the negative affect aroused by the stressor that produces the aggressive tendencies..." (Berkowitz, 1993, p.56). Agnew (1992) adopts a wider perspective and relates negative affect to crime in general. In his review of the relevant literature, he points out that many theories assume that: "... failure to achieve ... expectations may lead to such emotions as anger, resentment, rage, dissatisfaction, disappointment, and unhappiness -- that is, all the emotions customarily associated with strain in criminology" (Agnew, 1992, p. 52). In his own general strain theory, he emphasizes negative affect as a key concept in understanding and explaining crime and delinquency in general: "... Each type of strain increases the likelihood that individuals will experience one or more of a range of negative emotions...Anger... affects the individual in several ways that are conducive to delinquency" (Agnew, 1992, pp. 59-60). In an empirical test of the general strain theory, Agnew and White (1992), using self-report measures of delinquency among adolescents, found that strain variables (negative life events and life hassles) had the expected significant effect on both violent and non-violent offenses: fighting, robbery larceny, burglary, vandalism, etc. Similarly, Paternoster and Mazerolle (1994), using data from the National Youth Survey, reported that negative relations with adults, as well as feelings of dissatisfaction (with friends and school life) were positively related to delinquency. In a study on both adults and juveniles, Felson (1992) found that anger affects other forms of delinquency as strongly as it affects aggressive behavior.

On the social level of analysis, Haas (1968) presented a conceptual model in which economic stressors (unemployment and modernization) are positively associated with homicide and suicide (conceived by him as indicators of social strain) which, in turn, are linked to national aggressiveness (war). Linsky and Straus (1986) view violent crime as well as property crime as major possible responses to stress. In their comparative analysis of social stress in the 50 states of the United States, they report that "Stressful life events [based on objective aggregate measures] are positively correlated with all seven of the so-called 'index crimes,' that is, the higher the state stress level, the higher the crime rates for these states" (Linsky and Straus, 1986, p.77). In their more recent study of the 50 states of the United States, Linsky, Bachman, and Straus (1995) report a direct link between objective stress and violence. Brantingham and Brantingham (1984, pp. 146-148) present a model in which economic stress (unemployment) is related to both violent crime (due to increased strain) and property crime (due to real or perceived economic need).

According to Landau's (1997b) model, social support systems are conceived as having either a direct effect on, or as acting as mediators between, the social stressors and the reactions to which they are presumed to lead. Examples of social support systems are a sense of national solidarity (on the macro level), or family ties and stable social networks (on the micro level). Several previous studies (analyzed by Dooley and Catalano, 1980; Leavy, 1983; Linsky and Straus, 1986) have reported that social support appears to buffer the emergence of health and behavioral problems stemming from stressful life change. The basic assumption here is that the greater the strength and stability of the social support systems, the greater the ability of the individual and society to cope with stressful events and situations.

The importance of social support in the study of crime was emphasized by Cullen (1994), who proposed "social support" as a concept capable of organizing theory and research in criminology. Cullen's basic thesis is that "both across nations and across communities, crime rates vary inversely with the level of social support" (Cullen, 1994, p.537). The relevance of social support for crime and victimization was elaborated by him in a series of 14 propositions, and he urged criminologists to incorporate measures of support into their research designs. In the same vein, Goldstein (1994, pp. 63-64) emphasized the relevance of social support in the reduction of neighborhood crime and aggression and the facilitation of prosocial alternatives.

The applicability of the above conceptual models to the analysis of violent crime in Israel is demonstrated in the following section.

Stress and Violence in Israel: Some Empirical Evidence

Objective Stress Indicators

The sharp increase in crime (including violent crime) after the 1967 Six Day War, triggered criminological research into examining the relationship between wars and war-like situations and crime in Israeli society.

Hassin and Amir (1974) were the first to investigate the impact of war on crime in Israel. In their analysis of crime patterns during the 1973 (Yom Kippur) war, they found a decrease in the amount of crime during the first eleven days of the war. From the twelfth day on, there was an increase in all types of reported crime. In a similar study conducted on juveniles referred to the probation service in the Tel-Aviv area, Segev (1975) found that during the nineteen days of the 1973 War, there was a considerable increase in male juvenile delinquency in comparison to the equivalent immediate pre-war period. The level of delinquency after the war remained high and did not return to the immediate pre-war level.

Fishman (1983), comparing crime rates in the months before and after two major wars in Israel (the wars of 1967 and 1973), found that after the 1967 War (characterized by the acquisition of large enemy territories and very few casualties), there was a sharp increase in crimes against property, whereas after the 1973 War (characterized by a very high combat death toll), there was a large increase in homicide, attempted homicide, and crimes against the person in general. In another study focusing on juveniles in central Israel (Rehovot), Shoham (1985) also reported an increase in the relative level of violent offenses during the three years following the 1973 War in comparison to the equivalent pre-war period.

Unlike previous studies which focused on the major short wars, Landau and Pfeffermann (1988) analyzed the effect of prolonged security-related stress (measured by security-related casualties and incidents) on violent crime patterns over a period of 15 years (1967-1982). They reported that the number of casualties had a marginal positive effect on homicide. These findings provide support for the legitimation-habituation model (Archer and Gartner, 1984; Ross, 1985) according to which the loss of life during war provides legitimation for acts of aggression and to the perception of violence as a habitual way of behavior. It seems that in the long run, violence resulting from conflicts with out-groups ("enemies") is generalized and directed toward in-group members of society.

During the years of the Intifada, there was much public debate regarding its effects on Israeli society. Landau (1994) reported that during the first five years of the Intifada (1988-1992) 2,631 people were killed in Israel (within the pre-1967 borders) and the territories under Israeli control. Of these, only 17.7 percent (458 cases) were defined as "regular" (i.e., non-politically motivated) criminal homicides. It is of interest to note that during the above period, a strong similarity was found between the trends of politically motivated ("terrorist") homicides and "regular" criminal homicides. In addition, a sizable increase was found in homicides resulting from domestic conflict within Israel since the onset of the Intifada. These findings are not coincidental and can definitely be interpreted as being related to the increased exposure of Israelis to violence in the territories, thus lending additional support to the legitimation-habituation hypothesis.

The accumulated stresses of the Persian Gulf War (as specified earlier) were expressed in violent behavior only after it ended. An alarming rise in domestic violence in Israel was reported in the few months following the end of the war. Between February and August 1991, more than a dozen Israeli women were killed by their husbands (Greenberg and Stanger, 1991). These authors relate the increase in family violence to the psychological stress triggered by the war: "Shut up in tiny, sealed rooms under threat of Scud missile attacks, family tensions escalated....There was an emasculation of the Israeli male ...They felt fear and helplessness. Their anger built up." (p.15).

Objective economic stress factors have also been found to be related to violent crime in a number of Israeli studies. In an analysis of crime trends during 1951-1976, Fishman and Argov (1980) found a positive relationship between unemployment and homicide. In a multivariate analysis for the period of 1950-1981, Landau and Raveh (1987) reported that inflation and population density (as part of a unified stress measure) contributed positively to the rates of homicide, robbery, and total criminal activity and unemployment contributed in this direction to homicide rates.

In the aforementioned study of Landau and Pfeffermann (1988), it was found that increases in the inflation rate had a significant positive effect on both homicide and robbery, whereas the monthly relative changes in the unemployment rate had a significant positive effect on robbery.

Immigration is another stress factor found to be related to violent crime. A recent study on intimate femicide in Israel during 1990-1995 (Landau and Hattis-Rolef, 1998), reported that the two social groups with the highest representation in this violent crime were immigrants from the former Soviet Union, and from Ethiopia (58% and 922%, higher than their proportion in the population, respectively). The extremely high representation of the latter clearly reflects the difficulties entailed in their transition from their rural, traditional country of origin to the modern western-oriented Israeli society.

Subjective Perception of Stress and Support

The great majority of studies relating stress factors to crime on the aggregate level have attempted to find a link between two types of objectively defined sets of data: the stress factors (i.e., independent variables) on the one hand, and crime (i.e., the dependent variables) on the other. The "gap" between these two sets of objective data is usually "filled" with hypothetical intervening variables based on a variety of assumptions as to how these external stressors affect the populations encountering them. However, this line of research has tended to neglect a crucial link between the two sets of data, namely, the subjective perception of such stress factors (see, for example, Linsky and Straus, 1986). The lack of research on crime and subjective stress indicators is due mainly to the scarcity of repeated comparable survey data over prolonged periods, and over large population units.

Landau (1988a) introduced a new approach to the study of stress and violence by systematically investigating (on the aggregate level) the relationship between the subjective perception of social stress factors (as independent variables) and violence (homicide and robbery) in Israeli society. The perceptions of social stress and support were derived from continuing national public opinion surveys that have been conducted since 1967. The stress indicators related to the perception of the security, economic and political situation and solidarity indicators related mainly to the relationship between various groups in society (such as between those of

Eastern and Western origin, religious and secular groups, new immigrants and veteran Israeli, etc.).

The analysis was based on monthly data for the years 1967-1979. As predicted by the Landau and Beit-Hallahmi (1983) stress-support model, violent crime was positively related to most of the subjective stress indicators and negatively related to the subjective perception of national solidarity. Another study, using the same approach and research methods (Landau and Rahav, 1989) yielded similar results with regard to suicidal behavior: Suicide and attempted suicide were positively related to subjective stress indicators and negatively related to perceptions of social solidarity. In another study (Landau, 1988b), it was established that objective economic stressors (inflation and unemployment) were systematically and positively related to both subjective economic worries and dissatisfaction. Similarly, it was found that objective security-related stressors (security-related casualties and incidents) were positively related to the population's subjective worries and dissatisfaction regarding the security of the country. These findings provided validation of the subjective stress indicators and, because they constitute direct expressions of stress in the population, legitimation for their use as preferred substitutes for objective indicators.

In a follow-up study on homicide for the years 1979-1993, (Landau, 1997c), the above stress-support model received partial support regarding stress indicators and substantial support regarding solidarity indicators. A comparison between this study and the previous one (Landau, 1998a) reveals that economic stress has the most permanent and consistent effect over time on homicide. The effect of social solidarity on homicide is stable over time but changes in intensity. On the other hand, the effects of political and security-related stress on homicide were found to be inconsistent over time. Together, the results of the two studies (Landau, 1988a, 1997c) show that for more than 26 years (1967-1993), subjective indicators of stress and social solidarity have been significantly associated with homicide in Israeli society.

In three more recent studies on subjective indicators and crime (for the years 1967-1979), property offenses were added to the analysis, and the effects of subjective stress and support indicators on crime patterns were analyzed separately along the variables of gender (Landau, 1997b), ethnic origin (Landau, 1988a), and level of education (Landau, 2000). The results of these studies indicate that the above theoretical model applies to property offenses too. With regard to gender (Landau, 1997b), it was found that women's perceptions of stress and support are better predictors of violent and property crime rates than those of males. With regard to ethnic origin, Landau (1998a) reported that economic stress indicators had a greater effect on crime rates than security-related indicators, especially among respondents of Eastern (Asian or North African) origin. The perception of social solidarity among Eastern respondents was more related to crime than among their Western (European or American) counterparts. As to level of education, Landau (2000) reported that the relationship between violent and property crime rates and the subjective indicators were stronger in low education groups than in the medium and high education groups.

The above findings regarding respondents of Eastern origin, and those of low education indicate that for these weaker segments of society, whose contribution to criminality is disproportionately higher than their share in the population, (Landau 1998a, 2000), economic hardship and lack of social support/solidarity have a greater effect than security-related stress.

Social Divisions and Violence

The understanding of violence in Israel would be incomplete without referring to the major social divisions in Israeli society, and their relevance to the topic of this chapter. As indicated earlier, Israel is a multicultural society. Cultural norms have long been recognized as a key concept in understanding and explaining human behavior in general and violent behavior in particular (Berkowitz, 1993; Wolfgang and Ferracuti, 1967).

The main ethnic division in Israeli society is between the Jewish majority and the Arab minority. In 1998, Arabs (mostly Suni Moslems) comprised about one fifth (20.8%) of the Israeli population (Central Bureau of Statistics, 1999). The Jewish population of the country can be divided into two major ethnic groups: Eastern Jews (originating mainly from Middle Eastern and North African countries), and Western Jews (originating mainly from Europe and America). In 1998, one third (33%) of Israeli Jews were of Eastern origin, about two fifths (39.8%) were of Western origin, and more than a quarter (27.2%) were second generation Israelis (i.e. born in Israel to an Israeli-born father) (Central Bureau of Statistics, 1999).

Comparison between the Jewish and Arab population reveals that the prevalence of violence among Arabs is considerably higher than among Jews. The norms of traditional Arab culture "dictate" or "prescribe" violent actions in certain well-defined interpersonal situations or circumstances. Killing is culturally mandated to restore the good name of the family in the case of alleged sexual misconduct of a female in the family. Similarly, there is an obligation to participate in blood feuds and other individual or collective acts of violence between extended families (Kressel, 1981). From 1950 to 1964, the homicide rate in the Israeli Arab population (4.00 per 100,000) was almost four times higher than among Eastern Jews (1.07), and almost seven times than among Western Jews (0.59) Landau (1975a). More recent data reveal that the gap between the homicide rates of Jews and Arabs has remained quite similar: For the years 1981-1992, the average conviction rate for homicide and attempted homicide in the Arab population (3.37 per 100,000 population) was more than three times higher than in the Jewish population (1.1). Similarly, in 1997, the rate of conviction for homicide in the Arab population (6.9) was more than four times that of the Jewish population (1.7) (Central Bureau of Statistics, 1984-1995, 1999).

Comparison between Eastern and Western Jews reveals that the great majority of violent offenders (and most of the Jewish prison population) are of Eastern (especially North African) origin (Landau, 1975b; Giora-Shoham, Rahav, and Markovsky, 1987). This higher prevalence of violence among Arabs and Eastern Jews in Israel can be seen as closely related to the inferior position of these two ethnic groups in the Israeli social system. At the same time, these findings also reflect distinctive traditional cultural norms regarding violent behavior prevailing in these more traditional social groups.

It should be noted that the structural social conflicts between Arabs and Jews, and between Eastern and Western Jews constitute potential for violence on the collective level. Two additional potentially violent structural conflicts in Israeli society are those between religious and secular Jews and between the political left and right. The violent potential of the above social conflicts have been demonstrated on several occasions in Israel's history, the most dramatic example being the assassination of Prime Minister Yitzhak Rabin in 1995 (for more details on these conflicts, see Landau, 1997a).

Conclusions

The research presented here clearly shows that social stress is a valuable conceptual construct for the analysis and interpretation of patterns of violent crime in Israel. On the theoretical level, the adaptation of our stress-support model (Landau and Beit-Hallahmi, 1983; Landau, 1997b) to the aggregate level fits well into (and adds to) contemporary formulations of individual-level strain and support models (e.g., Agnew, 1992; Cullen, 1994). The advantage of our model is that stress and support are conceived as two complimentary parts of the same theoretical conceptualization. The methodology of utilizing subjective perceptions of stress and support also constitutes an original contribution in this area of research.

It is difficult to predict how the various stress factors in Israeli society will affect violent crime patterns in Israel in the future. It goes without saying that the generalizability of our theoretical model has to be tested across time and place. In this chapter we have provided the theoretical concepts together with the appropriate instruments for their measurement. This necessary strong connection between theory and the empirical measurement of its elements must surely be one of the main legacies of Marvin Wolfgang.

REFERENCES

Agnew, R. (1992). Foundation for a general strain theory of crime and delinquency. *Criminology*, 30: 47-87.

Agnew, R. and White, H.R. (1992). An empirical test of general strain theory. *Criminology*, 30:475-499.

Amir, M. (1971). *Patterns of Forcible Rape*. Chicago: The University of Chicago Press

Archer, D. and Gartner, R. (1984). *Violence and Crime in Cross-National Perspective*. New Haven, Conn.: Yale University Press

Berkowitz, L. (1993). *Aggression: Its Causes, Consequences, and Control*. New York: McGraw-Hill.

Brantingham, P. and Brantingham, P. (1984). *Patterns of Crime*. New York: Macmillan.

Central Bureau of Statistics, (1949-1999). *Statistical Abstract of Israel*. Jerusalem.

Brenner, M.H. (1977). Health costs and benefits of economic policy. *International Journal of Health Services*. 7:581-623.

Brenner, M.H. and Swank, R.T. (1986). Homicide and economic change: Recent analyses of the Joint Economic Committee Report of 1984. *Journal of Quantitative Criminology*, 2:81-103.

Coser, L.A. (1956). *The Function of Social Conflict*. New York: Free Press.

Cullen, F.T. (1994). Social support as an organizing concept for criminology: Presidential Address to the Academy of Criminal Justice Sciences. *Justice Quarterly*, 11: 527-559.

Dollard, J., Doob, L.W., Miller, N.M., Mowrer, O.H., and Sears, R.R. (1939). *Frustration and Aggression*, New Haven: Yale University Press.

Dooley, D., and Catalano, R. (1980). Economic change as a cause of behavioral disorder. *Psychological Bulletin*, 87:450-468.

Epstein, Y.M. and Babad, E.Y. (1982). Economic stress: Notes on the psychology of inflation. *Journal of Applied Social Psychology*, 12:85-99.

Farrington, K. (1986). The application of stress theory to the study of family violence. *Journal of Family Violence* 1:131-147.

Felson, R.B. (1992). 'Kick 'em when they're down': Explanations of the relationship between stress and interpersonal aggression and violence. *Sociological Quarterly*, 33:1-16.

Fishman, G. (1983). On war and crime. Pp. 165-180 in *Stress in Israel*, edited by S. Breznitz. New York: Van Nostrand Reinhold.

Fishman, G. and Argov, M. (1980). Trends of crime in Israel: 1951-1976. *Delinquency and Social Deviance*, 8:25-35. (Hebrew)

Goldstein, A.P. (1994). *The Ecology of Aggression*, New York: Plenum.

Haas, M. (1968). Social change and national aggressivenes, 1900-1960. Pp. 215-244 in *Quantitative International Politics: Insights and Evidence*, edited by J. D. Singer. New York: Free Press. .

Halleck, S. (1967). *Psychiatry and the Dilemas of Crime*. New York: Harper and Row.

Hassin Y. and Amir, M. (1974)."Business (crime) as usual," in wartime conditions among offenders in Israel. *Journal of Criminal Law and Criminology* 66:491-495.

Henry A.F. and Short, J.F. (1954). *Suicide and Homicide*. New York: Free Press.

Hertzog, S. (2000). Motor vehicle theft in Israel: An empirical analysis of the offense and the offenders. Unpublished paper.

Hovland, C.I., and Sears, B.R.. (1940). Minor studies of aggression: Correlation of lynching with economic indices. *Journal of Psychology* 9:301-310.

Katz, R. (1982a) Concerns of the Israeli: Change and stability from 1962 to 1975. *Human Relations*, 35:83-100.

Katz, R. (1982b). Dynamic patterning of concerns: A long-term comparison of the structure of hopes and fears of Israelis. *Social Indicators Research*, 10:359-388.

Kressel, G. M. (1981). Sorroricide/filiacide: Homicide for family honor. *Current Anthropology*, 22:141-158.

Landau, S.F. (1975a). Type of homicide and pathologies among homicide offenders: Some cultural profiles. *British Journal of Criminology*, 15:7-166.

Landau, S.F. (1975b). Future time perspective of delinquents and non-delinquents:The effect of institutionalization. *Criminal Justice and Behavior*, 2:22-36

Landau, S.F. (1984). Trends in violence and aggression: A cross-cultural analysis. *International Journal of Comparative Sociology* 25:133-158.

Landau, S.F. (1988a). Violent crime and its relation to subjective social stress indicators: The case of Israel. *Aggressive Behavior* 14:337-362.

Landau, S.F. (1988b). The relationship between objective and subjective stress indicators: Some Israeli findings. *European Sociological Review* 4:249-262.

Landau, S.F. (1989). The effect of objective social stress factors on subjective perception of well-being and social solidarity: The Israeli case. *Human Relations* 42:487-508.

Landau, S.F. (1994). Violent crime in a society at war: Israel and the Intifada. Pp. 63-84 in *Violence - Some Alternatives*, edited by J. M. Ramirez. Madrid: Centreur.

Landau, S.F. (1997a). Conflict resolution in a highly stressful society: The case of Israel. Pp. 123-136 in *Cultural Variation in Conflict Resolution: Alternatives for Reducing Violence*, edited by D. Fry and K. Bjorkqvist. Mahwah NJ: Lawrence Erlbaum Publishers.

Landau, S.F. (1997b). Crime patterns and their relation to subjective stress and support indicators: The role of gender. *Journal of Quantitative Criminology* 13:29-56.

Landau, S.F. (1997c). Homicide in Israel: Its relation to subjective stress and support indicators on the macro level. *Homicide Studies* 1:377-400.

Landau, S.F. (1998a). Crime, subjective stress and support indicators, and ethnic origin: The Israeli experience. *Justice Quarterly*, 15:244-272.

Landau, S.F. (1998b). Security-related stress: Its effects on the quality of life in Israel. In: D. Bar-Tal, D. Jacobson, A. Kleiman, (Eds.), *Concerned with Security: Learning from Israel's Experience*. Stamford, CN: JAI Press, pp. 289-310.

Landau, S.F. (2000). Violent crime, social stress and solidarity in Israel: The role of education. Paper presented at the 15th International Colloquium on the Brain and Aggression (C.I.C.A.), Miraflores (Madrid), Spain, July, 2000.

Landau, S.F., and Beit-Hallahmi, B. (1983). Aggression in Israel: A psychohistorical Perspective. Pp. 261-286 in *Aggression in Global Perspective*, edited by A. P. Goldstein and M. Segall. New York: Pergamon.

Landau, S.F. and Drapkin, I. (1968). Ethnic *Patterns of Criminal Homicide in Israel.* Jerusalem: Institute of Criminology, Faculty of Law, The Hebrew University.

Landau, S.F., Drapkin, I. and Arad, S. (1974). Homicide victims and offenders: An Israeli study. *Journal of Criminal Law and Criminology*, 65:390-396.

Landau, S.F. and Hattis Rolef, S. (1998). Intimate femicide in Israel: Temporal, social, and motivational patterns. *European Journal on Criminal Policy and Research*, 6:75-90.

Landau, S.F. and D. Pfeffermann, D. (1988). A time series analysis of violent crime and its relation to prolonged states of warfare: The Israeli case. *Criminology,* 26:489-504.

Landau, S.F. and G. Rahav. (1989). Suicide and attempted suicide: Their relation to subjective social stress indicators. *Genetic, Social and General Psychology Monographs*, 115:273-294.

Landau, S.F. and Raveh, A. (1987). Stress factors, social support and violence in Israeli society: A quantitative analysis. *Aggressive Behavior* 13:67-85.

Landau, S.F. and Sebba, L. (1998). Victimological research in Israel. In: Freedman, R. (ed.), *Criminal Justice and Criminology in Israel: Assessing the Knowledge Base Towards the 21st Century*. Albany, N.Y.: SUNY Press, pp. 359-387.

Leavy, R.L. (1983). Social support and psychological disorder: A review. *Journal of Community Psychology* 11:3-21.

Linsky, A.S., Bachman, R. and Straus. M.A.(1995). *Stress, Culture and Aggression*. New Haven CT: Yale University Press.

Linsky, A.S., and Straus, M.A. (1986*). Social Stress in the United States*. Dover MA: Auborn House.

MacEwen, K.E. and Barling, J. (1988). Multiple stressors, violence in the family of origin, and marital aggression: A longitudinal investigation. *Journal of Family Violence* 3:73-87.

Mayseles, O. (1989). Perceived stress in Israel due to terrorist acts and war: A national survey of high-school students. Paper presented at the Fourth International Conference on Psychological Stress and Adjustment in Time of War, Tel-Aviv, Israel, January, 1989.

Mimon, Z. (1983). *Public Attitudes on Living in Conditions of Galloping Inflation*, Tel-Aviv: The Institute for Social and Labor Research, Tel Aviv University. (Hebrew)

Paternoster, R., and Mazerolly, P. (1994). General strain theory and delinquency: A replication and extension. *Journal of Research in Crime and Delinquency* 31:235-263.

Ross, M.H. (1985). Internal and external conflict and violence. *Journal of Conflict Resolution*, 29:547-579.

Segev, H. (1975). *Patterns of Juvenile Delinquency During the Yom Kippur War in the Tel-Aviv area*. M.A. thesis. Tel-Aviv University.

Giora-Shoham, S., Rahav, G., and Markovsky, R. (1987). Family parameters of violent prisoners. *Journal of Social Psychology*, 127:83-91

Shoham, E. (1985). *Changes in the Behavior Patterns of Minors' Delinquency Before and After the Yom Kippur War*. M.A. thesis. Bar Ilan University, Ramat Gan.

Simmel, G. (1955). *Conflict and the Web of Group Affiliation*. Glencoe, Ill.: The Free Press.

Smooha, S. (1994). The effect of the mass immigration from the Commonwealth of Independent States on Israeli society. *Sociology Newsletter*. 6-7. (Hebrew)

Stone, R.A. 1982. *Social Change in Israel: Attitudes and Events*, 1967-79. New York: Praeger.

Wolfgang, M.E. (1958). *Patterns in Criminal Homicide*. Philadelphia: University of Pennsylvania Press.

Wolfgang, M. E. and Ferracuti, F. (1967). *The Subculture of Violence*. London: Tavistock Publications.

VIOLENCE AMONG RUSSIAN-GERMANS IN THE CONTEXT OF THE SUBCULTURE OF VIOLENCE THEORY

Elmar G.M. Weitekamp, Kerstin Reich
Institute of Criminology, University of Tuebingen

This research is supported by grant # WE 1446/6-1/6-2 from the German Research Foundation. Points of view or opinions expressed herein are our own and do not necessarily represent those of the German Research Foundation.

Introduction

After the fall of the iron curtain a tremendous number of Russian immigrants with German ancestors[1] came to Germany. Called Russian-Germans or the Aussiedler, they were granted German citizenship directly after their arrival. This process started in 1987 and reached a peak in 1990 with 400,000 immigrants from Romania, Poland, and the former Soviet Union. The total is now over 3 million and it is estimated that another 2 million people in those countries are still waiting to come to Germany. Recently, Germany enacted new laws to control and combat this massive immigration. All the welfare measures to help this group of immigrants were reduced in order to make it less attractive to emigrate. These reductions made it much more difficult for Russians of German descent to leave their respective countries. The most drastic measure is that persons who want to emigrate must take a language test in their country of origin to show that they have a German educational background and knowledge about the German culture. After introducing this measure one third of the people taking the language test failed and about 40 percent did not even dare to take it. In 1999 the German government enacted a law which allows only 100,000 Russian immigrants of German descent per year. In the past[2] Germany had used substantial aid packages in order to integrate the Aussiedler into German society. Among other types of aid they received "integration aid", a kind of unemployment payment, for 312 days and German language courses for 12 months. However, new laws enacted in 1993 reduced the amount of aid for the Aussiedler drastically. Integration aid is now paid for only 156 days and the language courses were reduced from 12 to 6 months. The "guarantee fund" which amounted to 450 million German marks in 1991 was reduced by

65 percent and is now 180 million marks per year. This reduction hurts young people the most, since this fund provided reeducation, job training programs, and social integration support programs (Reich et al. 1999). For young immigrants these measures led to severe social exclusion. Left in a "no man's land" or "enemy country" where they are involved in an intergenerational conflict with their parents and where legitimate means to succeed are blocked, the young Russians often rely on peer groups and subcultures, something they know about from their time in the former Soviet Union. Violence in these subcultures is an important and potent vehicle to find self-identity and to succeed in an unfriendly new home country, and even more important to have a sense of control.

This chapter explores the processes of immigration of the Russians of German descent and in particular the development of the intergenerational conflict caused by immigration and processes of social exclusion in the new home country which lead to the formation of youth groups and gangs. The theoretical model we use is the theory of subcultures and particularly the subculture of violence.

The Role of the Immigrant Family in Developing Ethnic Youth Groups

It is common sense that immigration is a critical and stressful life event which influences one's whole life. Immigration forces the immigrants to cope with a wide array of problems and uncertainties, and further to develop new schemes of behavior. Cognitive appraisals and coping strategies that were used are no longer valid and may even be ineffective (dysfunctional). Whether the integration process will be successful or not is dependent on other factors such as material and social sources of help.

The integration process of young immigrants mainly depends on social resources like social networks, family cohesion, and contact with native born residents (Hänze & Lantermann in Silbereisen 1999). Especially immediately after immigration, the family is the main source of emotional support for children, juveniles, and young adults when problems and uncertainties occur in the new environment. Aussiedler families are shaped by life experiences and the norms and values of their home countries. Socialized in a collectivistic-oriented society, family cohesion is traditionally very strong and highly valued. Family structures were able to support the social development of children and juveniles, on the one hand, through emotional attachment, and on the other hand, through autonomy. Both aspects, attachment and autonomy, are important as positive resources and effective protective factors, because they provide a high potential for coping and make the individual more resistant to stressful experiences (Hänze & Lantermann 1999). In sum, both aspects, autonomy and attachment, are positively related to psychosocial adjustment during adolescence (Noom et al. 1999), but they undergo changes because of the distinct event of immigration.

The first thing responsible for this change is that during the period immediately following migration, an inevitable decline in the social class or status of parents occurs. Second, immigrant families often have to shift from traditional forms of social organization to those of a modern industrial society. In addition they have to cope with the often contradictory norms and values of collectivistic versus individualistic societies. Besides the status loss, migration leads to a loss of competence of parents in essential daily life interactions because their learned skills and knowledge are mostly obsolete in the new home country. As a consequence parents often suffer from migration-related psycho-physical stress and this stress does not provide a supportive base from which adolescents can develop positive feelings about themselves the capabilities for responsible, independent action (Noom et al. 1999). The reaction of parents is to turn back to their traditions - meaning to strong family ties and responsibility for the community. This enables them to cope better with the losses they have suffered in every aspect of life. However, to a certain degree this reorientation blocks acculturation into the new society and this in turn influences the development of adaptational behavioral strategies and access to conventional opportunities for the children.

When family ties become overly strong, emotional warmth and support are still existent but there is less space for autonomy, meaning in this context self-worth and the ability to behave and to decide individualistically. The migrant youngsters are forced, particularly through institutions like schools and jobs, to assimilate as soon as possible to the new environment. They usually have a strong wish to do so and to internalize the cultural goals and expectations of the new home country. However, their wish to be integrated into German society is often too fast for their parents. This clash of the different paths of integration leads to new parental uncertainties, and as a consequence parents often try to restrain the autonomy of their children. In addition, this process upsets the parents, because their wish of family cohesion has been strengthened due to their migration experiences, and the efforts of the youngsters to become autonomous eventually leads to a loss of control for the parents.

What is described above is the intergenerational conflict emerging in immigrant families. Russian families who moved to Germany in recent years are at much higher risk for developing such an intergenerational conflict, because conditions have changed. The Aussiedler migration is a chain migration; this constitutes an important factor intensifying this particular conflict. Chain immigration means that large parts of the family clan are already in Germany and that the new immigrant waves, especially the elder generation, do not feel the necessity to adjust to the new environment. They simply want to join their own ethnic group with their traditional forms of living. Youngsters especially feel a great deal of stress because they realize that their parents are not able to socialize either themselves or their children into the host country's values and culture as the parents often reject them and want to stick to the old ones. In contrast, the youngsters are confronted with the demands of the host country which means they have to adapt to the new values and culture if they want to succeed in their new environment. This process leads to a widening of the gap between the way the parents want to live and the lifestyle the youngsters are trying to achieve, causing misunderstandings and creating intergenerational conflicts. In addition, the parents themselves are often overburdened with the effects of immigration. The following statements, expressed by our interviewees, demonstrate this quite clearly:

> *My parents have no time; they always work from early in the morning until late in the evening. They are not interested in what I am doing and they have no control about how and with whom I spend my time.*

> *They (parents) don't care. My mother works the whole day. Therefore I joined a gang where the elder ones taught us how to gain authority through the use of violence.*

Peer Contact after Migration

Young's studies (1932) suggest that for immigrant populations the causal factor for delinquency is not economic status, poverty, adolescence, or nationality, but the intergenerational conflict seemingly inherent to the process of social integration. This does not happen overnight. We try now to describe the pathway from intergenerational conflict to family detachment and involvement in delinquent activities or delinquent subculture groups. Problems such as lack of time for and attachment to children, weak supervision of the youngsters by their primary caregivers, and intergenerational conflict explain how families push their children to attempt to meet their social and emotional needs elsewhere (Miller 2001). There is not only this push but also a strong pull factor which leads to detachment from the family. Adolescents are in a developmental phase where the youngsters try to be free and independent from their parents and when they join peer groups not only for social interaction but also for support, feelings of belonging and recognition, and for having fun and action. Youth mention that relationships with their parents are often problematic in some way and, as a consequence, they begin to spend a lot of time away from home and hang out with other youngsters in public places (Miller 2001).

Young immigrants have an additional problem; they had to leave all their friends behind in their home country, and this kind of friendship is what they miss immediately after arriving in Germany. They now look for new friends who are suitable for mitigating migration-related problems. Besides parents, native born German youth could serve as an important social resource in this situation, and in addition they could supply the necessary knowledge for understanding daily customs, values, and norms. However, young Russian immigrants often fail to link up with young native Germans, because of their perceptions of each other and the related prejudices and ongoing stereotyping. There are many reasons why each group rejects the other one. Young Germans, for example, think that the cultural differences exhibited mainly through the obvious language problems make it impossible to communicate with the Russians. In addition they perceive the traditions and the value system of a collectivistic society which seems to have a deep influence on leisure time and friendships of young Russians as being strange. Another important factor is that the Germans look at the Russian youngsters as economic competitors since they are convinced that they are at a disadvantage in competing with the immigrants for jobs and any other kind of financial support from the welfare system (Eckert, Reis, and Wetzstein 1999 in Bade & Oltmer).

The Russian youngsters on the other hand mention that the Germans in general are unfriendly, that they spend their leisure time only with boring activities (meaning that they spend a lot of time at home and not in public places), and that they cannot communicate in a confidential or trustworthy way with them, since their behavior is considered to be too superficial and individualistic. The following statement by one of our interviewees illustrates this frustration:

> *I wanted to get in touch with native-born Germans because I really wanted to know what kind of fun they have. I couldn't imagine what that could be.*

What becomes clear is the fact that the negative social perceptions and attributes about the other group predominate over the positive aspects. This is a crucial fact since the negative perceptions prevent youngsters from contacting or getting in touch with members of the other group. Contact and spending time together, however, are important preconditions to reduce prejudices and stereotyping, thus allowing them to get to know each other and to learn from each other. According to Silbereisen and Schmitt-Rodermund (1999), peer rejection constitutes a risk factor for the development of problem behavior and/or delinquent behavior and it leads to social exclusion which consequently prevents integration. For many the answer to peer rejection is a tendency to join those peers who are similar and have similar experiences. For young immigrants these similarities are the use of the same language, being rejected by the dominant culture, and finding legitimate ways and paths being blocked.

As mentioned above, the migration of the Aussiedler is a chain migration and there are already many young people in Germany who have had such negative experiences in social interactions in their new home country. We know that young Russian people of German descent who came to Germany earlier know about the problems and needs of the youth who are coming now. In addition they know about the places where they can meet those newcomers. They use their insider knowledge and the situation of social deprivation to attract and recruit young people (usually males) to join them for delinquent activities to combat these migration-related problems. They form subcultural groups of youth who are at high risk to develop norms and attitudes which support the use of violence when they find themselves excluded from general patterns of life (Schagerl 2000). Consequently, there is a high likelihood that youth who are involved in those subcultural groups express negative emotions like rejection, helplessness, frustration, powerlessness, and low self-esteem through violent acts (Schagerl 2000). Indeed, statements from youth show great evidence that violent activities are a very potent solution for problems of social exclusion caused by immigration. It seems that youth can get attention, balance the loss of status (at least in their ethnic group), and keep the feeling of strength, power, and control through violent activities. The following statements by our interviewees demonstrate this important role of violence:

> *"It is normal to carry out conflicts with fists, above all, if you feel provoked".*

> *"If someone owns a lot of money, exhibits physical strength and is a good fighter we adore him and want to be like him."*

Subcultures and the Subculture of Violence in the Context of Russian Immigrants

Adler, Mueller and Laufer (2001, 158) defined a subculture the following way:

> "A subdivision within the dominant culture that has its own norms, beliefs and values. Subcultures typically emerge when people in similar circumstances find themselves isolated from the mainstream and band together for mutual support. Subcultures may form among members of racial and ethnic minorities, among prisoners, among occupational groups, among ghetto dwellers. Subcultures exist within a larger society, not apart from it. They share therefore some

of its values. Nevertheless, the lifestyles of their members are significantly different from those of individuals in the dominant culture."

The subculture of violence is based upon Sellin's (1938) culture conflict and crime theory. Sellin argued that criminology has to explain violations of conduct norms and noted that the legal definition of crime was inadequate to develop laws of human behavior, as social science requires. Sellin argued that different groups have different norms and that the conduct norms of one group may conflict with those of other groups. He saw culture conflict as one explanation for crime and delinquency. According to Sellin one could become criminal by behaving according to the norms and values of the group one belongs to, but that those norms and values could conflict with those of the dominant society. This means that the difference between criminals and noncriminals is that they respond to different sets of conduct norms. He focused his arguments on the immigration of persons to America and distinguished between primary culture conflict, which represents a collision of norms from distinct cultural systems, and secondary culture conflict, which occurs with the evolution of subcultures in a heterogeneous society. The secondary culture conflict characterizes law violations of groups and gangs in urban ghettos, drug-oriented subcultures, outlaw motorcycle gangs, and racist cliques.

Sellin's culture conflict theory was picked up by Cohen (1955), Miller, (1958), Cohen and Short (1958), and Cloward and Ohlin (1960) who tried to explain the criminal behavior of urban, male, and lower-class delinquency. Sellin's culture conflict theory also laid the foundation for the subculture of violence theory as developed by Wolfgang and Ferracuti in 1967. They argue that the social structure and other factors can be responsible for the emergence of subcultures and that once they exist a learning process is facilitated by positive reinforcement of violent behavior. According to Wolfgang and Ferracuti, the subculture of violence theory is not intended to explain all violent behavior, but tries to explain more spontaneous violence, which accounts for most of the violent crimes, rather than violence that is premeditated or of a psychopathological origin. Spontaneous violence in this context is mainly a domain of male juveniles and adolescents. Wolfgang and Ferracuti argue that the subculture of violence is only partly different from the parent culture and that violence is not the predominant mode of expression. It is a subculture in which a violent or physical response is either expected or required in some social situations, however. Members of the subculture of violence are obliged to resort to violence in order to defend their "honor", when there is an attack on one's manliness, physical prowess, or sexuality. In the context of a subculture of violence, personal assaults are not defined as wrong or antisocial. Quite the contrary: the quick resort to physical aggression is socially approved and expected concomitant to certain stimuli. Violence is a pervasive part of everyday life. According to Wolfgang and Ferracuti, lower-class males who inhabit the locale of a subculture of violence and who respond to perceived insults with violence, are accorded prestige, while those who use nonviolent means of conflict resolution are scorned and ostracized. Violence can be seen in this context as a central pillar around which a masculine identity can be constructed. Among the truly disadvantaged angry aggression develops as a consequence of racial or ethnic discrimination and low social position in the neighborhood, community, and urban environment.

Subcultures in the Former Soviet Union

According to Dobson (1990), before the iron curtain came down Soviet youth experienced problems similar to those in Western nations but they were different in three aspects. First, political control over the young people was much stronger and those who avoided and deviated from this control were considered to be political opponents. Second, the people of the former Soviet Union had to rely on the black market since the economy failed to provide sufficient consumer products. Third, the State was able to provide young people with jobs. The failure of the latter is usually linked to the development of juvenile delinquency and crimes committed by young adults. Finckenauer and Kelly (1992) convincingly argue that these characteristics led to the emergence of subcultures in the former Soviet Union. As they point out, in the Soviet context the concept of youth means persons from age 14 to 30, and instead of calling those groups youth subcultures the Soviets called them "informal youth associations". These associations could be official as well as unofficial and, according to Fain (1990), engaged in activities developed by and serving its members and not in activities ordered by some official decree. However, as Fel'dshtein (cited in Finckenauer and Kelly 1992) pointed out, the informal youth associations engaged in behaviors which were not accepted and which were quite distinct from the mainstream society. The young people expressed their opposition towards the official, conforming citizen through differences in dress, behavior, and lifestyle. Part of that opposing behavior could be delinquent and criminal but, according to Bushnell (1990), the criminal behavior was not a central part of their activities. At first glance these features fit the definition of typical American street gangs as defined by Klein et al. (2001). However, a major distinction is the fact that the Soviet youth groups used these forms of behavior for political protest and to reject openly the customs and values of mainstream society.

Finckenauer and Kelly (1992) point out that an important difference between the Soviet Union and other Western countries was that the Soviet Union tried to socialize their youth to be proper Communist citizens. The nation's youth organization, the Komsomol, was the main tool used to achieve this goal. Even though participation was voluntary, young people were forced to join if they wanted to move on to higher education, get better jobs, and come up for promotions (Riordan, 1989, Dobson 1990). According to Finckenauer and Kelly (1992), in the 1980's the Komsomol became too bureaucratic and corrupt, and basically lost touch with the needs of the Soviet youth, leading to a loss of credibility and a search for alternatives. Parallel to this development, the Soviet Union experienced an increasing orientation towards consumerism and self-orientation. Goods the Soviet economy was not able to produce led to black markets that became attractive for young people and youth groups since they could not find legitimate jobs. According to Dobson (1990) and Riordan (1989), the alternatives to State organized activities and the failing state economy were youth groups such as rock music fans, hippies, neo-fascist groups, hooligan groups, youth gangs, and vigilante groups. Many of those started to become involved in criminal behavior. This constitutes quite a change from opposing the dominant culture and turning to subcultures, where crime and violence become major features of daily life. Ovchinskii (1989) reports that almost half of the leaders of these subcultures, gangs, and youth groups had spent time in a correctional labor colony.

Salagaev (2001) describes gangs in Russia that fit Maxson and Klein's (1995) classification of a traditional gang: they are large, territorial, engaged in a wide variety of activities, have a history of self-regeneration, and have differentiated age or residence cliques. These gangs have a wide economic network, corrupt connections, and special security groups. The gangs are hierarchically structured with strict norms, and recruit their "fighters" from neighborhood youth. The gangs have a large pool of possible younger members, but only a small number become active gang members. The criminal gang activities include robberies, armed robberies, and the drug trade, but the main business is "solving problems" for businessmen inside their territory. This link to organized crime as described by Salagaev was also found by Finckenauer and Waring (1998) in their study on the Russian mafia in America.

Processes of Social Exclusion, Youth Abandonment, Youth Groups and Gangs in Europe

So far we have examined the processes of intergenerational conflicts emerging from immigration in the context of the Russians of German descent and how these processes lead to social exclusion and the formation of youth groups and gangs where violence could become a major form of gaining status and respect. In addition we introduced culture conflict theory and the subculture of violence theory to explain such developments and indicated that these forms of subculture already existed in the former Soviet Union. We will turn now to the situation in Europe, where we are experiencing massive immigration of Russians of German descent, particularly in Germany. Europe is facing similar developments in patterns of youth violence, and these patterns are particularly evident for immigrant groups and ethnic minorities. What we know from research is that youth groups, gangs, and subcultures develop easily if they have the following features:

- they exist in deprived communities
- they consist of minority or immigrant members of society either by race, nationality, or ethnicity
- they are predominantly male
- they are almost always alienated, marginalized youth who are socially excluded from society and whose opportunities are blocked
- they are usually young and typically adolescents or young adults
- they are involved in criminal activities with a wide range in the variation of delinquent and criminal behavior, and
- they are stable over time and can exist for long periods of time.

In his evaluation of juvenile crime and violence in Europe, Pfeiffer (1998) comes to the conclusion that since the mid 1980's there was a substantial increase in youth violence in the ten countries he evaluated. He sees the main cause for this as the shift of the European countries toward a "winner-loser culture" in which many disadvantaged youth appear to be the losers. Pfeiffer bases his argument on the findings of James (1995) who argues that at least three major elements are part of the creation of such "winner-loser" cultures:

"It is abundantly clear from many studies...that inequality in incomes combined with false promises of equality of opportunity, American-style of welfare support for the disadvantaged and poor job-quality are major causes of violence in developing and developed nations alike. From 1979 onwards in Britain, all three of these patterns were adopted as a deliberate government policy; the gap between rich and poor increased to pre-war levels, the amount and kind of state support for the disadvantaged was reduced dramatically; the quality of jobs available to young men decreased after union power to guarantee minimum wages and conditions of work was removed. These changes coincided with an unprecedented increase in violence against the person since 1987" (James, 1995, 74).

In this context, Polk and Weitekamp (1999) discuss youth abandonment. According to them, young people experience economic abandonment and are the losers in the contemporary winner-loser culture; therefore they are caught in a dreadful developmental trap. Polk and Weitekamp further point out that, historically, virtually all young people, at high, middle and low points of the class structure, could look forward to a process of moving from childhood through schooling into adulthood with some combination of work and family roles. These prospects are now less relevant and the problem of abandonment is greater for those young people who leave school early and enter the labor force with little to offer in the way of qualifications, skills, or experience. In his work about the new urban poor, Wilson (1996) describes a process in which work disappeared for this group of people. The lack of full-time work for this group leads to undesired consequences such as lack of money, delay of becoming independent from parents, the establishment of sexual relationships, marriage, and the establishment of a family. These individuals become stuck in a social and economic "no- man's land," one where a central feature of their existence is that normal supports for identity as an adult are not available. Polk and Weitekamp (1999) call this a developmental trap which forces young people to engage in complicated and innovative ways to struggle with their central identities as males or females. This developmental trap is even worse for members of minority groups by race, nationality, or ethnicity. Dubet and Lapeyronnie (1994) investigated the "winner-loser" hypothesis in France and found that a significant shift has occurred in social problems, including crime trends. They conclude that the social exclusion of marginal groups became the key problem of the 1990's. In addition, they consider the criminal acts by the marginalized youngsters as an expression of their helplessness about being unable to live a normal life and their inability to gain access to society.

It is here where we can see the clear connection to violence and youth groups, gangs, and subcultures. The situation of abandoned youngsters is such that issues of status and manhood are problematic and cry for a solution. According to Polk and Weitekamp (1999), the lack of traditional pathways to define "who I am as a man" makes it appealing to form or join a youth group, gang, or subculture, especially when comparing one's status to that of others. These groups or cultures can change the rules of the game and can make the loser into a winner again.

There are many signs in European countries that we are creating more "winner-loser" cultures which could serve as fertile ground for the formation of youth groups, gangs, and subcultures that resort to violence as a means of contesting masculinity. Pfeiffer's (1998) research clearly indicates that Europe is experiencing a substantial increase in violence. In addition, Dünkel and Skepenat (1998) found that for the State of Mecklenburg-Vorpommern, Germany, the increase in violent crimes is mainly caused by group offending. It is a small step from group offending or offending within a group to the formation of gangs and a subculture of violence, especially if processes of youth abandonment are not countered by any meaningful social policy and the opening of legitimate pathways for youth in order to allow them to participate in society.

This "dangerous" situation can be demonstrated with the example of the German Aussiedler. As mentioned in the introduction, the Aussiedler face severe financial restrictions to aid in their integration into the German society. To make matters worse, when they come to Germany the Aussiedler initially have to live in "temporary special housing arrangements". While theoretically they are supposed to leave these special housing units as fast as possible, according to Stoll (1999) they stay, for example, in Tübingen, an average of 2 years. These units are usually very crowded and the living conditions are very poor, reminding us of ghetto-like situations. There are no places for the young people; therefore, they are forced to hang out in the hallways or outside of the buildings and in general the people who live there have little privacy or common rooms which could be used for social activities.

The situation for the young Aussiedler is a particularly difficult one. While in Russia they were considered to be a minority group because of their German descent and labeled as German fascists, in Germany, even though they have a German passport, they are again a minority group and labeled Russians. In addition to their minority status, they often have language problems and difficulties in school. The school and/or job training they received in Russia is worth nothing in their new country of residence, thus blocking legitimate opportunities and marginalizing them even more. It is of no surprise that these young people form and join youth groups, gangs, and subcultures in order to find a place where they belong and have others to identify with. Hanging out in groups was already very much part of their culture in the former Soviet Union, since it was often too dangerous there to hang out alone and show one's opposition to the dominant society, as explained earlier. Here in Germany they perceive the German culture and environment as too dangerous and these circumstances force them to hang out together and to form gangs. Stoll (1999) reports, for instance, the existence of gangs and subcultures in the "temporary special housing units" of Tuebingen that can be considered neo-traditional according to the classification of Maxson and Klein (1995). The youth usually hang out in front of the housing unit, have a strong hierarchical order determined by age, and experience the new country of the "enemy". For the Aussiedler these housing units are often the only possibility to find friends, especially in rural areas. When families move away, the youth and young adults of these gangs and subcultures often come back and are admired by those who newly arrived or still live there according to the status symbols they were able to achieve. These status symbols are cars, clothes, and other forms which indicate wealth. These older gang members then recruit younger ones from the new arrivals and use them for their illegal activities. The gang and subculture members are involved in a variety of criminal activities and a quick look at juvenile correctional facilities reveals that a disproportionately high number of Aussiedler youth are incarcerated. The group cohesion of the "Russian gangs and subcultures" is particularly high, since in their country of origin they were already used to treating any outsiders, and especially the State, as the enemy and quite often controlled conflicts among themselves through violence. In addition the Aussiedler youth exhibit a very strong machismo culture and attitudes in which a high level of violence is considered normal (Reich et al. 1999).

The situation of being abandoned is especially bad for young Russians of German descent since they are so to speak "double losers"; they were outsiders in the former Soviet Union who could hardly succeed there and they are losers in the "promised land" again. The situation of abandoned youth thereby places them under a number of stresses which are likely to increase their willingness to use violence. Caught in conflict with others (native Germans and other immigrant groups such as the Turks) the abandoned young people cannot fall back on a wide network of other definitions of self as a way of asserting a self-concept which says "this is who I am". Violence is an apparent low-cost alternative and gangs and subcultures can be a great attraction. Membership in gangs and subcultures can change the rules of the game and make a loser into a winner.

Conclusion

This brief description of the situation of the Aussiedler in Germany clearly shows that in Germany we are creating a serious and long lasting street gang and subcultural problem in which violence constitutes a popular form of gaining an identity, status, and respect. We assume that similar developments can be found throughout Europe, since all European countries have serious minority problems, because members generally live in poor housing arrangements, drop out of schools (often because of language problems), are unskilled, hold low paying jobs, are socially excluded and marginalized, and often are looking for an identity. The Aussiedler in Germany are in some ways privileged compared to other minority groups since the State integrates them into the welfare system and provides them with resources that do not exist for other immigrants. An example of this is that they are treated as Germans with regard to the pension fund, meaning if they worked for 25 years in Russia as a carpenter, their German pension fund would show 25 years of payments into the German pension fund, even though, in reality, not a single mark was paid by that person into the pension fund. If the Aussiedler are forming gangs and subcultures of violence in order to cope with the circumstances of their new home country, the formation of gangs and subcultures and their respective activities seem to be an even more viable solution for other immigrant groups.

It seems to us that we in Europe have to open our eyes and tune our ears with regard to the emergence and existence of youth groups, gangs, subcultures, and subcultures of violence. Signs of emerging "winner-loser" cultures can be found in all European countries and the cultural influences on the use of violence to gain one's aims cannot be denied as well. The theory of the subculture of violence by Wolfgang and Ferracuti (1967) provides a useful vehicle in understanding these processes. We would like to conclude with a saying of Franz von Liszt (1905) who claimed at the end of the 19th century that "the best criminal policy is a good social policy", something which the European countries seem to have forgotten. This negligence can lead to serious problems and, with regard to youth groups, gangs, subcultures and their use of violence, we might be on a direct path to create a very serious problem in Europe.

REFERENCES

Adler, F., Mueller, G.O., Laufer, W.S. (2001). *Criminology*. Boston, McGraw Hill.

Bushnell, J. (1990). "Introduction: The History and Study of the Soviet Youth Subculture." In: *Soviet Sociology*, Vol 27, No 1, 3 – 10.

Cohen, A.K. (1955). *Delinquent Boys: The Culture of the Gang*. New York, The Free Press of Glencoe.

Cohen, A.K. and Short, J.F. Jr., Research on Delinquent Subcultures. (1958). In: *Journal of Social Issues* 14, 00. 20 – 37.

Cloward, R.A. and Ohlin, L.E. (1960). *Delinquency and Opportunity*. Glencoe, New York, The Free Press of Glencoe.

Dobson, R. (1990). "Youth Problems in the Soviet Union." In: Jones, A., Connor, W.D., Powell, D. (eds.) *Soviet Social Problems*. Boulder, Westview Press.

Dubet, F. and Lapeyronnie, D. (1994). *Im Aus der Vorstaedte: der Zerfall der demokratischen Gesellschaft*. Stuttgart, Klett-Cotta Verlag.

Dünkel, F. and Skepenat, M., Jugendliche und Heranwachsende als Taeter und Opfer von Gewalt. In: Schwind, H.-D., Kube, E., and Kuehne, H.-H. (Hrsg.). (1998). *Essays in Honor of Hans-Joachim Schneider: Criminology at the Threshold of the 21st Century*. Berlin, Walter de Gryter.

Eckert, R., Reis, C.,Wetzstein, T.A. (1999). Bilder und Begegnungen: Konflikte zwischen einheimischen und Aussiedlerjugendlichen. In K.J. Bade & J. Oltmer. *Aussiedler: Deutsche Einwanderer aus Osteuropa*. IMIS- Schriften, Bd.8.Osnabrück, Universitätsverlag Rasch.

Fain, A.P. (1990). Specific Features of Informal Youth Associations in large Cities. In: *Soviet Sociology* Vol. 27, No. 1, 19 – 42.

Finckenauer, J.O. and L. Kelley. (1992). "Juvenile Delinquency and Youth Subcultures in the Former Soviet Union". In: *International Journal of Comparative and Applied Criminal Justice.* Vol 16, No 2, pp 247 – 261.

Finckenauer, J.O. and Waring, E.J. (1998). *Russian Mafia in America: Immigration, Culture and Crime.* Boston, Northeastern University Press.

Hänze, M. & Lantermann, E.-D. Entwicklung und Anpassung. In Silbereisen, R. K., Lantermann, E.-D., Schmitt-Rodermund, E. (Hrsg.) (1999). *Aussiedler in Deutschland. Akkulturation von Persönlichkeit und Verhalten.* Opladen: Leske und Budrich.

James, O. (1995). *Juvenile Violence in a Winnder-Loser Culture.* London, Free Association Books.

Klein, M. W., Kerner, H.-J., Maxson, C. L. and Weitekamp, E.G.M. (eds.). (2001). *The Eurogang Paradox: Street Gangs and Youth Groups in the U.S. and Europe.* Dordrecht, Boston, London, Kluwer Academic Publishers.

Maxson, C.L and Klein, M.W. (1995). Investigating gang structure. In: *Journal of Gang Research* 3, (1), pp. 33 – 40.

Miller, J. (2001). *One of the Guys: Girls, Gangs and Gender.* Oxford: University Press.

Miller, W.B. (1958). Lower-Class Culture as a Generating Milieu of Gang Delinquency. In: *Journal of Social Issues,* 14, 5 – 19.

Noom, M. J., Dekovic, M., Meeus, W.H.J. (1999). Autonomy, Attachment and Psychosocial Adjustment During Adolescence: A Double-Edged Sword? *Journal of Adolescence,* 22. P. 771-783

Ovchinskii, V.S. (1989). Criminal Tendencies in the Youth Environment, In: *Soviet Sociology* 27, (4), pp 88 – 91.

Pfeiffer, C. Juvenile Crime and Violence in Europe. (1998). In: M. Tonry (ed.) *Crime and Justice: A Review of Research.* Volume 23. Chicago, the University of Chicago Press.

Polk, K. and E.G.M. Weitekamp. (1999). *Emerging Patterns of Youth Violence.* Paper presented at the American Society of Criminology Meetings, Toronto.

Reich, K., Weitekamp, E.G.M., Kerner, H.-J. (1999). Jugendliche Aussiedler: Probleme und Chancen im Integrationsprozess. In: *Bewährungshilfe,* Vol. 46, No 4, 335-359.

Riordan, J. (ed.). (1989). *Soviet Youth Culture.* Bloomington, Indiana, Indiana University Press.

Salagaev, A. (2001). Evolution of Delinquent Gangs in Russia. In: M. W. Klein, H.-J. Kerner, C.L. Maxson and E.G.M. Weitekamp (eds.) *The Eurogang Paradox: Street Gangs and Youth Groups in the U.S. and Europe.* Dordrecht, Boston, London, Kluwer Academic Publishers.

Schagerl,S. (2000). Aussiedler-Jugendliche. Integrationsanforderungen-
    Bewältigungsstrategien-Gewaltprävention. In: E. Gropper, H.-M. Zimmermann
    (Hrsg.) *Zuwanderung. Zugehörigkeit und Chancengleichheit für Kinder und
    Jugendliche.* Aktion Jugendschutz (ajs) Stuttgart, Landesarbeitsstelle Baden-
    Württemberg.

Schmitt-Rodermund, E. & Silbereisen, R:K. (1999). Differentielle Akkulturation von
    Entwicklungsorientierungen unter jugendlichen Aussiedlern. In: Silbereisen, R. K.,
    Lantermann, E.-D., Schmitt-Rodermund, E. (Hrsg.). *Aussiedler in Deutschland.
    Akkulturation von Persönlichkeit und Verhalten.* Opladen, Leske und Budrich.

Sellin, T. (1938). *Culture Conflict and Crime.* Bulletin No 41, New York, Social Science
    Research Council.

Silbereisen, R.K. and Schmitt-Rodermund, E. (1999). Wohlbefinden der jugendlichen
    Aussiedler. In Silbereisen, R.K., Lantermann E-D., Schmitt-Rodermund, E (Hrsg.)
    Aussiedler in Deutschland. Akkulturation von Personlichkeit und Verhalten.
    Opladen, Leske und Buderich.

Stoll, F. (1999). *Von Russland nach Württemberg: Eine Studie zur Integration jugendlicher
    Spätaussiedler.* Unpublished Master's Thesis. Faculty of Social and Behavioral
    Sciences, University of Tübingen, Germany.

von List, F. (1905). Das Verbrechen als sozial-pathologische Erscheinung. In: von List, F.
    Strafrechtliche Aufsätze und Vorträge, Zweiter Band, 1892 - 1904, Berlin, J.
    Guttentag.

Weitekamp, E.G.M. Straffällige junge Aussiedler - was kann die Justiz tun? In: Walter, J. (ed.)
    Jugendstrafvollzug am Ende des 20. und zu Beginn des 21. Jahrhunderts.
    Godesberg, Forum Verlag (forthcoming 2002)

Weitekamp, E.G.M. (2001). Gangs in Europe: Assessments at the Millennium. In: M. W.
    Klein, H.-J. Kerner, C.L. Maxson and E.G.M. Weitekamp (eds.) *The Eurogang
    Paradox: Street Gangs and Youth Groups in the U.S. and Europe.* Dordrecht,
    Boston, London, Kluwer Academic Publishers.

Wilson, W.J. (1996). *When Work Disappears: The World of the New Urban Poor.* New York,
    Vintage Books.

Wolfgang, M.E. and F. Ferracuti. (1967). *The Subculture of Violence.* Beverly Hills, Sage
    Publications.

Young, P. (1932). *The Pilgrims of Russian-Town.* Chicago: University of Chicago Press.

NOTES

[1] In this qualitative reserch project we interviewed 40 young Aussiedler who were incarccrated in a juvenile correctional institution and compared them with 40 young Aussidler in freedom. We will use some of the preliminary results to support our theoretical analyses.

[2] Germany always had people of German descent immigrating to Germany before 1987. However, the numbers were quite small compared to those of the people who immigrated after 1987.

ARREST CLEARANCES FOR HOMICIDE: A STUDY OF LOS ANGELES

Marc Riedel

Center for the Study of Crime, Delinquency and Corrections
Southern Illinois University

Introduction

At the time Wolfgang (1958) completed his classic research on homicide, arrest clearances for criminal homicide in Philadelphia were 94%. Of the 588 criminal homicides between 1948 and 1952, only 38 cases were listed as uncleared. On the basis of police reports requested by Wolfgang from 18 U.S. cities, percent cleared by arrest ranged from 84.1% in Seattle to 98.8% in Buffalo, except for Pittsburgh (1949-1953), the period covered by the clearance statistics was from 1948-1952. Although the number of cases was small, Wolfgang did a simple analysis comparing cleared and uncleared homicides in a short (10 pages) chapter.

Clearly times have changed. According to annual editions of *Crime in the United States* and *Sourcebook of Criminal Justice Statistics*, in 1960, 92% of murders and non negligent manslaughters were cleared by arrest. Arrest clearances reached their lowest point in 1994 (64.4%) and began to increase to 69.1% by 1999. While 69.1% clearances represent an increase, the practical consequence is that approximately 30% of people who murder other people are not apprehended.

Figure 1 gives the percent of homicides cleared from 1987 through 1998 for the United States and California, the state with the largest population. Figure 1 shows national and state time series trending downward until 1995 in the U.S. and 1994 in California when they begin an upturn. By 1998, California clearances had increased from 54.3% to 63.1% while United States clearances had increased from 64.4% to 68.7% The two series are roughly parallel until the mid-nineties although the California clearance percent is substantially lower than the U.S. percent. The mean U.S. clearance percent is 67.0% while the California mean percent is 59.8%. Put another way, while about 30% of homicide offenders in the United States are not arrested, 40% in California are not arrested.

Figure 1: Percent Homicides Cleared in U.S. and California: 1987-1998*

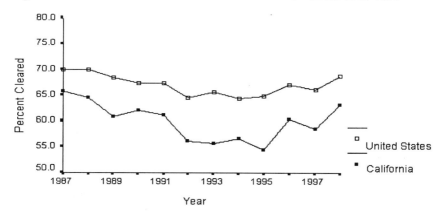

*Source: Annual Editions of UCR and Sourcebook of CJ Statistics

Understanding the reasons for a decline in homicide clearances is important for several reasons. First, whether the goals of the criminal justice system are incapacitation, deterrence, rehabilitation, retribution or any other purpose, the process begins with the arrest of offenders. Without arrests, there is neither further processing of offenders nor reduction of crime. Second, the declining percentage of clearances reduces public safety and contributes to deterioration in police morale. Third, the decline in clearances further traumatizes the victim's families and contributes to an increase in the fear of violent victimization. Finally, what are uncleared offenses to law enforcement become missing data to individuals seeking to understand homicide behavior. Studies reporting on offender related variables when one-third or more of the data are missing, need to consider the possibility of biased results(Riedel & Rinehart, 1996).

While research on clearances was done as early as 1931, (Stern, 1931) contemporary research began in 1992 with a paper by Cardarelli and Cavanagh (1992). Initial studies were descriptive, relying on the UCR and the Supplementary Homicide Reports (SHR) while the most recent (Wellford & Cronin, 1999) uses data gathered from police departments and is a sophisticated analysis of the contribution of circumstances and investigative variables to arrest clearances.

The present research uses homicide data from the California Criminal Justice Statistics Center to explore characteristics related to clearance by arrest. It differs from previous research in the following ways. First, unlike previous studies, I examine the hypothesis that the increase in percent cleared by arrest since the mid-nineties is the result of fewer homicides rather than more arrests. Second, while Wellford and Cronin had to promise the participating cities anonymity and strive to disguise their identity in the final report, this research focuses on the city of Los Angeles.

Review of Literature

Research exploring whether males or females are disproportionately represented in uncleared homicides shows mixed results.

Virtually every study of homicide from Wolfgang (1958) to the present has shown that males are the predominant victims and offenders. However, they are not always disproportionately represented among uncleared homicides. For property and violent crimes, Bynum, Cordner, and Greene (1982) found that gender of victim had little effect on clearances. Research by Cardarelli and Cavanagh (1992) using SHR for 1976 through 1986 found that males (24.5%) and females (24.6%) were almost equally represented among clearances. Riedel and Rinehart (1996) found no association between gender and clearances in Chicago.

On the other hand, Regoeczi, Kennedy, and Silverman (2000) using SHR and Statistics Canada data found that being a female homicide victim increased the probability of clearances in the U.S., Canada, New York and province of Ontario. Put another way, the Regoeczi et al. results suggest that males are over represented among uncleared cases.

There seems to be little agreement as to whether uncleared homicides are predominantly white or non-white victims.

While Bynum, Cordner, and Greene (1982) and Riedel and Rinehart (1996) found that race had little effect on clearances, Cardarelli and Cavanagh (1992) found that the highest percent of uncleared homicides were among Hispanics (30.5) followed by whites (26.1%), blacks (23.3%), and other (27.1%). In 55.8% of the cases, the race/ethnicity was unknown.

Regoeczi et al. found that the presence of non-white victims increased the probability of clearances in Canada and the United States, but not in Ontario or New York. For the final multivariate analysis, Wellford and Cronin (1999) found that the probability of closing the case was increased according to whether the offender was African-American or Hispanic.

Homicides with victims under the age of ten are more likely to be cleared by arrest while elderly victims of homicide are less likely to have their offenses cleared by arrest.

Cardarelli and Cavanagh found that while victims under the age of ten were frequently cleared, those over the age of 65 had very low clearance rates. Regoeczi et al found that the probability of clearing homicides increased for victims under the age of ten in three of the four jurisdictions studied. In comparison to clearances in Dade County (51.1%), Wilbanks, (1984) found that only 46.9% of the elderly homicides were cleared.

Riedel and Rinehart found that age interacts with whether felony homicides were the most difficult to clear by arrest. As victims age, their lifestyles change; children and adults gain greater freedom and are at greater risk of victim involvement in a felony. As age increases, a greater number were involved in a type of murder that was more difficult to clear. Hence, clearance percentages for older victims were lower than for younger victims, which supports the Cardarelli and Cavanaugh explanation, albeit in a slightly broadened form.

Research results suggest that handguns are not closely related to arrest clearances.

Perhaps because firearms are used in over half the homicides, it is easy to believe that firearms, especially handguns, would be the weapons closely related to uncleared homicides. In fact, the evidence suggests that other weapons are more closely related to clearances.

In what they characterize as a "surprising finding" Cardarelli and Cavanagh find that 47.9% of uncleared homicides involve strangulation/asphyxiation. Of the seven categories of weapons, firearms are the second from the bottom (23.2%); only bodily assault is lower (22.1%). Regoeczi et al. found that no-firearm-used increased the probability of clearing an offense in Canada and New York State, but not in the United States and Ontario.

Wellford and Cronin, (1999) found other weapons to be more important in closing a case than handguns. For the bivariate analysis, rifles, knives, and personal weapons led to arrest clearances more often than when a handgun was used.

One of the more consistent general results is that felony homicides are more difficult to clear by arrest than other kinds of homicides.

Riedel and Rinehart (1996) examined arrest clearances for 3,066 Chicago homicides from 1987 through 1991. They found homicides that involved concomitant felonies were less likely to be cleared than those that did not involve concomitant felonies (tau = 0.245). In their study of clearances in the United States and Canada, Regoeczi et al., (2000) found that the absence of a concomitant criminal act was the only variable that increased the probability of clearance in all four jurisdictions: U.S., New York State, Ontario, and Canada.

Wilbanks, (1984) found similar results in Dade County. In comparison to the county clearance percent (51.1%), fewer robbery (38.5%) and elderly (46.9%) homicides were cleared; and more homicides involving black (64.9%)*, female victims (61.0%) and victims under 15 (70.0%) were cleared. Similarly, using SHR data, Cardarelli and Cavanagh (1992) found a disproportionate number of felony homicides in the uncleared category.

A clearer indication of what the relationships between clearances and felony homicide means is found in the Wellford and Cronin, (1999) research. One of the most consistent relationships is whether the homicide involved drugs. One of the major factors increasing the probability of clearances was the absence of a drug-related homicide.

While the research consistently shows that intimate and family-related homicides are easily cleared by arrest, the evidence regarding stranger homicide is mixed.

The argument found in much of the research is that a low percentage of clearances results in a large number of missing values with respect to victim/offender relationships. Research suggests nonstranger homicides are cleared most frequently. Cardarelli and Cavanaugh found, for example, that more than 98 percent of all homicides among family, friends and acquaintances were cleared by arrest. Perhaps because a majority of felonies involve strangers, it was believed that missing values were primarily stranger homicides.

> "Consider two types of homicide clearances. The first is where a wife kills a physically abusive husband, calls the police, awaits their arrival, and freely confesses. Where this does not occur, family members may be witnesses and arguments and gunshots may be heard by neighbors. Clearing this type of case by arrest occurs easily and quickly.
>
> On the other hand, for felony related homicides, police may be called to the scene of a late night convenience store robbery homicide, sometimes hours after it occurs. Because of the time and location of the offense, there may be no witnesses, little or no third party cooperation, and little evidence. Facing such odds, even in the face of extensive investigation, it is likely that no offender will be arrested."(Riedel & Jarvis 1999 pp. 282-283).

Family related homicides are cleared disproportionately more often and quicker than other types. In a 1980 study of Dade County homicides, Wilbanks,(1984) found that while 51.1% of all criminal homicides in the county were cleared, 86.8% of husband and wife killings and 83.3% of killings involving domestic arguments were cleared. In a study of Memphis homicides from 1974-1978, Riedel, (1993) found that all family homicides were cleared within 24 hours. Eight-four percent of homicides involving friends and acquaintances and 69.2% of stranger homicides were cleared in the same period.

Although the evidence was sparse, most of the missing values were attributed to stranger homicides (Riedel, 1993). The difficulty is that a useful hypothesis is sometimes converted into exaggerated fact as when an FBI report implied that 53% of all homicides involved strangers(Riedel, 1998).

Recent evidence does suggest that family related homicides are among the homicides most easily cleared by arrest. However, the relationship between missing values and stranger relationships requires further research.

One approach to determining the identity of unknown relationships is a careful recoding of available records. Using all available paper records from the St. Louis Police Department from 1985 through 1989 and an expanded classification system, Decker, (1993) recoded 777 cases. Because of intensive data classification and reliability checks among three coders, only 4% of the victim/offender relationships remained unknown.

Decker recalculated the national percentages of victim/offender relationships omitting the category of unknowns (31%) and compared the results to the recoded St. Louis data for 1985-1989. He concluded that stranger homicides do not account for the majority of homicides classified as unknown relationships; indeed, they may be distributed among uncleared cases in the same proportions as they are among cleared homicide cases.

Using statistical imputation methods, Riedel and Regoeczi, (2000) found results for Los Angeles that were consistent with Decker's findings for St. Louis. However, in Chicago, the same expectation-maximization imputation method found a ten percent increase in stranger homicides. Using a weighting technique and multinomial logistic regression, Pampel and Williams, (2000) found a substantial increase in both acquaintances and strangers in 91 cities.

The small body of research on arrest clearances and homicides indicates that variables related to investigation may be positively related to clearances.

In most cases, arrest clearances are regarded as performance measures both within and external to a police department. The research by

Waegel, (1981-1982) indicates how police officers manage their workload to maintain a level of clearances satisfactory to their superiors.

While no arrest quotas were used in the department studied by Waegel, the informal understanding was that an officer should produce at least two arrests per week to remain in the detective division. These constraints lead to "skimming," that is, the practice of selecting out for vigorous investigative effort those cases, from the assigned workload, that were most likely to result in an arrest.

In determining law enforcement factors related to clearances, Greenwood (1970) and his associates (1975, 1977) placed primary responsibility for clearing cases on patrol officers who determine whether the necessary leads are present and conditions favorable for an arrest. By contrast, research done by Eck and the Police Executive Research Forum, (1983) concluded that both patrol officers and detectives make a substantial contribution.

Wellford and Cronin, (1999) found 51 characteristics of homicide events and investigative practices associated with arrest clearance. Of these, 37 were characteristics associated with police practices which suggests that law enforcement policies and practices can make a difference in clearing cases. Some of these included a computer check on decedent, witnesses, suspects, guns, use of the local Criminal Justice Information System, and using three or more detectives.

Method

The data for this study were all homicides reported to the California Criminal Justice Statistics Center from 1987 through 1998. Of the 42,163 California homicides for this 12 year period, 949 were justifiable homicides committed by civilians, 1,436 were police justifiable homicides, and 402 were manslaughters. This left a total of 39,376 willful murders for further analysis. I follow the practice in homicide research of referring to the latter events as homicides.

In addition to being available data, California is the largest state in the United States with an estimated 1998 population of 33,226,000. The largest city is Los Angeles with a 1998 population of about 3,716,000 people and a twelve year homicide total of 10,009 which is 53.5% of the homicides occurring in Los Angeles County.

To examine the characteristics of homicides and how they relate to clearances, I merged two files. As most readers will know, arrest clearances are reported monthly on an FBI form, Return A - Crimes Known to the Police, or a state-level facsimile. Characteristics of homicide, on the other hand, are reported individually on the Supplementary Homicide Reports (SHR). As a rule it is not possible to match the same homicides from the two forms on a month-by-month basis (Riedel, 1999a).

However, SHR data from the California Criminal Justice Statistics Center has two year and month dates. One is the month and year of incident and the other is the month and year it is submitted to the Uniform Crime Reporting Program. When the data are aggregated by the latter year and month, SHR data matches completely with Return A reports by year and month.

While the merging of the SHR file with Return A file insures that homicides reported in a single month on Return A are the same homicides described on the SHR, there is no way of knowing whether cleared homicides reported belong to homicides reported that month or previous months. To address that problem the dependent variable, monthly arrest clearances, are lagged in the multiple regression analysis.

The results of this study are divided into two sections. The first section examines the recent increase in percent arrest cleared and suggests that the increase may be the result of fewer homicides rather than more clearances. The second section is a multiple regression of arrest clearances in Los Angeles.

The dependent variable had two outliers. While the mean monthly clearances was 43.5, in September and December of 1991, the clearances were 95 and 105, respectively. Linear interpolation was used to replace these two extreme values.

Table 1 gives the monthly means and standard deviations for the independent variables used in the analysis. Some variables such as gender and number of victims are self-explanatory. The specific categories for others are given below.

Victim/Offender Relationships. Victim/offender relationships were coded into five variables with monthly frequencies.

> *intimate partners* (husband - legal or common-law; wife - legal or common-law; exhusband; exwife; boyfriend; girlfriend; homosexual couple);
> *other family* (which includes categories like father; mother; son; daughter; brother; sister; stepfather; in-law; stepmother; stepson; stepdaughter; other family);
> *other known* (which includes categories like; employer; employee; neighbor; acquaintance; other-known to victim);
> *strangers*;
> *gang members*. (Collected since 1992)

Weapons. Weapons were recoded into the four following variables.

> *handguns,*
> *long guns,*
> *knives* (includes sharp instruments)
> *other weapons.*

Locations. Locations were grouped as follows:

> *private indoor location* (victim's residence; offender's residence; other indoor residential location; shared residence);
> *public indoor location* (hotel; service station; liquor store; tavern; commercial business; financial institution; warehouse; jail; CYA;Department of Corrections; school grounds);
> *public outdoor location* (parking lot; street; highway or freeway; park; vacant field; other outdoor location);
> *vehicle (*cars; public transportation*)*.

Motive. The circumstances surrounding the offense were categorized into the following:

> *altercations* (brawls; arguments; domestic violence);
> *felonies* (robbery; rape; burglary; larceny; motor vehicle theft; arson; prostitution and commercial vice; other sex offense; abortion; narcotic drug laws; gambling; other felony);
> *organized crime/gangs* (gang altercation; drive-by shooting; organized crime; contract killing; contract arson);
> *other nonfelony* (child abuse; child killed by babysitter; institutional killings; sniper attack; other).

Table 1: **Monthly Mean and Standard Deviations of Independent Variables: Los Angeles, 1987-1998**

Variable	x	σ	Variable	x	σ
Homicides	69.5	20.2	Intimate Partners	2.8	1.9
One Victim	64.6	18.8	Other Family Victims	2.6	1.7
Two Victims	3.9	3.0	Other Known to Victim	17.7	9.2
Three or More	1.0	2.0	Strangers	22.0	7.8
Male Victims	59.5	18.1	Gang Member	9.4	10.0
Female Victims	10.0	4.4	Handguns	44.7	14.6
White Victims	7.5	3.3	Long Guns	8.1	4.9
Latino Victims	33.1	12.3	Knives	8.6	4.5
Black Victims	26.4	9.4	Other Weapons	8.0	3.6
Other Race	2.4	1.7	Location: Private Indoor	16.4	6.6
Victim Age: 1-14	2.7	2.2	Location: Public Indoor	3.9	2.6
Victim Age: 15-24	26.0	9.1	Location: Public Outdoor	42.4	13.4
Victim Age: 25-34	21.3	7.4	Location: Vehicle	6.3	3.7
Victim Age: 35-44	10.8	4.5	Altercations	22.1	7.8
Victim Age: 45-64	6.4	3.0	Felonies	16.5	7.5
Victim Age: 65-99	1.9	1.5	Organized Crime	21.5	9.1
One Offender	33.3	10.2	Other Non-Felonies	2.2	1.7
Three or More	6.4	4.3	Offender Age: 1-14	0.6	0.8
Male Offenders	45.1	14.9	Offender Age: 15-24	25.1	9.0
Female Offenders	2.6	1.9	Offender Age: 25-34	12.6	5.3
White Offenders	3.5	2.1	Offender Age: 35-44	5.1	2.5
Latino Offenders	22.6	8.5	Offender Age: 45-64	2.3	1.6
Black Offenders	20.5	8.2	Offender Age: 65-99	0.4	0.6
Offenders: Other Race	1.0	1.1			

Results

Are Arrest Clearances Increasing?

Arrest clearances are typically computed by dividing the number of homicide arrests by the number of homicides for the same year and jurisdiction. Multiplying the resulting proportion by 100 gives a clearance percent. However, clearance percentages can be misleading because an increase in percent cleared can be accomplished by having a larger denominator in relation to the numerator. Put another way, if homicides decrease more than clearances, the percent cleared will increase thereby giving a misleading view of police performance.

To explore this question, in addition to using clearance percentages as defined above, I compared them to clearance and homicide rates. In other words, to make the number of homicides and clearances comparable, I used a common metric: dividing each by the annual population and multiplying by 100,000. The jurisdictions used were the state of California and three cities: Oakland, San Diego, and Los Angeles. The three measures (clearance percentages, rates, and homicide rates) were calculated for 1993 and 1998 for each jurisdiction. I chose 1993 because it was a low year for clearance percentages. The comparisons are given in Table 2.

The results in Table 2 generally support two conclusions. First, while three of the four jurisdictions show an increase in clearance percentages between 1993 and 1998, all three show a decline in clearance rates. Second, when homicide rates are compared to clearance rates, there is a substantially greater decline in homicide rates than clearance rates. For example, Oakland clearance percentages increase by 19.7% - from 44.2% in 1993 to 63.9% in 1998. But clearance and homicide rates declined during the same period and homicide rates declined by a greater amount. Clearance rates only declined from 17.9 per 100,000 in 1993 to 11.6 per 100,000 in 1998 while homicide rates declined from 40.6 per 100,000 1993 to 18.1 per 100,000 in 1998. In the former case, the difference was a 6.2 point decline while in the latter, it was 22.5.

A limited exception to the results in Table 2 is found in Los Angeles. Clearance percentages, rates and homicide rates declined from 1993 to 1998. However, the decline in clearance percentages was 1.9% while the decline in homicide rates (18.2) was greater than the decline in clearance rates (11.2). These results suggest that recent increases in clearance percentages are probably a statistical artifact, reflecting a decline in the denominator, the number of homicides, rather than an increase in the numerator, the number of arrests.

Table 2: **Comparison of Clearance Percentages, Rates, and Homicide Rates for Four Jurisdictions**

Jurisdiction	1993	1998	Difference
State of California			
Clearance Pct.	55.5%	63.1%	+7.6%
Clearance Rate	7.2	4.1	-3.1
Homicide Rate	13.0	6.5	-6.5
City of Oakland			
Clearance Pct.	44.2%	63.9%	+19.7%
Clearance Rate	17.9	11.6	-6.2
Homicide Rate	40.6	18.1	-22.5
City of San Diego			
Clearance Pct.	45.9%	57.1%	+11.2%
Clearance Rate	5.3	2.1	-3.2
Homicide Rate	11.5	3.7	-7.8
City of Los Angeles			
Clearance Pct.	59.9%	58.0%	-1.9%
Clearance Rate	17.8	6.6	-11.2
Homicide Rate	29.7	11.5	-18.2

Multiple Regression Analysis: Victim and Event Variables

In order to determine what variables account for variations in arrest clearances, a multiple regression analysis was done using monthly clearances (N = 144) and aggregating SHR data to monthly units. Wellford and Cronin, (1999) found that 50% of the cases studied in four cities were cleared within one week; 66.7% within one month; and 88.1% within six months. In the present study, the independent variables are lagged up to three months to examine what characteristics are associated with clearances for each month.

It was decided that multiple regression was a more suitable analysis technique than ARIMA or autoregression for the 144 month series. There was very little evidence showing a trend in clearances. In exponential smoothing, the general parameter, alpha, controls the weight given to recent observations in the determining the overall level. When alpha = 0, old observations count as much as new ones while if alpha = 1, the single most recent observation is used exclusively (SPSS, 1994).

For the arrest clearance variable that had interpolated values, the smallest alpha is 0.2 which indicates a slight trend, probably found in the period from mid-1993 when the number (not the percent cleared) of monthly clearances turn downward.

To test for a significant amount of autocorrelation, the Durbin-Watson d-statistic was used for nonlagged data. The d-statistic for the data with 48 independent variables was 2.070 which was not significant for positive autocorrelation. The Durbin-Watson test was not used with lagged regressors (Kanjii, 1993; Ostrom, 1990).

Collinear variables were number of homicides, one victim, male victims, Latino victims, victims age 15-24, handguns, and public outdoor locations. The lowest correlation among these seven variables was 0.807. Although these variables were excluded in the multiple regression, most of the homicide research finds one or more of these to be important characteristics of homicide. One way to avoid the issue of collinearity was to create a victim composite variable by adding together the monthly number of seven variables, excluding monthly homicides (Allison, 1999).

A correlation matrix was computed using both victim and offender variables. While the correlations with victim and event variables were small, excluding the victim composite variable, they were larger than 0.80 for some offender gender, age, and race/ethnicity variables. Regression models were therefore calculated separately for offender variables and victim and event variables. Table 3 gives the final model for Los Angeles victim and event variables using stepwise regression.

Table 3: **Stepwise Multiple Regression Using Lagged and Unlagged Variables: Los Angeles Homicides, Victim and Event Variables, 1987-1998**

Unlagged			One Month Lag			Two Month Lag			Three Month Lag		
Variable	b	beta	Variable	b	beta	Variable	b	beta	Variable	b	beta
Victim Age: 25-34	0.778	0.405*							Victim Age: 25-34	0.744	0.397*
Altercation	0.621	0.341*							Other Weapons	0.513	0.132
Other Weapons	0.596	0.151*	Knives	0.794	0.252*				Public Indoor	1.013	0.179*
Two Victims	-0.778	-0.162*	Felonies	0.579	0.308*				Victim Age: 45-64	0.834	0.183*
Other Non-Felony	1.106	0.132*	Vehicle	0.967	0.252*	Victim Age: 25-34	0.956	0.508*	Organized Crime	-0.279	0.181*
R^2		0.600	R^2		0.388	R^2		0.253	R^2		0.365

*p < .05

Table 3 shows that for unlagged clearances, cases involving victims age 25-34 are positively related to arrest clearances for homicides. Consistent with research cited earlier, homicides involving altercations and other non-felonies are related to a larger number of arrest clearances.

The use of weapons other than knives and firearms is related to increased arrest clearances only for unlagged data. Wellford and Cronin (1999) found in a bivariate analysis that the use of personal weapons, included with "other weapons" significantly increased the probability of solving homicide cases. Table 3 shows that the presence of two victims is negatively related to the number of clearances. The victim composite variable did not enter into the final regression model.

With a one month lag, the use of knives, the presence of concomitant felonies and the location of homicides in a vehicle were related to increased arrest clearances. The use of knives in contrast to handguns was found to be associated with solving cases in the Wellford and Cronin research. The location of a homicide in a vehicle was also positively related to arrest clearances.

What is difficult to explain is the appearance of felonies as positively related to clearances. As previous research consistently indicated, felonies are among the most difficult offenses to clear.

With a two month and three month lag, cases with victims age 25-34 are significantly related to arrest clearances. With a three month lag, homicides occurring in public indoor locations with older victims (45-64) are more likely to be cleared by arrest. The use of other weapons was not significant at the three month lag. Wellford and Cronin also found that homicides were more likely to be solved if they occurred in a public indoor location such as a bar or a club. Homicides involving organized crime and gang activities were significantly less likely to be cleared by arrest.

Summary

An analysis of victim and event variables supports previous research to some extent. For arrest clearances occurring the same month as the homicide, the significant variables involve 25-34-year-old victims involved in altercations and other nonfelonies using other weapons. At a one month lag, vehicles become important as a location for the homicide and knives as weapons.

For the two and three month lags, victims age 25-34, and public indoor locations are related to arrest clearances. The appearance of older victims (45-64) at the third month lag suggest a time delay in clearing homicides where there may be few witnesses.

The negative relationship of organized crimes and gangs to clearances indicates the difficulty of clearing offenses where witnesses are unwilling to be involved. If the latter is the case, it is difficult to understand why this variable did not appear in the regression model sooner. The results reported here may reflect an accumulation of cases.

Multiple Regression Analysis: Offender Variables

Because of high correlations among independent variables, the regression model for offender variables used two composite variables. The first, a black composite variable, added together number of homicides one offender, black offenders, males, offenders age 15-24, and offenders age 25-34. The second, a Latino composite variable, added together number of murders, one offender, Latino offenders, males, and offenders age 15-24. The resulting regression models are given in Table 4.

Table 4 shows the results using the black composite variable; it indicates what might be expected: single black male offenders age 15-34 are positively related to arrest clearances. For the unlagged regression using a Latino composite variable, single Latino male offenders age 15-24, were positively related to arrest clearances.

In addition, for the unlagged regression using the black and Latino composite variable, the presence of two offenders and offenders age 35-44 were significantly related to arrest clearances. The age group 25-34 were not included in the Latino composite variable and was not significantly related to arrest clearances. However, in the Latino composite regression, black offenders were related to arrest clearances, although for the black composite variable, Latino offenders did not emerge in the final model. For the three month lagged regression using the Latino composite variable, black offenders also emerge in the final model.

The black composite variable is significantly related to arrest clearances for the first through the third month lagged analysis. For Latinos, three or more offenders were related to arrest clearances at the one month lag; otherwise, except for the appearance of black offenders at the third month lag, the Latino composite variable is significantly related to arrest clearances.

Table 4: Stepwise Multiple Regression Using Lagged and Unlagged Variables: Los Angeles Homicide Offenders, 1987-1998

	Unlagged			One Month Lag			Two Month Lag			Three Month Lag		
	Variable	b	beta	Variable	b	beta	Variable	b	beta	Variable	b	beta
	Black Composite	0.176	0.772*									
	Two Offenders Offender	-0.359	-.210*									
	Age: 35-44	0.893	0.159*	Black Composite	0.129	0.572*	Black Composite	0.109	0.488*	Black Composite	0.113	0.510*
	R^2		0.556	R^2		0.327	R^2		0.233	R^2		0.260
	Latino Composite	0.137	0.567*									
	Black Offenders	0.404	0.234							Black Offenders	0.553	0.328*
	Two Offenders Offender	-0.320	-0.187*	Latino Composite	0.102	0.426*	Latino Composite	0.111	0.470*	Latino Composite	0.005	0.026*
	Age: 35-44	0.808	0.385*	3 Offn +	0.638	0.195*						
	R^2		0.537	R^2		0.335	R^2		0.215	R^2		0.265

*p < .05

Conclusions

There are several conclusions supported by the analysis in this paper. First, any claims that percent cleared by arrest for homicide is increasing is largely a statistical artifact caused by a decrease in homicide rates more than by an increase in clearance rates.

Second, its worth considering the character of victim and event variables that are related to clearances: they are predominantly situational in nature. For example, in the unlagged model altercations is a significant predictor, but none of victim/offender relationships appear in the final model. Apparently, because altercations can characterize even stranger homicides, police investigators find prior relationships to be of little value in effecting arrests(Riedel, 1999b).

Third, knives and other weapons were found to be significantly related to arrest clearances, but not handguns. This was also true of the research done by Wellford and Cronin. It's likely there are so many handguns in circulation, many of which are stolen, that their appearance as a weapon simply does not discriminate between solved and unsolved cases.

Fourth, it's unclear in the analysis of the victim and event variables the relevance of certain age groups to clearances. Why is the victim age group 25-34 a significant variable in unlagged and the three lagged periods? Similarly, it's not clear why the victim age group 45-64 is positively related to clearances in the three month lag, but not earlier.

Fifth, in contrast to much of the previous research, felonies are positively, rather than negatively related to clearances, which is puzzling. It could be argued that "felonies" are too gross a classification, but other researchers have used similar classifications and found an inverse relationship.

Sixth, this research finds that a composite victim variable that include Latino victims and the variable of black victims was not related to solved homicides. However, demographic characteristics of offenders are among the most important variables related to clearances. Composite variables of black and Latino offenders were consistently related to clearances for unlagged and lagged clearances.

Finally, in doing research on arrest clearances there is a contradiction. On the one hand, it is clear that police departments are reluctant to be publicly identified when data is being gathered about arrest clearances. For example, the Wellford and Cronin research, which probably represents the best current study, would have benefited enormously by identifying and doing research on each of the four cities. They were prevented from doing that by signing an agreement not to reveal the identity of the cities.

On the other hand, Wellford and Cronin (1999) note that in a presentation of their results at a National Institute of Justice conference, a police administrator mentioned how useful the results would be in overcoming some of the shortcomings of the traditional clearance measure. However, the kinds of useful results that could eventuate from working with police departments is not going to occur if departments refuse to allow researchers to identify the department and set it in the social and historical context of a large city.

REFERENCES

Allison, P. (1999). *Multiple Regression: A Primer*. Thousand Oaks: Pine Forge Press.

Bynum, T. S., Cordner, G. W., & Greene, J. R. (1982). "Victim and Offense Characteristics." *Criminology, 20*, 301-318.

Cardarelli, A. P., & Cavanagh, D. (1992). Uncleared Homicides in the United States: An Exploratory Study of Trends and Patterns. Paper presented at the American Society of Criminology, New Orleans, LA.

Decker, S. H. (1993). "Exploring Victim-Offender Relationships in Homicide: The Role of Individual and Event Characteristics." *Justice Quarterly*, 10, 585-612.

Eck, J. E. (1983). Solving Crimes: The Investigation of Burglary and Robbery. Washington, D.C.: Police Executive Research Forum.

Greenwood, P. (1970). An Analysis of the Apprehension Activities of the New York City Police Department. New York: Rand Institute.

Greenwood, P., Chaiken, J., & Petersilia, J. (1977). *The Criminal Investigation Process*. Lexington, MA: Lexington Books.

Greenwood, P. W., & Petersilia, J. (1975). The Criminal Investigation Process: Vol. 1. *Summary and Policy Implications* (R-1776-DOJ): Rand Corporation.

Kanjii, G. K. (1993). *100 Statistical Tests*. London: Sage Publications.

Ostrom, C. W., Jr. (1990). *Time Series Analysis: Regression Techniques*. (2nd ed.). Newbury Park: Sage Publications.

Pampel, F. C., & Williams, K. R. (2000). "Intimacy and Homicide: Compensating for Missing Data in the SHR." *Criminology*, 38(2), 661-680.

Regoeczi, W. C., Kennedy, L. W., & Silverman, R. A. (2000). "Uncleared Homicides: A Canada/United States Comparison." *Homicide Studies*, 4, 135-161.

Riedel, M. (1993). Stranger Violence: A Theoretical Inquiry. New York: Garland Publishing Co.

Riedel, M. (1998). "Counting Stranger Homicides: A Case Study of Statistical Prestidigitation." *Homicide Studies*, 2, 206-219.

Riedel, M. (1999a). "Sources of Homicide Data: A Review and Comparison." In M. D. Smith & M. A. Zahn (Eds.), *Homicide: A sourcebook of social research* (pp. 75-95). Newbury Park: Sage Publications.

Riedel, M. (1999b). "Toward a Perspective on Stranger Violence." *Advances in Criminological Theory.* 12, 19-35

Riedel, M., & Jarvis, J. (1999). "The Decline of Arrest Clearances for Criminal Homicide: Causes, Correlates, and Third Parties." *Criminal Justice Policy Review*, 9, 279-305.

Riedel, M., & Regoeczi, W. (2000, November). Estimating Stranger Homicides: Los Angeles and Chicago. Paper presented at the American Society of Criminology, San Francisco, CA.

Riedel, M., & Rinehart, T. A. (1996). "Murder Clearances and Missing Data." *Journal of Crime and Justice*, 19, 83-102.

SPSS. (1994). SPSS Trends 6.1. Chicago: SPSS, Inc.

Stern, M. (1931). "A Study of Unsolved Murders in Wisconsin from 1924-1928." *Journal of Criminal Law, Criminology, and Police Science*, 21, 513-536.

Waegel, W. B. (1981). "Case Routinization in Investigative Police Work." *Social Problems*, 28, 263-275.

Waegel, W. B. (1982). "Patterns of Police Investigation of Urban Crimes." *Journal of Police Science and Administration*, 10, 452-465.

Wellford, C., & Cronin, J. (1999). *An Analysis of Variables Affecting the Clearance of Homicides: A Multistate Study* . Washington, DC: Justice Research and Statistics Association.

Wilbanks, W. (1984). *Murder in Miami: An Analysis of Homicide Patterns and Trends in Dade County (Miami) Florida* 1917-1983: Lanham, Md.: University Press of America.

Wolfgang, M..E. (1958). *Patterns in Criminal Homicide*: Philadelphia: University of Pennsylvania Press.

TRENDS AND PATTERNS OF HOMICIDE IN AUSTRALIA

Satyanshu Mukherjee

In the criminal codes of nations, murder is the crime that attracts the most severe punishment. Nations that still have capital punishment in their statute books use it more often for this crime than any other. The United Nations state that "the number of homicides in a country can reflect a true level of violence. The reasons for this recognition are that there is no significant difference in definitions of a completed murder across countries, the reportability rate of murder is usually close to 100 percent, and homicide trends can be accepted as a measure of change in social behavior" (UNCJIN 1997).

It is not only the abominable nature of the crime that has fascinated scholars and researchers for decades, but homicide exposes various manifestations of violence in a society. Ten years of Australian homicide data reveal the existence of the following types of homicides involving different degrees of criminality; involving violence of different nature and degree; involving victims of different age, gender, marital status, occupation, life style, etc.; in different locations; and under different circumstances: intimate homicide, child killing, homicide arising from sexual rivalries, victim precipitated homicide, internecine conflict, hired killings, unintended homicide, drug-related homicide, and hate homicide.

Gottfredson and Hirschi suggest that "despite popular and scholarly opinion to the contrary, homicide is perhaps the most mundane and, in our view, most easily explainable crime" (1990:31). Others, Riedel, (1999) suggest that homicide is a statistically rare phenomenon. If one is interested in analyzing homicide trends, particularly from secondary data, both of these views may be correct. But an examination of details of homicide incidents, like the ones by Wolfgang, (1958) and Silverman and Kennedy, (1993), and the various types of homicides listed above soon makes it clear that the crime of homicide is neither mundane nor can it be explained easily. Similarly, 'statistically rare' is a relative and comparative term. In a ten-year period, 1989 to 1998, almost 218,000 individuals fell victim to homicides in the United States. In the same period 3,386 people became victims of homicide in Australia.

Homicide is a human tragedy. Although an incident of homicide ends the life of a victim, it launches a prolonged period of trauma and suffering for the victim's family, close friends, workmates, classmates, and many others. A single incident of homicide affects many more individuals than single incidents of robbery, rape, or serious assault. A close examination of some of the homicide cases in Australia reveals that on average at least 25 individuals, including families of the victim and the offender, are intimately affected by each incident of homicide. Then there are rare cases like the primary care physician, a father of four who practiced in the same community for over 20 years, gunned downed on his way to a home visit, which affects many more individuals (Burnley, Edmunds, Gaboury, and Seymour, 1998). This is why the phenomenon of homicide needs to be carefully and continuously researched.

Trend analysis of aggregate homicide rates provides the general pattern and identifies the convergence or divergence with social, economic, and demographic aspects of a society. Unless the data is disaggregated and analyzed, however, it cannot assist in enhancing our understanding of the problem. Has the nature of homicide in Australia changed over time? Are there more intimate killings now than before? How do drug-related homicides influence the overall homicide rate? Is stranger homicide increasing? What role does the presence of alcohol play in homicide? Following a brief overview of a long-term trend in homicide in Australia, this paper will present a snapshot of homicide in the ten-year period 1989-90 to 1998-99.

The Homicide Trend in Australia

Homicide as described in this paper includes murder, manslaughter (not by driving), and infanticide. Between 1915 and 1998 the Australian homicide rate has remained below two per 100,000 population for most years. Only in four years (1919, 1920, 1988 and 1990) has the rate exceeded two. Overall, the trend in homicide, considering events like the two world wars and the Depression of the 1930s, has been a stable one. If one were to fit a curve, the trend fits a dish-shaped curve. The homicide trend also appears to portray a long cycle and the declining trend in the 1990s could be the beginning of a new cycle. Figure 1 shows that during the 84 year period the lowest homicide rate of 0.8 per 100,000 was recorded in 1941, in the middle of the Second World War, and the highest rate of 2.4 was recorded in 1988, Australia's bicentennial year. In 1998 the recorded homicide rate was 1.7 per 100,000 population.

Figure 1: AUSTRALIA, Trends in Homicide 1915 – 1998

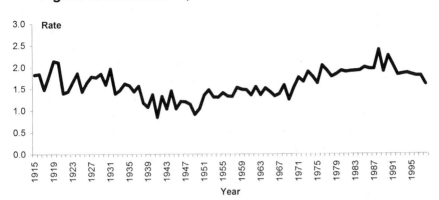

Source: Adapted from *Causes of Death* data, Australian Bureau of Statistics

Research literature on homicide offers a number of explanations for homicide trends. Income inequality, unemployment, and inflation may influence homicide rates (Brenner, 1976). Social disorganization, particularly in large urban centers, could account for an increase in certain types of homicide (Blumstein and Rosenfeld, 1998; Fagan, Zimring, and Kim, 1998). In recent years, some research appears to show an association between illicit drug dealing and trafficking and homicide (Blumstein and Rosenfeld 1998). Rosenfeld, Bray and Egley, (1999) found "concentrated disadvantage and racial isolation" as major sources of youth homicide in urban areas. Of course, whether these factors have a direct or an indirect influence and whether they vary over time need to be examined. However, homicide trend data from a few industrialized countries present some interesting possibilities.

The Australian trend in homicide rate appears remarkably similar to that in Canada and the United States; the differences lie in the magnitude. Zahn and McCall, (1999) and Silverman and Kennedy, (1993) present long-term trend data for homicide in the United States and Canada respectively. Homicide rates peaked in the early 1930s in the United States and in Canada; I observe the same in Australia. The rates declined gradually until about the mid 1940s and then plateaued in all the three countries. Between the mid-1960s and the mid-1970s homicide rates increased in all three countries, but the increase was much sharper in the United States and Canada than in Australia. A trough and then decline followed this increase. Is it possible that the same factors are influencing homicide trends in the United States, Canada, and Australia? Of course the point to be noted is the high homicide rate in the United States, several times that in Australia and Canada.

Silverman and Kennedy, (1993) label the United States homicide rate "as an aberration among industrial nations". Analyzing violence in the United States, Zimring and Hawkins, (1997) write about this aberration thusly: "What separates the United States from the rest of the industrial Western world is not particularly high rates of crime generally or even much higher rates of the fist fights, purse snatchings, and street level extortions that constitute the bulk of violent crimes in most developed countries. The distinctive violence problem in the United States is the relatively small number of life-threatening attacks, usually shootings, and not infrequently attacks that occur in the course of armed robbery."

Indeed, the presence of firearms in homicide appears to separate the United States from other industrial nations. Consider the data in Figure 2. England and Wales displays one of the lowest homicide rates in the industrial world; this has been so for decades. Homicide rates of Australia and Canada have converged in recent years. In 1974 for each homicide in Australia there were 5.4 homicides in the United States (population adjusted). In 1998 the ratio declined to 1: 3.7. Similar relationships are obtained between Canada and the United States and England and Wales and the United States. This ratio change has taken place primarily because of declines in the rate of homicide in the United States in the 1990s. In spite of the decline, the difference between homicide in the United States and the other three countries remains.

Figure 2: **Total homicide rate in selected countries, 1974-1998**

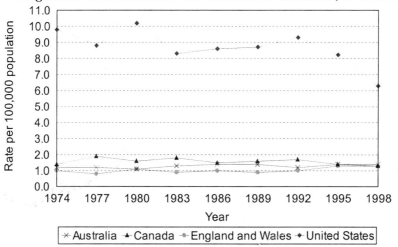

Firearms kill a majority of homicide victims in the United States and this has been the situation for almost the last 90 years. In 1910 the total homicide rate in the United States was 4.6 per 100,000 population and over 54 percent of homicides were committed by firearms. It is interesting to note how this proportion has oscillated over the years. Total homicides increased until the early 1930s, and so did the proportion of homicides by firearms: in 1930 this proportion was almost 68 percent. Homicides declined until the early 1950s, and so did the proportion of firearm-related homicides, reaching a low of 52.6 percent in 1950. Again, almost 67 percent of all homicides were by a firearm in 1970, when the homicide rate had jumped to 8.3 (U.S. Bureau of the Census, 1975). The homicide rate continued to increase gradually and in 1990 homicides by firearms still accounted for 65 percent of all homicides. Up to this point it would appear that firearms drive the homicide rate in the United States. The substantial decline in the homicide rate in the United States since 1993 needs to be examined carefully.

Relative to the United States, homicides by firearms account for a small proportion of homicides in Australia, Canada, and England and Wales. An overwhelming majority of firearm-related homicides in the United States are committed with handguns. Since 1930 Australia has had strict controls on handguns and by 1998 promulgated laws in each State and Territory on a uniform basis. Canada in the 1990s tightened its firearm legislation. England and Wales, for a long time, have had strict gun control. Consider the data in Figure 3 which charts non-firearm-related homicide rates in the four countries. The total homicide rate in the United States in 1974, as shown earlier, was about five and a half times that of Australia; once firearm-related homicides are excluded, the United States rate was only two and a half times that of Australia. In 1998, for each non-firearm-related homicide in Australia there was only 1.6 in the United States. Similar patterns are observed in the relationships between the non-firearm homicide rates of Canada and England and Wales and the United States. Figure 3 makes a powerful point: the non-firearm-related homicide rates in all four countries are close and getting closer. In 1998 this rate was 1.4, 1.3, 1.3 and 2.2 per 100,000 population in Australia, Canada, England and Wales, and the United States respectively.

Figure 3: **Non-firearm homicide rate in selected countries, 1974-1998**

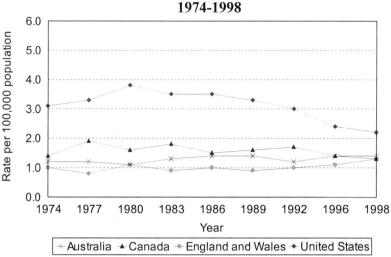

Assaults by firearms are considered more serious that those by other weapons. Vinson found that "gun attacks in New South Wales are 2.7 times more likely to result in death than the reported knife attacks" (1974: 80-81). Although a higher portion of homicides in Australia and England and Wales are committed by knives than guns, the homicide rate remains low. Thus lethality of guns is an important issue.

It is relevant to point out that in the United States a much higher proportion of homicides than in the other three countries are between strangers. Similarly, a substantial portion of these could be part of robbery or drug-related encounters or gang fights in the United States. It is interesting to note that, since 1996, the non-firearm robbery rate in the United States has reached a level lower than that in England and Wales. The point that emerges is that lax gun control laws appear to significantly influence the level of violent crime, including homicide, in the United States. Since homicide is often an unintended consequence of a robbery or assault gone wrong, it is important to analyze trends in these crimes while examining homicide.

Patterns of Homicide in Australia

The long-term trend data presented in Figure 1 are important for our understanding of changes in rates in different periods. But the trend data do not provide details of types of homicides, victim-offender relationships, motives, location, characteristics of unsolved homicides, etc. Details of homicides for the last 10 years are available and can be used to examine these issues, however.

Following a few tragic incidents in Melbourne in 1987, the governments of Australia convened a National Committee on Violence to assess and investigate violence in Australia. In its report (1990) the Committee made a number of recommendations, one of which was to establish a National Homicide Monitoring Program (NHMP) at the Australian Institute of Criminology. The main objective of the NHMP is to collect, on an ongoing basis, detailed information on incidents, victims, and offenders of homicide in Australia. So far the Institute has collected data for 10 years, 1 July 1989 to 30 June 1999, involving 3150 homicide incidents, 3481 identified offenders, and 3386 victims. This part of the paper relies on the NHMP data set.

First, a few general comments. In these 10 years the number of homicide incidents in Australia has fluctuated between a low of 297 and a high of 327 per year. Although this may appear small, the fluctuation amounts to about 10 percent of the total number of homicides in a year. In relation to population, there has been less than one homicide for 50,000 people. Also, the figures are susceptible to sharp movements should rare incidents of mass killings occur. The Port Arthur massacre of April 1996, when a lone gunman killed 35 people and injured 19 within a few minutes, is one such incident. If this incident had not taken place, the number of homicides would have been the lowest since the early 1960s.

Approximately 86 percent of all the homicides occurred in urban areas, almost the same proportion as the population living in urban areas. The number of homicides also appears to be related to the size of each State and Territory, with one exception. The Northern Territory has only one percent of the country's population, but over five percent of homicides occurred in this area. Aborigines account for over a quarter of the Northern Territory's population and they are involved in 70 percent of the Territory's homicide incidents.

Homicide in the North American context is a street crime, often of a random nature. This may be because a much larger proportion of homicides in the United States than in Australia, New Zealand, and the United Kingdom occur in open areas, between strangers, in the process of crimes like robbery, assault, rape, etc., and brawls between gangs. In Australia, homicide is not considered to be a random event (Wallace 1986; Mouzos 2000). An overwhelming majority of homicide incidents are between offenders and victims known to each other, occur in private dwellings, and occur between 6 p.m. and 6 a.m. The hours between 6 a.m. and noon are the most unlikely time for a homicide. Over four out of five incidents involve a single offender and a single victim.

Profile of Homicide in Australia

Unsolved Homicides

Like violent crimes such as robbery and assault, homicide incidents are dominated by males, both as offenders and victims. Even though homicide is one of the most serious offenses, not all incidents are cleared. Thus, whereas details of all incidents, including where, how, when, and under what circumstances they occurred, and detailed characteristics of all victims are available, details of offenders involved in unsolved homicides are missing. In the ten-year period 347 homicide incidents in Australia, or 11 percent of 3,150, still remain unsolved. No research in Australia has examined the issue of unsolved homicides. Recent research in the United States notes that factors that influence the clearance rate of homicides are changes in the nature of homicides, police resources, and citizens' behaviors (Cardarelli and Cavanaugh, 1992). Wellford and Cronin (2000) support the significance of these factors in clearing homicides and list a large number of specific factors concerning police resources and case characteristics. (See also the chapter by Riedel in this volume.)

While detailed analysis of the unsolved homicides in Australia is not possible, certain incident and victim characteristics of uncleared homicides can be presented. Of all the homicide incidents where the place of occurrence was known almost 63 percent occurred in either the victim or suspect's home; of the unsolved homicide incidents only 46.7 percent occurred in homes. Conversely, while just over 21 percent of all incidents occurred on the streets and in open areas, well over a third of unsolved homicides occurred there. This appears logical because one would expect that homicides occurring inside homes would be between people who know each other well and relatives/friends of victims may be of assistance to police in locating suspects. As can be expected in more than four out of ten unsolved homicide incidents the motive was unknown and in another third no apparent motive could be established.

Victims of unsolved homicides did not differ from victims in general in age, gender, or employment status. However, the distribution of the race of victims in unsolved incidents does appear to differ from the distribution of racial categories in the general victim population. An overwhelming majority of homicides are intra-racial and in this sense racial differences of victims in unsolved and solved homicides are significant. Wellford and Cronin, (2000) observed that a homicide case was more likely to be solved if the suspect was an African American or Hispanic. The Australian data show that only a very small proportion of homicides where the victim was an Aborigine remained unsolved. However, where a victim was an Asian, particularly an Indo-Chinese, the likelihood that the case remained unsolved was substantial. It is interesting to note that the involvement of this group in drug and drug-related offenses in Australia is significantly higher than that of any other group. Indeed, prisoner data show that almost half of the 474 prisoners of Indo-Chinese background in Australian prisons in 1998 were in prison for drug dealing and trafficking (Mukherjee, 1999).

Solved Incidents and Their Participants

During the ten-year period under study, there were, in all, 3150 homicides in Australia. These were generally distributed evenly according to populations of States and Territories. Approximately two-thirds of homicide incidents occurred in homes. Nearly four out of ten homicides occurred between six in the evening and midnight and over a third occurred on Saturdays and Sundays. Almost 81 percent of the incidents involved one offender and one victim, and in just over 14 percent there was one victim but more than one offender.

Victim Profile

In all there were 3,386 homicide victims in the period between 1 July 1989 and 30 June 1999, including those for unsolved incidents. About 63 percent of the victims were males and about 37 percent were females. In relation to population the female and male victimization rates per 100,000 were 1.4 and 2.4 respectively. Homicide research literature in Australia suggests that the gender distribution of homicide victims has not changed over the past several decades.

In all age groups, except infants under the age of one year, victimization rates show a set pattern, that is, the female rate is slightly more than half of the male rate. For infants the risk of becoming a victim of homicide was similar for males and females, 2.8 and 2.6 per 100,000 relevant population respectively; for male infants the rate was higher than the rate of all males but for female infants the rate was almost twice the rate of all females. Also, the homicide victimization rate of female infants was higher than that of females of any other age; for males, the highest victimization rate was for adults between 18 and 41 years of age.

The racial appearance of close to 4 out of 5 homicide victims over the 10-year period was Caucasian; they also make up over three-quarters of Australian population. On the other hand, Aborigines and Torres Strait Islanders (Indigenous Australians) account for about two percent of the Australian population but about 13 percent of homicide victims. Asians accounted for 6.3 percent of homicide victims, similar to their proportion in the population. Racial appearance details are based on the perception of the police officers recording the incident.

Almost 53 percent of male victims were never married as compared to only about 27 percent of female victims. While only one-third of the male victims were married and living with their partners at the time of their death, about half of the female victims were married. A large majority of both male and female victims were unemployed or not in the work force.

A firearm was the third most frequently used weapon to commit homicide (23%); the most common weapon was a knife or a sharp instrument (35%). The choice of a weapon to kill did not vary according to the gender of the victim. However, almost a third of the female victims as compared to a quarter of male victims died as a result of severe beating or kicking.

Offender Profile

Even in a serious crime like homicide a substantial number of incidents remain unresolved and no offender is apprehended. Furthermore, of those suspected and arrested for committing homicide some may never face trial because of lack of evidence and some may be acquitted. It is important to note that the offender data portrayed below suffer from these deficiencies.

Of the 3,150 homicide incidents in Australia over the ten-year period 2,803 were cleared and offenders were apprehended. For these 2,803 incidents 3,481 offenders (actually suspects or alleged offenders) were arrested and charged. About 87 percent of the offenders whose gender was known were males and about 13 percent were females. This is not unusual considering that violence is a predominantly male phenomenon. Males between the ages of 18 and 26 showed the highest gender-age specific homicide rate (9 per 100,000), and this was nine times that of their female counterparts.

Racial appearance of offenders as determined by the police reveals that over three quarters were Caucasians. However, gender distribution of offenders points out that only 68.5 percent of female offenders as compared to 76.6 percent of male offenders were Caucasians. Australia's indigenous population is grossly over-represented in the offender population. Sixteen percent of offenders whose racial appearance was known were of indigenous appearance, yet the indigenous people constitute only two percent of the total population. Of all the male offenders 15.5 percent were of indigenous appearance whereas almost a quarter (24.1%) of female offenders belonged to this category. The over-representation of the indigenous population among homicide offenders reveals another special feature. About 27 percent of the population of the Northern Territory are indigenous but they account for approximately 73 percent of homicide offenders in the Territory. Similarly in Western Australia where 3.1 percent of the population are indigenous, about 29 percent of the State's homicide offenders belong to this group.

Like the victim population, almost three out of five male offenders were single and over half of the female offenders were married or living in a de-facto relationship. A much larger proportion of the offender population as compared to victim population was unemployed or not in the work force.

Discussion

Research on homicide, particularly in the last two decades has significantly enhanced our understanding of this phenomenon. This enhanced understanding emphasizes that profiles of homicide incidents, victims, and offenders are important but these profiles drawn separately from each other fail to establish causality. Causality can best be explained through an analysis of interpersonal relationships between victims and offenders of homicide, interactions between them, and circumstances surrounding the incidents. Especially in the Australian setting the data appear to suggest that homicide is not an unplanned act of aggression. Indeed, in an overwhelming majority of incidents the victim and the offender are known to each other, and very often they are intimate partners living together, members of a family, friends and acquaintances. Unlike in the United States, relatively few homicides in Australia occur between strangers and in the process of other crimes such as robbery and rape.

Violence in humans is not an ingrained or deeply rooted habit; very often it is learned. Many factors can trigger violence and aggression in humans. Most humans, however, can manage and avoid engaging in violent acts. In this context it is perhaps useful to analyze wanton homicides separately from homicides of intimates and close relatives. The data collected under the National Homicide Monitoring Program do not enable us to examine these issues but they point to distinct characteristics of different types of homicides. In this section an attempt is made to examine three aspects of homicide.

First, the data reveal that females are grossly over-represented as victims of homicide. Secondly, approximately two-thirds (63%) of all homicides in Australia in the last ten years involved intimates (21%), family members (14%), and friends (28%). Most homicides are also intra-racial and the Aboriginal community of Australia shows an unusually high rate of homicide.

Females as Victims

Although it is claimed that violence and homicide are predominantly male phenomena, males are also responsible for most female victims of homicide. Consider the data in Table 1.

Table 1: **Offender-Victim Distribution of Solved Homicides**

Offender		Victims		
		Male	Female	Total
Male	N	1631	1037 (563)	2668
	%	85.8	92.3	88.2
Female	N	270 (203)	86	356
	%	14.2	7.7	11.8
Total	N	1901	1123	3024
	%	62.9	37.1	100.0

Numbers in parentheses represent intimates.

The data in Table 1 show that male offenders killed about 92 percent of female victims and 86 percent of male victims. Violence is a male phenomenon but the fact that males kill an unusually large number of females, raises questions as to their motives and circumstances. Do males kill females for different reasons? This leads us to the second issue, i.e. intimate homicide.

Intimate Homicide

The participants in this type of homicide are spouses, ex-spouses, persons in current or former de-facto relationships, current and former boy/girl friends, and extra-marital lovers. The data in Table 1 show that their intimate partners killed 50 percent of all female victims. Indeed over 54 percent of female victims of male homicide were killed by their partners. However, a majority of victims of male homicide are males. When women kill, a large majority, over 75 percent, of their victims are males, and an equal proportion of male victims are their intimate partners. Overall, as the data in Table 1 show 766 victims, or 25 percent of solved homicides, were killed by their intimate partners. While this type of homicide is different from all other types, it is a difficult area for further study. Because the victim's exact role in the incident is difficult to verify.

Over-Representation of Aborigines in Homicides

About 13 percent of the victims and almost 17 percent of the offenders of homicide in Australia over the last ten years were Aborigines. These proportions are several times their representation in the total Australian population. Furthermore, Aborigine women account for almost a quarter of all female offenders of homicide. Like minorities in many countries, Aborigines of Australia also suffer serious disadvantages in areas such as health, education, employment, housing, income, and justice. Violence, in particular assault and domestic assault, in the Aboriginal communities prevail at a much higher rate than in other communities. Suicide is also unusually high in the Aboriginal communities.

Conclusion

The homicide rate in Australia has remained fairly stable since the early 20th century. The highest rate of 2.4 per 100,000 population was recorded in 1988, the 200th year of European settlement in Australia. The Australian data reveal patterns and trends in homicide similar to those observed in some industrialized countries. Although strict handgun control was implemented in the early 1930s, one in five homicides still involve guns. Jealousy, arguments, revenge, alcohol, drugs, and money appear to be related to homicide. Females are three times as likely to be victims of homicide as offenders and Aborigines are significantly over-represented as offenders and victims of homicide. When a female kills, three out of four victims are a male and three out of five times the victim is her intimate partner. About two-thirds of all homicides are between intimates, family members and friends and about the same proportion occurs in private homes. The very personal nature of this crime thwarts any community action to deal with the problem.

REFERENCES

Blumstein, A. and R. Rosenfeld. (1998). "Explaining Recent Trends in United States Homicide Rates," *Journal of Criminal Law and Criminology*, 88: 1175-1216.

Brenner, M.H. (1976). Estimating the Social Cost of National Economic Policy: Implications for Mental and Physical Health and Criminal Aggression. Study prepared for the use of the Joint Economic Committee, Congress of the United States, Paper No. 5. Washington, D.C.: UNITED STATES Government Printing Office.

Burnley, J.N., C. Edmunds, M.T. Gaboury and A. Seymour. (1998). "Homicide: Its Impact and Consequences", in *National Victim Assistance Academy*, Office for Victims of Crime, Office of Justice Programs, United States Department of Justice.

Cardarelli, A.P. and Cavanaugh, D. "Uncleared Homicides in the United States: An Exploratory Study of Trends and Patterns." Paper presented at the Annual meeting of the American Society of Criminology, (1992) (Cited in Wellford and Cronin 2000).

Fagan, J., F.E. Zimring and J. Kim. (1998). "Declining Homicide in New York City: A Tale of Two Trends," *Journal of Criminal Law and Criminology*, 88: 1277-1323.

Gottfredson, M.R. and T. Hirschi. (1990). *A General Theory of Crime*, Stanford, CA: Stanford University Press.

Mouzos, J. (2000). Homicidal Encounters: A Study of Homicide in Australia 1889-1999, Canberra: Australian Institute of Criminology.

Mukherjee, S.K. (1999). Ethnicity and Crime: An Australian Research Study. A report prepared for the Department of Immigration and Multicultural Affairs, Canberra: Australian Institute of Criminology, November.

National Committee on Violence. (1990). Violence: Directions for Australia, Canberra: Australian Institute of Criminology.

Riedel, M. (1999). "Sources of Homicide Data" in M.D. Smith and M.A.Zahn (eds.) *Studying and Preventing Homicide: Issues and Challenges*. Thousand Oaks: Sage Publications.

Rosenfeld, R., T.M. Bray, and A. Egley. (1999). "Facilitating Violence: A Comparison of Gang-Motivated, Gang-Affiliated, and Non-gang Youth Homicides," *Journal of Quantitative Criminology*, 15:495-516.

Silverman, R. and L. Kennedy. (1993). *Deadly Deeds: Murder in Canada*, Scarborough, Ontario: Nelson Canada.

UNCJIN. (1997). "Trends in violence and crime prevention strategies throughout the world". *Crime and Justice Letter*. Vienna: United Nations Office at Vienna.

US Bureau of the Census. (1975). *Historical Statistics of the United States Colonial Times to 1970, Bicentennial Edition, Part 1*, Washington, D.C.

Vinson, T. (1974). "Gun and Knife Attacks", the *Australian Journal of Forensic Sciences*, December: 80-81.

Wallace, A. (1986). *Homicide: The Social Reality. Sydney: New South Wales Bureau of Crime Statistics and Research*.

Wellford, C. and Cronin, J. (2000). "Clearing of Homicide Clearance Rates", *National Institute of Justice Journal*, April: 2-7.

Wolfgang, M.E. (1958). *Patterns in Criminal Homicide*, Philadelphia: The University of Pennsylvania Press.

Zahn, M.A. and P.L. McCall. (1999). "Homicide in the 20th-Century United States: Trends and Patterns", in M.D. Smith and M.A. Zahn (eds.) *Studying and Preventing Homicide: Issues and Challenges*. Thousand Oaks: Sage Publications.

Zimring, F.E. and G. Hawkins. (1997). *Crime is Not the Problem: Lethal Violence in America*, New York: Oxford University Press.

INVESTIGATING RACE AND GENDER DIFFERENCES IN SPECIALIZATION IN VIOLENCE

Alex R. Piquero
University of Florida

Stephen L. Buka
Harvard School of Public Health
Harvard University

Introduction

Contemporary interest in the study of criminal careers and career criminals can be traced back to the work of Chicago sociologist Clifford Shaw (1930) and his associates (Sutherland, 1937) continuing along with seminal works by the Gluecks (Glueck and Glueck, 1940), Lemert (1951), Becker (1963), and Goffman (1963) (e.g., Bursik, 1989). Perhaps the most seminal treatment of the concept of criminal careers and career criminals was established by Wolfgang and his colleagues (1972) in their book, *Delinquency in a Birth Cohort*, a study that traced the delinquent careers of 9,945 males who were born in 1945 and who lived in Philadelphia throughout the course of their juvenile years.

As most readers are aware, one of the central findings emerging from the Philadelphia Birth Cohort Study was that a very small percentage of offenders (6% of the cohort, 18% of the delinquent subset) was responsible for 52% of all the delinquency in the cohort through age 17. Some scholars have characterized the finding of the chronic offender to be among the "most important and enduring findings of the research" (Tracy and Kempf-Leonard, 1996:6).

According to Bursik (1989:390), "the structure of [the original Wolfgang et al.] data set enabled [the authors] to use sophisticated stochastic models to examine some long-standing but untested assumptions concerning the dynamics of specialization in illegal behavior and developmental trends in the seriousness of that behavior." In this vein, their book also presented the first empirical examination of offense specialization, or the tendency of criminal offenders to repeat the same offense type on successive offenses.

Although several methods to study specialization exist (Britt, 1996; Paternoster et al., 1998; Piquero et al., 1999), Wolfgang and his colleagues (1972:206) employed transition matrices and found that (1) "the probabilities associated with the commission of an offense, when that offense is classified by its components, depend...on the type of the offense just committed", and that (2) "the offense history up to the immediately previous offense...has no bearing on the observed probabilities of committing the next offense" (i.e., knowledge of the number and type of offenses prior to the current offenses provides no aid in predicting the type of next offense).

When these analyses were carried out separately across race, they found that when white juveniles were re-arrested, the overall probability was .17 of a next arrest for theft, and among those re-arrested after an arrest for theft, the probability that the next arrest also was for theft was .30 (Blumstein et al., 1986:81). Among black offenders, the comparable probabilities were .18 and .25, respectively. In terms of serious offenses, while arrests for violent offenses were more likely for nonwhites than for whites, they were no more likely to follow previous arrests for violent offenses than to follow arrests for any other offense types. In sum, perhaps the most important finding of the book was that there was "no systematic specialization...over time" (Erickson, 1973:367).

When Erickson (1973) commented that the "total impact of this book in establishing a new trend in American criminological research must await the test of time," little did he realize just how much of an impact the Philadelphia Birth Cohort study would have. In addition to being one of the most cited pieces of research (Cohn and Farrington, 1996), Walker (1998:60) has noted that *Delinquency in a Birth Cohort* is "one of the most important pieces of criminal justice research in the last twenty-five years [and] has had a profound influence on thinking about crime policy." Even longitudinal study protagonists Gottfredson and Hirschi (1986:215) commented that the Philadelphia Birth Cohort Study has been a major inspiration for researchers interested in criminal careers and career criminals.

Since the publication of the Philadelphia Birth Cohort results, a number of studies have attempted to map out the criminal trajectories of chronic offenders. These studies have proceeded along both qualitative (Irwin, 1970; Inciardi, 1975; Baskin and Sommers, 1998; Shover, 1996) and quantitative (Spelman, 1994; Tracy et al., 1990; Tracy and Kempf-Leonard, 1996; Nevares et al., 1990) tracts. A comprehensive review of the criminal career literature, *Criminal Careers and 'Career Criminals'*, was issued by the National Research Council in the mid-1980s (Blumstein et al., 1986). The report identified several dimensions that were important for the study of criminal careers and career criminals including: participation, frequency, seriousness, specialization, persistence, and career length (desistance). In this report, the authors claimed that there were distinct dimensions of offending and that the characterizations of the dimensions likely varied across demographic groups based on gender and race.

Much information has been learned regarding patterns of offending within the criminal career dimensions of onset (Farrington et al., 1990; Tolan, 1987; Tibbetts and Piquero, 1999), prevalence and frequency (Elliott, 1994; Nagin and Land, 1993; Nagin and Smith, 1992), offense seriousness (Blumstein et al., 1988), chronicity (Piquero, 2000a), specialization (Blumstein et al., 1988; Britt, 1996; Bursik, 1989; Klein, 1984; Mazerolle et al., 2000; Piquero et al., 1999), offense frequency and persistence (Blumstein and Cohen, 1979; Chaiken and Chaiken, 1982; Horney and Marshall, 1992; Dean et al., 1996; Canela-Cacho et al., 1997; Piquero et al., 2001), as well as desistance (Bushway et al., 2001; Laub and Sampson, 2001; Laub et al., 1998; Maruna, 2001; Sommers et al., 1994; Shover and Thompson, 1992; Farrington and West, 1995), and career length (Blumstein et al., 1982; Spelman, 1994; Shinnar and Shinnar, 1975; Greenberg, 1975). The study of criminal careers and career criminals has also led to the development of several theoretical models, developmental in nature, that focus on the etiology and course of the chronic offender. These include theories advanced by Moffitt (1993), Patterson and Yoerger (1993), and Loeber and Hay (1994) suggesting that a small group of offenders is responsible for a significant portion of criminal activity, especially those types of offenses that are violent in nature.

Current Focus

Although much has been learned from the study of criminal careers, except for a few expositions (Elliott, 1994; Tracy et al., 1990; Wolfgang et al., 1972), little attention has been paid toward race and gender comparisons regarding criminal career dimensions, especially those related to specialization in violence (Blumstein et al., 1988; Mazerolle et al., 2000; Rojek and Erickson, 1982; Tracy et al., 1990; Tracy and Kempf-Leonard, 1996). A concerted focus along demographic lines, particularly with regard to race (Hawkins et al., 1998), is important because any serious theory of antisocial and criminal behavior must account for offending patterns associated with age, race, and gender (Tonry et al., 1991). In this paper, we examine the extent to which specialization in violence exists according to groups defined by gender, race, and gender by race categorizations.

Data

The study sample was drawn from the Providence cohort of the National Collaborative Perinatal Project (NCPP) (Niswander and Gordon, 1972). The majority of the Providence cohort (86%) was recruited from a 50% sampling of all registered clinic patients at a major maternity hospital in Rhode Island. The study sample consists of all members of the cohort who were born from March 1960 to August 1966 (N=3,828), excluding those known to have died prior to age seven. Approximately half (49.6%) of the study sample were male, with over 77% white subjects and about 23% non-white (almost all-black) subjects.

The NCPP was a major interdisciplinary study of the pre- and perinatal antecedents of childhood mental, neurological, and physical abilities. It followed prospectively the course of over 56,000 pregnancies enrolled between 1959 and 1966 at fifteen university-affiliated medical schools in the United States. Major findings from the NCPP have been published by Niswander and Gordon (1972), Broman et al. (1975), and Nichols and Chen (1981). Studies regarding criminal history information have also been published, primarily with the Philadelphia (Denno, 1990; Gibson et al., 2000; Piquero and Tibbetts, 1999; Tibbetts and Piquero, 1999; Piquero, 2000a, 2000b, 2000c), Providence (Lipsett et al., 1990), and Baltimore NCPP cohorts (Hardy et al., 1997)

By January 1, 1985 all members of the Providence cohort had reached age eighteen and were no longer under the jurisdiction of the juvenile court system. Through the cooperation of the Chief Judge of the Family Court of Rhode Island, which has statewide jurisdiction over juveniles, all NCPP cases with court contact were identified, with proper safeguards of confidentiality and anonymity. Subjects with court records were identified by linking names and birthdates with computerized court listings. Mother's names, sibling's names, and in some cases home addresses and father's names were used for verification where possible.

Among the cohort of 3,828 subjects, 38% of the sample included white males, 11% non-white males, 39% white females, and 11% non-white females. Twelve percent (N=459) of the sample was identified as having at least one court-reported "true" arrest (i.e., non-status, non-dependency). These 459 offenders were responsible for 1,164 arrests, of which 252 were violent arrests. In addition, 180 of the 459 offenders were arrested for a violent crime. To assess the reliability of the juvenile arrest data obtained through this process, a random 5% sample of the entire cohort was reclassified by the same process. There was a 100% concordance for classification as having a court record or not.

To be sure, we must acknowledge that our data are based solely on official records. Although several researchers argue in favor of **self-report** data (Thornberry and Krohn, 2000), others have noted substantive limitations with their use (Lauritsen, 1998). For purposes of this paper, use of official data does not appear to pose a fatal concern because researchers have found that self-reports and official records produce "comparable and complementary results on such topics as prevalence, continuity, versatility, and specialization in different types of offenses" (Farrington, 1989:418; see also Weis, 1986). Second, since our data contain information for different race and gender groups, it is also important to bear in mind the research by Hindelang and colleagues (1979:995) showing that self-reports and official measures "provide valid indicators of the demographic characteristics of offenders within the domain of behavior effectively tapped by each method."

Results

We begin our investigation by exploring three criminal career dimensions (prevalence, frequency, and violence) across gender, race, and gender-race categorizations (see Table 1). Regarding gender, male arrest prevalence in the Providence cohort is a little over 19% versus 5% for females ($\chi^2_{(1)}$ =189.07). In addition, males are significantly more likely than females to incur a higher frequency of arrest (T=10.70). Violent offender prevalence was also significantly different across the genders with males being more likely than females to register a violent arrest by age 18 ($\chi^2_{(1)}$ = 48.61).

Table 1: **Criminal History Information**

VARIABLE	N	PREVALENCE* (Mean)	FREQUENCY** (Mean)	VIOLENCE*** (Mean)
Sex				
Male	1,900	.192	.528	.071
Female	1,928	.048#	.083#	.023#
		$(\chi^2_{(1)}=189.07)$	(T=10.70)	$(\chi^2_{(1)}=48.61)$
Race				
White	2,957	.108	.260	.034
Non-White	871	.157#	.453#	.090#
		$(\chi^2_{(1)}=14.93)$	T=2.89)	$(\chi^2_{(1)}=48.00)$
Categories				
White-Male	1,470	.181	.464	.054
White-Female	1,487	.037	.057	.014
Non-White Male	430	.232	.746	.127
Non-White Female	441	.083#	.167#	.054#
		(F=71.88)	(F=45.08)	(F=34.55)

*   For prevalence, 0=non-offender, 1=offender.
**   Frequency is measured by a count of the number of arrests by age 18.
***   Violence measures the proportion of the sample who was arrested for a violent offense by age 18, 0=not arrested for violence, 1=arrested for violence.
#   p<.05

When examining race differences across the same three dimensions, Table 1 shows that arrest prevalence ($\chi^2_{(1)}=14.93$) and frequency (T=2.89) is significantly higher for non-whites compared to whites. Results for violence are substantively similar; that is, non-whites (9%) are significantly more likely than whites (3%) to be arrested for violence ($\chi^2_{(1)}=48.00$).

The bottom portion of Table 1 also presents the arrest analysis for the four race-gender categorizations. Arrest prevalence is highest among non-white males (23%), followed by white males (18%), and non-white (8%) and white (3.7%) females (F=71.88). Tukey's B tests of significance revealed that non-white males were significantly different from the other three categorizations. Substantively similar results are obtained for arrest frequency. Non-white males were responsible for the majority of arrests by age eighteen in the cohort, followed by white males, and non-white and white females, respectively (F=45.08). Tukey's B tests of significance revealed that the number of arrests engaged in by non-white males was significantly higher than the other three categorizations. Finally, violent arrest prevalence was significantly higher for non-white males (12.79%) relative to non-white females (5.4%), white males (5.4%), and white females (1.4%), respectively (F=34.55). In sum, these results suggest that non-white males are significantly more likely to incur higher arrest prevalence in general, and for violence in particular, as well as incur a higher number of arrests than any other race-gender categorization. These results are consistent with extant research, including results from the two Philadelphia birth cohort studies (Tracy et al., 1990; Wolfgang et al., 1972).

Specialization

An important question in criminal career research is the extent to which individuals specialize in the types of offenses they commit (Blumstein et al., 1986; Wolfgang et al., 1972). The next set of analyses investigate the extent to which sample members who are arrested for a violent offense are also arrested for a nonviolent offense. Given findings from previous research showing that with an increasing frequency of offending there is a higher tendency for a violent offense to be committed (Farrington, 1998; Piquero, 2000b), we begin our investigation of specialization with the assumption that violent offenses are committed at random in criminal careers (Farrington, 1998:429). Herein, we employ the binomial distribution to examine how the probability of committing a violent offense increases as the total number of offenses increases. If offenders specialize, the actual number of violent offenders should be significantly fewer than expected, and each one should commit more violent offenses (on average) than expected. On the other hand, if there were complete generality in offending, the probability of committing a violent offense would increase with the number of offenses committed.

In the full cohort, 252 of the 1,164 arrests were for a violent crime (21.65%). Assuming that different types of offenses were committed at random (probabilistically), it might be expected that 21.65% of the 236 offenders who committed only one offense would commit a violent offense. Table 2 shows that the observed number of violent offenders (69) was somewhat close to the expected value of 51.09 violent offenders Moving onto the next offense category, it might be expected that 38.61% (i.e., a proportion equal to $1-(.7835)^2$) of the 88 offenders who committed two offenses would commit at least one violent offense. The actual number of violent offenders, 32, is quite close to the expected number of violent offenders, 33.97. For the third offense category, it might be similarly expected that 51.9% (i.e., a proportion equal to $1-(.7835)^3$) of the 40 offenders who committed three offenses would commit at least one violent offense. The actual number of violent offenders, 19, is very close to the expected number of violent offenders, 20.76. As one proceeds along the offense categories, it can be observed that the predicted number of violent offenders is very close to the actual number of violent offenders.

Assuming complete generality in offending, it might be expected that 38.6% (177.23) of the 459 offenders would commit at least one violent offense – quite close to the actual figure of 39.22% (180). Had there been a

Table 2: Specialization Full Sample

OFFENSE CATEGORY	OFFENDERS	VIOLENT OFFENDERS	EXPECTED NON-VIOLENT OFFENDERS	EXPECTED NON-VIOLENT PERCENT	EXPECTED VIOLENT OFFENDERS	EXPECTED VIOLENT PERCENT
1	236	69	184.906	0.783	51.094	0.216
2	88	32	54.020	0.613	33.979	0.386
3	40	19	19.238	0.480	20.761	0.519
4	26	15	9.797	0.376	16.202	0.623
5	24	12	7.086	0.295	16.913	0.704
6	15	11	3.469	0.231	11.530	0.768
7	6	4	1.087	0.181	4.912	0.818
8	7	4	0.994	0.142	6.005	0.857
9	5	4	0.556	0.111	4.443	0.888
10	2	2	0.174	0.087	1.825	0.912
11	3	2	0.204	0.068	2.795	0.931
12	1	1	0.053	0.053	0.946	0.946
13	2	2	0.083	0.041	1.916	0.958
14	1	1	0.032	0.032	0.967	0.967
16	1	1	0.025	0.025	0.974	0.974
17	1	1	0.020	0.020	0.979	0.979
37	1	0	0.015	0.015	0.984	0.984
TOTAL	459	180	281.768	0.613	177.231	0.386

tendency to specialize in violent offending, the number of violent offenders would have been significantly fewer than expected, and each one would have committed more violent offenses (on average) than expected. However, a chi-square goodness-of-fit test showed that the actual numbers were not significantly different from the expected numbers ($\chi^2_{(16)}$=10.20).[1] Thus, there appears to be no detectable tendency for offenders to specialize in violence.

Tables 3 and 4 present the specialization in violence analysis for males and females, respectively. Among males, 19.7% of the arrests were for a violent crime, while among females, 33.7% of the arrests were for a violent crime. As can be seen from both tables, the predicted number of violent offenders is remarkably similar to the actual number of violent offenders for males (predicted=137.78, actual=135) and females (predicted=43.32, actual=45). Chi-square goodness-of-fit tests for both males ($\chi^2_{(16)}$=7.06) and females ($\chi^2_{(5)}$=1.32) showed that the actual number of violent offenders was not significantly different from the expected number of violent offenders. The same analyses were completed for race groups defined as white/non-white, and these results may be found in Tables 5 and 6, respectively. Among whites, 17.3% of the arrests were for a violent crime while for non-whites, 30.1% of the arrests were for a violent crime. Both tables reveal that the predicted number of violent offenders is similar to the actual number of violent offenders for both whites (predicted=102.81, actual=101), and non-whites (predicted=69.01, actual=79). Chi-square goodness-of-fit tests for both whites ($\chi^2_{(13)}$=6.59) and non-whites ($\chi^2_{(11)}$=7.72) showed that the actual number of violent offenders was not significantly different from the predicted number of violent offenders.

Though not shown, the specialization-in-violence analysis was performed for four different race-gender categorizations (white males, white females, non-white males, and non-white females). In none of these analyses did we find evidence of specialization in violence. Thus, it can be concluded that there is no detectable tendency for individuals in the Providence NCPP cohort to specialize in violence, at least as measured by arrest records.

Discussion and Conclusion

Wolfgang and colleagues' (1972) *Delinquency in a Birth Cohort* was the first large-scale birth cohort study of delinquency undertaken in the U.S. based upon a generalizable, urban population (Tracy et al., 1990:1) and it represented a "turning point in criminological research [much] like the Shaw and McKay area studies in the 1930s" (Morris, 1972:vii). These scholars presented one of the first systematic and sophisticated mathematical analyses of delinquency written at that time, as well as the first substantial empirical analysis of career patterns, especially those related to specialization in

Table 3: Specialization Males

OFFENSE CATEGORY	OFFENDERS	VIOLENT OFFENDERS	EXPECTED NON-VIOLENT OFFENDERS	EXPECTED NON-VIOLENT PERCENT	EXPECTED VIOLENT OFFENDERS	EXPECTED VIOLENT PERCENT
1	183	47	146.912	.802	36.087	.197
2	62	19	39.958	.644	22.041	.355
3	33	15	17.074	.517	15.925	.482
4	21	11	8.722	.415	12.277	.584
5	23	11	7.669	.333	15.330	.666
6	15	11	4.015	.267	10.984	.732
7	6	4	1.289	.214	4.710	.785
8	7	4	1.207	.172	5.792	.827
9	4	3	.554	.138	3.445	.861
10	2	2	.222	.111	1.777	.888
11	3	2	.267	.089	2.732	.910
12	1	1	.071	.071	.928	.928
13	2	2	.115	.057	1.884	.942
14	1	1	.046	.046	.953	.953
16	1	1	.037	.037	.962	.962
17	1	1	.029	.029	.970	.970
37	1	0	.023	.023	.976	.976
TOTAL	366	135	228.217	.623	137.782	.376

Table 4: Specialization Females

OFFENSE CATEGORY	OFFENDERS	VIOLENT OFFENDERS	EXPECTED NON-VIOLENT OFFENDERS	EXPECTED NON-VIOLENT PERCENT	EXPECTED VIOLENT OFFENDERS	EXPECTED VIOLENT PERCENT
1	53	22	35.112	.662	17.887	.337
2	26	13	11.411	.438	14.588	.561
3	7	4	2.035	.290	4.964	.709
4	5	4	.963	.192	4.036	.807
5	1	1	.127	.127	.872	.872
9	1	1	.024	.024	.975	.975
TOTAL	93	45	49.674	.534	43.325	.465

Table 5: Specialization Whites

OFFENSE CATEGORY	OFFENDERS	VIOLENT OFFENDERS	EXPECTED NON-VIOLENT OFFENDERS	EXPECTED NON-VIOLENT PERCENT	EXPECTED VIOLENT OFFENDERS	EXPECTED VIOLENT PERCENT
1	168	39	138.936	.827	29.064	.173
2	63	15	43.087	.683	19.912	.316
3	29	11	16.402	.565	12.597	.434
4	15	8	7.016	.467	7.983	.532
5	19	9	7.349	.386	11.650	.613
6	10	7	3.199	.319	6.800	.680
7	4	2	1.058	.264	2.941	.735
8	4	2	.875	.218	3.124	.781
9	2	1	.361	.180	1.638	.819
10	2	2	.299	.149	1.700	.850
11	3	2	.371	.123	2.628	.876
12	1	1	.102	.102	.897	.897
14	1	1	.069	.069	.930	.930
16	1	1	.057	.057	.942	.942
TOTAL	322	101	219.187	.680	102.812	.319

Table 6: Specialization Non-Whites

OFFENSE CATEGORY	OFFENDERS	VIOLENT OFFENDERS	EXPECTED NON-VIOLENT OFFENDERS	EXPECTED NON-VIOLENT PERCENT	EXPECTED VIOLENT OFFENDERS	EXPECTED VIOLENT PERCENT
1	68	30	47.511	.698	20.488	.301
2	25	17	12.204	.488	12.795	.511
3	11	8	3.752	.341	7.247	.658
4	11	7	2.621	.238	8.378	.761
5	5	3	.832	.166	4.167	.833
6	5	4	.581	.116	4.418	.883
7	2	2	.162	.081	1.837	.918
8	3	2	.170	.056	2.829	.943
9	3	3	.119	.039	2.880	.960
13	2	2	.018	.009	1.981	.990
17	1	1	.003	.003	.996	.996
37	1	0	.002	.002	.997	.997
TOTAL	137	79	67.980	.496	69.019	.503

criminal offending, over the entire span of adolescent years of a cohort (Erickson, 1973:362,367).

Following in their tradition, we set out to examine the arrest patterns across several criminal career dimensions for sample members of the Providence portion of the National Collaborative Perinatal Project. Several findings are noteworthy. First, males were significantly more likely than females to (1) be arrested, (2) incur a higher number of arrests, and (3) be arrested for at least one violent offense by the age of 18. Second, non-whites were significantly more likely than whites to (1) be arrested, (2) incur a higher number of arrests, and (3) be arrested for at least one violent offense by the age of 18. Third, in exploring the extent to which specialization in violence existed according to groups defined by gender, race, and gender by race categorizations, our analysis failed to detect any tendency for specialization in violence through age 18. Thus, arrest careers were marked by generality, as opposed to specificity in violence. This finding is consistent with those of other scholars who obtained similar results with different data sets and different sample compositions (Capaldi and Patterson, 1996; Farrington, 1991; Piquero, 2000b; Tracy et al., 1990; Wolfgang et al., 1972).

Several directions for future research are warranted. First, extant research does not provide evidence on the extent to which substantive conclusions regarding specialization differ according to self-report and official records (Farrington, 1998). This is especially the case for self-report and official records drawn from the same data set. Given the controversial nature of validity issues related to official and self-reported race differentials (Elliott, 1994), distinct measurement protocols could influence the detection of specialization (or generality) across crime measures. Second, little remains known about offending patterns during the adult years. For example, Piquero and his colleagues (1999) found that there was a tendency for offenders to become more specialized in their offending behavior over time regardless of the age at which they initiated offending. Yet, more work is needed before any general conclusions can be drawn. Third, although our effort provided some estimates of specialization (or lack thereof) across race, much of the specialization research has been conducted on white samples. Thus, further study of the life-course patterns of specialization across minority group members, especially African-Americans and Hispanics is important. This is especially so in light of Moffitt's (1994) provocative hypothesis that life-course-persistent offenders are likely to be comprised of minority group members. To the extent that her hypothesis is correct, evidence should show that minority group members are likely to exhibit the most diverse offending patterns. Clearly, these and other future research directions hold promise for a more complete understanding of criminal career patterns.

REFERENCES

Baskin, D.R., and I.B. Sommers. (1998). *Casualties of Community Disorder: Women's Careers in Violent Crime.* Boulder, CO: Westview Press.

Becker, H. (1963). *Outsiders: Studies in the Sociology of Deviance.* New York: Free Press.

Blumstein, A. and J. Cohen. (1979). "Estimation of Individual Crime Rates from Arrest Records." *Journal of Criminal Law and Criminology* 70:561-585.

Blumstein, A., J. Cohen, J. Roth, and C. Visher. (1986). *Criminal Careers and "Career Criminals".* Washington, D.C.: National Academy Press.

Blumstein, A., J. Cohen, S. Das, and S.D. Moitra. (1988). "Specialization and Seriousness during Adult Criminal Careers." *Journal of Quantitative Criminology* 4:303-345.

Britt, C.L. (1996). "The Measurement of Specialization and Escalation in the Criminal Career: An Alternative Modeling Strategy." *Journal of Quantitative Criminology* 12:193-222.

Broman, S.H., P.I. Nichols, and W.A. Kennedy. (1975). *Preschool IQ: Prenatal and Early Developmental Correlates.* New York: Halstead Press.

Bursik, Jr., R.J. (1989). "Erickson Could Never have Imagined: Recent Extensions of Birth Cohort Studies." *Journal of Quantitative Criminology* 5:389-396.

Bushway, S., A. Piquero, P. Mazerolle, L. Broidy, and E. Cauffman. (2001). "An Empirical Framework for Studying Desistance as a Process." *Criminology,* 39:491-515.

Canela-Cacho, J.A., A. Blumstein, and J. Cohen. (1997). "Relationship between the Offending Frequency of Imprisoned and Free Offenders." *Criminology* 35:133-175.

Capaldi, D.N. and G.R. Patterson. (1996). "Can Violent Offenders be Distinguished from Frequent Offenders: Prediction from Childhood to Adolescence". *Journal of Research in Crime and Delinquency* 33: 206-231.

Chaiken, J.M. and M. Chaiken. (1982). *Varieties of Criminal Behavior.* Santa Monica, CA: Rand.

Cohn, E.G. and D.P. Farrington. (1996). "Crime and Justice and the Criminal Justice and Criminology Literature." In M. Tonry (ed.), *Crime and Justice: An Annual Review of Research,* Volume 20. Chicago: University of Chicago Press.

Dean, C.W., R. Brame, and A.R. Piquero. (1996). "Criminal Propensities, Discrete Groups of Offenders, and Persistence in Crime." *Criminology* 34:547-574.

Denno, D. (1990). *Biology and Violence.* Cambridge: Cambridge University Press.

Elliott, D.S. (1994). 1993 "Presidential Address: Serious Violent Offenders: Onset, Developmental Course, and Termination." *Criminology* 32:1-21.

Erickson, M.L. (1973). "Delinquency in a Birth Cohort: A New Direction in Criminological Research". *Journal of Criminal Law and Criminology* 64:362-367.

Farrington, D.P. (1991). "Childhood Aggression and Adult Violence: Early Precursors and Later Life Outcomes." In D.J. Pepler and K.H. Rubin (eds.), *The Development and Treatment of Childhood Aggression.* Hillsdale, NJ: Erlbaum.

Farrington, D.P. (1998). "Predictors, Causes, and Correlates of Male Youth Violence." In M. Tonry and M.H. Moore (eds.), *Youth Violence: Crime and Justice, An Annual Review of Research.* Chicago, IL: University of Chicago Press.

Farrington, D.P. and D.J. West. (1995). "Effects of Marriage, Separation, and Children on Offending by Adult Males." In Z.B. Smith and J. Hagan (eds.), *Current Perspectives on Aging and the Life Cycle.* Volume 4: *Delinquency and Disrepute in the Life Course.* Greenwich, CT: JAI Press.

Farrington, D.P., R. Loeber, D. S. Elliott, J.D. Hawkins, D. Kandel, M. Klein, J. McCord, D. Rowe, and R. Tremblay. (1990). "Advancing Knowledge about the Onset of Delinquency and Crime." In B. Lahey and A. Kazdin (eds.), *Advances in Clinical and Child Psychology* Volume 13. New York: Plenum.

Gibson, C.L., A.R. Piquero, and S.G. Tibbetts. (2000). "Assessing the Relationship between Maternal Cigarette Smoking during Pregnancy and Age at First Police Contact." *Justice Quarterly* 17:519-542.

Glueck, S. and E. Glueck. (1940). *Juvenile Delinquents Grown Up.* New York: The Commonwealth Fund.

Goffman, E. (1963). *Stigma: Notes on the Management of Spoiled Identity.* Englewood Cliffs, NJ: Prentice-Hall.

Gottfredson, M.R. and T. Hirschi. (1986). "The true value of lambda would appear to be zero". *Criminology* 25:581-614.

Greenberg, D. (1975). "The Incapacitative Effect of Imprisonment: Some Estimates." *Law and Society Review* 541-580.

Hardy, J.B., S. Shapiro, E.D. Mellits, E.A. Skinner, N.M. Astone, M. Ensminger, T. LaVeist, R.A. Baumgardner, and H. Starfield. (1997). "Self-Sufficiency at Ages 27 to 33 Years: Factors Present between Birth and 18 Years that Predict Educational Attainment among Children Born to Inner-City Families." *Pediatrics* 99:80-87.

Harnett, D.L. and A.K. Soni. (1991). *Statistical Methods for Business and Economics.* Fourth Edition. Reading, MA: Addison-Wesley Publishing Company.

Hawkins, D.F., J.H. Laub, and J.L. Lauritsen. (1998). "Race, Ethnicity, and Serious Juvenile Offending." In R. Loeber and D.P. Farrington (eds.), *Serious and Violent Juvenile Offenders.* Thousand Oaks, CA: Sage Publications.

Hindelang, M.J., T. Hirschi, and J.G. Weis. (1979). Correlates of Delinquency: the Illusion of Discrepancy between Self-Report and Official Measures. *American Sociological Review* 44:995-1014.

Horney, J. and I.H. Marshall. (1992). "Measuring Lambda through Self-Reports." *Criminology* 29:471-495.

Inciardi, J.A. (1975). *Careers in Crime*. Chicago: Rand McNally College Publishing Company.

Irwin, J. (1970). *The Felon*. Toronto: Prentice-Hall.

Klein, M. (1984). "Offense Specialization and Versatility among Juveniles." *British Journal of Criminology* 24:185-194.

Laub, J.H. and R.J. Sampson. (2001). "Understanding desistance from crime." In M. Tonry (ed.) *Crime and Justice: An Annual Review of Research*. Chicago: University of Chicago Press.

Laub, J.H., D.S. Nagin, and R.J. Sampson. (1998). "Trajectories of Change in Criminal Offending: Good Marriages and the Desistance Process." *American Sociological Review* 63:225-238.

Lauritsen, J.L. (1998). "The Age-Crime Debate: Assessing the Limits of Longitudinal Self-Report Data." *Social Forces* 77:127-155.

Lemert, E. (1951). *Social Pathology*. New York: McGraw-Hill.

Lipsitt, P.D., S.L. Buka, and L.P. Lipsitt. (1990). "Early Intelligence Scores and Subsequent Delinquency: A Prospective Study." *The American Journal of Family Therapy* 18:197-208.

Loeber, R. and D.F. Hay. (1994). "Developmental Approaches to Aggression and Conduct Problems." In M. Rutter and D.F. Hay (eds.), *Development through Life: A Handbook for Clinicians*. Malden, MA: Blackwell Scientific.

Maruna, S. (2001). *Making Good: How Ex-Convicts Reform and Rebuild Their Lives*. Washington, DC: American Psychological Association.

Mazerolle, P., R. Brame, R. Paternoster, A. Piquero, and C.W. Dean. (2000). "Onset Age and Offending Versatility: Comparisons across Gender." *Criminology*, 38:1143-1172.

Moffitt, T.E. (1993). "Adolescence-Limited and Life-Course Persistent Antisocial Behavior: A Developmental Taxonomy." *Psychological Review* 100:674-701.

Moffitt, T.E. (1994). "Natural Histories of Delinquency." In E. Weitekamp and H. Kerner (eds.) *Cross-National Longitudinal Research on Human Development and Criminal Behavior*. Netherlands: Kluwer Academic Publishers.

Morris, N. (1972). "Foreward". In M.E. Wolfgang, R. Figlio, and T. Sellin (eds.), *Delinquency in a Birth Cohort*. Chicago: University of Chicago Press.

Nagin, D.S. and K.C. Land. (1993). "Age, Criminal Careers, and Population Heterogeneity: Specification and Estimation of a Nonparametric, Mixed Poisson Model." *Criminology* 31:327-362.

Nagin, D.S. and D.A. Smith. (1992). "Participation in and Frequency of Delinquency Behavior: A Test for Structural Differences." *Journal of Quantitative Criminology* 6:335-356.

Nevares, D., M.E. Wolfgang, and P.E. Tracy. (1990). *Delinquency in Puerto Rico: The 1970 Birth Cohort Study*. New York, NY. Greenwood Press.

Nichols, P.L. and T. Chen. (1981). *Minimal Brain Dysfunction: A Prospective Study*. Hillsdale, NJ: Erlbaum.

Niswander, K., and M. Gordon. (1972). *The Women and Their Pregnancies*. Washington, D.C.: U.S. Department of Health, Education, and Welfare.

Paternoster, R., R. Brame, A. Piquero, P. Mazerolle, and C.W. Dean. (1998). "The Forward Specialization Coefficient: Distributional Properties and Subgroup Differences." *Journal of Quantitative Criminology* 14:133-154.

Patterson, G., and K. Yoerger. (1993). "A Model for Early Onset of Delinquent Behavior." In S. Hodgins (ed.), *Crime and Mental Disorder*. Newbury Park, CA: Sage.

Piquero, A. (2000a). "Are Chronic Offenders the Most Serious Offenders? Exploring the Relationship with Special Attention to Offense Skewness and Gender Differences." *Journal of Criminal Justice* 28:103-115.

Piquero, A. (2000b). "Frequency, Specialization and Violence in Offending Careers." *Journal of Research in Crime and Delinquency* 37:392-418.

Piquero, A. (2000c). Testing Moffitt's "Neuropsychological Variation Hypothesis for the Prediction of Life-Course Persistent Offending." *Psychology, Crime, and Law.* 7:193-216

Piquero, A. and S. G. Tibbetts. (1999). "The Impact of Pre/perinatal Disturbances and Disadvantaged Familial Environments in Predicting Criminal Offending." *Studies on Crime and Crime Prevention* 8:52-70.

Piquero, A., R. Paternoster, P. Mazerolle, R. Brame, and C.W. Dean. (1999). "Onset Age and Specialization." *Journal of Research in Crime and Delinquency* 36:275-299.

Piquero, A., A. Blumstein, R. Brame, R. Haapanen, E.P. Mulvey, and D.S. Nagin. (2001). "Assessing the Impact of Exposure Time and Incapacitation on Longitudinal Trajectories of Criminal Offending." *Journal of Adolescent Research* 16:54-74.

Rojek, D.J. and M.L. Erickson. (1982). "Delinquent Careers: A Test of the Career Escalation Model." *Criminology* 20:5-28.

Shaw, C. (1930). *The Jack-Roller: A Delinquent Boy's Own Story*. Chicago: University of Chicago Press.

Shinnar, R. and S. Shinnar. (1975). "The Effect of the Criminal Justice System on the Control of Crime: A Quantitative Approach." *Law and Society Review* 9:581-612.

Shover, N. (1996). *Great Pretenders*. Boulder, CO: Westview Press.

Shover, N. and C.Y. Thompson. (1992). "Age, Differential Expectations, and Crime Desistance." *Criminology* 30:89-104.

Sommers, I., D.R. Baskin, and J. Fagan. (1994). "Getting Out of the Life: Crime Desistance by Female Street Offenders." *Deviant Behavior* 15:125-149.

Spelman, W. (1994). *Criminal Incapacitation.* New York, NY. Plenum Press.

Sutherland, E. (1937). *The Professional Thief,* Chicago: University of Chicago Press.

Thornberry, T.P. and M.D. Krohn. (2000). "The Self-Report Method for Measuring Delinquency and Crime." In D. Duffee (ed.), *Measurement and Analysis of Crime and Justice,* Volume 4. Washington, DC: U.S. Department of Justice.

Tibbetts, S. G. and A. Piquero. (1999). "The Influence of Gender, Low Birth Weight, and Disadvantaged Environment in Predicting Early Onset of Offending: A Test of Moffitt's Interactional Hypothesis." *Criminology* 37:843-877.

Tolan, P. (1987). "Implications of Age of Onset for Delinquency Risk." *Journal of Abnormal Child Psychology* 15:47-65.

Tonry, M., L.E. Ohlin, and D.P. Farrington. (1991). *Human Development and Criminal Behavior.* New York: Springer-Verlag.

Tracy, P. E. and K. Kempf-Leonard. (1996). *Continuity and Discontinuity in Criminal Careers.* New York, NY: Plenum Publishing Company.

Tracy, P.E., M.E. Wolfgang, and R. Figlio. (1990). *Delinquency Careers in Two Birth Cohorts.* New York: Plenum.

Walker, S. (1998). *Sense and Nonsense About Crime and Drugs.* Belmont, CA: Wadsworth.

Wolfgang, M.E., R. Figlio, and T. Sellin. (1972). *Delinquency in a Birth Cohort.* Chicago: University of Chicago Press.

Wolfgang, M.E., T. P. Thornberry, and R. Figlio. (1987). *From Boy to Man, From Delinquency to Crime.* Chicago: University of Chicago Press.

NOTES

[1] The value for χ^2 is given by $\Sigma(O_i\text{-}E_i)^2/E_i$, where O_i is the observed number of violent offenders and E_i is the expected number of violent offenders. The degrees of freedom are given by $c\text{-}1$ where c is the number of categories. Some readers may observe that an expected value of at least one or more in each category is needed (Harnett and Soni, 1991:690). In an effort to determine if the small number of expected violent offenders in the present analysis beginning at offense category 10 biased the test, we created a category 10+ that took all of the offenders at or above 10 and combined them into one category. The observed number of violent offenders for this category became 12, while the expected number was 10. A re-calculation of the χ^2 yielded a value of 9.29 with 10-1 (or 9) degrees of freedom because there were 10 categories. This alternative goodness-of-fit test yielded results that were similar to those obtained with the unaltered arrest distribution; that is, since the actual numbers are not significantly different from the expected numbers, it can be concluded that there is no detectable tendency for offenders to specialize in violence.

CARRYING GUNS AND INVOLVEMENT IN CRIME

Alan J. Lizotte, Trudy L. Bonsell, David McDowall,
Terence P. Thornberry
School of Criminal Justice, University at Albany

Marvin D. Krohn
Department of Sociology, University at Albany

This article was prepared under Grant 86-JN-CX-0007(S-3) from the Office of Juvenile Justice and Delinquency Prevention, Office of Justice Programs, U.S. Department of Justice; Grant 5 R01 DA0551202 from the National Institute on Drug Abuse; and Grant SBR09123299 from the National Science Foundation. Work on this project was also aided by grants to the Center for Social and Demographic Analysis at the University at Albany from NICHD (P30 HD32041) and NSF (SBR-9512290). Points of view or opinions in this document are those of the authors and do not necessarily represent the official position or policies of the funding agencies.

Introduction

Firearm assaults are an important source of injury among young people in the United States. In 1997, persons aged 13 to 19 comprised 9.75% of the population, but they accounted for 14% of the nation's 10,369 firearm homicide victims (U.S. Federal Bureau of Investigation, 1997). National Electronic Injury Surveillance System (NEISS) estimates for 1992-1993 show that those aged 15 to 19 accounted for 22% of the 57,500 hospital emergency department visits for assaultive gunshot wounds, although they account for only 7.2% of the population (Zawitz, 1996).

Besides their role as victims, juveniles also are often the offenders in gun-related violence. In 1997, 17.6% of the arrests for firearm homicides were of persons 13 to 19 years old (Fox and Zawitz, 1998). A study of arrestees in 11 cities found that juveniles were more likely than adults to report that they used a gun to commit a violent criminal offense (Decker et al., 1997).

Accompanying the high levels of youth violence are high levels of illegal gun carrying. Survey estimates of the prevalence of gun carrying by young people vary with the population and reference period (Arria et al., 1995; Callahan and Rivara, 1992; Callahan et al., 1993; Centers for Disease Control, 1991; Hemenway et al., 1996; Kann et al., 1996; Lizotte et al., 1997; Webster et al., 1993) but they range as high as 84% for incarcerated juveniles (Sheley and Wright, 1995). The existing evidence indicates that youth who carry firearms are more apt to be involved in activities that involve a high risk of injury, such as drug dealing and predatory crime (Bjerregaard and Lizotte, 1995; Lizotte et al., 1994; Lizotte et al., 2000). Little is known, however, about whether rates of criminal offending rise when juveniles carry guns. Youths may be more frequently involved in crime and other high-risk behaviors when they arm themselves with guns, but for the types of youths who choose to carry guns, these incidents may occur equally often when they do not carry firearms (Blumstein and Cork, 1996; Cook and Laub, 1998). That is, the relationship between gun carrying and violence could be spurious.   It is also possible that firearm use could lower the number of crimes committed by offenders.   Offenders may commit fewer armed robberies because guns allow them to select fewer hardened targets with bigger payoffs. Without a gun it would be necessary to victimize many soft targets for the same financial outcome (Kleck, 1991).   The latter is undesirable to the offender because it increases the risk of capture.

We use longitudinal self-report data to investigate the relationship between firearm carrying and criminal offending in a sample of urban youths. We examine the stability of gun carrying patterns over time, and compare crime rates during periods when sample members carried guns to periods when they did not carry them.

Our hypotheses are the following. First, boys who carry guns will have elevated levels of serious violent crime because guns are most useful in potentially violent situations.   Second, drug selling will be higher when offenders carry guns because offenders need them for protection against rivals and would-be thieves. This should be especially true at older ages when the most serious drug selling occurs (Lizotte et al., 1997). Third, property crimes should show smaller differences by gun carrying because guns are generally not necessary to commit many types of property crime (e.g., larceny).

Methods

The Rochester Youth Development Study (RYDS) is a longitudinal panel study designed to examine the development of juvenile delinquency and other related behaviors in an urban sample. Interviews were conducted with the youths and their primary caregivers (in 95% of cases the mother or stepmother). Data also were collected from the Rochester schools, police, and other agencies that serve youth.

Sampling and Cohort Formation

The total panel consists of 1000 students who attended Grades 7 and 8 of the Rochester, New York public schools during the 1987-1988 academic year. Beginning in the spring of 1988 the subjects were interviewed every six months for 9 interview waves between 1988 and 1992. The present analysis is based on student interviews from Waves 1 through 9. This period roughly corresponds to the increase in juvenile gun homicides in the U.S. (1986 to 1992). At Wave 1 the students were on average 13.5 years of age, while at Wave 9 they were 17.5 years old.

To ensure that serious chronic offenders would be included in the study, the investigators stratified the overall sample. Males are overrepresented 75% to 25% because they are more likely than females to engage in serious delinquency. Furthermore, students were selected in proportion to the resident arrest rates of the census tracts in which they lived at the beginning of the study. These rates estimate the proportion of the general population in each tract arrested in 1986. Students from the tracts with the highest resident arrest rates are overrepresented in the sample because they are at greater risk for serious delinquency. Similarly, students in tracts with low resident arrest rates are underrepresented. Because the probability of a youth living in a particular census tract is known, this sampling strategy provides a means of weighting cases to represent the total Grade 7 and 8 cohorts.

A total of 4,013 students were enrolled in Grades 7 and 8 in spring 1988, of whom 3,372 (84%) were eligible for the sample. Students were considered ineligible if they moved out of the Rochester school district before Wave 1 cases were fielded, if neither English nor Spanish was spoken in the home, if a sibling already was in the sample pool, or if they were older than the expected age for Grade 8 pupils under the Rochester schools' admission policy. All eligible cases were assigned to their census tract of residence at the beginning of sample selection. To generate a final panel of 1,000 students, the investigators selected 1,334 students on the basis of an estimated nonparticipation rate of 25% (Elliott et al., 1983). First, students in the census tracts with the highest resident arrest rates, approximately the top one-third, were selected with certainty. Second, students in the remaining census tracts were selected at a rate proportionate to the tract's contribution to the overall resident arrest rate. Proportionately fewer members of the sample were drawn from tracts with lower resident arrest rates. Once the number of students to be selected from a tract was determined, the student population in the tract was stratified by gender and grade, and students were selected at random from those strata. If a student refused to participate, a replacement of the same grade, gender, and race/ethnicity was selected from the same census tract as the student who refused.

Data Acquisition and Management

The current analysis is based on 638 boys who remained in the panel at Wave 9. Girls are excluded from the analysis because they rarely carry guns. The retention rate for males at Wave 9 is 87.5%. Characteristics of boys who remain in the sample at Wave 9 compare favorably with those in the initial sample. Only slight and statistically non-significant differences exist in age, race/ethnicity, Wave 1 self-reported delinquency and drug use, and resident arrest rates of census tracts. As a result, the boys remaining in the sample at Wave 9 are an accurate representation of those sampled initially (Thornberry et al., 1993; Krohn and Thornberry, 1999). The sample is not only urban but also largely minority: 63% of the respondents are African-American, 18% are Hispanic, and 19% are white. The families have low levels of parental education and low incomes: nearly 75% of the parents did not complete high school, and at Wave 4 (1990) the median income was $15,964.

The sample used in this analysis is weighted to represent the total population. We multiply each case by the sampling fraction for the entire population divided by the sampling fraction for a particular census tract. The sampling fraction for the entire sample is the number of boys sampled, divided by the number of boys in the population. Similarly, the sampling fraction for a tract is the number of boys sampled in the tract, divided by the number of boys living in the tract. Our statistical methods require a random sample and the weighting procedure produces a random sample from a stratified sample.

RYDS interviewers conducted interviews with adolescents in private rooms at the schools. Youths who had dropped out of school, moved from the city, or were institutionalized remained in the sample and were interviewed in person either at home or in other appropriate settings. Each interview lasted about an hour.

Measurement of Delinquency and Gun Carrying

The delinquency measures are derived from the study's self-reported delinquency inventory. Respondents were asked whether they had engaged, during the past six months, in a series of 44 delinquent behaviors, adapted largely from the National Youth Survey (Elliott et al., 1985) as modified by the Denver Youth Survey (Huizinga et al., 1991). If a respondent answered in the affirmative to a particular delinquency item, he was asked how often he did so and also was asked to describe the most serious incident. Coders screened the descriptions to determine whether they were in the proper category of delinquency and to ensure that they were "actionable" offenses rather than trivial acts that law enforcement officials would ignore. Interrater reliability for coding actionable offenses ranges from 90% to 95%. Prior research (Hindelang et al., 1981; Huizinga and Elliott, 1986), as well as research with the Rochester project (Thornberry and Krohn, 2000), has shown that self-report measures have adequate validity and reliability.

We use three indices of delinquency in the analysis: Serious Violence, Drug Sales, and Property Crimes. Weapons carrying was excluded from all indices so that hidden gun carrying would not be confounded with crimes committed. Serious violent crimes include attacking someone with a weapon, gang fights, and robbery. These crimes put offenders and victims at very high risk for injury. Therefore, a criminal would benefit greatly from carrying a gun to commit these crimes. The drug sales variable includes the sale of both marijuana and other hard drugs. As mentioned earlier, drug dealers may use guns to protect the money that they make and the drugs that they sell. Finally, property crimes include offenses such as breaking and entering, dealing in stolen goods, auto theft, credit card fraud, forgery, joyriding, larceny, arson, and property damage.

As part of the self-reported delinquency battery, subjects were asked whether they had carried a hidden weapon since the time of the last interview and, if they had, if any of the weapons were firearms. Our hypotheses focus on the link between involvement in crime and carrying *illegal* guns. For a number of reasons our question is likely to tap into information about carrying illegal guns as opposed to carrying for sporting reasons.   First, we ask the question as part of a battery that includes 43 other self-reported delinquency items.   Second, the screening question asks about *hidden weapon* carrying in general, before asking about firearms. Other studies have simply asked if respondents carried a gun, misleadingly counting *any* gun carrying as illegal. Thus, our wording also eliminates bb guns, toy guns, and the like.

Respondents who answered in the affirmative to hidden weapon carrying were then asked to identify the type of weapon that they had carried. On this measure subjects do not need to own the firearms that they carried. As a result, the measure is better, especially for adolescents, than one that asks if the respondent owns a gun, and then if it is carried. Our measure is conservative in its count of gun carriers because the subjects may not report some guns carried in cars because they were not carried on the person. In spite of the conservative nature of our measure, for Waves 1 through 9, between 4% and 8% of the subjects carried a gun depending upon the wave. Furthermore, more than 1% (8) of our original 729 boys have died from gunshots since the inception of the study. Similarly, there are currently six boys in prison for committing homicides. So, nearly 2% of boys in the sample have either been a victim of firearm homicide or committed a homicide.

Hidden gun carrying is somewhat transitory. Table 1 shows that of those boys who ever carry a hidden gun, 43.5% only carry during one six-month period. Another 40.5% carry at two or three different waves (or up to 12 and 18 months respectively). Only 14.3% carry consistently for two to three years and less than 2% carry longer than this. In other words, during adolescence nearly half of the hidden gun carriers are short term carriers and about half are longer term (if intermittent) carriers (Webster et al., 1993). In addition, only about one-third of the boys carry hidden guns in adjacent 6-month waves, the other two-thirds stop carrying after only six months. Thus, there are many boys who at some point in their adolescent lives carry guns and at other, somewhat proximate points in time, do not carry guns. This suggests that most of these boys are not strongly committed to persistent, long-term gun carrying. We wish now to determine if the level and type of crime that they commit is the same or different during periods of time when they carry hidden guns compared to periods of time when they do not.

Table 1
Numbers of Waves Subjects Carry Guns

Number of Waves	Number of Subjects	%	Cumulative %
1	61	43.5	43.5
2	39	28.1	71.6
3	17	12.4	84.0
4	11	7.5	91.5
5	2	1.6	93.1
6	7	5.2	98.3
7	1	1.0	99.3
8	1	0.7	100.0

Our data cannot tell us if the boy is carrying a gun at the moment he is committing a crime. It can tell us whether involvement in crime changes during the six-month time period when he reports carrying a gun. However, offenders need not actually carry a gun at the instant of committing a crime for the gun to be efficacious for use in the crime. For example, street level drug dealers need not, and frequently do not, actually have drugs or guns in their possession on the street. The gun and drugs can be tucked away inside a doorway out of reach of a police officer or a larcenous buyer. However, both the drugs and the gun are easily accessible for sale or use. Therefore, measuring gun carrying at the instant the crime is committed would overlook many offenses that are committed because the gun is available to be carried, although not actually carried. If offenders actually had to carry the gun to use it, we would expect our measure of gun carrying to underestimate the relationship between gun carrying and the number of crimes committed. Therefore, finding significant increases in the number of crimes committed for periods of gun carrying compared to no gun carrying should be a low-end estimate of the true difference.

Statistical Analysis

The analysis for this paper is organized as follows. For each of the first eight waves of data we count the number of crimes committed by the boys who reported carrying guns in that particular wave for each of the three delinquency indices. We then count the number of crimes committed by those same gun carriers in the next wave at which they did not carry a gun. For those boys who carried guns in both Waves 1 and 2, we compare their Wave 1 rate with their Wave 3 rate. If they also carried in Wave 3, we compare their Wave 1 crimes to their Wave 4 crimes, and so on. We do this for each of Waves 2 through 8 and we sum the results across the waves. We then calculate crime rates and rate ratios indicating the elevation or decline in the number of crimes committed when the boys are carrying guns and when they are not carrying guns.

It is conceivable that the boys may commit more crimes as they mature, and that this maturation effect accounts for any differences in the amount of crime committed when the boys carry guns and when they do not carry. Most of the comparisons are across six-month data collection periods, and it would be unusual to find maturation effects in such short intervals. Still, to allow for possible maturation, we also reverse the process just described, comparing the amount of crime that gun carriers commit to their level of crime at the most recent preceding wave when they did not carry. For example, we calculated the number of crimes that gun carriers commit when carrying a gun in Wave 9. We then calculated the number of crimes that these carriers commit in the most recent preceding wave at which they did not carry. For the boys who carried in both Waves 9 and 8, we compare Wave 9 and Wave 7, and so on. We do this for all waves for comparisons to the past, summing across the waves. Again we calculate crime rates, rate ratios, and tests of statistical significance to determine the size and importance of the effect of gun carrying on the amount of crime committed. If a boy dropped out of the study subsequent to the wave that he carried but before he had an opportunity to not carry, he was dropped from the analysis.

As a result, exactly the same subjects are compared when carrying and when not carrying. A similar procedure was used for estimating the rate of crimes in the analysis of the past. In this analysis boys are counted at each wave of carrying. This means that a boy carrying at two waves will be included in the analysis twice. These comparisons to the future and the past provide estimates of the range of enhancement (or reduction) in crimes committed due to gun carrying.

Results

There are 219 incidents of boys carrying illegal hidden guns for comparison to future periods of non-carrying. Similarly, there are 239 incidents of boys carrying guns for comparison to past periods of non-carrying. Table 2 shows that the rate of serious violent crimes is higher during periods when the boys carry hidden guns than during periods when they do not. This is true for comparisons to the future and to the past. For future comparisons boys commit 5.1 times the number of serious violent crimes when they carry guns than when they do not. The mean paired difference for boys carrying compared to not carrying is 3.3 more crimes for gun carriers (Mean Paired Difference = MPD = 3.3), a statistically significant difference. Multiplying the number of incidents times the mean paired difference in violent crimes shows that the gun carriers commit 723 more serious violent crimes during periods when carrying guns than during periods when not carrying over the 4.5 year period (219 x 3.3 = 723). Results are obtained similarly for the comparison to past waves of not carrying guns. When carrying, these boys commit 2.9 times as many serious violent crimes as when not carrying in the prior wave. On average they commit 2.3 more crimes when carrying a gun (MPD = 2.3), for a total of 539 more serious violent crimes over the period. This difference is also statistically significant.

As predicted, drug sales are elevated for gun carriers at later waves when the boys are older and more likely to be serious drug dealers. In other words, the increase in drug selling is largest when compared to the past wave not carrying a gun as opposed to the future wave not carrying. This is because boys are more likely to sell drugs as they age. In the future comparison, the boys transact 2.1 times more drug sales during periods of time when carrying guns, or about 5.2 more sales per subject (MPD = 5.2), a statistically significant difference. However, for the past comparison gun carriers transact 9.7 times more drug sales or about 18.3 more sales per subject (MPD = 18.3). The number of drug sales associated with gun carrying is startling, between 1130 (future comparison) and 4371 (past comparison) more drug sales occur during time periods when the boys carry guns.

Table 2
Difference in Crimes Committed During Periods of Carrying and Periods of Not Carrying Guns

Type of Delinquency	Forward Comparisons (n = 219)				Backward Comparisons (n = 239)			
	Ratio of Carrying to Not Carrying Periods*	Mean Paired Difference**	95% Confidence Interval	Crimes During Gun Carrying Periods***	Ratio of Carrying to Not Carrying Periods*	Mean Paired Difference**	95% Confidence Interval	Crimes During Gun Carrying Periods***
Serious Violence	5.1	3.3	1.8-4.8	723	2.9	2.3	1.0-3.5	539
Drug Sales	2.1	5.2	1.3-9.0	1130	9.7	18.3	11.7-24.9	4371
Property Crimes	2.0	3.5	1.0-6.1	777	1.5	2.0	-0.7-4.7	487

* Ratio of number of crimes committed during periods of time carrying to number committed during periods of time not carrying.
** Mean paired differences in crimes when carrying and not carrying.
*** Number of crimes committed during periods of carrying

Finally, property crimes do not show the same strong relationships between gun carrying and offending. For the future comparison the boys are twice as likely to commit property crime when carrying (MPD = 3.5), a statistically significant difference. However, for the past comparison there is no significant difference between periods of gun carrying and non-carrying. This suggests that the findings from the future comparison could be because over time the boys tend to decrease the number of property crimes committed and this could provide the appearance that not carrying a gun in the next wave is responsible when it is not.[1] Firearms are not as necessary to commit property crimes. Therefore, boys are less likely to commit property crimes, compared to other crimes, during periods when they are also carrying hidden guns.

Conclusion

Depending upon the wave of data, about 4% to 8% of boys in Rochester carry hidden guns. Most boys who carry guns do so for relatively short time periods and nearly half carry for 6 months or less. This suggests that they may not be highly motivated to carry guns. Rather, gun carrying is short lived and episodic. When the boys do carry guns, however, they are high rate offenders for crimes that are most likely to produce injury to either the perpetrator or the victim. When the boys discontinue carrying guns, their rate of offending is greatly reduced. Thus, gun carrying seems to be associated with many dangerous crimes committed by a small, specific group of high rate offenders. For example, although the gun carrying boys represent about 25% of the sample across all 9 waves, during the periods of time that they carry guns they are responsible for about 37% of serious violent crimes and 64% of drug sales in all 9 waves. This is especially remarkable considering that most only carry the gun in one or two waves.

It is not possible to ascertain whether this facilitation is opportunistic (e.g., when boys carry guns they happen to encounter opportunities to use them) or premeditated (e.g., boys know that they are going to be involved in criminal activity and obtain guns in order to commit the crime). Of course, both factors could operate in concert. Juveniles who plan to engage in dangerous activities such as drug dealing, armed robbery, and the like, or when traveling among other dangerous people (Wright and Rossi, 1986), probably feel a need for protection that carrying a gun affords. When doing this, opportunities arise to commit crime that would not be realistic without the gun. In other words, criminals probably carry guns because they travel in a dangerous world, intend to commit crime, do not want to miss golden opportunities, see the protective efficacy of hidden gun carrying, and, relative to all of this, they see little cost.

Taken together these findings suggest that preventing, discouraging, or deterring even a few boys from carrying guns could have a dramatic impact on reducing violent crime. Policies that are specifically directed at gun carriers are likely to have the largest impact. Since these boys appear to carry guns to reduce their risks when committing dangerous crimes, raising the perceived costs of gun carrying could have a powerful impact on their criminal offending rates.

In addition to raising the perceived costs, policies also might attempt to reduce the perceived necessity for carrying guns. Past research has shown that a strong predictor of boys' gun carrying is having peers who do the same (Lizotte et al., 1994, 1997; Bjerregaard and Lizotte, 1995). This peer group of gun carriers is the embodiment of traveling among dangerous people mentioned above. Reducing gun carrying in this peer group therefore might be helpful in lowering the necessity of gun carrying for others.

While this strategy would have the impact of removing illegal guns from the streets, the real motivation is to remove boys from the street who carry guns in order to reduce their high rates of offending and in order to deter others from carrying. The guns themselves are easily replaced since there are so many guns in the U.S. (probably about 250 million) (Kleck, 1991). However, convincing a criminal that the cost of gun carrying is higher and the necessity is lower could deter and dissuade the perceived need.

In the last few years the New York City police have instituted policies that address these concerns (Citizens' Crime Commission of New York City, 1996). They have dramatically increased "pat downs" for violators of other ordinances and laws. In the process they have increased the number of persons arrested for illegal gun carrying. They have also encouraged those arrested for carrying guns to report others whom they know carry guns in exchange for leniency. The change has been impressive but we do not yet know if it is due to the policy.[2] Between 1990 and 1998 in New York City the number of homicides dropped from nearly 2,300 to less than 633 per year. Most of this decline was in firearm homicides. Similarly, from 1992 to 1997 the percent of violent crimes committed with a handgun dropped from about 33% to about 16%.

A strategy of increasing the costs and reducing the need for illegal gun carrying and use also has been implemented in Boston. It targets a specific population of serious youthful offenders and initial evidence suggests that it has successfully reduced youth violence (Kennedy et al., 1996). In St. Louis, authorities have obtained parental permission to search and seize guns from the homes of these high-risk boys (Rosenfeld and Decker, 1996). Not all interventions need to be law enforcement based. For example, education programs could be effective if they communicate the associated risks of gun carrying to these boys.

Because the boys' gun carrying is short-term and transitory, it seems that they are not highly committed gun carriers. This suggests that they may be easily deterred. Furthermore, because a relatively small number of boys carry guns and because they are such high rate offenders, convincing even a few to stop carrying guns could greatly reduce crimes and the assaultive injuries that accompany them. These facts provide empirical support for a spectrum of strategies for reducing gun violence, from the law enforcement tactics mentioned above to prevention through education. Whatever the intervention, it must begin early in the life course because boys as young as 13 years of age are already carrying hidden guns.

REFERENCES

Arria, A.M., N.P. Wood, and J.C. Anthony. (1995). "Prevalence of Carrying a Weapon and Related Behaviors in Urban Schoolchildren, 1989 to 1993." *Archives of Pediatric Adolescent Medicine* 149:1345-1350.

Bjerregaard, B. and A.J. Lizotte. (1995). "Gun Ownership and Gang Membership." *Journal of Criminal Law and Criminology* 86:37-58.

Blumstein, A. and D. Cork. (1996). "Kids, Guns and Homicide: Policy Notes on an Age-Specific Epidemic." *Law and Contemporary Problems* 59:5-24.

Callahan, C.M. and F.P. Rivara. (1992). "Urban High-School Youth and Handguns: A School-Based Survey." *JAMA* 267:3038-3042.

Callahan, C.M., F.P. Rivara, and J.A. Farrow. (1993). "Youth in Detention and Handguns." *Journal of Adolescent Health* 14:350-355.

Centers for Disease Control. (1991) "Weapon-Carrying among High School Students – United States, 1990." *MMWR* 40:681-684.

Citizens' Crime Commission of New York City. (1996). "Reducing Gun Crime in New York City: A Research and Policy Report." Citizens' Crime Commission of New York City.

Cook, P. J. and J. H. Laub. (1998). "The Unprecedented Epidemic in Youth Violence." Pp. 27-64 in M.H. Moore and M. Tonry (eds.) *Crime and Justice*. Chicago, IL: University of Chicago Press.

Decker, S.H., S. Pennell, and A. Caldwell. (1997). *Illegal Firearms: Access and Use by Arrestees*. Washington, DC: U.S. National Institute of Justice.

Elliott, D.S., S.S. Ageton, D. Huizinga, B.A. Knowles and R.J. Cantor. (1983). The Prevalence and Incidence of Delinquent Behavior 1976-1980. Boulder, CO: Behavioral Research Institute.

Elliott, D.S., D. Huizinga, and S.S. Ageton. (1985). *Explaining Delinquency and Drug Use*. Beverly Hills: Sage Publications.

Fox, J.A. and M.W. Zawitz. (1998). Homicide Trends in the United States. Washington, DC: U.S. Bureau of Justice Statistics.

Hemenway, D., D. Prothow-Stith, J.M. Bergstein, R. Ander, and B.P. Kennedy. (1996). "Gun Carrying among Adolescents." *Law and Contemporary Problems* 59:39-53.

Hindelang, M.J., T. Hirschi, and J.G. Weis. (1981). *Measuring Delinquency.* Beverly Hills: Sage Publications.

Huizinga, D. and D.S. Elliott. (1986). Reassessing the Reliability and Validity of Self-Report Delinquency Measures. *Journal of Quantitative Criminology* 2:293-327.

Huizinga, D., F-A. Esbensen, and A. Weiher. (1991). "Are There Multiple Paths to Delinquency?" *Journal of Criminal Law and Criminology* 82:83-118.

Kann, L., C. Warren, W. Harris, J. Collins, B. Williams, J. Ross, and L. Kolbe. (1996). "Youth Risk Behavior Surveillance – United States, 1995." *MMWR* 45:1-63.

Kennedy, D.M., A.M. Piehl, and A.A. Draga. (1996). "Youth Violence in Boston: Gun Markets, Serious Youth Offenders, and a Use-Reduction Strategy." *Law and Contemporary Problems* 59:147-196.

Kleck, G. (1991). *Point Blank.* New York: Aldine de Gruyter.

Krohn, M.D. and T.P. Thornberry. (1999). "Retention of Minority Populations in Panel Studies of Drug Use." *Drugs & Society* 4:185-207.

Lizotte, A.J., G. J. Howard, M. D. Krohn, and T. P. Thornberry. (1997). "Patterns of Illegal Gun Carrying among Young Urban Males." *Valparaiso University Law Review* 31:375-393.

Lizotte, A.J., M. D. Krohn, J. C. Howell, K. Tobin, and G. J. Howard. (2000). "Factors Influencing Gun Carrying among Young Urban Males over the Adolescent - Young Adult Life Course." *Criminology,* 38: 811-834.

Lizotte, A.J., J. Tesoriero, T.P. Thornberry, and M.D. Krohn. (1994). "Patterns of Adolescent Firearms Ownership and Use." *Justice Quarterly* 11:51-74.

Rosenfeld, R. and S.H. Decker. (1996). "Consent to Search and Seize: Evaluating an Innovative Youth Firearm Suppression Program." *Law and Contemporary Problems* 59:197-220.

Sheley, J.F. and J.D. Wright. (1995). *In the Line of Fire: Youth, Guns, and Violence in Urban America.* New York: Aldine de Gruyter.

Thornberry, T.P., B. Bjerregaard, and W. Miles. (1993). "The Consequences of Respondent Attrition in Panel Studies: A Simulation Based on the Rochester Youth Development Study." *Journal of Quantitative Criminology* 9:127-158.

Thornberry, T. P. and M. D. Krohn, (2000). "The Self-Report Method for Measuring Delinquency and Crime." Pp. 33-83 in D. Duffee, R. D. Crutchfield, S. Mastrofski, L. Mazerolle, and D. McDowall (eds). *Criminal Jusitce 2000 (V.4): Innovations in Measurement and Analysis.* Washington, D.C.: U. S. Department of Justice.

U.S. Federal Bureau of Investigation. (1997). *Crime in the United States.* Washington, DC: U.S. Federal Bureau of Investigation.

Webster, D.W., P. S. Gainer, and H.R. Champion. (1993). "Weapon Carrying among Inner-City Junior High School Students: Defensive Behavior vs. Aggressive Delinquency." *American Journal of Public Health* 83:1604-1608.

Wright, J.D. and P.H. Rossi. (1986). *Armed and Considered Dangerous: A Survey of Felons and their Firearms*. Hawthorne, NY: Aldine de Gruyter.

Zawitz, M.W. (1996). *Firearm Injury from Crime*. Washington, DC: U.S. Bureau of Justice Statistics.

NOTES

[1] In fact, the mean number of property crimes declines rather rapidly over the 9 waves for boys in general and for boys who carry guns in particular.

[2] Of course, many other factors such as the strong economy, low unemployment, welfare reform, and the like could be responsible for decreasing rates of firearms crime. Many other places have experienced a similar decline absent this policy. Detailed analyses, well beyond the scope of this research, would have to be conducted to adequately determine the causes of this decline in firearm crime.

VICTIM CATEGORIES OF CRIME REVISITED

Simon I. Singer
College of Criminal Justice, Northeastern University

Introduction

When Marvin Wolfgang asked me to co-author *Victim Categories of Crime* (Wolfgang and Singer 1978), he transformed my status as an anonymous graduate student into one that was committed to his way of doing criminology. *Victim Categories of Crime* set the stage for my dissertation, and a research agenda that saw crime less as a product of the actions of an offender, and more as an event to be described and understood in ways that go beyond any simple, unidirectional analysis. Previously, I had completed a proseminar paper on the development of the National Crime Panel victimization surveys. I came into the graduate program in sociology at the University of Pennsylvania after having completed a Master's thesis at Northeastern University on the elderly as victims of crime. Wolfgang knew of my interest in the emerging study of victims, and for that reason I believe asked me to join him in revising his article. The original version of *Victim Categories of Crime* had first appeared a decade earlier in a German publication honoring Hans von Hentig (Wolfgang 1967). Wolfgang wanted to see an English version of the article published, and one that would take into account recent developments in the emerging study of the victim.

But much of the literature on victims then, and today, moved away from the concept of crime as a complex event. This victimological literature often neglects the possibility that the offender could also be a victim; missing all too often is the interactive element to crime (Miers 1990). But Wolfgang was precise in his thinking about "victimization." He wanted it to be a criminological term, insisting in the first draft of our article that victimization be used in a criminological context to describe the impact of crime on the victim. Otherwise, he argued it would be difficult to separate conceptually the act of victimization from the act of crime. As a consequence, it stimulated the work of a long line of homicide studies, most recently Luckenbill's (1977) research on homicide as a situated transaction.

In the pages that follow, I revisit several victim categories of crime and in so doing revisit Wolfgang's way of doing criminology. My revisit of an article that was written several decades ago is selective. I will focus on how Wolfgang moved criminology through his victim categories. I wish to show how several categories reflected his way of seeing crime as related to a complex set of social interactions. Informed by victim categories of crime, I see Wolfgang's vision of criminology as generating a dynamic, interactionist approach to modern criminology.

To highlight what I see as a dynamic, interactionist perspective, I begin where Wolfgang (1958) began in his study of *Patterns in Criminal Homicide,* and the victim category of victim-precipitated crime. I then consider the way in which the victim allowed Wolfgang to theorize a subculture of violence. I further highlight how victimization is used to classify crime for the purpose of creating an offense severity scale (Sellin and Wolfgang 1964). Finally, I consider briefly the consequences of thinking about victims without offenders. I conclude by considering the way various cohort studies fit a dynamic interactionist perspective, particularly in showing the extent to which there is variation in the social context of crime and victimization.

Victims Who Precipitate Crime

The term victim-precipitated crime appeared in Wolfgang's first book, *Patterns in Criminal Homicide.* In the forward to the book, Sellin states that it "is the first of many that will enhance his reputation as a careful, imaginative and productive scholar." The careful and imaginative came in the way that Wolfgang was able to draw on Von Hentig's speculative comments regarding the victim's contribution to crime. Von Hentig (1948), in a chapter titled "the victim's contribution to the genesis of crime," states that

> "The relationships between perpetrator and victim are much more intricate than the rough distinctions of criminal law. Here are two human beings. As soon as they draw near to one another male or female, young or old, rich or poor, ugly or attractive—a wide range of interactions, repulsions as well as attractions, is set in motion (383-384)."

The qualitative, interactive dimension in von Hentig's statement is without direction, and as it stands is not conducive to empirical testing. Wolfgang (1958) takes von Hentig's speculative comments a step further to the point where a victim category emerges for testing the interaction between victim and offender. This comes in the form of his definition of victim-precipitated homicide:

> "Those cases in which the victim is a direct, positive precipitator in the crime — the first to use physical force in the homicide drama" (326).

There are several dimensions to Wolfgang's definition of victim-precipitated homicide that go beyond the more speculative statements of von Hentig. The first is one in which there is an action that can be measured in a particular direction—where the offender was "the first to use physical force." This provides a hypothesis and the opportunity to quantify relationships that previously were delegated simply to the intent of the offender. The second dimension is one in which the victim and offender are an event, part of the "homicide drama," and in so doing the role of one could easily be reversed with that of the other.

The qualitative, interactive dimension is reflected in Wolfgang's homicide case files. By bringing into the picture the victim, Wolfgang is able to operationalize a dimension of social interaction in which victim and offender confront one another. What is of particular significance is not the action of the offender to the exclusion of the victim, or for that matter the action of the offender to the exclusion of the victim. Wolfgang moves a step further towards another category of victim and that is one in which a push or shove is taken as a serious threat, a threat to one's masculinity (assuming the offender is male) and indicative of more serious violence.

Wolfgang draws on case records to theorize the significance of a "jostle," and to show how one set of actions reproduces another. How behavior is reproduced by structures of action is a key element to contemporary social theory (Giddens 1984). The "jostle" represents the reflexivity of social action. Wolfgang is able to draw on the jostle to provide a dynamic interpretation of how offenders are a product of more than their personal characteristics. Still those characteristics come into play when considering the structure of social action. That is, the significance of a jostle as a precipitating action is reproduced in the attitudes and values of individuals towards the use of violence. This is further reflected in variation in the demographic characteristics of offenders. According to Wolfgang

> "Intensive reading of the police files and of verbatim reports
> of interrogations, as well as participant observation in these
> interrogations by the author suggest that the significance of a
> jostle, a slightly derogatory remark, or the appearance of a
> weapon in the hands of an adversary are stimuli
> differentially perceived and interpreted by Negroes and
> whites, males and females. Social expectations of response
> in particular types of social interaction result in differentially
> definitions of the situation, p188."

Based on a victim category of crime, Wolfgang is able to describe the interaction between structure and action. Although the structuration of behavior is now a common sociological concept (Giddens 1984), the jostle is a micro level variable reflecting the macro level demographics of culture. Through the victim, structures of criminal behavior are reproduced. The significance of a jostle placed Wolfgang into the social interactionist school of thought. Wolfgang draws on W.I. Thomas, one of the founding members of the Chicago school of sociology, to make his point on differential "definitions of the situation." But while Thomas relied on qualitative data to illustrate definitions of the situation (see particularly his book *The Unadjusted Girl* (1923), Wolfgang is able to draw on the victim to produce a quantitative criminology, one that builds on a critical social interactionist perspective.

Wolfgang might have been mixing too many levels of analysis. Definitions of the situation operate in the minds of individuals. They are a product of the way communities and societies control the "hedonistic selection of activity" of individuals (Thomas 1923: 43). The definition of the situation is a restraining influence. Culture has a positive influence. According to Thomas, for example, the Polish immigrant's definition is rooted in family, church, and community. These definitions of the situation come into conflict with the impulses that drive the search for adventure, money, love, and fame. However, Wolfgang takes Thomas' dictum a step further to suggest that definitions of the situation can be deviant, and reflect deviant communities. This is not that far removed from Edwin Sutherland's theory of differential association with a ratio of definitions favorable or unfavorable to violation of the legal code (Sutherland and Cressey 1978). But for Wolfgang definitions of the situation tell how offenders act in anticipation of their possible victimization.

In suggesting that demographic characteristics predict who is more likely to use violence, Wolfgang moves away from a micro level concern with the victim to provide a macro level, structured account. This minimizes the dynamic interpretation of the offender and victim suggesting that there are deviant cultures that in the final analysis predict criminal behavior. Violence is now a product of group norms and values, and no longer a consequence of the offender's interaction with the victim. This is reflected in the way that age and gender are related to the use of violence as a means of protecting one's honor.

> A male is usually expected to defend the name and honor of his mother, the virtue of womanhood (even though his female companion for the evening may be an entirely new acquaintance and/or a prostitute), and to accept no derogation about his race (even from a member of his own race), his age, or his masculinity (188).

The gendered attitudes of males define the situation so that violence is a socially approved form of action. The expectation of using violence to defend one's honor suggests a particular kind of culture, one that fails to restrain the actions of others. Indeed the culture is one that pushes rather than restrains behavior. This is illustrated through the victim categories in the action of victims as well as offenders. In other words, they are in it together. They are all part of the same generating milieu in which violence is seen as a direct consequence of culture. But this is the more static, normative side of a culture of violence. It conflicts with that part of victim categories which suggest a dynamic, event-oriented theory of violence, one that is specific to certain social situations. This interactive, situation-specific form of culture can be seen in the hyphenated "sub-culture" with which Wolfgang concludes *Patterns of Criminal Homicide:*

> There may be a sub-culture of violence which does not define personal assaults as wrong or antisocial; in which the quick resort to physical aggression is a socially approved and expected concomitant of certain stimuli; and in which violence has become a familiar but often deadly partner in life's struggles. Attacks against the person are made without compunction, despite the middle-class value-system which views such acts as the most heinous of crimes. A conflict or inconsistency of social norms is most apparent, and the value–system of the reference group with which the individual differentially associates and identifies, determines whether assaultive behavior is necessary, expected or desirable in specific social situations. 329

In other words, the subculture is not always there in all situations but only in certain situations. This lifts whatever restraining influence may exist in the dominant culture making it possible for a new set of expectations to operate in "specific social situations."

So Wolfgang was able to move from the quantitative to the qualitative, and from the data to the theory. In so doing, he stimulated a considerable amount of scholarly work. Although the concept of victim-precipitation was used by others (e.g., Normandeau 1968; Amir 1967; Fattah 1967), it was never as successfully operationalized to the extent that Wolfgang was able to do (Silverman 1974). This is because Wolfgang was more specific and narrow in how far he wanted to go in producing an empirically grounded criminology. Victim precipitation was a concept that emerged to understand patterns in homicide. The bottom line for Wolfgang was criminological not victimological. As a victim category of crime, victim precipitation was one way to empirically identify patterns in homicide.

Victims Who are Also Offenders

The category of victims who are also offenders suggests a dynamic subculture in which the victimization experience, whether in the form of a push or a shove, is one that allows its members to define certain situations as warranting a violent response. This category also suggests that one experience leads to another. This moves beyond the incident of crime, such as that which is suggested through a victim-precipitated offense. There is a history to consider in the way that individuals can alternate between being a victim and offender involved in crime. The overlap of victim and offender experiences reveals a dynamic life course process in which the victim experience is one of the many experiences that shape one's willingness to use violence.

A more static interpretation of subculture that ignores this victim category implies that there is a singular normative value system that differentiates victims from their offenders. The offender is something other than the victim, and the victim is one who has no potential of ever becoming an offender. The more static view of subculture is shaped by a normative structure in which commitment to crime is shaped early in the life course of individuals. A less dynamic view of subculture allows for the prediction of crime based on background factors, such as race, gender, and age. This static interpretation of subculture is circular and based exclusively on demographic characteristics. There is little in the way of life experiences to be considered and to suggest otherwise. Definitions of the situation cannot be viewed exclusively as products of race, gender, and age characteristics. These attributes of individuals are only proxy indicators for the higher probabilities that can lead to one falling into a victim category of crime.

But victim categories of crime provide the added punch to see how issues of masculinity in the context of patriarchy may produce the situational responses that Wolfgang saw as part of a subculture. The victimization experience does not eliminate the importance of background factors, such as gender, it only highlights the means by which such factors are reproduced. Without the category of victims as offenders, there is little more than patriarchy to describe issues of masculinity and the reasons for violence. But not all patriarchal households are the same. It is not just masculinity and defending one's honor that produce the definitions of the situation that Wolfgang sees as leading to a violent response. The significance of a jostle comes into play in how patriarchy and honor are enforced through the threat and use of violence.

To ignore the violent aspects of patriarchy or maintaining honor is not only to ignore those definitions of the situation that are intended to act as a mechanism of control, but also to ignore how being the victim of patriarchy and honor can lead to crime. To rely exclusively on race, gender, and age characteristics to describe a subculture is to produce a circular argument, as critics of the subculture of violence thesis have repeatedly argued (see for instance Ball-Rokeach 1973). A less circular dimension is one that takes into account prior interaction between victim and offender to provide a more dynamic interpretation of how structural characteristics are reproduced to reflect newly created definitions of the situation.

In their book, *The Subculture of Violence,* Wolfgang and Ferracuti (1967) stress that subcultures are a product of norms and values that are developed through social interaction. Early on in their book, they argue that racial characteristics cannot be considered the only indication of a subculture. Race is only presented as a proxy variable for the learned behaviors that are hypothesized to produce a culture of violence. Based on aggregate data on lethal acts of violence, they state that

> "Whatever may be the learned responses and social conditions contributing to criminality, persons visibly identified and socially labeled as Negroes in the United States appear to possess them in considerably higher proportions than do persons labeled white (Wolfgang and Ferracuti 1967:264)."

The learned responses and social conditions are inclusive of victim categories in which the experiences of offenders are coupled with that of their experiences as victims. For instance, in my work, (Singer 1986) I have found that being the victim of violence as a juvenile is a significant predictor of adult criminality. The greater prevalence of blacks involved in adult criminality correlates with their more frequent victimization as juveniles. That is, the victim experience explained the effect of race. Moreover, the victimization experience accounts for significantly more of the variance in the probability of adult criminality than other foreground factors, such as gang membership or weapon use. Others have similarly found a strong and significant relationship between being a victim of crime and subsequent criminal behavior (Widom 1989).

But victim categories of crime move beyond legal categories if we extend the concept of victimization to include perceived injustices. Victim categories and much of the victimological literature are not confined to the actual experience of victims. Perceptions of victimization are just as important. An act of crime may be viewed as an act of righting a perceived wrong or injustice. But this requires taking into account the perspective of offenders and the possibility of their perceived direct and indirect victimization. It is a perspective that suggests there is a dynamic on going process that reproduces itself; a criminology that moves in the mind of offenders and victims to create new structures and new "definitions of the situation."

Victims of a Subculture of Crime

Theories of subculture can be divided into those that recognize their structural and contextual properties. In the more structured analysis, norms and values are determined by a given set of conditions.   There is little movement and the victimization experience is generally absent from the analysis. There is less focus on the event. Instead offenders are seen simply as life course delinquents or criminals without considering why individuals desist from their criminal behavior. In the normative view of a subculture, life course experiences account for few deviant values and norms. The normative is set early on with respect to what is acceptable. Thus an interpretation of subculture as one in which life experiences and expectations are not a product of social interaction is one which sees a violent subculture rather than a subculture of violence.

A violent subculture is one where lethal violence is an attribute that stays with its members. Commitment to violence is believed, in the more normative, structured view of a subculture, to be routinely handed down from one generation to the next. Members of a violent subculture are born into their definitions of the situation.   There is little movement during the life course of individuals.   The definitions of the situation stick from one generation to the next. A violent subculture suggests a tight conceptualization of the normative and the actions that reproduce criminal behavior.

In contrast to the more normative view of subculture, "a subculture of violence," drawing on victim categories of crime, is more dynamic, suggesting that the social interaction between victim and offender predicts high levels of violence. In this sense, Wolfgang and Ferracuti's use of the term "subculture of violence" is similar to the way that Matza (1964) uses the term "subculture of delinquency" to contrast a delinquent subculture. In both the subculture of violence and the subculture of delinquency, there is a dynamic aspect to the determinants of crime. For Matza, it is one that mainly happens in the mind of delinquents through their rationalization of delinquent behavior.   There is no readily identifiable instrumental or visible form of control. Instead, techniques of neutralization minimize the moral bond of the law by being specific to life course events, such as those that emerges through perceived acts of victimization. Matza is not so much concerned with the initiation of delinquency, what produces the initial act of deviance, although he makes some passing reference to its determinants in his conclusion. Rather how deviance happens and the way individuals justify it and its repeated conduct are a product of a culture in which delinquency is more or less common knowledge. So too with Wolfgang and Ferracutti's subculture of violence. The use of violence is in response to a perceived physical or psychological threat. As every good defense attorney knows, the explanation of that threat can make the criminal look more like a victim than an offender. In Matza's (1964: 174) terms there is the "denial of the victim."

But there is more to Wolfgang's victim categories to suggest that they loosely sensitize us to the determinants of crime. The victim as an offender exists through a state of frustration that is institutionally driven. It is institutional in the sense that among certain groups, there is little to regulate perceived injustices except to act as offender. In the more recent revisions of anomie theory, offenders are victims of their inability to achieve the "American dream" and its stress on monetary success (Messner and Rosenfeld 1994). Those who are unable to achieve a slice of the American pie are believed to pursue other ways of adapting to their perceived victimization through acts of crime.

Similarly, the victim plays a significant role in a strain theory of delinquency. Agnew (1985) has argued that limiting strain theory simply to the disjunction of aspirations and expectations or actual achievements ignores the life course dimensions of strain. His revised strain theory draws on the social psychology of victimization to suggest that if you treat people badly they behave badly. He further states that "the anger/frustration experienced by the individual energizes the person for action, creates a desire for revenge, and lowers inhibitions—including concern for the long-term consequences of one's behavior (Agnew 1995)." In this sense, victimization is not totally unrelated to what Wolfgang earlier observed in the significance of a jostle.

The Measurement of Crime and Delinquency and Categories of Victimization

In developing a weighted index of crime to take into account the complex dimensions that reflect offense seriousness, Sellin and Wolfgang (1964) created a measurement index with offense severity weights. The actual amount of harm inflicted could be measured based on the concept of victimization. It is a way of classifying the offense and it is an aspect of criminal law. The graduated sets of legal penalties that are inflicted based on types of felony offenses are ingrained in making the punishment fit the crime. Yet a more sensitive measure is one that goes beyond legal categories to take into account the elements of victimization. There is a distinction between robbery in the first and second degree based on the use of a weapon that reflects offense seriousness, but from a victim categories point of view, seriousness may be better defined by taking into account the extent of injury and monetary loss as well as weapon use. A broader perspective of victimization to the measurement of crime is the psychological harm that might be inflicted as well as physical injuries.

Where does the measurement of crime fit in with victim categories of crime? First, Sellin and Wolfgang's book *the Measurement of Delinquency* is rooted in the concept of victimization. They suggested a classification of victimization for their own and further studies: a) "Primary victimization" is used to refer to a personalized or individual victim, who may be directly assaulted and injured in a vis-a-vis offense, who is threatened, or who has property stolen or damaged. b) "Secondary victimization" generally refers to commercial establishments such as department stores, railroads, theatres, chain stores, churches and the like. This victim is impersonal, commercial and collective, but is not so diffusive as to include the community at large. c) "Tertiary victimization" excludes both primary and secondary types and refers to a very diffusive victimization that extends to the large community and includes offenses against the public order, social harmony, or the administration of government. Regulatory offenses and violations of city ordinances are typical. d) "Mutual victimization" excludes all of the above categories and refers to those cases in which the participants engage in mutually consensual acts, such as fornication, adultery or statutory rape. E) "No victimization" was used as a category for offenses that could not be committed by an adult and which are now commonly referred to as "juvenile status" offenses (such as running away from home, truancy from school, being declared "incorrigible").

As a scheme for analyzing victimization rates, the measurement of delinquency attempts to go beyond legal labels attached to offense by providing a way of seeing the event and all its complexity. The type of victimization tells us about victim and offender interaction and relates to a dynamic criminology. A more static interpretation is one that ignores victim categories and assumes that the offense can simply be measured by the intent of the offender, or the degree to which the offender is criminally responsible. On the other hand, a dynamic interpretation of crime sees offense variation in seriousness based on victimization; the measurement of crime moves away from the offender's intention or responsibility towards the consequences of the offense on the victim.

Victims Without Offenders

There is an additional victim category of crime that I wish to raise that was not included in the original article. It is criminology without the interaction between victim and offenders. It is purely victimological in that the end result is to present victims as other than offenders. Current support for harsher penalties, including the death penalty and the recriminalization of delinquency (Singer 1996), appear related to a victim-rights movement that views offenders as other than victims. Victim categories of crime allow us to empathize with offenders as possible victims. That kind of empathy is on the decline in a society that classifies its offenders in ways that simply ignore their possible victimization. Marcus Dubber (1998) has noted the risk in a society that increasingly sees the offender as somehow different than the population of victims.

He states:

> The absence of mutual identification, that is, of empathy, has resulted not only in the public's failure to check the state's exercise of its punishment right. More disturbingly, it has deprived modern punishment of its central claim to legitimacy based on the right to be punished. Offenders who do not identify themselves with the institutions that threaten, impose, and inflict punishment on them will not regard their punishment as autonomous, that is, as self-threatened, self-imposed, and, most important, self-inflicted. Instead of viewing punishment as the recognition of their membership in the community of rational persons, these offenders perceive it as the heteronomous and therefore illegitimate use of community violence against an outsider. As a result of the differentiation between observers and offenders, to which rehabilitationism has contributed by transforming punishment from the recognition of identity into the treatment of deviance, the state's exercise of its punishment power today is both unchecked by empathy and unjustified by autonomy (Dubber 1998:146).

Why should we be less likely to empathize with the offender? I want to suggest that it is related to broader structural characteristics, such as, the political and organizational interests that have given birth to the victim rights movement without considering victim categories of crime. The public is more often satisfied with a language of governmental control that shows the offender to be other than a victim. The politicization of crime control policies is also impacted by the organizational interests that emerge in the form of victim advocacy groups. Space precludes the opportunity to review the long list of ways in which the victim has emerged as a professional topic of concern by service providers.

But contrary to the direction of Wolfgang's research, the victim has been redirected in ways that highlight the need to separate offenders from their communities. This has produced a larger population of long-term prisoners, and the reinstatement of the death penalty as a way to permanently remove the offender. There is little consideration of victim categories of crime particularly in the way that offenders might also be the victims of crime.

Conclusion

I would like to conclude my revisit of victim categories of crime with what I see as the lasting impact of Wolfgang's criminological scholarship. It is a scholarship that produced a dynamic, interactive criminology. The victim was one way to get at the interaction between offenders and their social environment. Wolfgang moved criminological scholarship to think beyond the label of offender. This was always the case in the early sociological perspectives on deviance, particularly in the qualitative work of the Chicago school of sociology. But through victim categories of crime Wolfgang was able to quantify what previously was left to the more speculative arguments of early criminologists, such as von Hentig. In moving beyond qualitative data, Wolfgang was able to think about the characteristics of an event and dimensions of seriousness that related to the complex consequences of victimization.

Wolfgang, Figlio and Sellin's (1972) study of delinquency in a birth cohort followed the path set in Wolfgang's dissertation and in his work on victim categories of crime. It is one that recognizes the importance of a dynamic life course history in which individuals are influenced by their social experiences. Wolfgang quantified part of that relationship in ways that previously was left to speculation. He could say it with a degree of precision that was not the case in more qualitatively generated sets of research. To do so he relied on a dynamic conception of crime that was event oriented and was coded for dimensions of an offense that related to the characteristics of victimization.

Wolfgang's cohort studies gave birth to other cohort studies, and the dynamic aspects of subcultural theory gave rise to more explicit theoretical statements on the determinants of delinquency. This is clearly illustrated in Thornberry's (1996; 1987) interactionist theory of delinquency. It is a theory that moves; that takes into account the dynamic aspects of the life course of delinquents and non-delinquents. It is a theory that emphasizes non-recursive relationships. The unidirectional, normative model of delinquency is absent in Thornberry's interactionist analysis. There is a reverse causal ordering similar to that which was first suggested by Wolfgang in his operationalization of the concept of victim-precipitated homicide.

The structural is still retained in a dynamic, interactionist analysis on the determinants of crime. Longitudinal, cohort analyses, however, are sensitive to life course dimensions that might structure behavior. There are generational effects and even effects that are limited to shifts in the life course of adolescents. A different set of reciprocal relationships operates for those juveniles early in adolescence as opposed to those late into adolescence. For instance, the influences of peers have been found to be greater later in adolescence (Thornberry 1996: 232).

Still significant parts of Wolfgang's work have been used to justify a normative, static conception of criminology. Perhaps the most frequently cited aspect of the "delinquency in a birth cohort" studies is their support for the notion of a chronic violent offender. By ignoring victim categories of crime we are left with a static conception of a criminal as a super-predator from birth.

In short, Wolfgang anticipated and stimulated the work of those who followed him in writing about victimization and victim categories. Most important, the inclusion of victim categories enhances our understanding of the criminal event. Wolfgang's way of doing criminology generated the life course cohort studies that now form a significant part of the criminological literature. To ignore those life course experiences would be to ignore the act of victimization, and for that matter any reason to revisit victim categories of crime.

REFERENCES

Agnew, Robert. (1985). "A Revised Strain Theory of Delinquency." *Social Forces* 64:151-66.

Agnew, Robert. (1995)."Stability and Change in Crime Over the Life Course: A Strain Theory Explanation." *In Advances in Criminological Theory, Volume 7: Developmental Theories of Crime and Delinquency.* Thornberry Terence, ed. New Brunswick, NJ: Transaction.

Amir, Menachem. (1967). "Victim Precipitated Forcible Rape." *Journal of Criminal Law,* Criminology and Police Science 44: 93-502.

Ball-Rokeach, S. (1973). 'Values and Violence: A Test of the Subculture of Violence Thesis', *American Sociological Review*, 38, 736-50.

Cohen, A. K. (1955). *Delinquent Boys: The Culture of the Gang.* New York: The Free Press.

Dubber, M. (1998). 'The Right to Be Punished: Autonomy and Its Demise in Modern Penal Thought', Law and History Review, 16:113-46.

Fattah, E. A. (1967). "Towards a Criminological Classification of Victims." *The International Journal of Criminal Police* 209.

Giddens, A. (1984). The Constitution of Society: Outline of the Theory of Structuration. Berkeley and Los Angeles: University of California Press.

Matza, D. (1964). *Delinquency and Drift.* New York: John Wiley.

Messner, S. F., and Rosenfeld, R. (1994). *Crime and the American Dream.* Belmont, California: Wadsworth Publishing Company.

Miers, D. (1990). 'Positivist Victimology: A Critique Part 2: Critical Victimology, *International Review of Victimology*, 1: 219-30.

Normandeau, A. (1968). "Patterns in Robbery." *Criminologica*, November : 2-15.

Singer, Simon I. (1996). Recriminalizing Delinquency: Violent Juvenile Crime and Juvenile Justice Reform. New York: Cambridge University Press

Singer, Simon I. (1986). "Victims of Serious Violence and their Criminal Behavior: Subcultural Theory and Beyond." *Victims and Violence* 1:61-70

Silverman, Robert A. (1974). 'Victim Precipitation: An Examination of the Concept' in I. Drapkin and E. Viano. *Victimology: A New Focus*. Lexington, Mass: D. C. Heath.

Sutherland, Edwin H., and Donald R. Cressey. (1978). *Criminology*. Tenth Edition. Philadelphia: Lippincott.

Sellin, Thorsten and Marvin E. Wolfgang. (1964). The Measurement of Delinquency. Montclair, New Jersey: Patterson, Smith.

Thomas, W. I. (1923). The Unadjusted Girl: With Cases and Standpoint for Behavior Analysis. Boston: Little, Brown, and Company.

Thornberry, Terence P. (1996). 'Empirical Support for Interactional Theory: A Review of the Literature', in D. J. Hawkins, ed., Delinquency and Crime: Current Theories, 198-235. Camridge: Cambridge University Press.

Thornberry, Terence P. (1987). "Toward an Interactional Theory of Delinquency." Criminology 4:863-891.

von Hentig, Hans. (1948). The Criminal and His Victim: Studies in the Sociobiology of Crime. New Haven: Yale University Press.

Widom, Cathy S. (1989). "Child Abuse, Neglect, and Adult Behavior: Research Design and Findings on Criminality, Violence, and Child Abuse." *American Journal of Orthopsychiatry* 59:355-67.

Wolfgang, Marvin, Robert Figlio and Thorsten Sellin. (1972). *Delinquency in a Birth Cohort*. Chicago: University of Chicago Press.

Wolfgang, Marvin. (1958). *Patterns in Criminal Homicide*. Montclair, N.J.: Patterson Smith.

Wolfgang, Marvin and Simon I. Singer. (1978). "Victim Categories of Crime." *Journal of Criminal Law and Criminology* 69:379-394

Wolfgang, Marvin E. and Franco Ferracuti. (1967). *The Subculture of Violence*. London: Tavistock Publications.

Wolfgang, Marvin E. (1967). *Analytical Categories for Research in Victimization*. Germany: Kriminologische Wegzeichen.

A MINIMUM REQUIREMENT FOR POLICE CORRUPTION

Carl B. Klockars
University of Delaware

Maria R. Haberfeld
John Jay College of Criminal Justice

Sanja Kutnjak Ivkovich
Harvard University

Aaron Uydess
University of Delaware

Challenges in the Study of Police Corruption

Corruption is extremely difficult to study in a direct, quantitative, empirical manner. Because most corruption incidents are never reported or recorded, official data on corruption are better regarded as measures of police agency anti-corruption activity than as measures of the actual level of corruption. Moreover, police officers are unlikely to be willing to candidly report their own or other officers' corrupt activities, even with assurances of confidentiality by researchers.

In order to overcome the difficulties inherent in attempts to measure corruption, we chose to invert the problem and measure corruption's conceptual opposite: integrity. We define integrity as *the normative inclination to resist temptations to abuse the rights and privileges of their occupation.*[1] The concept of integrity involves questions of *fact* and *opinion* that can be explored directly and without the resistance that direct inquiries about corrupt *behavior* are likely to provoke. It is, for example, possible to ask non-threatening questions about officers' *knowledge* of agency rules and questions of officers' *opinions* about the seriousness of their violation, the punishment they deserve or are likely to receive, and their estimates of the willingness of officers to report such behavior without asking them directly about their own or others' corrupt *behavior*.

Moreover, a vision of a police agency of integrity contrasts in a most important way with one that is free of corruption. The corruption-free police agency is one from which all morally defective individual officers have been removed and in which the agency remains vigilant and active in preventing their entry or emergence. By contrast, the idea of a police agency of integrity envisions an institution whose organizational culture is highly intolerant of corruption.

The administrative implications of these very different visions are, of course, enormous. The mandate for the administrator of an institution that would be corruption free is to engage in vigorous efforts to screen out morally defective candidates for police careers, detect the misconduct of those who manage to slip through the screening, and remove them from careers in police service. It is a highly individualistic concept of the idea of police corruption that calls for highly individual responses to it.

By contrast, the vision of the police agency of integrity involves quite different administrative goals and objectives. The objective of the leader of a police agency of integrity is to create an occupational culture that is intolerant of corruption. Doing so requires attention to how agency rules are created, communicated, and learned, how deviations from those rules are discovered, investigated, and disciplined, and how ready police officers themselves are to report misconduct when it comes to their attention. This is a profoundly social and organizational mandate for police leaders that stands in stark contrast with the individual focus and obligations that spring from the vision of a corruption-free police agency.

Finally, the methodological consequences of these different visions are critical. Measuring the level of corrupt behavior, the number of morally defective police officers, and agency vigilance in their discovery may not be impossible, but the obstacles are enormous. Measuring how seriously officers regard misconduct, how willing they are to support the punishment of it, and how willing they are to tolerate it in silence – the occupational culture of police integrity – is well within the capacities of modern social science.

Measuring Integrity

In order to measure police integrity we designed a questionnaire that sought to answer in a systematic, standardized, quantitative manner five very basic organizational questions that are fundamental to a general theory of police integrity. At the same time, the questionnaire was intended to satisfy some basic informational needs of any practical police administrator who wants to create an occupational culture intolerant of corruption:

1. Do officers in this agency know the rules?
2. How strongly do they support those rules?
3. Do they know what disciplinary threat this agency makes for violation of those rules?
4. Do they think the discipline in this agency is fair?
5. How willing are they to report misconduct?

The questionnaire presented police officers with eleven hypothetical case scenarios. The scenarios, displayed in Exhibit 1, cover a range of corrupt behavior from that which merely gives an appearance of a conflict of interest (Case 1) to incidents of bribery (Case 3) and theft (Cases 5 and 11).

Respondents were asked to evaluate each of these case scenarios by responding to seven core questions. Six questions were pairs of questions reflective of a dimension of police integrity. Two questions pertained to their own and other officers' perceptions of the *seriousness* of each case; two pertained to the severity of *discipline it should* and *would* receive; and two to their own and other officers' *willingness to report* it (See Exhibit 2). The remaining question asked if the behavior described in the scenario was a violation of official policy in the agency.

In designing the scenarios we sought to describe incidents that were not only plausible and common forms of police misconduct, but ones that were uncomplicated by details that might introduce ambiguity into either the interpretation of the behavior or the motive of the officer depicted in the scenario. In designing some scenarios we drew from previously published work that had employed a case-scenario approach (Fishman, 1978; Martin, 1994; Huon, Hesketh, Frank, McConkey, and McGrath, 1995; Miller and Brasswell, 1992). For other scenarios we drew upon our own experience. Respondents were asked to assume that the officer depicted in the scenarios had been a police officer for five years, had a satisfactory work record, and had no history of previous discipline.

Exhibit 1: Case Scenarios

Case 1.   A police officer runs his own private business in which he sells and installs security devices, such as alarms, special locks, etc. He does this work during his off-duty hours.

Case 2.   A police officer routinely accepts free meals, cigarettes, and other items of small value from merchants on his beat. He does not solicit these gifts and is careful not to abuse the generosity of those who give gifts to him.

Case 3.   A police officer stops a motorist for speeding. The officer agrees to accept a personal gift of half of the amount of the fine in exchange for not issuing a citation.

Case 4.   A police officer is widely liked in the community, and on holidays local merchants and restaurant and bar owners show their appreciation for his attention by giving him gifts of food and liquor.

Case 5.   A police officer discovers a burglary of a jewelry shop. The display cases are smashed and it is obvious that many items have been taken. While searching the shop, he takes a watch, worth about two days pay for that officer. He reports that the watch had been stolen during the burglary.

Case 6.   A police officer has a private arrangement with a local auto body shop to refer the owners of the cars damaged in the accidents to the shop. In exchange for each referral, he receives a payment of 5% of the repair bill from the shop owner.

Case 7.   A police officer, who happens to be a very good auto mechanic, is scheduled to work during coming holidays. A supervisor offers to give him these days off, if he agrees to tune-up his supervisor's personal car. Evaluate the SUPERVISOR'S behavior.

Case 8   At 2 A.M. a police officer, who is on duty, is driving his patrol car on a deserted road. He sees a vehicle that has been driven off the road and is stuck in a ditch. He approaches the vehicle and observes that the driver is not hurt but is obviously intoxicated. He also finds that the driver is a police officer. Instead of reporting this accident and offense he transports the driver to his home.

Case 9.   A police officer finds a bar on his beat which is still serving drinks a half hour past its legal closing time. Instead of reporting this violation, the police officer agrees to accept a couple of free drinks from the owner.

Case 10.   Two police officers on foot patrol surprise a man who is attempting to break into an automobile. The man flees. They chase him for about two blocks before apprehending him by tackling him and wrestling him to the ground. After he is under control both officers punch him a couple of times in the stomach as punishment for fleeing and resisting.

Case 11.   A police officer finds a wallet in a parking lot. It contains the amount of money equivalent to a full-day's pay for that officer. He reports the wallet as lost property, but keeps the money for himself.

Exhibit 2: Case Scenario Assessment Options

1.   How serious do YOU consider this behavior to be?

        Not at all   Very
        serious   serious
         1   2   3   4   5

2.   How serious do MOST POLICE OFFICERS IN YOUR AGENCY consider this behavior to be?

        Not at all   Very
        serious   serious
         1   2   3   4   5

3.   Would this behavior be regarded as a violation of official policy in your agency?

        Definitely   Definitely
        not   yes
         1   2   3   4   5

4.   If an officer in your agency engaged in this behavior and was discovered doing so, what if any discipline do YOU think <u>SHOULD</u> follow?

        1. None
        2. Verbal reprimand without pay
        3. Written reprimand
        4. Period of suspension
        5. Demotion in rank
        6. Dismissal

5.   If an officer in your agency engaged in this behavior and was discovered doing so, what if any discipline do YOU think <u>WOULD</u> follow?

        1. None
        2. Verbal reprimand without pay
        3. Written reprimand
        4. Period of suspension
        5. Demotion in rank
        6. Dismissal

6.   Do you think YOU would report a fellow police officer who engaged in this behavior?

        Definitely   Definitely
        not   yes
         1   2   3   4   5

7.   Do you think MOST POLICE OFFICERS IN YOUR AGENCY
          would report a fellow police officer who engaged in this behavior?

Definitely				Definitely
not				yes
1	2	3	4	5

The Sample of U.S. Police Officers

          Our sample consisted of 3,235 officers from thirty U.S. police
agencies. Some characteristics of the samples from each of the thirty
agencies are summarized in Table 1. In order to prevent identification of
specific agencies we have assigned each agency a random number from 1-30
and reported only an approximate number of sworn employees. It is for this
reason that we provide only approximate individual agency response rates.
          Although these agencies were drawn from many different parts of
the U.S. and the sample is quite large, it is a convenience sample that over
represents certain types of police agencies. While one of the reasons why we
opted to study integrity instead of studying police corruption was precisely to
weaken the reluctance of the police agencies to participate in the study and to
curtail the potential resistance by the police officers to fill out the
questionnaires, police agencies were careful about opening their doors to us.
Potential reasons for their caution may include their paramilitary nature,
acceptance of the rotten-apple theory, and fear that we might uncover
something negative for the agency. Consequently, a systematic bias probably
exists in our sample because not all agencies we approached to participate in
the study accepted our invitation (seven agencies we approached turned
down our request). Some rejections came straight from the office of the chief
of the agency; others were based on objections from the local police union.
In one instance we completed a survey of an agency, but before the
questionnaires could be returned to us a union official came into the office of
the liaison that had collected them and demanded that they be destroyed
immediately and before his eyes. Our assumption is that many, if not all of
these agencies refused to participate because they believed they had
something to hide. Fear of revealing something untoward was a serious
concern to these agencies, despite the fact that we assured them we would
keep their participation confidential, assured all individual respondents of
anonymity, and asked only about opinions and not about actual misconduct.
          This is not to say that our sample does not include some seriously
troubled police agencies. We were fortunate to have friends and former
students of considerable influence in a number of such agencies. Some were
senior officers who knew how to influence what might otherwise have been a

highly resistant chief. Others were high ranking union officials who eliminated both potential and actual resistance from that quarter. In one such case a highly influential union contact granted us entree to an agency to which their powerful union had previously flatly denied us access.

It is also the case that we approached some agencies knowing that they were quite receptive to research. Most of them had strong reputations not only as very good police agencies, but, as part of that reputation, quite honest ones as well. The combined effect of these systematic biases is that our sample may, to a degree, disproportionately represent police agencies that are not only receptive to research but believe that the survey will not reveal anything that might embarrass them.

Furthermore, being a convenience sample, it includes no state police agencies, only one sheriff's agency, and only one county police agency. Thus, it over represents municipal police agencies. While our sample also over represents police agencies from the Northeastern United States, it does contain agencies from the South, Southeast, and Southwest, but none from West Coast, Northwestern, or Midwestern cities.

In each agency we relied upon the efforts of a liaison officer to distribute the questionnaires and collect those that had been completed. In some agencies this was done by distributing the questionnaires to all agency personnel through the agency's internal mail system and having officers return the completed questionnaires by mail directly to the liaison officer. In other agencies the questionnaires were distributed to unit or division supervisors and they assumed responsibility for distributing and collecting them within their respective units or divisions. In still others, an officer assumed direct responsibility for distributing and collecting the surveys and did so personally, visiting shifts, and standing by while officers completed the surveys.

Since our goal was to study aspects of police culture in an agency, instead of obtaining a representative sample of, for example, 10% of police officers in a larger number of agencies, we tried to survey all police officers employed in a selected sample of police agencies. Although with the purpose of increasing the police officers' willingness to participate we guaranteed anonymity to the respondents and asked a limited number of questions about their demographic characteristics in order to dispense of their fear that they might be identified using these factors, we ultimately relied on their willingness to participate in the study – the participation in the study was voluntary. In addition, some of the police officers could not be included in the study (i.e., they could not even be given the opportunity to participate) because they were either on vacation, sick leave, or appearing in the court on the day when the questionnaires were distributed.

In the end, the response rates vary from 16% to 93% (Table 1).[2] However, in over one-half of the agencies in the sample (57%), the *majority* of police officers employed by the agency participated in the study. Furthermore, in additional one-quarter of the agencies (23.3%) between 40% and 50% of the police officers participated, and in only 20% of the agencies a response rate was lower than 40%.

The issues of sampling bias could be raised particularly for the 6 agencies in which the response rates were below 40%. Indeed, are the characteristics of police officers who participated different from the those of the police officers who refused to participate? For example, supervisors (whose opinion might be somewhat different from that of line officers) could be over-represented in our sample, compared to the overall population of police officers in a particular agency, especially in the agencies with lower response rates. Our results indicate that, if supervisors are over-represented, this is occurring *consistently* across the agencies in the sample and *is not related* to the response rates (i.e., the percentage of supervisors in the agencies is not related to the response rates),[3] nor to the ranking of the agencies in the sample.[4]

Another type of sampling bias can possibly affect our results. In particular, line officers with higher levels of normative inclination to resist corruption (i.e., higher levels of integrity) in the agency could be the ones who might be more likely to participate in the study. In other words, samples from agencies with substantially higher response rates could contain a larger percentage of police officers on the other end of the integrity scale, pulling the agency's overall means toward lower values. If this were the case, we would expect a negative relationship between the response rates and the agency's ranking on our integrity scale. It did not seem that the variation in response rates had a significant effect on the results; in particular, the ranking of agencies based of their integrity score (see Table 4) was not significantly correlated with their response rates.[5]

Table 1: Agency-Specific Characteristics of the Sample of Thirty U.S. Police Agencies

Agency Number	Approximate Agency Size (Sworn Officers)	Sample Size: Sworn Officers	Approximate Response Rate	% Supervisors	% Patrol	Mean Length of Service
1	315	171	54%	36.1%	53.7%	10.87
2	510	371	73%	15.4%	58.5%	13.86
3	445	387	87%	18.4%	58.1%	14.24
4	130	60	46%	18.3%	65.0%	11.06
5	1210	758	63%	12.6%	69.7%	9.42
6	150	110	73%	27.3%	61.8%	12.48
7	30	27	90%	35.6%	65.4%	15.23
8	35	24	69%	39.1%	62.5%	9.71
9	40	20	50%	40.0%	61.1%	13.08
10	15	14	93%	53.8%	61.5%	15.54
11	10	6	60%	16.7%	100%	14.00
12	20	16	80%	37.5%	75.0%	14.16
13	15	11	73%	9.10%	90.9%	6.94
14	65	47	72%	38.3%	63.0%	10.97
15	70	37	53%	18.9%	70.3%	13.64
16	30	15	50%	40.0%	60.0%	17.14
17	20	5	25%	100%	25.0%	19.40
18	985	458	46%	17.7%	57.8%	11.82
19	25	20	80%	45.0%	75.0%	11.50
20	105	20	19%	45.0%	50.0%	14.39
21	120	55	46%	22.2%	48.1%	13.42
22	150	68	45%	30.9%	60.3%	13.45
23	850	350	41%	15.5%	65.9%	11.70
24	100	39	39%	38.5%	68.4%	11.83
25	385	80	21%	19.2%	84.0%	9.55
26	45	7	16%	28.6%	57.1%	15.71
27	35	22	63%	36.4%	95.5%	11.31
28	25	13	52%	0.0%	15.4%	5.67
29	25	8	32%	50.0%	62.5%	9.50
30	30	16	53%	37.5%	50.0%	10.31

Validity of Officer Responses

Before reporting the results of the survey we must give some consideration to the question of whether our police officers answered the survey questions honestly. While we asked officers only about their attitudes and not about their actual behavior or that of other police officers and assured them that their responses would be confidential, police respondents are naturally suspicious of such promises. To further allay officer fears that their identity might be discovered we asked only the most minimal background facts about them: rank, length of service, assignment, and whether or not they were supervisors. We did not ask standard questions about age, race, gender, or ethnicity for fear that our police respondents might consider that disclosing that information in combination with their rank, assignment, and length of service would make it possible to identify them.

In addition, we asked all of our police respondents two questions about validity at the end of the survey. The first was "Do you think MOST POLICE OFFICERS would give their honest opinion in filling out this questionnaire?" The second was "Did you?" To the first question 84.4% of our police respondents (N =2679 of 3175) reported that they thought most officers would answer the questions honestly and 97.8% of our police respondents (N = 3107 of 3176) reported that they themselves had done so. We took our respondents at their word. When analyzing the results of the survey, we discarded the responses of the 2.2% of police officers (N= 69) who reported that they had not answered honestly.

We also take some comfort from the fact that each of the questions invited officers who might consider manipulating their responses to create a favorable impression on the public or their supervisors to do so in a somewhat different direction. For example, while officers might be inclined to report that they thought certain types of misconduct were more serious than they actually thought them to be, we believe that they would be unlikely to report that misconduct should be punished more severely than they thought appropriate for fear that their reports might be used against them.

If there were this kind of manipulation of answers taking place to any substantial degree, it should be evident in differences in correlation coefficients between the answers to questions about seriousness, discipline, and willingness to report. In fact, as Table 2 illustrates, the correlations between all six questions are extraordinarily high. The more serious police officers regarded a behavior, the more severely they thought it should and would be punished, and the more willing they were to report it. One could, in fact, predict with great accuracy the rank or mean answer to any one of the six questions by knowing the rank or mean answer to any other one of them. This finding lends support to our contention that all of the core six questions on the survey – the two on seriousness, the two on discipline, and the two on willingness to report – all tap the same phenomenon – the degree of police intolerance for misconduct.

Table 2: **Spearman Correlation Coefficients – U.S. Police Officer Rank Ordering of Own and Others' Views of Seriousness, Punishment Should and Would Receive and Own and Others' Willingness to Report**

	OWN View of Seriousness	OTHERS' View of Seriousness	Punishment SHOULD Receive	Punishment WOULD Receive	OWN Willingness to Report	OTHERS' Willingness to Report
OWN View of Seriousness						
OTHERS' View of Seriousness	1.00 p< .001					
Punishment SHOULD Receive	.973 p< .001	.973 p< .001				
Punishment WOULD Receive	.973 p< .001	.973 p< .001	1.00 p< .001			
OWN Willingness to Report	.973 p< .001	.973 p< .001	.982 p< .001	.982 p< .001		
OTHERS' Willingness to Report	.980 p< .001	.980 p< .001	.989 p< .001	.989 p< .001	.998 p< .001	

Survey Results

The general results of the survey of 3,235 police officers from thirty U.S. police officers are displayed in Table 3 below. Elsewhere we have compared the results of our survey of U.S. officers with similar surveys of 1,649 Croatian, 1,477 Polish, and 767 Slovenian police officers (Haberfeld, Klockars, Ivkovich, and Pagon, 2000). Here we should like to set the responses of our U.S. police officers in context by comparing them, first, with the responses of officers in the samples drawn from each agency and then with a sample of 375 U.S. undergraduate university students.

Table 3: U.S. Police Officer Perceptions of Offense Seriousness, Punishment, and Willingness to Report

CASE NUMBER & DESCRIPTION	SERIOUSNESS				DISCIPLINE						WILLINGNESS TO REPORT			
	Own View		Other Officers		Should Receive			Would Receive			Own View		Other Officers	
	x̄	(rank)	x̄	(rank)	x̄	(rank)	(Mode)	x̄	(rank)	(Mode)	x̄	(rank)	x̄	(rank)
Case 1 Off-Duty Security System Business	1.46	1	1.48	1	1.34	1	None	1.51	1	None	1.37	1	1.46	1
Case 2 Free Meals, Discounts on Beat	2.60	2	2.31	2	2.13	2	Verbal Reprimand	2.37	2	Verbal Reprimand	1.94	2	1.82	2
Case 3 Bribe from Speeding Motorist	4.92	10	4.81	10	4.92	9	Dismissal	4.86	9	Dismissal	4.19	9	3.92	9
Case 4 Holiday Gifts from Merchants	2.84	3	2.64	3	2.53	3	Verbal Reprimand	2.82	3	Written Reprimand	2.36	4	2.28	3.5
Case 5 Crime Scene Theft of Watch	4.95	11	4.88	11	5.66	11	Dismissal	5.57	11	Dismissal	4.54	11	4.34	11
Case 6 Auto Repair Shop 5%Kickback	4.50	7	4.26	7	4.40	8	Suspend w/o pay	4.46	8	Suspend w/o pay	3.95	8	3.71	8
Case 7 Supervisor: holiday for tune-up	4.18	6	3.96	6	3.59	5	Written Reprimand	3.43	5	Written Reprimand	3.45	6	3.29	6

Table 3 (cont.): U.S. Police Officer Perceptions of Offense Seriousness, Punishment, and Willingness to Report

CASE NUMBER & DESCRIPTION	SERIOUSNESS Own View x̄	(rank)	Other Officers x̄	(rank)	DISCIPLINE Should Receive x̄	(rank)	(Mode)	Would Receive x̄	(rank)	(Mode)	WILLINGNESS TO REPORT Own View x̄	(rank)	Other Officers x̄	(rank)
Case 8 Cover-Up of Police DUI Accident	3.03	4	2.86	4	2.81	4	Suspend w/o pay	3.21	4	Suspend w/o pay	2.34	3	2.28	3.5
Case 9 Drinks to Ignore Late Bar Close	4.54	8	4.28	8	4.02	7	Suspend w/o pay	4.08	7	Suspend w/o pay	3.73	7	3.47	7
Case 10 Excessive Force on Car Thief	4.05	5	3.70	5	3.76	6	Suspend w/o pay	4.00	6	Suspend w/o pay	3.39	5	3.07	5
Case 11 Theft from Found Wallet	4.85	9	4.69	9	5.09	10	Dismissal	5.03	10	Dismissal	4.23	10	3.96	10

Differences in Environments of Integrity

To display the differences in the environments of integrity among the 30 U.S. police agencies, we devised a system that would permit us to compare and rank the responses of officers in that agency with those of officers from the other agencies in the national sample. To determine an agency's summary ranking on the question that asked about officers' own perceptions of the seriousness of the behavior described in each case, the mean score of each agency's responses for each of the eleven cases was rank ordered from highest (1) to lowest (30). An agency was then awarded three (3) points if its mean score placed it among the top ten agencies on any question, two (2) points if it scored among the middle ten, and one (1) point if it scored among the bottom ten. These scores were then summed for all eleven cases. Using this scaling system agency scores could range on questions of officers' own perceptions of seriousness from eleven (11), for an agency that scored in the lowest third of agencies on all eleven questions, to thirty three (33), for an agency that scored among the highest third of agencies on all eleven questions.

An alternative summary ranking system could, of course, be based upon the full range of 30 point rankings for each of the 11 scenarios. This would create a scale that could range from 330 for an agency that scored the lowest of all thirty agencies on all six questions for all eleven scenarios to 1980 for an agency that scored the highest of all thirty agencies on all six questions for all eleven scenarios. Such a scoring system would, however, magnify small and largely meaningless differences in mean scores, creating a false sense of precision. The ranking system we developed intentionally seeks to blunt any false sense of precision by allowing agencies to score, in a sense, only "high," "middle," or "low" on any given question.

Exactly the same procedure was used to calculate a summary score and ranking for each agency's responses about most officers' perceptions of seriousness, discipline should receive, discipline would receive, own willingness to report, and other officers' willingness to report. The summary scores we developed formed the basis on which the agencies were placed in rank order from 1 to 30 (Table 4).

Table 4: Seriousness, Discipline, and Willingness to Report Scores Rank Ordered by Total Agency Integrity Score

AGENCY	OWN OPINION OF SERIOUS-NESS	OTHERS' OPINION OF SERIOUS-NESS	DISCIPLINE SHOULD RECEIVE	DISCIPLINE WOULD RECEIVE	OWN WILLING-NESS TO REPORT	OTHERS' WILLING-NESS TO REPORT	TOTAL INTEGRITY RANK SCORE	
CHARLESTON	3	3	3	3	3	3	1	18
3	3	3	3	3	3	3	1	18
4	3	3	3	3	3	3	1	18
6	3	3	3	3	3	3	1	18
10	3	3	3	3	3	3	1	18
17	3	3	3	3	3	3	1	18
30	3	3	3	3	3	3	1	18
ST. PETERSBURG	3	2	3	3	3	3	8	17
18	2	2	3	3	3	3	9	16
7	3	2	2	2	3	3	10	15
11	3	3	2	2	2	2	11	14
12	3	3	3	1	2	2	11	14
CHARLOTTE MECKLENBURG	2	2	2	3	2	2	13	13
19	3	2	2	2	2	2	13	13
20	3	2	2	2	2	2	13	13
29	2	3	2	1	2	2	16	12
26	3	2	2	2	1	1	17	11
27	2	2	2	1	2	2	17	11
24	2	2	1	1	2	2	19	10
21	1	1	2	3	1	1	20	9
22	1	1	2	2	1	2	20	9
9	2	1	2	1	1	1	22	8
16	1	1	1	1	2	2	22	8
13	1	2	1	1	1	1	24	7
14	1	1	1	2	1	1	24	7
15	1	1	1	1	2	1	24	7
23	1	1	1	2	1	1	24	7
25	1	1	1	2	1	1	24	7

AGENCY	OWN OPINION OF SERIOUS- NESS	OTHERS' OPINION OF SERIOUS- NESS	DISCIPLINE SHOULD RECEIVE	DISCIPLINE WOULD RECEIVE	OWN WILLING- NESS TO REPORT	OTHERS' WILLING- NESS TO REPORT	TOTAL INTEGRITY RANK SCORE	
8	1	1	1	1	1	1	29	6
28	1	1	1	1	1	1	29	6

Contrasting Environments of Integrity

Four rows on Table 4 are shaded, three of which bear the name of the police agency which participated in the survey. Police agencies in Charleston, South Carolina, St. Petersburg, Florida, and Charlotte-Mecklenberg, North Carolina are identified because subsequent to our survey each volunteered to make its results public and, as agencies of integrity, open themselves up to a year and a half of highly detailed scrutiny by us. They see themselves as agencies of high integrity, are appreciated as such by the communities they serve, and gave us full access to their complaint, discipline, personnel, and internal affairs records. For more than a year we met monthly with "study groups" of officers dedicated to the study of integrity in each agency and interviewed hundreds of police officers from those agencies to corroborate the findings of our survey. Everything we have learned about these agencies from studying them closely for a year and a half confirms the findings of our survey, that these are police agencies of high integrity in which the occupational culture is very intolerant of corruption.

We have also shaded the ranking of Agency 23. It ranked in a five-way tie for 24th position in our ranking ordering of the integrity environments of 30 U.S. police agencies. Only 3 police agencies surveyed ranked lower. Agency 23 has a long history of scandal. Despite various reform efforts, it continues to carry a reputation as an agency with persistent corruption problems. Initially, though the administration approved, our request to survey this agency was flatly turned down by the police union. However, we happened to have a supportive former student who was a high-ranking official in the union and he managed to have their decision reversed.

The University Student Sample

While there is ample independent evidence that tends to corroborate our survey findings of markedly different officer opinions about seriousness, appropriate and expected discipline, and willingness to report between agencies of high and low integrity, one further comparison will prove especially helpful. This comparison involves a sample of 375 university students all of whom were enrolled in introductory level sociology or criminal justice courses.

Proposing a direction in which we expect student and police officer opinions about corruption scenarios to differ is somewhat challenging. To begin with, there are no prior studies comparing the opinions about police corruption cases by both police officers and college students. Second, the results of prior research studies about crime seriousness (not necessarily focusing on police misconduct) differ. In particular, Selling and Wolfgang found that the estimates of seriousness provided by police officers and college students differed in absolute terms, but their relative rankings turned out to be quite similar.[6] Kelly and Winslow (1970) also found college students' and police officers' ratings to be alike. On the other hand, Hsu's study of crime seriousness (1973), conducted in Taiwan, suggested that culture may play an important role in the evaluations of seriousness; there was a strong gender effect on the ratings of the seriousness by college students, police officers, and judges. Third, the opinion about police and police misconduct is not uniform across communities and individuals (Robert and Stalans, 2000; Flanagan and Longmire, 1996); just as the level of corruption and the media exposure differ from community to community, public opinion, tolerance of police misconduct, and own involvement in corruption vary as well. In addition, public reaction in the same community could range from mild disapproval to a full-blown scandal, despite the substantial level of similarity in the corruption cases triggering the public attention.[7] Fourth, demographic characteristics of individual respondents and their actual experience with the police could have an impact on their opinion about the police (Flanagan and Longmire, 1996; Robert and Stalans, 2000) and possibly, the level of their tolerance of police misconduct. While age, as some of the studies suggested, might be an important factor affecting the overall opinion about the police, actual experience with the police could be an even stronger one. College students tend to be younger than the overall adult population and, although not necessarily as frequent in the official crime rates recorded by the police as their non-college counterparts, they belong to the age group among the most frequently arrested by the police (Maguire and Pastore, 1999). Furthermore, college students belong to the age group that, compared to the older generations, tends to underestimate the risks of engaging in deviant behavior[8] and, therefore, may be more likely to tolerate it. Fifth, having in mind that the characteristics of a particular community a respondent is coming from may have an impact on the respondent's tolerance of corruption, the prediction of the size and direction of differences in opinions between police officers and students is further complicated by the fact that the police officers in our sample come from 30 different police agencies and college students, probably coming from an equally large number of communities, almost surely do not come from these same 30 communities.

Consequently, since our sample of police officers over-represents police agencies of high integrity (which would probably make a stronger and realistic deterrent threat), we conjecture that, if there were some differences in their opinions, police officers would perceive the scenarios as more serious than college students would; they would also likely advocate more severe discipline as appropriate, and would be more willing to report misconduct by fellow officers. The cases in which we would expect smaller differences are the ones in which college students could envision themselves participating on the opposite side of the transaction, e.g., as bribe-givers (Case 3) or gift-givers (Cases 2 & 4).

All students surveyed attended the University of Delaware; 25.9% were freshmen; 31% were sophomores; 21.4% were juniors; and 18.7% were seniors. About half (53.1%) were criminal justice majors, but only 12.8% had plans to become police officers. There were no significant differences between the answers of the criminal justice majors and other student respondents. The university student responses to the survey are displayed in Table 5.

We chose to collect the university student sample to employ it as a rough indicator of middle-class public perceptions of police integrity. Admittedly, the sample is neither random nor representative of the age distribution of the U.S. middle class. However, both of these shortcomings are, in our opinion, outweighed by considerations of cost and convenience and the modest inference we ultimately plan to draw from the comparison.

Table 5: U.S. Police Officer and University Student Reports of OWN Seriousness, Discipline SHOULD, and OWN Willingness to Report

	Police (X_1) vs Student (X_2) OWN Seriousness				Police (X_1) vs Student (X_2) Discipline SHOULD				Police (X_1) vs Student (X_2) OWN Willingness to Report			
	X_1	X_2	X_1-X_2	t-test	X_1	X_2	X_1-X_2	t-test	X_1	X_2	X_1-X_2	t-test
Case 1- Off Duty Security System Business	1.46	1.37	0.09	2.04 - p<.05	1.34	1.47	-0.13	-2.60 - p<.05	1.37	1.34	0.03	0.64 NS**
Case 2- Free Meals, Discounts, on beat	2.60	2.05	0.55	9.65 - p<.001	2.13	1.87	0.26	5.33 - p<.001	1.94	1.50	0.44	9.05 p<.001
Case 3- Bribe from speeding Motorist	4.92	4.12	0.80	17.22 - p<.001	4.92	3.72	1.20	22.10 - <.001	4.19	3.22	0.97	14.79 p<.001
Case 4- Holiday Gifts from Merchants	2.84	1.81	1.03	17.99 - p<.001	2.53	1.53	1.00	19.67 - <.001	2.36	1.46	0.90	18.44 p<.001
Case 5- Crime Scene Theft of Watch	4.96	4.69	0.27	8.58 - p<.001	5.66	4.76	0.90	15.65 - p<.001	4.54	3.92	0.62	9.85 p<.001
Case 6- Auto Repair Shop 5% Kickback	4.50	3.34	1.16	19.32 - p<.001	4.40	3.21	1.19	17.11 - p<.001	3.95	2.90	1.05	15.04 p<.001
Case 7- Supervisor: Holiday for Tune-Up	4.18	3.10	1.08	17.40 - p<.001	3.59	2.60	0.99	14.20 - p<.001	3.45	2.55	0.90	12.75 p<.001
Case 8- Cover-Up of Pol. DUI and Accident	3.03	3.43	-0.40	-5.78 - p<.001	2.81	3.13	-0.32	-4.32 - p<.001	2.34	2.71	-0.37	-5.01 p<.001
Case 9- Drinks to Ignore Late Bar Closing	4.54	3.73	0.81	13.74 - p<.001	4.01	3.22	0.79	13.10 - p<.001	3.73	2.93	0.80	11.64 p<.001
Case 10- Excessive Force on Car Thief	4.05	3.99	0.06	0.92 NS**	3.76	3.92	-0.16	-2.11 p<.05	3.39	3.32	0.07	0.85 NS**
Case 11- Theft from Found Wallet	4.85	4.15	0.70	14.84 p<.001	5.09	3.85	1.24	19.69 p<.001	4.23	3.32	0.91	12.59 p<.001

** not significant

Comparisons Between the Police and the Student Sample

Differences in Opinions about Seriousness

With respect to perceptions of seriousness, there were statistically significant differences between police and student assessments in ten of the eleven cases (Table 5). The only scenario in which there were no significant differences in the perceptions of students and police officers (Case 10) involves the use of excessive force on a car thief following a foot pursuit. Police officers gave it a mean rating of 4.05 on a five-point seriousness scale, while university students gave it a nearly identical mean score of 3.99. An additional case, Case 1, involving a police officer who conducted an off duty security business showed a statistically significant difference, although the actual difference was not meaningful (a mean difference of .04 on the five-point scale).

In eight of the remaining cases there were significant and quite substantial differences between police officer and student opinions of seriousness. In only one instance, Case 8, in which a police officer covers up a minor accident and drunk driving by a police officer, university students rate this conduct an average of 4/10ths of a point higher than the police officers. However, on the remaining seven cases police officers rated those cases as substantially more serious than the university students did.

Differences in Opinions about Discipline

There were significant differences between student and police officer opinions on the discipline a police officer *should* and *would* receive for the behavior described in each of the eleven cases. In four cases, (Case 1 – Off Duty Security System Business; Case 2 – Free Meals and Discounts on Beat; Case 8 – Cover Up of Police DUI; and Case 10 – Excessive Force on Car Thief) the differences between the discipline police officers and students thought a police officer *should* receive were significant but not meaningful (less than a 1/3 point difference on a five-point scale.) In the remaining seven cases the discipline police officers thought police officers *should* receive was substantially greater than what the students thought appropriate.

Differences in Opinions about Willingness to Report

There were no significant differences in student and police officer estimates of their own willingness to report a police officer who ran an off-duty security business (Case 1) or who used excessive force on a car thief following a pursuit (Case 10). University students reported that they were somewhat more likely to report a police officer who covered up a police officer DUI and minor accident (Case 8). However, in the remaining eight cases university students reported that they would be substantially less willing to report the officer described in the scenario than police officers did. With one exception, Case 1 – the scenario describing a police officer who ran an off duty security system business – police officers also estimated that in all ten other scenarios other police officers would be more likely to report the misconduct described in the scenarios than did the university students we surveyed.

Conclusion: A Minimum Requirement for Police Corruption

In order to overcome the challenges associated with the empirical study of police corruption and other forms of police misconduct, we decided to measure their opposite – the level of integrity in police agencies. Consequently, with the goal of tackling the level of normative inclination to resist temptations to abuse the rights and privileges of police office, we were able to ask non-threatening questions of fact and opinion about the seriousness of violations, punishment such behavior deserves, and the willingness to report misconduct.

The questionnaire we designed was distributed to a convenience sample of 30 U.S. police agencies. We detected the differences in the environments of corruption-related integrity across the agencies and ranked these agencies in terms of our estimates of their integrity. A question addressed in this research is where would college students, whose opinion is often taken to represent the opinion expressed by the middle class, rank on our scale of integrity relative to police agencies in our sample?

Our results indicate that, with a few exceptions, the students thought that the behaviors described in the scenarios were less serious, should and would receive less discipline, and that they would be less likely to report it than the police officers who participated in the survey were. Indeed, if the same procedure used to rank the environments of integrity in the police agencies we surveyed were used to rate the university student sample, the student sample would have ranked dead last.

This finding turns the spotlight on an issue that is at the core of the problem of understanding police integrity. While popular conceptions of the nature of police corruption attribute it to the actions of morally defective police officers, our research suggests that this approach belies a fundamental misunderstanding and misconception of the problem. Corrupt police agencies need not be staffed with morally defective individuals. Our findings demonstrate that even a considerably stronger benchmark –

standards of integrity of the average, middle-class college student – is unlikely to ensure that the agency is intolerant of corruption.

One implication of this finding bears heavily on the scholars in the area of policing. In particular, scholars who have tried to understand police corruption by studying corrupt police agencies have been looking in the wrong place; instead of focusing our scholarly attention on the agencies of low integrity, we should look at what the agencies of high integrity do in order to create and maintain the police culture intolerant of corruption.

A second implication is crucial for police administrators. It is that corruption will not be effectively reduced merely by screening out those candidates who are morally defective. It is now empirically demonstrable that the police agency of integrity must either select candidates who are morally superior and/or socialize those who become police officers to new and elevated standards of integrity. Our research demonstrates that for a police agency to become corrupt, all it needs to do is nothing.

REFERENCES

Fishman, Janet E. (1978). *Measuring Police Corruption.* New York: John Jay College of Criminal Justice.

Flanagan, Timothy J. and Dennis R. Longmire. (1996). *Americans View Crime and Justice: A National Public Opinion Survey.* Thousand Oaks, CA: Sage.

Haberfeld, Maria R., Carl B. Klockars, Sanja Kutnjak Ivkovich, and Milan Pagon. (2000). "Police Officer Perceptions of the Disciplinary Consequences of Police Corruption in Croatia, Poland, Slovenia, and the United States," *Police Practice and Research, An International Journal* 41.

Hsu, Marlene. (1973). "Cultural and Sexual Differences on the Judgment of Criminal Offenses," *Journal of Criminal Law, Criminology and Police Science.*

Huon, Gail F., Beryl L. Hesketh, Mark G. Frank, Kevin M. McConkey, & G.M. McGrath. (1995). *Perceptions of Ethical Dilemmas.* Payneham, Australia: National Police Research Unit.

Kelly, Delos H. and Robert W. Winslow. (1970). "Seriousness of Delinquent Behavior: An Alternative Perspective," *British Journal of Criminology.*

Klockars, Carl B., William A. Geller, Sanja Kutnjak Ivkovich, Maria R. Haberfeld, and Aaron Uydess. (2001). Enhancing Police Integrity, *A Report to the National Institute of Justice.*

Maguire, Kathleen and Ann L. Pastore. (1999). *Sourcebook of Criminal Justice Statistics* 1998. Washington, D.C., USGPO.

Martin, Christine. (1994). *Illinois Municipal Officers' Perceptions of Police Ethics*, Chicago: Illinois Criminal Justice Information Authority.

Miller, Larry S. and Michael C. Brasswell. (1992). "Police Perceptions of Ethical Decision-Making: The Ideal vs. The Real," *American Journal of Police*.

Robert, Julian V. and Loretta J. Stalans. (2000). *Public Opinion, Crime, and Criminal Justice*. Boulder, CO: Westview Press.

Sellin, Thorsten and Marvin E. Wolfgang. (1964). *The Measurement of Delinquency*. New York: Wiley.

Sherman, Lawrence W. (1978). *Scandal and Reform*. Berkeley, CA: University of California Press.

Weisberg, Herbert F., Jon A. Krosnick, and Bruce D. Bower. (1996). *An Introduction to Survey Research, Polling, and Data Analysis*. Thousand Oaks, CA: Sage.

NOTES

[1] For a detailed discussion of the definition of integrity, see Klockars, Geller, Ivkovich, Haberfeld, and Uydess (2001).

[2] If our sample were a probabilistic sample, we could try to determine the sampling error. However, the chances of error cannot be calculated for a convenience sample such as ours (Weisberg, Krosnick, and Bower, 1996).

[3] The Spearman's correlation coefficient measuring the relationship between the response rates and the percentage of supervisors in an agency is -.087 (p>.05, n.s.), indicating no systematic bias associated with the lower response rates.

[4] The Spearman's correlation coefficient is -.139 (p>.05, n.s.), indicating no correlation between the percent of supervisors in our sample and the agency's ranking on the integrity scale.

[5] The Spearman's correlation coefficient of the integrity rankings and the response rates is -.253 (p>.05, n.s.), suggesting no significant relationship between the two variables.

[6] Sellin and Wolfgang (1964) used 286 police officers of different lengths of service, age, and diversity of experience as one of the groups of respondents in their pioneering study. They explained that the police officers were a particularly interesting group because they were perceived to belong to the lower stratum of the society based on their education, occupation, and income. At the same time, they needed to enforce legal rules which embody middle-class values. College students were used in the same study as representatives of middle-class values and of the general population. The results suggested that police officers as a group provided higher absolute scores of seriousness for the descriptions of the crimes presented to them than college students. However, Sellin and Wolfgang (1964, p. 275) concluded upon comparing the results for various groups that,

> "...although absolute numerical scores varied among rating groups, with the police scores generally higher, the inherent ratio quality of the magnitude judgments means that the numbers used by the raters are not particularly relevant and that the only fact of real importance is the ratios of offense seriousness which are preserved intact."

[7] Sherman reported that in Oakland, California (one of the four research sites) there was a "little scandal" – resulting in "a brief, shallow reaction of public disapproval – which preceded the "big scandal." However, the severity of the allegations of corruption and the event were, "serious enough to have been the subject of a 'big' scandal, but no big scandal occurred" (Sherman, 1978).

[8] The results of the 1997 National Household Survey on Drug Abuse indicated that people in the age group 18 to 25 were less likely than people in the age group 35 years and older to agree that people risk harming themselves if they smoke marijuana once a month, use cocaine ones a month, try heroin once or twice, consume four or five drinks nearly every day, or smoke one or more packs per day (Maguire and Pastore, 1999).

COMMUNITY POLICING IN CANADA: AN EVALUATION FOR MONTREAL

André Normandeau
Police Research Group, Université de Montréal

Introduction

In France and Quebec, they call the model: "Une Police de Proximité." In Spain and Latin America, the common expression is "Policia de Barrio." In Great Britain, Australia, New Zealand, Canada and the United States, the term is usually: "Community Policing." The acronym in North America is almost a pun: C.O.P./P.O.P. ("Community-Oriented Policing"/ "Problem-Oriented Policing"). However, for the public, it is simple: "the police is the police," a kind of insurance policy against violence and theft.

Community policing proposes a new philosophical, organizational and operational approach to policing. It suggests a partnership between the community and the police in "managing crime and public order" as well as developing crime prevention programs. This partnership aims at resolving problems of public security. The intellectual leader of this approach is Herman Goldstein through his seminal book on "Problem-Solving Policing" (1990). The partnership is symbolized by the image of the G-7 or G-8 (like the famous economic group of the major industrialized countries). It relates to the main following partners: police managers and officers, elected officials, the media, citizens' associations and pressure groups, business people, churches' representatives, other public services (social services, education, health, housing, work...), other justice services (courts, corrections...), and the important field of private security. The problem-solving approach is symbolized by the acronym: S.A.R.A., that is: a) scanning the problem; analysis, response and assessment (evaluation).

In the context of this article, we will not go into the details of the community policing model. The literature on the subject is quite abundant as we see in the prize-lists of the "best-sellers" of more than 30 books in the United States and 12 in Canada from 1975 to 2000 (see Table 1). The two most recent ones are those of Palmiotto (2000) for the United States and McKenna (2000) for Canada.

Table 1
List of the "Best-Sellers" on Community Policing: United States and Canada (1975-2000)

I.   The Prize-List in the United States

1.	Goldstein	1977, 1979, 1990
2.	Wilson and Kelling	1982
3.	Police Executive Research Forum	1985-2000
4.	Police Foundation	1985-2000
5.	National Institute of Justice	1985-2000
6.	National Center for Community Policing	1985-2000
7.	Skolnick and Bayley	1986, 1988
8.	Eck and Spelman	1987
9.	Greene and Mastrofski	1988
10.	Skogan	1990
11.	Sparrow, Moore and Kennedy	1990
12.	Trojanowicz and Bucqueroux/Kappeler and Gaines	1990, 1998
13.	Klockars and Mastrofski	1991
14.	Toch and Grant	1991
15.	Friedman	1992
16.	Moore	1992
17.	McElroy, Cosgrove and Sadd	1993
18.	Trojanowicz and Bucqueroux	1994, 1998
19.	Rosenbaum	1994
20.	Lurigio and Rosenbaum	1994
21.	Bayley	1994
22.	Miller and Hess	1995
23.	Kratcoski and Dukes	1995
24.	Cordner, Gaines and Kappeler	1996
25.	Fielding	1996
26.	Peak and Glensor	1996, 1999
27.	Kelling and Coles	1996
28.	Dunham and Alpert	1997
29.	Skogan and Hartnett	1997
30.	Stretcher	1997
31	Thurman and McGarrell	1997
32.	Albert and Piquero	1998
33.	Williams	1998
34.	Watson, Stone, Deluca	1998
35.	Oliver	1998, 2000
36.	Carter and Radelet	1999
37.	Glensor, Correia and Peak	2000
38.	Palmiotto	2000

II.   The Prize-List in Canada

1.	Murphy and Muir	1985
2.	Canadian Police College Journal	1987-1992
3.	Brodeur	1990, 1991
4.	Normandeau and Leighton	1990, 1991
5.	Chacko and Nancoo	1993
6.	Solicitor General of Canada	1994
7.	Seagrave	1997
8.	Brodeur	1995, 1998
9.	Chalom	1998
10.	Normandeau	1998
11.	Prévost	1999
12.	McKenna	2000

Our contribution will strictly be oriented to the assessment and evaluation of community policing in one large North American Metropolitan Area: Montreal, Province of Quebec, Canada. This empirical contribution would have pleased my mentor Marvin Wolfgang who did so many concrete empirical studies in his criminological lifetime.

Community Policing in Montreal, Quebec/Canada (1990-2000)

Montreal was founded in 1642 by French settlers, as was Canada as such in 1534 and Quebec City, the first "city" in Canada, in 1608. Nowadays, the Montreal Metropolitan Area, about 500 miles north of New York City and 50 miles north of New York State, has a population of 3.5 millions. Within the area we find the "Island of Montreal" (25 miles by 75) in the middle of the Saint Lawrence River. Half of the population of the area lives on the Island under the label: "Montreal Urban Community" (1.75 millions). Canada, as a whole, now has a population of 30.5 millions. The Province of Quebec, the second largest in Canada (out of 10 provinces), has a population of 7.5 millions. Montreal, the largest metropolitan area within the Province of Quebec, is also the second largest metropolitan area in Canada, after Toronto, Ontario (4.5 millions) but before Vancouver, British Columbia (2.0 millions). If 25% of the total Canadian population is French-speaking, within the Province of Quebec French citizens represent 85% of the population. Within the Montreal Metropolitan Area, they represent 75% and within the Montreal Urban Community the comparable figure is 70%.

Our study covers the territory of the Montreal Urban Community (1.75 millions) where one unified police department presides over public security since 1970: the "Montreal Urban Community Police Service" or, in French, since the official documents are in this language: "Service de police

de la Communauté urbaine de Montréal" (SPCUM). The community policing
model in Montreal goes by the label: "Police de Quartier" (PDQ) which
means "Neighborhood Policing". The police service has 4150 police officers
and 850 civilians, that is 5000 employees. The territory is divided in 49
districts (PDQ no. 1 to no. 49).

The Montreal police service began experimenting with the community
policing model at the beginning of the 1990's with five pilot projects in five
Neighborhoods. In 1994-95, a new police chief and a new mayor decided
that the "whole" department would go "community-oriented" and "problem-
solving-oriented" beginning in 1997. A "white paper" or task-force report
was written and publicly discussed and approved by the police top-
management and the elected officials on the board of the police department
(see Service de police de la Communauté Urbaine de Montréal, 1995, 150
pages). The year 1996 was devoted to the special training of all the
employees, police officers as well as civilians, to prepare such a major
organizational change. New police stations were built. Publicity went at large
to the public about the change. For example, an important advertisement
campaign in the media, in the subway and buses, as well as a brochure
highlighting the key components of "La police de quartier" (PDQ) which was
distributed in one million copies. In 1997 and 1998, all 49 new police
districts were opened and the "real work" began. The five main components
on which Montreal community policing is founded are the following:

Problem-solving

Policemen and women use an approach that goes beyond merely
responding to a call. Working with the community, they concentrate their
efforts on identifying and analyzing the underlying causes of problems in
order to solve them in a durable manner.

Geographical Responsibility

Led by a commander, an autonomous team of policemen and women
assumes responsibility for a given neighborhood. This new way of
functioning encourages knowledge of a neighborhood's needs and resources
as well as staff stability. Thus employees and the community get to know
each other better.

A Service Approach

Staff makes it a point of honor of satisfying citizens. They are thus committed to provide their "customers" with services that efficiently meet their needs.

Partnership with the Community

The community plays an important role in matters regarding public security. Indeed, by joining forces with neighborhood residents, institutions and community groups, the police department wishes to develop modern tools adapted to local characteristics. For the prevention of crime and disorder, for example, in each police district, there will now be created a committee of 12 citizens ("comité aviseur de citoyens") that will act as a local board, in the spirit of the administration board in private enterprises.

Staff Recognition

This approach represents a major change in the organization's structure and culture, promoting greater empowerment and staff autonomy. Moreover, staff will be given the opportunity to devise a career plan and to fully develop their potential. They thus will evolve in a stimulating and rewarding work environment.

With this major shift represented by these five components, the police department intends to rally citizens and partners to promote a feeling of security and develop a peaceful and secure quality of life in the neighborhoods. Modern in design, the new police stations facilitates closer ties with the community. It has a reception area and a community room for citizens' use.

This being said, does it work?

An Evaluation of Community Policing for Montreal: 1990-2000

In general, looking at the studies in the United States and Canada since 1990, scientific results show that "victimization" rates and "fear of crime" have dropped from 10 to 40 percent in cities which have "seriously" implemented community policing. Levels of satisfaction among citizens as well as police officers have increased by 15 to 35 percent in the same cities (Normandeau, 1998; see also Rosenbaum, 1994; Skogan and Hartnett, 1997).

As a case study, research on the impact of community policing in Montreal comes to similar conclusions. However, there is often a major gap between levels of satisfaction of front-line officers versus middle and upper managers.

Public Opinion and Community Policing

In 1990, we developed a public opinion questionnaire (about 60 items) which we used thereafter, with on-going adaptation, in the next ten years, up to 2000. The questionnaire is about victimization, fear of crime, satisfaction with regard to policing in their neighborhoods... We did the survey four times: a) in 1991 and 1995, before and after the "pilot projects"; b) in 1996, after the pilot project but before the police department-wide re-organization; c) in 1999 after the first phase of the implementation of community policing in Montreal.

We will report in this article several main highlights of our study. A book is in preparation for the analysis of the whole ten-year study (Normandeau, 2002).

Surveys 1991-1995

Tables 2, 3 and 4 compare three of the five neighborhoods where community policing pilot projects were introduced between 1991 and 1995 with three adjacent neighborhoods where traditional policing continued. These results show that two out of three neighborhoods (Tables 2 and 3) were successful in decreasing significantly victimization and fear of crime, increasing significantly citizen feeling of security and satisfaction of the police work, as well as increasing business people satisfaction. In the third comparison (table 4), which was not significant, we discovered that the pilot project was not properly implemented because of wavering local police leadership, thus contributing, in our opinion, to the near-failure of the experiment.

Table 2: Community Policing in Montreal, 1991-1995

Comparisons between Three Community Policing Pilot Neighborhood Projects and Three Adjacent Traditional Police Neighborhoods

Neighborhoods #1 (Experimental) Versus #4 (Traditional)

Indicators	Differences (± Δ) between 1991 and 1995 - Δ = diminution; + Δ = increase		
	Neighborhood #1	Neighborhood #4	Differences
I. Official Crime rates (police data)	- Δ 18%	+ Δ 5%	23%
II. Victimization crime rates (survey)	- Δ 23%	+ Δ 11%	34%
III. Feeling of security (survey)	+ Δ 40%	+ Δ 9%	31%
IV. Citizen satisfaction (survey)	+ Δ 38%	+ Δ 11%	27%
V. Business people satisfaction (survey)	+ Δ 44%	- Δ 7%	37%

Note 1:   The sample (N=) was around 100 to 125 persons for each group and in each neighborhood.
Note 2:   Statistical test: chi-square (.05) All differences are «Significant» in Table 2.

Table 3: Community Policing in Montreal, 1991-1995

Comparisons between Three Community Policing Pilot Neighborhood Projects and Three Adjacent Traditional Police Neighborhoods

Neighborhoods #2 (Experimental) Versus #5 (Traditional)

Indicators	Differences (± Δ) between 1991 and 1995 - Δ = diminution; + Δ = increase		
	Neighborhood #2	Neighborhood #5	Differences
I. Official crime rates (police data)	- Δ 14%	+ Δ 8%	22%
II. Victimization crime rates (survey)	- Δ 21%	+ Δ 10%	31%
III. Feeling of security (survey)	+ Δ 35%	+ Δ 8%	27%
IV. Citizen satisfaction (survey)	+ Δ 32%	+ Δ 2%	30%
V. Business people satisfaction (survey)	+ Δ 29%	- Δ 5%	34%

Note 1:   The sample (N=) was around 100 to 125 persons for each group and in each neighborhood.
Note 2:   Statistical test: chi-square (.05). All differences are «Significant» in Table 3.

Table 4: **Community Policing in Montreal, 1991-1995**

Comparisons between Three Community Policing Pilot Neighborhood Projects and Three Adjacent Traditional Police Neighborhoods

Neighborhoods #3 (Experimental) Versus #6 (Traditional)

Indicators	Differences (± Δ) between 1991 and 1995 - Δ = diminution; + Δ = increase		
	Neighborhood #3	Neighborhood #6	Differences
I. Official Crime rates (police data)	- Δ 2%	+ Δ 6%	8%
II. Victimization crime rates (survey)	+ Δ 5%	+ Δ 9%	4%
III. Feeling of security (survey)	+ Δ 4%	- Δ 8%	12%
IV. Citizen satisfaction (survey)	+ Δ 9%	+ Δ 2%	7%
V. Business people satisfaction (survey)	+ Δ 4%	- Δ 5%	9%

Note 1:   The sample (N=) was around 100 to 125 persons for each group and in each neighborhood.
Note 2:   Statistical test: chi-square (.05). All differences are «Non-Significant» in Table 4

Surveys 1996-1999

Tables 5, 6 and 7 report on comparisons between six other neighborhoods but this time in a "before" (1996) department-wide implementation of the community policing model with the "after" (1999) implementation. We presented three measures: a) victimization crime rates; b) citizen feeling of security; c) citizen satisfaction of the police work. The results show that victimization crime rates decreased significantly in the six neighborhoods; citizens' feeling of security increased significantly in five of the six neighborhoods; citizen satisfaction increased significantly again in five of the six neighborhoods. The Côte-des-Neiges neighborhood is the particular city district which is out-of-the-pattern. Additional in-depth interviews with citizens of the district lead us to believe that one particular homicide could explain the difference. It was a high-profile and media-attention "disgusting" (to the public) homicide in the district in 1996, known as the "Harvey's restaurant armed robbery and murder" where two of three young adult employees were strangled and killed by having their throats slit by knives and "machetes." The third one, a young adult woman, was very badly maimed and "left for dead" in her blood with her throat deeply cut. She was hospitalized for a year and will remain handicapped for the rest of her life. The case was in the news from 1996 to 1999 because the suspects were only arrested in 1998 and the trial took place only in 1999 (three young men were finally found guilty). Objectively, though, the victimization crime rate in this district was as low and had not increased more, between 1996 and 1999, than in the other five districts. The "perception" of crime and violence was thus, in our opinion, a significant factor explaining differences between this neighborhood and the other five.

Table 5: **Victimization Crime Rates in Montreal**

Percentage of the Population in Each Neighborhood Which Have Been Victimized by Crime in the Last Twelve Months

NEIGHBORHOODS	1996		1999	
	%	N	%	N
#1 Cartierville	19 %	105	12%	135
#2 Ahuntsic	15%	121	10%	141
#3 Côte-des-Neiges	23%	115	18%	140
#4 Notre-Dame-de-Grâce	25%	101	15%	149
#5 Rosemont	28%	119	15%	136
#6 Nouveau Rosemont	26%	107	16%	148

Note 1: The sample (N=) was around 100 to 150 citizens in each neighborhood.
Note 2: Statistical test: chi-square (.05). All differences are «Significant» in Table 5.

Table 6: **Citizen Feeling of Security in Montreal**

If You Were to Walk Alone in your Neighborhood at Night, How Would You Feel?

NEIGHBORHOODS	1996		1999	
	Feel secure ("quite" or "a lot")	Insecure ("quite" or "a lot")	Feel secure ("quite" or "a lot")	Insecurity ("quite" or "a lot")
#1 Cartierville	60 %	40%	72%	28%
#2 Ahuntsic	51%	49%	66%	34%
#3 Côte-des-Neiges	46%	54%	36%	64%
#4 Notre-Dame-de-Grâce	44%	56%	59%	41%
#5 Rosemont	65%	35%	78%	22%
#6 Nouveau Rosemont	71%	29%	82%	18%

Note 1: The sample (N=) was around 100 to 150 citizens in each neighborhood.
Note 2: Statistical test: chi-square (.05). All differences are «Significant» in Table 6.

Table 7: **Citizen Satisfaction of the Police Work in Montreal**

Level of Satisfaction in each Neighbourhood, with regards to the Montreal Urban Community Police Service

NEIGHBORHOODS	1996		1999	
	Satisfied ("quite" or "a lot")	Not satisfied ("quite" or "a lot")	Satisfied ("quite" or "a lot")	Not satisfied ("quite" or "a lot")
#1 Cartierville	76 %	24%	84%	16%
#2 Ahuntsic	75%	25%	83%	17%
#3 Côte-des-Neiges	68%	32%	59%	41%
#4 Notre-Dame-de-Grâce	71%	29%	81%	19%
#5 Rosemont	82%	18%	88%	12%
#6 Nouveau Rosemont	78%	22%	89%	11%

Note 1: The sample (N=) was around 100 to 150 citizens in each neighborhood.
Note 2: Statistical test: chi-square (.05). All differences are «Significant» in Table 7.

Police Officers/Civilians and Community Policing: Survey 1998

In 1998, at the end of the first phase of the implementation of community policing, the Montreal Urban Community Police Service undertook a survey of their personnel (officers and civilians). The results are presented in Table 8 around 43 issues. Exactly 2,702 subjects out of 5000 answered: 2318 police officers out of 4150, and 384 civilian employees out of 850.

This survey (1998) measured the "morale" of the personnel, the degree of adhesion by employees to the community policing model, as well as the comprehension of the role of each member. The pursued objectives were to lay a situational diagnostic and then to develop, in partnerships, the proper strategies, including the necessary adjustments. The aim was to involve each member of the organization and to bring recognition of his/her contribution to the working of community policing in Montreal.

The main findings of the personnel survey are reflected in Table 8.

Table 8: Results of the Survey of the Personnel of the Montreal Urban Community Police Service (SPCUM, 1998)

Percentage of the Personnel who agree with the statement

STATEMENTS	Police managers	Unionized police officers	Civilian managers	Unionized civilians
	N = 115	n = 2203	n = 49	n = 335
1.The prevailing mood in my unit is excellent	89.5	65.3	63.3	68.1
2. I am proud to work in the SPCUM	95.6	84.7	95.9	88.2
3. I feel supported by the SPCUM	79.8	50.8	66.7	59.9
4. I feel supported by my association or union in my job	74.1	75.3	33.3	53.4
5. I find the current changes in the SPCUM "exciting" and "justified"	80.0	33.3	89.6	55.6
6. I estimate that the SPCUM is managing conveniently the changes (in the circumstances)	63.5	39.7	63.3	48.6
7. Between what I am told to do and what I really do, it is concordant	56.5	43.0	59.6	54.4

STATEMENTS	Police managers	Unionized police officers	Civilian managers	Unionized civilians
	N = 115	n = 2203	n = 49	n = 335
8. My work is allowing me to use fully my knowledge and abilities	71.3	61.8	63.3	63.6
9. I estimate that my work is appreciated properly	56.5	56.7	59.2	64.8
10. In my unit, personnel are efficiently managed	75.2	55.0	69.4	55.6
11. I have the necessary resources to execute my work: office, computer, equipment...	53.9	28.4	69.4	69.3
12. The offices in which I work are adequate	90.4	69.9	83.7	67.3
13. Overall, I like my work at the SPCUM	92.2	84.6	91.8	88.9
14. I estimate that it is possible to have a career at the SPCUM up to my expectations	89.6	67.9	70.8	54.9
15. At the SPCUM, the employees have the will to surpass themselves	65.8	35.7	59.2	39.1
16. Community policing has changed my tasks	97.3	72.8	76.3	81.7
17. Community policing has changed my responsibilities	94.7	68.6	74.4	75.8
18. I succeed to adapt to the new ways of functioning	95.6	77.2	93.2	88.7
19. I am willing to strive for the implementation of community policing	98.2	74.1	95.6	89.2
20. At this stage of its implementation, community policing is a success	67.5	22.4	63.0	47.4
22. I have received all the necessary information to implement community policing through my work	78.8	53.5	79.5	56.5
23. I have received all the necessary training to implement community policing through my work	76.1	50.0	47.1	58.7

STATEMENTS	Police managers	Unionized police officers	Civilian managers	Unionized civilians
	N = 115	n = 2203	n = 49	n = 335
24. I have the necessary knowledge to implement community policing through my work	94.8	69.2	90.7	77.4
25. My work is more rewarding since the implementation of community policing	64.5	24.7	43.2	42.7
26. Since the implementation of community policing, there is a better collaboration between the units of the service	42.5	12.9	26.7	32.5
27. We have the necessary personnel so that community policing will work	33.0	5.9	29.3	14.7
28. I feel that I contribute a lot to the success of community policing	83.3	43.1	68.3	56.6
29. Community policing aims at increasing the quality of the services to citizens	98.3	67.0	93.9	78.6
30. Community policing allows us to offer better services to the population, tailored to their needs	86.7	41.8	85.7	65.5
31. I believe that the changes at the SPCUM are running smoothly for the citizen	83.0	47.7	93.6	65.2
32. I understand the five components of community policing - problem-solving - geographical responsibility - a service approach - partnerships - staff recognition	100.0 95.6 100.0 99.1 99.1	86.2 87.0 85.0 83.4 69.0	98.0 97.9 95.8 93.8 87.5	85.8 86.5 84.9 84.8 69.1
33. Within my activities, I apply the five components of community policing - problem-solving - geographical responsibility - a service approach - partnerships - staff recognition	96.1 87.0 100.0 97.1 97.1	68.4 70.0 79.1 62.2 57.4	97.1 87.0 100.0 84.8 89.2	77.1 63.2 85.5 73.1 69.0

STATEMENTS	Police managers	Unionized police officers	Civilian managers	Unionized civilians
	N = 115	n = 2203	n = 49	n = 335
34. The changes within my unit are coherent with those elsewhere in the SPCUM	88.0	72.8	74.4	74.9
35. I am sufficiently informed of the impact of community policing on my work, my tasks, my responsibilities	80.0	59.5	70.5	64.8
36. The lines of authority in my unit are sufficiently clear (for example: there are only a few contradictory guidelines)	78.4	65.3	60.4	58.0
37. The roles and responsibilities of each unit at the SPCUM are well defined (each unit well understands the role of other units)	28.7	36.0	29.2	34.2
38. When I must deal with other units, I know whom to contact	74.6	38.4	63.3	45.7
39. The working methods between different units at the SPCUM are coherent	33.0	30.0	25.5	38.2
40. There is sufficient cooperation between the different units to answer to the needs and priorities of internal and external "customers"	49.1	34.6	44.7	44.4
41. When it happens, problems between units are treated and resolved like it should	58.0	47.9	43.5	56.7
42. Top management develops guidelines, procedures, tools... which answer the needs of my unit	61.9	45.1	48.9	55.8
43. I know what my immediate superior expects from me at work	84.3	87.2	77.6	88.0

Source: Montreal Urban Community Police Service (SPCUM, 1998)
Note: The questionnaire was in French. This is our personal translation (A.N.)

"Zone Of Agreement" Between Police Managers, Police Officers And Civilians

On numerous important statements a strong majority of the personnel (police and civilian) share common perception, a "common vision", that is, for example:

1. "Community policing aims at increasing the quality of the service to citizens": from 63% to 90% (Q. #29).

2. "I am proud to work in the SPCUM": from 85% to 96% (Q. #2).

3. "Overall, I like my work at the SPCUM": from 85% to 92% (Q. #13).

4. "I succeed to adapt to the new ways of functioning": from 77% to 96% (Q. #18).

5. "I am willing to strive for the implementation of community policing": from 74% to 98% (Q. #19).

6. "I understand the five components of community policing": from 69% to 100% (see for each component in Q. #32).

They even share some "critical observations":

7. "We have the necessary personnel so that community policing will work": from 6% to 33% only (Q. #27).

8. "The roles and responsibilities of each unit at the SPCUM are well defined": from 29% to 36% only (Q. #37).

9. "The working methods between different units at the SPCUM are coherent": from 26% to 38% only (Q. #39).

10. "Since the implementation of community policing, there is a better collaboration between the units of the service": from 13% to 43% only (Q. #26).

In addition, even if it is positive, those who think that their work is well recognized is not that strong:

11. "I estimate that my work is appreciated properly": from 57% to 65% (Q. #9).

"Zone Of Disagreement" Between Police Managers and Police Officers

This being said, there are several highly "significant differences" between police managers and front line unionized police officers on key issues, especially with regard to "the management of change", the available "resources", the "level of success of community policing", the perception of the "service approach" to citizens as well as the "feeling" that their work is of "real value". For example:

1. "I feel supported by the SPCUM in my job": from 51% (officers) to 80% (managers) (Q. #3).

2. "I find the current changes in the SPCUM exciting and justified": from 33% (officers) to 80% (managers) (Q. #5).

3. "I estimate that the SPCUM is managing conveniently the changes (in the circumstances)": from 40% (officers) to 64% (managers) (Q. #6).

4. "I have the necessary resources to execute my work": from 28% (officers) to 54% (managers) (Q. #11).

5. "At the SPCUM, the employees have the will to surpass themselves": from 36% (officers) to 66% (managers) (Q. #15).

6. "At this stage of its implementation, community policing is a success": from 22% (officers) to 68% (managers) (Q. #20).

7. "I have received all the necessary training to implement community policing through my work": from 50% (officers) to 76% (managers) (Q. #23).

8. "My work is more rewarding since the implementation of community policing": from 25% (officers) to 65% (managers) (Q. #25).

9. "I feel that I contribute a lot to the success of community policing": from 43% (officers) to 83% (managers) (Q. #28).

Evident overall in these responses is that managers agree with the management of change (64%) and a vision of "success" (68%) for community policing while officers have very strong reserves on success (22%), on resources (28%), and on the feeling of rewarding work (25%).

Conclusion: Quality Policing at the Millennium

As the "father-figure" of community policing, Herman Goldstein, once wrote (1990, p. 3):

> "While problem-oriented policing builds on the best of the past, it is obviously much more than just a new tactic or program to be added on to prevalent forms of policing. It entails more than identifying and analyzing community problems and developing more effective responses to them. In its broadest context, it is a whole new way of thinking about policing that has implications for every aspect of the police organization, its personnel, and its operation. With an ever-present concern about the end product of policing as its central theme, it seeks to tie together the many elements involved in effecting change in the police so that these changes are coordinated and mutually supportive. It connects with the current move to redefine relationships between the police and the community. Fully implemented, it has the potential to reshape the way in which police services are delivered."

Looking at the results of our surveys, we see that the implementation will not necessarily be smooth since the visions of the public, the police managers and the police officers are sometimes quite contradictory. But, do we have really a choice? We must continue to develop the community policing model. At the outset we asked: "Does it work?" The answer is:

"Yes, community policing works"... even if it is not a new religion, not a new panacea; it is simply a tool, a better tool to reach public security in a democratic society. There will be no miracle, but if community policing passes in the next few years the test of evaluation, it will be a sign of a better insurance policy (and police) for all citizens in this new century. The label "community" policing is now a good "pretext for change." One day, however, this adjective will not be necessary: the day where police officers and citizens will have understood that, in any case, "quality policing" in a democratic country is automatically professional, problem-oriented and community-oriented. It is "public policing" at its best, it is simply "policing at the millennium."

REFERENCES

Alpert, G.P.; Piquero, A.L., editors (1998). *Community Policing: Contemporary Readings.* Illinois, Waveland Press.

Bayley, D. (1994). *Police for the Future.* New York, Oxford University Press.

Brodeur, J.P., editor (1998). *How to Recognize Good Policing.* California, Sage.

Brodeur, J.P., editor (1995). *Comparisons in Policing: An International Perspective.* Brookfield, Vermont, Ashgate.

Brodeur, J.P. (1991). Policer lapparence, *Revue canadienne de criminologie*, vol. 33, 3-4, 285-332.

Brodeur, J.P. (1990). Police et sécurité en Amérique du Nord, *Les Cahiers de la sécurité intérieure*, 1, 1, 203-240.

Canadian Police College Journal (1987-1992). Many Articles on Community Policing. Ottawa: Solicitor General of Canada. All bilingual issues.

Carter, D.; Radelet, L. (1999). *The Police and the Community.* New Jersey, Prentice-Hall. Sixth edition.

Chacko, J.; Nancoo, S., editors (1993). *Community Policing in Canada.* Toronto, Canadian Scholars' Press Inc.

Chalom, M. (1998). Le policier et le citoyen: pour une police de proximité. Montréal, Liber.

Cordner, G.; Gaines, L.; Kappeler, V. (1996). Police Operations: Analysis and Evaluation. Cincinnati, Anderson. See section V: *"Community policing and problem-solving,"* p. 365-522.

Dunham, R.G.; Alpert, G.P., editors (1997). Critical Issues in Policing. Illinois, Waveland Press. See section VI: *"Community-Based Policing"*, p. 391-503. Third edition.

Eck, J.E.; Spelman, W. (1987). Problem-Solving/Problem-Oriented Policing in Newport News. Washington, D.C., *Police Executive Research Forum* (P.E.R.F.).

Fielding, G. (1996). *Community Policing*. New York, Oxford University Press.

Forcese, D. (1999). *Policing Canadian Society*. Toronto: Prentice-Hall. Second edition.

Friedman, R. (1992). Community Policing: Comparative Perspectives and Prospects. New York, St-Martin's Press.

Glensor, R.W.; Correia, M.E.; Peak, K.J., editors (2000). *Policing Communities/Understanding Crime and Solving Problems*. Los Angeles, Roxbury.

Goldstein, H. (1990). *Problem-Oriented Policing*. New York, McGraw-Hill.

Goldstein, H. (1979). Improving Policing: A Problem-Oriented Approach, *Crime and Delinquency*, 25, 2, 236-258.

Goldstein, H. (1977). *Policing a Free Society*. Cambridge, Mass., Ballinger.

Greene, J.; Mastrofski, S, editors (1988). *Community Policing: Rhetoric of Reality*. New York, Praeger.

Griffiths, C.; Whitelaw, B.; Parent, R. (1999). *Canadian Police Work*. Toronto: Nelson.

Kelling, G.; Coles, C. (1996). *Fixing Broken Windows/Restoring Order and Reducing Crime in our Communities*. New York, Free Press.

Klockars, C.; Mastrofski, S., editors (1991). *Thinking About Police: Contemporary Readings*. New York, McGraw-Hill.

Kratcoski, P.C.; Dukes, D., editors (1995). *Issues in Community Policing*. Cincinnati, Anderson.

Laplante, L. (1991). La police et les valeurs démocratiques. Québec, IQRC.

Lurigio, A.; Rosenbaum, D., editors (1994). Community Policing. Special issue of *Crime and Delinquency*, 40, 3, 299-468.

McCormick, K.; Visano, L., editors (1992). *Understanding Policing. Toronto, Canadian Scholars' Press.*

McElroy, J.; Cosgrove, C.; Sadd, S. (1993). *Community Policing: The CPOP in New York. California*, Sage.

McKenna, P. (2000). *Foundations of Community Policing in Canada*. Toronto, Prentice-Hall.

McKenna, P. (1998). *Foundations of Policing in Canada*. Toronto, Prentice-Hall.

Miller, L.; Hess, K. (1994). *Community Policing: Theory and Pr*actice. Minneapolis/St-Paul, West.

Moore, M. (1992). Problem-Solving and Community Policing, in M. Tonry and N. Morris, editors, *Modern Policing*. Chicago, University of Chicago Press, 99-158.

Murphy, C.; Muir, G. (1985). *Community-Based Policing: A Review of the Critical Issues.* Ottawa, Solicitor General of Canada. Also in French.

National Center for Community Policing (1985-2000). Many Publications on Community Policing. University of Michigan.

National Institute of Justice/Department of Justice (1985-2000). Many Publications on Community Policing. Washington, D.C.

Normandeau, A. (2002). La police de quartier à Montréal, 1990-2000: est-ce que ça marche? Montréal, in preparation.

Normandeau, A., editor (1998). Une police professionnelle de type communautaire. Montréal: Editions du Méridien, 2 volumes.

Normandeau, A.; Leighton, B. (1990). A Vision of the Future of Policing in Canada/Police-Challenge 2000. Ottawa: Solicitor General of Canada, 2 volumes. Also in French.

Normandeau, A.; Leighton, B., editors (1991). Police and Society in Canada. Special issue of the *Canadian Journal of Criminology*, 33, 3-4, 239-585. A bilingual issue.

Oliver, W.M., editor (2000). *Community Policing/Classical Readings.* New Jersey, Prentice-Hall.

Oliver, W.M. (1998). *Community-Oriented Policing: A Systemic Approach to Policing. New Jersey*, Prentice Hall.

Palmiotto, M. (2000). *Community Policing/A Policing Strategy for the 21st Century.* Maryland, Aspen.

Peak, K.J.; Glensor, R.W. (1996). *Community Policing and Problem Solving: Strategies and Practices.* New Jersey, Prentice Hall. Second edition in 1999.

Police Executive Research Forum/P.E.R.F. (1985-2000). Many Publications on Community Policing. Washington, D.C.

Police Foundation/P.F. (1985-2000). Many Publications on Community Policing. Washington, D.C.

Prévost, L. (1999). Résolution de problèmes en milieu policier. Montréal, Modulo.

Rosenbaum, D., editor (1994). *The Challenge of Community Policing: Testing the Promises. California,* Sage.

Seagrave, J. (1997). *Introduction to Policing in Canada.* Toronto, Prentice-Hall.

Service de police de la Communauté urbaine de Montréal (1995). Vers la police de quartier. Montréal, SPCUM, 3 volumes.

Skogan, W.; Hartnett, S. (1997). *Community Policing*, Chicago Style. New York, Oxford University Press.

Skogan, W. (1990). *Disorder and Decline: Crime and the Spiral of Decay in American Neighborhoods*. New York, Free Press.

Skolnick, J.; Bayley, D. (1988). Theme and Variation in Community Policing, in M. Tonry et N. Morris, editors, *Crime and Justice: A Review of Research* (volume 10). Chicago, University of Chicago Press, 1-37.

Skolnick, J.; Bayley, D. (1986). *The New Blue Line: Police Innovation in Six American Cities*. New York, Free Press.

Solicitor General of Canada, editor (1994). *Community Policing Series*. Ottawa, Solicitor General of Canada. Also in French.

Sparrow, M.; Moore, M.; Kennedy, D. (1990). Beyond 911: *A New Era for Policing*. New York, Basic Books.

Stansfield, R. (1996). *Issues in Policing/A Canadian Perspective*. Toronto, Thompson.

Stretcher, V. (1997). *Planning Community Policing: Goal Specific Cases and Exercises*. Illinois, Waveland Press.

Thurman, Q.; McGarrell, E., editors (1997). *Community Policing in a Rural Setting*. Cincinnati, Anderson.

Toch, H.; Grant, D. (1991). *Police as Problem Solvers*. New York, Plenum.

Trojanowicz, R.; Kappeler, V.; Gaines, L.; Bucqueroux, B. (1998). *Community Policing: A Contemporary Perspective*. Cincinnati, Anderson. Second edition with new co-authors.

Trojanowicz, R.; Bucqueroux, B. (1990). *Community Policing: a Contemporary Perspective*. Cincinnati, Anderson.

Trojanowicz, R.; Bucqueroux, B. (1994). *Community Policing: How to Get Started*. Cincinnati, Anderson. Second edition in 1998.

Watson, E.M.; Stone, A.R.; De Luca, S.M. (1998). *Strategies for Community Policing*. New Jersey, Prentice-Hall.

Williams, B. (1998). *Citizen Perspectives on Community Policing/A Case Study in Athens, Georgia*. Albany, State University of New York Press.

Wilson, J.Q.; Kelling, G. (1982). *"Broken Windows: The Police and Neighborhood Safety"*, Atlantic Monthly, 249, 29-38.

THE WOLFGANG LEGACY ON THE INTERSECTION OF RACE AND THE DEATH PENALTY

Ruth-Ellen M. Grimes

Behavioral Sciences Department
California State Polytechnic University, Pomona

This paper was presented at the annual meeting of the American Society of Criminology, San Francisco, November 16, 2000.

Introduction

A persistent concern of Marvin Wolfgang's professional criminological journey was the impact of racial disparities in the criminal justice process. In his first major work Wolfgang (1958) analyzed data from police records on 588 criminal homicide cases in Philadelphia between 1948-1952. He found 73% of these 588 victims were black and 75% of the 621 offenders were black. The question then became one of why such a disproportionate number of blacks were represented in these homicide statistics, given their overall 18% representation in the general population. Detailed analysis revealed that blacks were more likely than whites to be charged with first degree homicide (blacks 20%, whites 15%) and were more likely to be convicted in all homicide cases (blacks 81%, whites 62%). This study neither focussed on nor reported on racial differentials in capital sentencing.

Wolfgang first examined disparities in capital sentencing in 1962 (Wolfgang, Kelly, and Nolde). This study considered 439 persons sentenced to death for first degree murder and placed on death row in Pennsylvania between 1914 and 1958. Three significant findings emerged from this research: type of murder, race of offender and type of counsel were all linked to race. While blacks were not disproportionately represented on death row, they were executed at significantly higher rates than white inmates. Wolfgang et al., (1962) found that black, publicly defended, felony murderers suffered the death penalty at a significantly higher proportion than whites. Conversely, whites were more likely to have their death sentences commuted to lesser penalties.

Wolfgang's continuing concern with patterns of racial discrimination would ultimately take him to the courts in an effort to bring quantitative social science data to bear directly on the problem.

Setting the Stage

Wolfgang's seminal work on rape, race, and the death penalty introduced into court evidentiary statistical data which showed a clear pattern of racial discrimination in the sentencing of convicted rapists in the U.S. South between 1945 and 1965.

In 1965 Wolfgang and Anthony Amsterdam undertook a project, under the auspices of the National Association for the Advancement of Colored People (NAACP)'s Legal Defense Fund to:

1. bring cases to the United States Supreme Court challenging imposition of the death penalty;
2. utilize social science statistical evidence; and
3. attempt to halt executions.

Data were gathered from eleven Southern states to examine the relationship between race and sentencing where rape was a capital offense. These jurisdictions were chosen because of the substantial numbers of persons actually executed for rape, compared to seven other states where capital punishment could also then be imposed for rape.

In their pioneering analysis of these data on race, rape and the death penalty, Marvin Wolfgang and Marc Riedel (1973) focussed on investigating social differentials which may have masked racial discrimination. They chose the death penalty as the vehicle for exposing specific discrimination against blacks because it had long been noted that blacks were disproportionately sentenced to death and executed in the United States. Their belief that general social differentials may not alone denote racial discrimination, defined as failure of blacks to receive due process in the administration of criminal justice, was systematically tested.

The initial finding was that a disproportionate number of blacks were sentenced to death. The authors noted however that the obvious differential sentencing by race does not in itself prove discrimination. Therefore they introduced twenty-nine nonracial variables to examine further the association between race and imposition of the death penalty. Their social, legal, and procedural variables included offender and victim characteristics, items pertaining to the nature of the defendant-victim relationship, and circumstances related to the offense and trial.

None of the over two dozen possibly aggravating nonracial factors withstood their tests of statistical significance. For example, they found that blacks were more frequently sentenced to death even when prior record, use of force, contemporaneous offense, forced entry, presence of weapon, accomplice, impregnation of the victim, or statutory rape were controlled.

The only variable that remained significant was defendant's race. In the jurisdictions studied, it was clear that the death penalty had been inflicted disproportionately on blacks without statutory or other legally accepted grounds. This led Wolfgang and Riedel to conclude that their study demonstrated a patterned, systematic and customary differential imposition of the death penalty, and that the pattern of differential justice is a product of racial discrimination.

Maxwell V. Bishop 398, F 2d 138 (1968)

Wolfgang employed these findings in 1968 in Maxwell v. Bishop 398, F 2d 138. His deposition in this case, based on his research on the relationship between race and sentencing for rape, was presented in Maxwell to support the petitioner's claim of racial discrimination.

William Maxwell was an Arkansas defendant given the death penalty for raping a white woman. On appeal Judge Harry Blackmun (U.S Ct. of Appeals 8th Circuit) reviewed statistical evidence offered by Wolfgang and denied relief primarily on the grounds that the defendant's county was not literally represented in the random sample of counties in the study; and therefore found the findings were not applicable.

Although the Wolfgang data were derived from a representative sample of nineteen counties, inclusive of more than forty-seven percent of the population of Arkansas, Judge Blackmun disallowed the arguments that Maxwell was denied due process and equal protection because he was:

1. Sentenced under statutes discriminatorily enforced against Negroes; and
2. Denied due process and equal protection of the laws because Garland County jury lists revealed race differences and were compiled from racially designated poll tax books.

The Court argued that "the statistics revealed very little about the details of the cases" where capital punishment was handed down in a black offender/white victim situation as compared with other racial situations.

The Legacy

David Baldus, George Woodworth and Charles Pulaski continued in the Wolfgang tradition when in 1980 lawyers at the NAACP Legal Defense and Educational Fund requested them to undertake an empirical study that might prove useful in the NAACP's challenge to the post-Furman application of the death penalty. Baldus and his colleagues accepted, and chose Georgia as the venue because of their finding of its prominence as a death-sentencing jurisdiction in their own Procedural Reform Study Project, and due to the high quality of the data on homicide cases that were available in that state (Baldus, Woodworth, and Pulaski, 1990: 310).

In their acknowledgments, the authors express their gratitude to Wolfgang for generously sharing data collection instruments, and to Anthony Amsterdam for providing assistance, guidance, and inspiration. The three links, Wolfgang, Amsterdam and the NAACP Legal Defense Fund, are once again all present.

McCleskey V. Kemp 107, S.Ct. 1756 (1987)

In 1982 the Legal Defense Fund used findings from the Procedural Reform Study to support requests in a number of cases for post-conviction hearings on the issue of arbitrariness and discrimination in the application of the death penalty in Georgia's post-Furman sentencing process. Only one request was granted. In Atlanta on October 8, 1982 federal district judge J. Owen Forrester ordered an evidentiary hearing on the issue in the case of Warren McCleskey, a black man who had been convicted of the murder of white police officer Frank Schlatt during the commission of a robbery.

Various constitutional claims were addressed in McCleskey's post-conviction hearing, the most relevant being the assertion that his death sentence was unconstitutional because it had been imposed on the basis of the interracial offender-victim dyad. McCleskey's petition argued that the evidence to be presented would show that Georgia had applied its capital penalty discriminatorily, which violated the Fourteenth Amendment's equal protection clause in purposefully discriminating against black defendants whose victims were white. Employing language from the Furman decision, it was further alleged that such a discriminatory application of the death penalty constituted an arbitrary, capricious, and irrational application of the death sentence and violated the Eighth Amendment of the federal Constitution.

Judge Forrester rejected McCleskey's claims, declaring that the data were not "essentially trustworthy" and did "not in substantial degree mirror reality." He held that "multi-variate analysis is ill-suited to provide the court with circumstantial evidence of the presence of discrimination, and it is incapable of providing the court with measures of qualitative difference in treatment which are necessary to a finding that a prima facie case has been established with statistical evidence" (quoted in Baldus et al., 1990: 340-341). In essence Judge Forrester held that multiple-regression analysis did not "compare identical cases." Nonetheless, he set aside McCleskey's murder conviction and death sentence and ordered a retrial.

The 11th Circuit Court of Appeals reversed Judge Forrester's granting a retrial, but agreed that neither arbitrariness nor discrimination had been demonstrated. Ironically, the Court did assume the "validity of the research" and its findings. Still, the Court found that "the statistical evidence of discrimination does not contain the level of disparity...so great as to inevitably lead to a conclusion that the disparity results from intent or motivation" (quoted in Baldus et al., 1990: 343).

The McCleskey decision was appealed (with an amici curiae brief filed by Marvin Wolfgang and others), and in a 5-4 decision the Supreme Court, affirmed the 11th Circuit's ruling. In an interesting and somewhat contradictory opinion, Justice Powell, writing for the majority, acknowledged that the "study is valid statistically" but still appeared to accept the lower court's finding that "the methodology of the study was flawed" (quoted in Baldus et al., 1990: 345).

The Court's problem was to reconcile the accepted use of statistical evidence in discrimination cases involving employment or selection of jury venires with denying the use of such evidence in capital cases. Powell's solution was simply to identify the three "limited contexts" in which the Court "has accepted statistics as proof of intent to discriminate." These include cases where the quantitative evidence of discrimination is "stark," and in employment and jury selection cases. In regard to death penalty cases, he argued that there were two dimensions of the capital sentencing process in Georgia that make death penalty cases significantly different. First, trial juries are uniquely constituted, and second, they have to consider "innumerable factors that vary from case to case" (Gross and Mauro, 1989: 174). Specifically, Powell wrote: "The application of an inference drawn from the general statistics to a specific decision in a trial and sentencing simply is not comparable to the application of an inference drawn from general statistics to a specific venire-selection or a Title VII case. In those cases, the statistics relate to fewer entities, and fewer variables are relevant to the challenged decisions" (quoted in Baldus et al., 1990: 346). In short, quantitative evidence is insufficient to demonstrate "stark" discrimination in capital sentencing. The Court's decision may therefore be interpreted as there is no common standard in individual death penalty cases.

McCleskey lost, but in-roads were made. Justices Brennan and Blackmun (Blackmun also sat on the Furman and Maxwell cases) wrote dissenting opinions, with Justices Marshall and Stevens generally concurring. Justice Brennan argued that Georgia's capital processing was characterized by racial discrimination, amply demonstrated by historical as well as statistical evidence, and was therefore in violation of the cruel and unusual clause of the Eighth Amendment. Justice Blackmun found Powell's reasoning untenable, and accepted the evidence that in McCleskey's case race had been a factor. Yet, he differed with Brennan in that he accepted the Georgia process, by limiting death eligibility to only particularly heinous cases in which no race effect could be shown.

It is of particular note to witness the transition in the life course of Justice Harry Blackmun in regard to death-sentencing. In Maxwell he clearly rejected the claim of racial discrimination based on statistical evidence. In Furman he dissented from the majority's decision to base their opinion rejecting Georgia's procedures on constitutional grounds, and indicated his own belief that the death penalty serves no legitimate penal purposes.

In his McCleskey opinion, Justice Blackmun reflected on his earlier position in Maxwell: "McCleskey's evidence . . . is of such a different level of sophistication and detail that it simply cannot be rejected on those grounds" (referring to the purported inadequacies of the statistical data offered in Maxwell), and "it is this experience, in part, that convinces me of the significance of the Baldus study" (quoted in Gross and Mauro, 1989: 164).

And finally, in 1994, in Callins v. Collins, 114 S.Ct.1127, Blackmun's epiphany is complete. The case involved the Supreme Court's rejection of a Texas inmate's appeal for a stay of execution. In ringing words he declared, in his dissent, that "the death penalty experiment has failed" and referred to the Court's delusionary belief that capital sentencing could be meted down in any constitutionally acceptable manner. He bluntly stated, "from this day forward, I no longer shall tinker with the machinery of death."

Conclusion

There has been a recent resurgence of interest in the wanton and freakish application of the death penalty in the United States. In essence, the new millennium is witnessing a call for a moratorium on capital punishment. Polls show a decrease in citizen support from 80% of the citizenry two decades ago, to percentage figures hovering in the low 60's in 2001. Illinois' Governor George Ryan ordered cessation of executions, 13 other states have pending legislation to do so, and 11 bills are floating nationwide in consideration of abolishing the death penalty (NBC Nightly News, Tuesday, May 1, 2001).

In the most recent volume of *Social Problems*, Michael Radelet calls for employment of our sociological imagination to distinguish the issue of capital punishment from an insulated vengeful response to low-lifes who commit particularly nasty murders, to a question of who we are as a nation, as a people, and as human beings. He argues that "viewing the death penalty as a battle between the forces of good versus solitary bad apples – the only viewpoint that can make executions possible – ends up dehumanizing us all." (Radelet, 2001:86).

Not only in his research but also in his teaching, Wolfgang made a special effort to underscore the prevalence of racial discrimination in the United States. He impacted students, fellow colleagues, justices, and politicians alike. He imparted his eloquent style of language to many of us. In closing, here are passages from Wolfgang and Cohen's (1970: 2-3) much used text on crime and race:

- It is obvious even to the most casual observer that some minority groups, particularly Negroes, experience a narrower range of life's alternatives, or choices, and encounter more restrictions than whites.
- When crime and color converge, the person is in double jeopardy. To the visible badge of color is added the label criminal, reinforcing attitudes of prejudice and compounding acts of discrimination.
- What is most regrettable is that many people–partly from exaggeration of a few facts, partly from a readiness to believe–strongly associate the two factors of color and crime...The effects of this mental association go far beyond a seize-and-search police policy. The private citizen clinging to a false premise is soon beset by a host of false fears and driven to hasty reprisals that damage society's efforts to integrate community life.
- If information is an aid to understanding, and if correct information leads to better understanding, then there is merit in sifting facts from flaws in the ideas associated with race and crime. To do so, we must examine the meaning of race, the meaning of crime and criminal statistics, the interpretations of that convergence, the most plausible explanations of criminal conduct among minority groups, the relations between the criminal justice system and minority groups, and the efforts needed to effect change.

The legacy has been heard.

REFERENCES

Baldus, David C., George Woodworth, Charles A. Pulaski, Jr. (1990). *Equal Justice and the Death Penalty: A Legal and Empirical Analysis.* Boston: Northeastern University Press.

Gross, Samuel R. and Robert Mauro (with a foreword by Marvin Wolfgang). (1989). *Death and Discrimination: Racial Disparities in Capital Sentencing.* Boston: Northeastern University Press.

Radelet, Michael L. (2001). "Humanizing the Death Penalty." *Social Problems* 48: 83-87.

Wolfgang, Marvin E. (1958). *Patterns in Criminal Homicide.* London: Oxford University Press.

Wolfgang, Marvin E., Arlene Kelly, and Hans C. Nolde. (1962). "Comparison of the Executed and the Commuted among Admissions to Death Row." *Journal of Criminal Law, Criminology and Police Science* 53: 301-311.

Wolfgang, Marvin E. and Bernard Cohen. (1970). *Crime and Race: Conceptions and Misconceptions.* New York: Institute of Human Relations Press.

Wolfgang, Marvin E. and Marc Riedel. (1973). "Race, Judicial Discretion, and the Death Penalty." *Annals of the American Academy of Political and Social Science* 407: 119-133.

SHOULD THE JUVENILE COURT SURVIVE?

Barry Krisberg
National Council on Crime and Delinquency

Introduction

Nearly two decades ago Marvin Wolfgang called for radical reform of the juvenile court (Wolfgang, 1982). He proposed that youths over the age of 16 years be tried in criminal courts, and that younger children be handled in family courts. He further proposed that juvenile status offenses such as truancy, running away, and incorrigibility be decriminalized. This proposal appeared in a journal designed for members of the California Bar Association. Fortunately, Dr. Wolfgang's bold proposal never received wide circulation among criminologists or national policy-makers as he later reconsidered these views, and often privately decried the fact that his research was misinterpreted to justify crackdowns on youthful offenders. As a long-time board member of the National Council on Crime and Delinquency (NCCD), Dr. Wolfgang was a strong advocate in the Council's fight against the movement to prosecute ever younger children in criminal courts.

The call to radically alter the juvenile court was based on a number of research findings, as well as Dr. Wolfgang's strong adherence to the philosophy of "just deserts" (von Hirsch, 1993). For example, Wolfgang's birth cohort research had demonstrated that a vast majority of the clientele of the juvenile justice system consisted of youths who had only one or two official contacts with the police during their teen years. A very small percentage (around 7%) tended to have extensive involvement with police and court agencies. This latter group of chronic offenders accounted for the vast majority of all arrests in his birth cohort studies. Further, the chronic offenders accounted for most of the violent offenses (Wolfgang, Figlio, and Sellin, 1972). Wolfgang's Philadelphia birth cohort study also suggested that strong court intervention with first or second time offenders did not seem to deter the continued criminal behavior of the chronic offenders.

Today, the movement to abolish the juvenile court is at full sail. Since 1992 over forty states have stiffened laws permitting more children to be tried in criminal courts, imposing mandatory incarceration for selected offenses, and reducing the protections of confidentiality for youths tried in juvenile courts (Torbet et al., 1996). Just this year, California voters overwhelmingly supported a ballot proposition that would give more discretion to prosecutors to file juvenile cases in adult courts, enhance penalties for "gang-related" offenses, diminish confidentiality, and increase penalties for very minor crimes. For instance, Proposition 21 reduced the threshold of a felony charge for property to damage of $400 or more — the cost of repairing a broken window or minor dent in a late model car.

Federal legislation that would encourage states to try more children as adults almost passed this year, but was stalled in a partisan dispute about the bill's gun control provisions. Neither Democrats nor Republicans have seriously questioned the "get tough on juvenile offenders" aspects of the federal crime bill. Media coverage has emphasized tragic shootings at several suburban high schools. The fact that juvenile violent crime rates have been declining for several years has received scant attention. The centennial celebration of the American juvenile court received little media or public policy attention. Some would argue that Dr. Wolfgang's proposal has been adopted de facto without the requisite national public policy discussion that such a radical reform should demand.

A Brief History

How did we get to this place, are the critics of the juvenile court correct, and are there alternatives to the political rush to kill the juvenile court? A brief review of the evolution of juvenile justice in this nation is instructive.

During the early part of the 19th century voluntary organizations such as the Society for the Prevention of Juvenile Delinquency advocated for the separation of juveniles from adult offenders. These Jacksonian era reformers created "houses of refuge" as special prisons for wayward youths, emphasizing education, industry and moral training (Picket,1969). These early specialized juvenile facilities were conceived of as preventive institutions, accepting destitute children, youth who had committed crimes, and children with unfit parents. Early judicial reviews of the new houses of refuge granted them virtually unrestrained powers to intervene in children's lives. The courts enunciated the doctrine of parens patriae that viewed the state as the ultimate parent of children whose parents were deemed inadequate (see for example, *Ex Parte Crouse,* 1838).

The reformers who created the houses of refuge were motivated by both religious bigotry and concerns about class conflict. A new wave of immigrants (especially Irish and Italian) seemed to these reformers to threaten the social order. Anti-Catholic bias was a strong factor in the perceived need to control these youths. African-Americans were excluded from the first houses of refuge and continued to be held in jails and adult workhouses until a decade later when several cities opened segregated juvenile facilities for these youths (Mennel, 1973).

The Jacksonian reformers defined poverty as a product of individual character flaws that included loose morals, weak family structures, illiteracy, and alcohol abuse. Houses of refuge theoretically produced a regime of work, education, and discipline through corporal punishment that might counteract some of these character flaws. Despite a strong tradition of propaganda proclaiming the successes of these early juvenile facilities, they were often places of extreme violence and brutality with frequent reports of excessive use of solitary confinement and physical abuse of the wards by their caretakers. Mennel, (1973) estimates that as many of 40 per cent of the youth ran away.

The industrial portion of the house of refuge included large workshops that produced shoes, brass nails, and caned chairs. Young women were put to work spinning cotton and doing laundry. This captive child labor was sold to private contractors. Upon release, the youths were assigned to involuntary apprenticeships as domestic workers, or in some cases, as seamen in the merchant marine. Efforts of the youth to reunite with their families were discouraged.

By the mid-nineteenth century, critics were already exposing scandals occurring in the houses of refuge. As a result, many states established state-run juvenile facilities instead of the private refuges. In 1847, Massachusetts was the first state to open a training school to confine and educate wayward youths. Massachusetts also established the precursor of contemporary probation systems, authorizing representatives of the state Board of Charities to advise the court on appropriate sanctions and to supervise youth until they appeared in court.

Despite intensified efforts to supervise the new state juvenile facilities, there were repeated instances of riots and frequent reports of staff violence against youthful inmates. Newly formed labor unions seized on the issue of the exploitation of inmate labor, citing very low wages and harsh working conditions at the training schools. Catholic groups complained that incarcerated children were denied freedom to practice their religion (Mennel, 1973). Many states conducted independent investigations of the training schools and sought alternative placements for wayward youngsters.

In Illinois, these forces culminated in the passage of the Juvenile Court Act of 1899 — the first comprehensive American child welfare legislation. Child advocates such as Jane Addams and Lucy Lathrop joined forces with powerful civic organizations, including the Chicago Bar Association and the Chicago Women's Club (Platt, 1969) to push through legislation to end the longstanding practice of housing children in the Cook County Jail. The Juvenile Court Act created a separate Illinois juvenile court authorized to deal with both dependent and delinquent youths. Juveniles who were charged with truancy, running away, curfew violations, and chronic disobedience of their parents were also under the jurisdiction of the new "children's court." The new law gave juvenile court judges broad discretion to remove children from their homes, or to monitor them in the community. The philosophy of the court emphasized rescuing children from bad families or dangerous neighborhood environments. Court processes were designed to be informal, flexible, and closed to public view. Confidentiality and privacy were stressed as methods of protecting vulnerable children, and giving them a chance at rehabilitation.

The idea of a "children's court" spread across the nation rapidly. By 1925, all but two states had enacted specialized court procedures for children. Proponents believed that they had ushered in a new era of sensitive and humane care for troubled youngsters. Others viewed the juvenile court as little more than an administrative remedy to rationalize the growing number of dispositional options created for wayward youths. The new court also sought to utilize the new knowledge technologies of the biological and social sciences to deal with its clients (Sutton, 1988). This historical period, sometimes referred to as "The Progressive Era," placed increasing faith in the emerging disciplines of science and engineering to solve social problems. The concept of a "hands-off" government was being gradually replaced with notions of a more activist State that would ameliorate some of the problems created by the marketplace.

Some early observers of the juvenile court expressed concern about its unrestrained powers. The new courts were soon overwhelmed with children and families whose needs were enormous. The goal of individualized treatment was soon abandoned in practice, with juvenile courts often devoting less than ten minutes to new case hearings (Krisberg and Austin, 1993). Youth advocates attempted to launch clinics attached to the court to provide more in-depth case studies and to fine tune the court's dispositions and treatment services. However chronic under-funding and lack of powerful political support doomed the juvenile court to inadequate legal and treatment responses for delinquent and dependent youths. For example, there was minimal support for training of juvenile court judges, and several states insisted that probation staff be unpaid volunteers. The National Council on Crime and Delinquency (NCCD) was created in 1907 to fight for standards for the court, to lobby for enactment of state laws creating paid court staff, and to establish minimum standards for the education and training of court personnel.

Establishing the children's court did not end the stories of abuse and scandal that plagued juvenile correctional facilities. However, the basic jurisprudence of the juvenile court went largely unquestioned in political, legal, and academic arenas until the mid-1960s. In the latter half of the 20th century, American society was confronted by many difficult issues, including the spread of adolescent drug use and the growing violence of urban street gangs. Clients of the juvenile court were, increasingly, impoverished youngsters whose cultural identities and experiences differed dramatically from those of most judges and court staff. Some expressed doubt about the presumed benevolence of the children's court (Tappan, 1947).

America in the early 1960s was still in the midst of an intense struggle for civil rights for its disenfranchised citizens. Many of the participants in the civil rights protests in the South were teenagers, leading to large numbers of youngsters being held in Southern jails. Race riots occurred in many large cities; urban communities were aflame. Abuses of power by law enforcement agencies received increased scrutiny from the media and the judicial system. Even more privileged adolescents expressed their dissatisfaction with the established order through drug experimentation, civil disobedience against the Viet Nam War, and the sexual revolution.

Conservatives tended to view these developments as evidence of a fundamental breakdown of morality and social order. Presidential candidates such as Barry Goldwater and, later, Richard Nixon, urged middle America, to help restore "law and order." Liberals felt that the criminal justice apparatus needed to be regulated and restrained. They emphasized the pursuit of social justice and of economic opportunity as the main solutions for the nation's struggles.

Growing doubts about the broad powers of the juvenile court led to a series of significant U.S. Supreme Court decisions that radically altered the children's court. *Kent v. United States* (383 U.S. 541, 1966) and *Breed v. Jones* (421 U.S.519, 1975) challenged the informality of decisions that transferred youths to the adult court system. Then, in the landmark decision in *In re Gault* (387 U.S. 1, 1967) the Supreme Court outlined a set of rights that must be accorded to juveniles. The *Gault* decision focused on the requirement that youths be notified of the charges against them, that defendants in the juvenile court had the right to confront witnesses, and were protected against self-incrimination. For the first time, the Supreme Court specified that juvenile court hearings must have written transcripts, an obvious predicate for appellate review of these proceedings. The *Gault* decision was rendered by the same court that extended the guarantee of legal representation to indigent persons, limited police interrogation of defendants, and expanded protections against illegal search and seizures. Many juvenile court officials warned that the new rights afforded children in the juvenile court would transform the humane and individualized court processes into a junior criminal court (Lemert, 1972).

In the late 1960s, the President's Commission on Law Enforcement and the Administration of Justice (1967) proposed programs to divert large numbers of offenders away from the juvenile court system to community-based programs. The Commission urged that the number of youths in detention centers and training schools be greatly reduced. The U.S. Senate began a long series of hearings on juvenile justice that culminated in the passage of the Juvenile Justice and Delinquency Prevention Act of 1974. This legislation provided funding for communities to separate confined juveniles from adult offenders, and remove juvenile status offenders from locked facilities. Federal funds were primarily intended to support community groups wishing to set up prevention and diversion programs. Adding emphasis to this trend, Massachusetts closed the nation's first training school, and went on to transfer nearly 1000 youths from state institutions to community-based programs (Miller, 1998).

The traditional paradigm of juvenile justice was in almost complete disarray. It was now argued that the court negatively stigmatized youngsters, and delivered second-class justice. Critics of the juvenile court urged a policy of "radical non-intervention," that is, when at all possible, do nothing (Schur, 1973). The new view of juvenile justice emphasized the value of community resources to solve family and youth problem behavior. Diversion programs were initiated at both the police and court level and community-based treatment was encouraged in lieu of institutional placements. Juveniles who were truant, violated curfew laws, ran away from home, or committed other "status offenses" were to be removed from the jurisdiction of juvenile justice system to the largest extent possible. Every effort was to be made to expand the legal protections afforded to juveniles. Federal funding priorities favored non-profit agencies rather than criminal justice agencies. The juvenile court was viewed in a new light. No longer the "helping agency," the juvenile court was now viewed with suspicion and mistrust.

Over the next ten years, the optimism of liberals waned that America's system of juvenile justice could be radically reformed. Such knowledgeable observers as Rubin (1979) suggested that the rights of juveniles around the country remained significantly compromised in large measure because of inadequate legal representation for accused youths. Others worried that diversionary programs actually "widened the net" of social control by drawing in youngsters whose minor misconduct had not previously brought them under state supervision (Austin and Krisberg, 1981; Lerman, 1975; Cohen, 1979; and Scull 1977). Some national data suggested that there was a small reduction in the number of confined juveniles during the 1970s, however the decline in incarceration had the greatest impact on white youngsters. Incarceration rates for children of color continued to rise, even during the heyday of the diversion and decarceration movement (Krisberg et al., 1987).

There were also signs that the liberal critique of juvenile justice was being trumped by more conservative advocates of reform. Even as the national juvenile justice agenda in the 1970s continued to be dominated by the ethos of diversion and deinstitutionalization, developments in the states presaged another radical shift in national thinking on juvenile justice policy. States such as New York and California enacted legislation making it easier to transfer juveniles to the adult court system. Scholars and policy makers began speculating about the need to improve methods of dealing with very dangerous young offenders (*20th Century Fund Task Force on Sentencing Policy toward Young Offenders*, 1978).

The Reagan Administration brought a decidedly punitive perspective to national juvenile justice policy. They sought to enact harsh new penalties for serious and violent juvenile offenders. Reagan officials asserted that liberal juvenile justice policies were "ideas whose vogue had run ahead of solid knowledge" (*National Advisory Committee for Juvenile Justice and Delinquency*, 1984:8). The new conservative juvenile justice reform agenda encompassed vigorous prosecution of serious juvenile offenders, new and harsher mandatory penalties, national crusades against drugs, gangs, and pornography; and a new focus on the plight of missing and exploited children (Regnery, 1986). Both the Reagan and Bush Administrations recommended the de-funding of the federal juvenile justice program, which survived due to the support of Congressional Democrats.

Shifts to the right in juvenile justice policy at the federal level mirrored changes in the states. Since 1992, nearly all states have made it easier to punish juveniles in the criminal court system, and have significantly reduced the juvenile court's ability to protect the confidentiality of its clients (Torbet, et. al., 1996). Federal and state courts also reflected a sterner attitude toward juvenile offenders. For instance in *Schall v. Martin* (467 U.S. 243 1984) the Supreme Court upheld the constitutionality of preventive detention of juveniles for their protection and to avert pretrial crimes.

During the 1990s, the juvenile court was under constant attack by critics from both the left and the right. While there was something of a renaissance of the federal Office of Juvenile Justice and Delinquency Prevention during the Clinton Administration, Congress largely supported the "get tough on juveniles" policies of the past decade. Federal juvenile crime legislation passed both the House and Senate, but was mired in debate over gun control provisions added to the bills after the tragic shootings at Columbine High School. The juvenile crime legislation is still pending. Voters across the nation continue to support ballot propositions that favor harsher treatment of juvenile offenders.

As one key indicator of this "get tough" trend, the number of persons under age 18 who were sent to state prisons grew by 118 per cent between 1985-1997. There was a corresponding growth in the number of minors placed in adult jails. This rise in incarceration continued even as rates of violent juvenile crime were declining in the mid-1990s. Exemplifying this new assault on the juvenile court, prosecutors in California and Michigan have attempted to try children as young as six and seven years old in criminal courts.

Should the Juvenile Court Survive?

Is it time to take the juvenile court off life support and to heed Dr. Wolfgang's early advice? I would argue that this would be a tragic public policy mistake that Americans would regret and for which our youngest and most vulnerable citizens would pay a terrible price.

Dr. Wolfgang raised three very important criticisms of the contemporary juvenile court. First, he noted that research on adolescent development suggested that, in general, youngsters over the age of 16 possessed the intellectual capacity to discern whether their acts were right or wrong. While this observation is correct, it should be noted that there are many areas in which American law still prohibits persons under age 18 years from exercising their free will. For example, persons under 18 may not enter into binding contracts without parental permission; they cannot join the military. The sexual behavior of persons under age 18 is often regulated by criminal laws. Most significantly, no state permits persons younger than age 18 to vote. It is hard to discern why this arguably arbitrary age threshold that applies to so many crucial aspects of the law should not be applied to the criminal law. As we noted earlier, virtually all states have created mechanisms through which younger adolescents can be transferred to the criminal courts. While it does not make absolute sense to establish an arbitrary cut off age for juvenile court jurisdiction, more relevant is the argument that some minimum standard of intellectual functioning should be applied in a criminal law system that assumes that defendant's exercise their free will. The criminal law system has struggled mightily in dealing with defendants with mental illness, developmental disabilities, language, and, even cultural differences that may inhibit their full participation in the legal process. The difficulties notwithstanding, it is still more logical to preserve a jurisprudence that concerns itself with individual differences in lieu of a legal system that pretends that such differences are irrelevant.

A second concern about the juvenile court emanates from the principles of "just deserts" and proportionality of punishment. Critics of the juvenile court have long complained that young people are often punished de facto for offenses that would be virtually ignored if committed by adults. Some have expressed concern that similar offenses will be treated very differently in the juvenile court because of its ethos of individualized justice (Feld, 1988). These observations certainly have some merit. However, the contemporary criminal law system has not fully avoided these concerns. Localized law enforcement policies have cracked down on minor law breaking in certain communities while ignoring the same behavior in other neighborhoods. The recent political popularity of the hypothesis of "broken windows" policing is a case in point. The "broken window" advocates speculate that aggressive responses to minor misconduct (e.g. arresting "Squeegee men" or graffiti scrawlers) can lead to significant improvements in public safety (Kelling, 1999). Studies have consistently documented disparities in criminal court policies that seem better explained by race, gender, age, geographic, and other non-legal variables than by legitimate legal factors (Tonry, 1994; McDonald and Carlson, 1994). Put simply, the record of the criminal law system in meting out proportionate and fair penalties is quite disappointing. The adult sentencing system is dominated by plea bargaining to such an extent that even apparently "mandatory" sentencing laws are administered with broad discretion (Miethe, 1987). Why would we suppose that moving the docket of the juvenile court over to the criminal courts would produce any net benefit in terms of the principles of "just desserts"?

Another aspect of the "just desserts" concern is that the limited upward age limit of juvenile court jurisdiction means that there is not enough time for adequate punishment of youthful offenders before they "age out" of the juvenile system. One problem with this line of reasoning is that there is no objective calculus that equates punishment time with offense severity. Interestingly, this very issue was pursued by Dr. Wolfgang in his classic research reported in *The Measurement of Delinquency* (Sellin and Wolfgang, 1964). A recent Florida case involving 12-year-old Lionel Tate illustrates this problem. After the family turned down a plea bargain that would have required Lionel to spend three years in a juvenile correctional facility, the adult court judge was forced to follow Florida's mandatory sentencing laws and send the young boy to prison for the rest of his life. In another California case, in which a 15-year-old killed or injured several high school students, the alleged offender is expected to be tried as an adult and to receive a sentence of 500 years. If this occurs, this child will be the youngest inmate in the California prison system. These two examples illustrate that the criminal sentencing system is more like a meat axe than a surgical tool. There is no consensus on how much punishment time is enough. The political imperative seems to drive all criminal sentences up to ever staggering levels. Dr. Wolfgang advocated for the principle of "just desserts" as a way to limit governmental excesses and to preserve human rights. The application of current adult sentencing patterns to delinquent children seems to be a perverse application of his thinking.

Perhaps Dr. Wolfgang's most significant concern about the juvenile court rested on his renowned cohort studies showing that most adolescents did not reoffend after one or two contacts with the police. There was, however, a small group of offenders that accounted for a very large percentage of all crimes, especially violent offenses. It has been inferred by some that these research findings prove that the juvenile court is too lenient on these hardcore offenders. This conclusion does not seem warranted (Krisberg and Jones, 1994). For example, it could be argued that the juvenile justices system's limited response to minor offenders works well for the vast majority of youths (Howell, 1997). Other studies of chronic offenders show that selective incapacitation strategies are of limited utility in stopping the crime committing patterns of chronic offenders, in fact, incarceration may exacerbate their law-breaking activities (Haapanen, 1990; Krisberg, 1997). There is a growing body of research indicating that youths sent to adult prisons have higher recidivism rates than comparable offenders handled in juvenile facilities (Bishop, et. al. 1997; Fagan, 1995; and Howell, 1997). Thus, the findings of the Wolfgang research on chronic offenders lend little or no support to the policy direction of abolishing the juvenile court.

During the early years of the juvenile court movement, renowned American philosopher George Herbert Mead articulated the theoretical quandary faced by the "children's court." Mead noted that crime control is sought through "hostile procedures of law and ... through comprehension of social and psychological conditions" (Mead, 1961:882). He understood that the juvenile court was attempting to reconcile these two approaches. "The social worker in the court is the sentimentalist, and the legalist in the social settlement, in spite of his learned doctrine, is the ignoramus (ibid)."

The juvenile justice system, at its best, represents a delicate balancing act of the demands of distributive justice with the need that interventions with troubled children be individualized and flexible. This balancing act is constantly threatened by inadequate resources given to the court, and hostile societal attitudes towards the families and children who are brought to justice.

Another famous American social thinker, Roscoe Pound, asserted that "the American juvenile court was the greatest step forward in Anglo-American law since the Magna Carta." Nonetheless, Professor Pound worried that the virtually unrestrained powers of the court could make it a "Star Chamber" (Pound, 1957). Contemporary juvenile justice reformers continue to struggle with this duality (Schwartz, 1988).

The current political climate seems quite hostile to young people and it is unlikely that more enlightened treatment of troubled adolescents will triumph in the short term. The aging of the general population means that a smaller proportion of citizens are young people themselves, or are currently parents of teenagers. The media continues to demonize the young by highlighting the most violent and sexually explicit aspects of popular music, films, and computer games. There are too few positive media portrayals of the contributions of young people to society. Sadly, too many Americans live in fear of young people, especially those with darker skins. Our children have been transformed into "super predators" by publicity-hungry academics and cynical elected officials. However, if we abandon the concept of redemptive justice that is the heart and soul of the juvenile court philosophy, we do so at our peril.

The key question we each must ask is, "What kind of justice system would we desire if our own children were arrested?" I suspect that most of us would want the values of juvenile court to be applied to our children. Why, then, should not these values apply to "other people's children"? I believe that because of his deep and lifelong commitment to social justice, Marvin Wolfgang understood this core moral issue very well. I suspect that Dr. Wolfgang would have vigorously opposed the present political frenzy to kill the "children's court."

REFERENCES

Austin, James and Barry Krisberg. (1981). "Wider, Stronger, and Different Nets: The Dialectics of Criminal Justice Reform." *Journal of Research on Crime and Delinquency*, 18:165-196.

Bishop, Donna M. and Charles Frazier, Kaduce Lonn Lanza, et. al. (1996). "The Transfer of Juveniles to Criminal Court: Does It Make a Difference?" *Crime and Delinquency*, 42(2):171-191.

Bishop, Donna and Lawrence Winner, Lonn Lanza Kaduce, et. al. (1997). "The Transfer of Juveniles to Criminal Court: Reexamining Recidivism Over the Long Term," *Crime and Delinquency*, 43(4):548-563.

Cohen, Lawrence E., James R. Kluegel. (1979). "Selecting Delinquents for Adjudication: An Analysis of Intake Screening Decision in Two Metropolitan Juvenile Courts." *Journal of Research in Crime and Delinquency*. 16 (1): 143-163.

Fagan, Jeffrey. (1995). "Separating the Men from the Boys: The Comparative Advantage of Juvenile Versus Criminal Court Sanctions on Recidivism Among Adolescent Felony Offenders," Source book: *Serious, Violent & Chronic Juvenile Offenders*, Thousand Oaks, CA: Sage Publications.

Feld, Barry C. (1988). "*The Juvenile Court Meets the Principle of Offense: Punishment, Treatment and the Difference It Makes.*" Boston University Law Review, 68(5):821-915.

Haapanen, Rudy A. (1990). Selective Incapacitation and the Serious Offender: *A Longitudinal Study of Criminal Career Patterns*, New York: Springer-Verlag

Howell, James C. (1997). *Juvenile Justice and Youth Violence*, Thousand Oaks, CA: Sage Publications.

Kelling, George. (1999). *Broken Windows and Police Discretion*, Washington, DC: United States National Institute of Justice.Krisberg, Barry and James Austin. (1993). *Reinventing Juvenile Justice*. Newbury Park, CA: Sage Publications.

Krisberg, Barry and Michael Jones. (1994). *Images and Reality: Juvenile Crime, Youth Violence and Public Policy*, San Francisco, CA: National Council on Crime and Delinquency

Krisberg, Barry and James Austin. (1981). *The Unmet Promise of Alternatives to Incarceration.* San Francisco: National Council on Crime and Delinquency.

Krisberg, Barry and Ira Schwartz, Gideon Fishman, Ziv Eisikovits, Edna Guttman, Karen Joe. (1987). "The Incarceration of Minority Youth." *Crime and Delinquency*, 33 (2):173-205.

Lemert, Edwin. (1972). *Social Action and Legal Change*. Chicago:Aldine.

Lerman, Paul. (1975). *Community Treatment and Social Control: A Critical Analysis of Juvenile Correctional Policy*. Chicago: University of Chicago Press

McDonald, D.C. and K.E. Carlson. (1994). "Why Did Racial/Ethnic Sentencing Differences in Federal District Courts Grow Larger Under the Guidelines?" *Federal Sentencing Report.*

Mead, George H. (1961). "The Psychology of Punitive Justice," *Theories of Society*, Glencoe: Free Press

Mennel, Robert M. (1973). *Thorns and Thistles: Juvenile Delinquents in the United States*, 1825-1940. Hanover, NH: University Press of New England

Miethe, T.D. (1987). "Charging and Plea Bargaining Practices Under Determinate Sentencing: An Investigation of the Hydraulic Displacement of Discretion." *Journal of Criminal Law and Criminology*, 78(1)

Miller, Jerome G. (1998). Last One Over the Wall. Columbus: Ohio State University Press

National Advisory Committee for Juvenile Justice and Delinquency Prevention. (1984). "Serious Juvenile Crime: A Redirected Federal Effort." Washington, D.C. Office of Juvenile Justice and Delinquency Prevention.

Picket, Robert S. (1969). *House of Refuge: Origins of Juvenile Reform in New York State*, 1815-1857. Syracuse: Syracuse University.

Platt, Anthony M. (1969). *The Child Savers*. Chicago and London: University of Chicago Press.

Pound, Roscoe. (1957). *Guides for Juvenile Court Judges*. New York: National Probation and Parole Association.

Regnery, Alfred S. (1986). "A Federal Perspective on Juvenile Justice Reform," *Crime and Delinquency*, 32:39-52.

Rubin, H. Ted. (1979). *Juvenile Justice: Policy, Practice and Law*. Santa Monica, CA, Goodyear Publishing.

Schur, Edwin M. (1973). *Radical Non-Intervention: Rethinking the Delinquency Problem*, Englewood Cliffs,NJ: Prentice-Hall

Schwartz, Ira. (1988). "The Jailing of Juveniles in Minnesota: A Case Study," *Crime and Delinquency*, 34(2):133-149.

Scull, Andrew T. (1977). "Social Control in Historical Perspective: From Private to Public Responses to Crime," in *Corrections and Punishment*. Beverly Hills: Sage Publications.

Sutton, John R. (1988). Stubborn *Children: Controlling Delinquency in the United States*, 1640-1981. Berkeley, CA: University of California Press

Tappan, Paul. (1947). *Delinquent Girls in Court*. New York: Columbia University Press.

Tonry, Michael. (1994). "Racial Politics, Racial Disparities, and the War on Crime*," Crime and Delinquency*, 40(4):475-494.

Torbet, Patricia, Richard Gable, Hunter Hurst, et. al. (1996). "State Responses to Serious and Violent Juvenile Crime," Washington, D.C.: Office of Juvenile Justice and Delinquency Prevention

Twentieth Century Fund Task Force on Sentencing Policy Toward Young Offenders. (1978). *Confronting Youth Crime*. New York: Holmes & Meier Publishers.

Von Hirsch, Andrew. (1993). *Censure and Sanctions*. Oxford, UK: Clarendon.

Wolfgang, Marvin. (1982). "Abolish the Juvenile Court," *California Lawyer*, November: 12-13

Wolfgang, Marvin, Robert M. Figlio, Thorsten Sellin. (1972). *Delinquency in a Birth Cohort*, Chicago: University of Chicago Press.

THE LIFE OF LIFERS: WOLFGANG'S INQUIRY INTO THE PRISON ADJUSTMENT OF HOMICIDE OFFENDERS

Hans Toch
School of Criminal Justice, University of Albany

In 1958, Marvin Wolfgang published his monumental first book, *Patterns in Criminal Homicide*. The study reported in the book focused on offenders who had been arrested for acts of homicide in Philadelphia between 1948 and 1952. Three hundred and eighty-seven of these offenders were slated for follow-up, and 44 were studied after they had spent nine years as inmates of the Eastern State Penitentiary. Almost all of the offenders in the prison were serving life sentences.

Wolfgang entitled his prison study "quantitative analysis of adjustment to the prison community." One way in which the study was quantitative was in its use of an "adjustment index" that had been invented by Wolfgang for the occasion. This index combined positive and negative indicators (measures of misbehavior and achievement) into a single score. The score was calculated as a deviation from the group mean. This procedure categorized each inmate as being better- or worse-adjusted than the group of 44.

The second connotation of quantitative in the title of the paper had to do with comparisons between the prisoners who had been thus dichotomized. Despite small numbers (there were only 17 "maladjusted" prisoners) differences appeared to emerge in line with Wolfgang's tentative expectations.

The most salient of these differences also happens to be the most interesting one, in that it is polymorphous, ubiquitous, obdurate and pervasive. No matter what measure of prison adjustment has been invoked, nor where it has been used, nor to whom it has been applied, younger prisoners invariably have been deemed to adjust less well than older prisoners. In Wolfgang's case, this observation was in fact remarkable, because he studied lifers, who tend to be the cream of prison society, and whose behavior was probably exemplary. Wolfgang was nevertheless able to conclude that "whatever other factors may be involved, there is no doubt that there is a significant association between age and prison adjustment for this particular group of offenders" (Wolfgang, 1961, p. 614). Wolfgang also noted that it is the youthful offender "who contributes most disproportionately to crime in the community and who persists in his maladjustment in the prison community" (p. 617).

Of the variables Wolfgang explored in his study, several bit the dust because they proved to be highly correlated with age. Felony murderers thus seemed to adjust less well to the prison, but almost all the inmates serving time for felony murder fell into the young age group. The same held for the prisoners who had never been married before coming to prison. Only prior imprisonment (which facilitated adjustment) proved unrelated to age.

As far as aging itself is concerned, Wolfgang contended that "more concentrated attention should be given to an analysis of the components that make up this variable" (p 617). He also recorded a roster of implications of his findings for prison management. He wrote that "perhaps encouragement of older-younger inmate relationships might function in a constructive manner to spread adjustment patterns throughout a larger portion of the inmate population (p. 618). This suggestion has been regarded by some as either silly or brave, given publicized concerns about prisons becoming "schools of crime." Prison administrators at the time, however, would have been neither shocked nor surprised by Wolfgang's suggestion, because they regarded older, long-term prisoners (and lifers, in particular) as a stabilizing force in the inmate community.

Given Wolfgang's primary concern with constructing a measure of prison adjustment and demonstrating its utility, he may have transcended his goal by concluding with a prescriptive inference. One wonders, however, whether in the same connection he considered the corollaries of his prescription. If pairing older prisoners with younger prisoners could exercise a beneficent influence on the latter, how would the pairing affect the older prisoners? And if our focus is primarily on the inception of the aging (or maturational) process, what can we say about the later stages of this process, in which a mature, "adjusted" inmate—the over-35 member of Wolfgang's cohort—faces long years in the prison? While criminology has every reason to center on criminogenic individuals, no-longer-young and no-longer criminogenic offenders who have matured out but are languishing in the system deserve a measure of criminological attention, especially in an Age of Sentencing Reforms which populates our prisons with increasing numbers of such offenders.

Aging and Other Beneficent Changes

Wolfgang's prisoner-subjects were not representative of their prison population, which we know consisted mainly of younger inmates serving shorter sentences. These prisoners would have experienced many more serious adjustment problems than Wolfgang's subjects. And since Wolfgang's subjects were prison senior citizens, relatively speaking, the fact that he was able to ratify well-trodden findings related to age and adjustment is a testimonial to the sensitivity of the criterion measure he invented. The same point relates to sentence length. We know that long-term prisoners tend to experience fewer disciplinary problems, and Wolfgang's prisoners were as long-term as they come. We also know that the problems of most prisoners are concentrated early in their prison terms, and Wolfgang's subjects had served hefty amounts of time.

The three variables (age, sentence length, and time served) are, of course, related to each other, but they are far from redundant. While young inmates consistently have high infraction rates, they also exhibit dramatic changes in misbehavior rates over time. The prison problems of young inmates decline—more or less sharply, depending on remaining time-to-serve. In contrast, the low misbehavior rate of the older prisoners (the sort of prison inmates studied by Wolfgang) is apt to remain low from admission to release. Young, short-term inmates have the highest infraction rates in prisons by a very wide margin.

But while age exercises the dominant influence, it is not the only show in town. When one computes infraction rates for age-equivalent groups at various junctures of any type of prison term, one can show that prison experience tempers misbehavior, allowing for the fact that the inmates grow older while incarcerated (Toch and Adams, 1989, pp. 18-19). Young inmates especially adapt over time, though they admittedly have appreciable room for improvement. Inmates over 25 (a ripe age in prison) show no equivalent changes when we rely on infraction rates, which almost follows from the fact that older prisoners engage in few prison violations. A more differentiated picture might emerge if we invoked a different set of criterion measures, such as program involvement and relationships with staff.

The Prison Adjustment of Long-term Inmates as a Set of Transactions

When we think of prison adjustment we must never imply that the prison—the world to which the prisoner must adjust—is a dependable constant. Prisons, and settings within prisons, vary in the challenges and opportunities they present to the prisoner. There are prisons (admittedly, few) that have a panoply of programs, while others are stultifying paragons of sterility; some prisons are tense places, and others lower-pressure; some have relaxed regimes as prisons go, and others are tightly regimented. There are prisons with extremely structured routines, and others that provide limited degrees of freedom to their inmates.

It follows that the attributes of individual prisons (and settings within prison) will vary in their compatibility or incompatibility with the needs and coping skills of individual prisoners. The pressures and challenges presented by a given prison may thus handily exceed the coping capacity of one inmate, but not of another, and where challenges or pressures overtax an inmate, his "prison adjustment" is apt to suffer. Where a prison provides only limited opportunities for an inmate to pursue his goals, the adjustment of that inmate may thus appear unimpressive, or much less impressive than it would if the inmate were fully engaged in constructive pursuits.

Many of the adjustment problems of longer-term inmates—if we could sensitively measure them—have their origin in a lack of correspondence between the needs of the inmates and the attributes of most prisons. This is dramatically the case at the inception of long prison terms—where the inmate must adjust without much support or assistance to spending most of his life in prison. A contrasting set of unaddressed problems will show up imminently preceding release—where the inmate must face a now-unfamiliar world. But prisons are most consistently unhelpful during the mid-stage of long prison careers, where inmates are offered static modules of segmented activity, with no continued opportunities for achievement and personal development. In other words, prisons are set up to provide short-term involvements for their short-term prisoners (if they provide any involvements at all), and make negligible provision for persons who must spend a good part of their lives - including their mature years - in confinement.

The "New Wave" Long-term Inmate

At present, the situation relating to the long-term prisoners is exacerbated by the response of some prison administrators to the influx of prisoners who are arriving in large numbers under draconian determinate sentences, including life without parole. These "new wave" long-term prisoners are often prejudged by these administrators to be singularly violence-prone, though no data exist to undergird such preconceptions.

Based on undocumented assumptions of dangerousness and risk, many prisoners are over-cautiously classified and placed in highest-available custody settings, which tend to be Spartan and tightly supervised. The range of inhospitable settings has even been expanded to encompass supermaximum or "maxi-maxi" prisons, which feature protracted isolation and substantially circumscribed privileges. One particularly sad indication of the consequence of such measures for the range of "prison-adjustment" is a set of symptoms, resembling serious mental illness that has begun to appear among residents of supermaximum settings. The problem is in fact consistent and prevalent enough to have been labeled the "SHU (Special Housing Unit) Syndrome" (Grassian, 1983).

In New York, where some eight percent of the prison population are locked down in confinement cells (Goord, 2000), prison administrators recognize the fact that mental health-related consequences, short of an SHU

Syndrome can occur on a substantial scale, and have responded by assigning mental health teams to segregation settings. A chaplain who has worked in New York prisons has described the effects of solitary confinement on the more youthful prisoners segregated in New York State who are liable to be disproportionately frustrated. He writes:

> "It might take a few weeks or a few months, but there was a defining moment when the most youthful prisoners in isolation units regressed into something less than human.

> 'The light went out in their eyes,' said Romano, a retired Roman Catholic prison chaplain. "They became like zombies. I'd talk to them through the food slot, and all I got back was a blank stare" (Grondahl, op cit., p. B8).

That is not to say that most long-term prisoners end up sitting in super maximum confinement cells where their sanity is compromised. But most do tend to spend decades in prison fortresses where regimes are unnecessarily stringent and program opportunities sparse. As a paradoxical fact, the prisoners who spend the most time in prisons and lead the most problem-free existence tend to experience the highest degree of deprivation and enjoy the fewest opportunities.

Of course, some recently arrived long-term prisoners (including lifers who now have no real hope of parole) can be expected to generate prison problems—especially at the inception of their terms. One reason this is the case is because many of these inmates are still young men as they begin serving their long sentences. Some are also embittered by a knowledge or perception of unfairness, given the disproportionateness of their penalties. A sense of hopelessness can diminish any incipient resolve to get constructively involved or to cooperate with staff.

The onset of long prison terms is, however, the worst juncture for long-term classification decisions. Impressions of longer-term prisoners that are formed when they enter the system are bound to be colored by their serious (mostly violent) commitment offenses, though these bear no relationship to prison behavior. This makes it hard to confirm that lifers who are not reacted to with classificatory overkill and are afforded opportunities to program are demonstrably well-behaved. Risk-tolerant classification decisions are rare in the United States, but such moderate decisions are typical for Canadian prisons, and Luciano (2000) has pointed out that

> "While incarcerated, [Canadian] lifers tend to be the most well-adjusted, co-operative offenders who maintain and even strengthen their community resources while making the most of program opportunities to address criminogenic needs, improve their educational and employment skills... The higher proportion of

lifers [subsequently] assigned lower security ratings reflects the positive adjustment and ability of lifers to utilize incarceration opportunities to lower their risk profile." (pp. 22-23).

Confrontations and Escalations

Prisoners under disproportionate sentences who arrive with a frame of mind dominated by feelings of bitterness, discouragement, disgruntlement, and hopelessness could in theory still be appeased or reconciled if they elicited empathetic responses from sensitive prison administrators. Unfortunately, an aversive cycle may unfold, with results that can be messy and counterproductive. Heavy-handed treatment premised on predictions of poor adjustment contributes to poor adjustment. Prisoners who may have entered the prison gate with concerns about the legitimacy of their sentence can now come to evolve concerns about the legitimacy of their harsh conditions of confinement.

There are unquestionably some long-term prisoners in American prisons who behave very destructively and who cause substantial problems for their keepers. But prison staff often treat such obdurate long-termers harshly for prolonged periods of time. The checkered prison careers that result raise interesting chicken-and-egg questions. Roy King (1999) has recently written that

> *"The possibility should at least be examined that the reason for the high levels of violence in American prisons may have as much to do with the way in which prisons have been managed and staffed on the cheap, and the fairness and dignity with which prisoners are treated, as it has with the qualities that criminals bring with them into prison. It is at least a plausible hypothesis that the ever more repressive response to violence - of which supermax is but the latest expression - sets up a vicious circle of intolerance which is doomed to make matters worse."* (p. 183).

The ugliest escalations occur where prisons respond to disgruntled reactions of inmates with smug and self-satisfied asperity. Such escalations are apt to reach ridiculous extremes. As example, after a Washington State prison disturbance, inmates were left without clothing, mattresses or blankets, and were deprived of hot food. After the next escalation, one of the participants reported, "They put us back with no water because we broke the faucets. We had no lights because we broke the lights. And we were naked and in shackles and on two sack lunches a day" (Vogel, 1998, p. 16). Meanwhile, in New York State, a disgruntled SHU resident who protested by throwing feces at a counselor had 15 years to life added to his prison sentence. The judge then told the prisoner, "whether one agrees with the nature of the type of maximum facility that [your prison] has become in terms of limited release of inmates, that is not a subject for this court to address…that in no manner justifies your acting out in the manner in which you have been convicted" (Judge, 1999). The disgruntled prisoner was thus relegated to lifetime confinement in the very setting that had inspired the explosion for which he stood convicted.

More circumscribed polarizations can occur on a daily basis, and may easily reach points-of-no-return. In the Washington State setting that had experienced the riot, a resident who is adjudged to stand too close to his door when a meal is served, is left hungry until his next meal arrives. The warden of the prison defended this practice in an interview, after conceding that it could sometimes be abused.

> *"[The warden] admits that an inmate may be denied a meal if he's not standing far enough from the cuff port when it's opened. "If they are not behind the line, they don't get their meal. We don't want people working there who only give the inmate a second to get to the line and walk away, but sometimes that happens. Then the inmates make a huge deal about it. If the inmate would have followed the rules, he would have gotten his meal"* (Vogel, 1998, p. 17).

Staff justifications for circumscriptions (such as "if the inmate would have followed the rules, he would have gotten his meal") are apt to ring hollow to targeted prisoners. One resident of the Washington setting indicated in a letter:

> *"Most prisoners can understand and go along with legitimate rules. It's a prison, after all."*

> *"On the other hand, what are perceived as malicious and arbitrary policies give rise to problems."* (LaRue, 2000).

In a second letter, the same prisoner wrote:

> *"Discipline needs to be maintained, and there is a way to do that in all U.S. prisons. Loss of good time, isolation, loss of minimum or medium custody, etc., etc. [But] denying people adequate showers, recreation or visits with friends goes too far and is malicious in the extreme. I feel as strongly about reading material and food supplements when you're in your cell 23 hours a day and seven days a week and there's nothing to keep you occupied."* (ibid).

The prisoner concluded in his letter that deliberately inculcating suffering must be an explicit prison policy. "Why else" he asks, "would you deny a person visits with friends if not to induce psychological torment over the loss of such visits?"

"Why else?" is a legitimate question. One could answer it by inventing bureaucratic justifications for deprivations that are arbitrarily arrived at. Such justifications are bound to sound silly because rules consist of subtle differentiations among unnecessary strictures such as allowing only two magazine subscriptions rather than one or three, five sheets of paper rather than ten or fifteen, and three showers rather than two or five. Prisons also engage in exercises of custodial overkill, such as superfluous "skin searches" followed by massive force used against the prisoners who object to being humiliated (Conover, 2000). Such insensitive practices cannot be justified to their disgruntled or injured targets.

The range of prison restrictions, rules, and rule enforcements cries out for thoughtful review and ameliorative reform. An ideal move, in an ideal world, would be to involve staff and prisoners in the process of rule revision, but this presupposes trust and goodwill, which one cannot generate in hopelessly polarized settings. De-escalation of conflict must therefore precede the exploration of constructive solutions in back-to-the-wall environments such as segregation settings.

At the moment, the opposite trend is in evidence, and prisoners' resentment is cumulating, provoking counterpart feelings (such as disdain, fear, or cynicism) among officers (Corcoran, 2000). But even in better times, constructive solutions to problems in prisons are difficult to achieve because staff relate to prisoners in quasi-parental fashion. Prison staff make rules, enforce restrictions, confer privileges and provide amenities. Prisoners follow (or fail to follow) rules, and use (or fail to use) the amenities and resources. Interactions between staff and prisoners take stereotypical forms such as, "I want, you can't have;" "I formally request, we shall take your request under consideration;" "you must do what I tell you, why should I have to?" and so forth. These interactions are of the kind that transactional analysts call Child-Parent transactions, as opposed to the sort of transactions (Adult-Adult) which are requisites for constructive problem solving (Berne, 1967).

Child-Parent transactions vary along dimensions such as permissiveness-authoritarianism, but they are invariably asymmetrical. One party gives or demands or allows, and the other plays the role of supplicant or recipient. In corrections, Child-Parent transactions often turn predictably acrimonious. Outcomes are apt to be demeaning to prisoners, even where staff makes concessions (such as relaxed rules or expanded privileges) desired by the inmates. Where prisoners gain concessions through the courts, Child-Parent transactions now occur between the courts and the prison staff, and may become demeaning to the staff.

Some of the prison staff may also feel it is demeaning to spend time on handmaiden work or "babysitting" functions such as serving food to prisoners, or delivering their mail. One way to counter such feelings can be to stage demonstrations of one's power over the lives of the inmates. One prisoner recalls:

> *"Let's say you asked for something earlier in the day, like toilet paper. They wouldn't give it to you or would wait until the end of the day. Dinner would come and you would ask, what happened to my toilet paper? And the guard would say, 'Oh, you don't want to eat?' And take your meal away."* (Vogel, 1998, p. 14).

Daniel Bergner (1998), in a book about Angola, which is Louisiana's legendary prison for inmates sentenced to life without parole, described activities by some officers at the prison who self-consciously exercised power over prisoners they adjudged to be serious offenders. He writes that

> *"The lowliest guard could tell a great number of men what to do.... And if he was put on one of the shakedown teams he could...ransack their 'houses' their locker boxes, leaving everything from rolls of toilet paper to photo albums scattered across the floor along with the upturned benches (to check for contraband stashed in screw holes) and the contents of overturned garbage cans. In fact, he <u>would</u> do this, was <u>expected</u> to leave their homes torn through, and probably couldn't help being aware that he had this control over <u>killers</u>, couldn't help feeling, as one assistant warden put it, 'that superpower,' like your chest grew six inches under that badge".* (pp. 83-84).

The problem of staff-prisoner relations is an obdurate problem, but can be ameliorated by deparentifying actions of prison staff and treating older adult prisoners in ways more appropriate to their chronological age or their level of psychological maturity. To move in this direction, staff must avoid viewing prisoners as congenital miscreants whose reluctant compliances must be forcefully compelled (creating a system of punitive Child-Parent transactions).

Maturing and Maturing Out

Recent statistics suggest that untoward incident rates in New York prisons are steadily decreasing. Administrators argue from these data that the numbers demonstrate the efficacy of segregated confinement and the incapacitation of troublemakers (Goord, 2000). Understandably, the conclusion that the data may suggest a reduced need for segregation settings is not equally emphasized. Neither is the fact that long-term sequestration must inevitably reach the point where confinees no longer pose a risk.

As American correctional populations age, the "dangerous long-term prisoner" myth becomes difficult to sustain. It strains anyone's credulity to conceive of confined arthritic old men as violence-prone. While prison administrators may not accept age 35 as the "great divide"—as Wolfgang did, and as did Sheldon and Eleanor Glueck (1937)—at some point prisoners obviously become old enough so that they must be viewed as special-need inmates rather than as high-risk ones.

To be sure, few prisoners (or other persons, for that matter) become instantaneously transmuted from ebullient youth to sedate senescence, or veer sharply from being problems to having problems. "Great divides" in most people's lives are in fact long bumpy slopes along which age-related changes occur. There may be physiological contributions to such age-related changes—the juices of life may slow and infirmities may start to impinge—but most personal development is a function of learning or maturation. And learning or maturation can be facilitated or retarded by the environment to which a person is exposed.

Where the environment in the prison consists of other youthful offenders in full flower of offending—as it does through membership in a gang engaged in drug trafficking or internecine warfare—no maturation can be expected. The same holds for a sterile existence in which the older prisoner plays checkers, watches television programs and stamps license plates for three hours a day. Under such circumstances, a "Great Divide" (admittedly a statistical artifact) would occur late in the chronological sequence.

It is, however, axiomatic that where any person is extensively exposed to a learning environment, his or her maturation can be accelerated. In prisons, learning environments can consist of all manners of constructive experiences, ranging from formal education and vocational training to association with peers who are dedicated fellow-gleaners. Key ingredients of learning environments for prisoners are prison staff who are concerned with creating learning environments. Such staff can contribute in a variety of ways to fostering maturation, by providing support and encouragement, serving as role models, and showing that they care.

Maturation, Stultification, and the Long-term Inmate

The maturation process for long-term prisoners poses special problems. What one expects is a long flat slope in that the environment offers few incentives for change. The standard recipe for long-term prison adjustment—keeping one's nose clean, doing trouble-free time, staying by oneself—is hardly a prescription for personal development. A lifer's life typically offers only a protracted stultifying and redundant existence, consisting of rigidly invariant daily routines. As one long-term prisoner explained, "the lifer at mid-life...can fill his time, but if that time is without markers the years are long and meaningless.... The mid-life lifer is trapped. He revolves on the wheels of sameness.... His future only can be seen through the wrong end of a telescope" (Healy, 1996, pp. 17, 19). Such an existence is insipid and boring, has no high points, and provides no directionality, purpose, or sense of progression. Even where program opportunities exist, there is no premium in most such programs on learning or involvement in something that matters.

The lifer is bound to sense that his life is dissipating, and is being wasted. For some, this experience is alienating. An individual who feels disowned or abandoned is apt to reciprocate by withdrawing all psychological allegiance and losing trust. At best the result is a stance of self-insulation and a sharply constricted routine (Zamble, 1992). At extremes, there emerges the caricature of the "old con," who has lost the capacity to care about anything but immediate survival issues. At the other extreme is the "angry lifer," who nurtures the rejection he feels for those who have rejected him. The angry lifer's stance is one of chip-on-the-shoulder suspiciousness and smoldering resentment. A long-term prisoner-turned-journalist, Dennie Martin, describes the chronological sequence of feelings culminating in this perspective:

> *"The first thing a convict feels when he receives an inconceivably long sentence is shock. The shock usually wears off after about two years, when all his appeals have been denied. He then enters a period of self-hatred because of what he's done to himself and his family. If he survives that emotion—and some don't—he begins to swim the rapids of rage, frustration, and alienation. When he passes through the rapids, he finds himself in the calm waters of impotence, futility, and resignation. It's not a life one can look forward to living. The future is totally devoid of hope, and people without any hope are dangerous—either to themselves or others."*
> (Martin and Sussman, 1993, p. 259).

If we imprison more convicted offenders for longer periods of time, we must consider the question of how the experiences of these prisoners can be enriched to prevent stultification or embitterment. The challenge is to think of activities that offer experiential variety and purpose, as well as providing interlocking learning experiences and opportunities for advancement.

Lifers' Clubs

An example of an intervention that can include meaningful activity is that of so-called "lifers' clubs" sponsored by some prison administrators. The term "lifers' club" is a misnomer, because it evokes images of sedate socializing by elder statesmen. The idea, in fact, is not that of a vehicle for congeniality, but of a setting in which action projects can be designed and implemented. "Club" members belong to the same club in that they share a common fate: each must deal everyday with heavy-hanging time, ostracism by society, abandonment by those in the outside world, the prospect of being psychologically institutionalized and the lack of meaningful activities. Such problems weigh heavily on lifers, but lifers are unlikely to surface these concerns or discuss them openly as a group because prisoners (in male prisons, at least) are enjoined by cultural norms to keep their feelings to themselves.

One substitute for verbalizing one's frustrations is to try to reduce them through ameliorative action. Rather than dwelling on issues of rejection and abandonment, one can seek ways of establishing contact with persons outside the prison. Rather than complaining about being bored, one can devise projects that are time-consuming, interesting, and meaningful. Rather than wallowing in the purposelessness of one's existence, one can find ways of being useful and deploying one's capabilities.

Lifers' clubs can serve such purposes, and their efficacy can be enhanced through supportive staff sponsorship. Designating a lifers' group as a "club" makes it appropriate to pair the group with a staff (faculty) advisor, who can serve to legitimize, facilitate, and coordinate its activities. The staff advisor can serve as a liaison between the inmates and the warden or prison administration, and as a link with civilians who may want to work with the inmates, or who may benefit from the inmates' activities.

Lifer projects may vary in kind, but the delivery of services that have social utility is especially important. For one, being useful is a respite from uselessness. Projects that are useful can also provide a means for the inmates to atone for past transgressions. The link is direct where projects have targets (such as predelinquent youths) that are expected to profit from the prisoners' sadder-but-wiser experience. Didactic crime-centered projects have thus become popular as interventions for lifers. Revealingly, the subtitle of a book about one such project (the New Jersey Juvenile Awareness project) reads, "Learn the Truth at the Expense of Our Sorrow" (Wormser, 1991).

The sorrow at issue in New Jersey would include both the offenders' transgressions and their consequences. The lifers running the project had indicated that "we are using ourselves as examples to prove the fact of what crime and its involvement is really about" (Finckenauer and Gavin, 1999, p. 21). They had written that "we are far from being experts on life and its problems, but we do feel that our prison experiences put in the proper perspective just might turn a young person away from crime and the following in our poor footsteps" (Ibid., p. 22).

In a delinquency-prevention project the offender makes amends by serving as a negative role model. He presents himself, and the prison, as something to be avoided. He tells the consumers of his message, "if you don't watch it, there, but by the grace of God, go you—and as you see, I am not what you wish to become." The prisoner can then contend—as did the participants in the New Jersey project—that if a single delinquent can be deflected from a criminal career, the lifers' lives gain a measure of redeeming value.

There are obviously many other ways of making contributions to the community that have redemptive benefits for prisoners. Many disadvantaged groups—sick children, handicapped persons, the infirm and elderly—can gratefully use products or services that originate in the prison. While such products and services assist persons in need, they provide satisfaction to the prisoners who supply the products and services, and can take pride in their accomplishment (Toch, 2000).

In-house Prison Careers

I have asked the question, Should lifers (and other long-term prisoners) have in-house careers in the prison? (Flanagan, 1995; Toch, 1997). This question has struck some as ludicrous, given the dictionary definition of a career as "a profession for which one trains, and which is undertaken as a permanent calling." Being a prisoner is not regarded as a profession, and lifers are not trained to be lifers, though most may end up with a "permanent calling." But there does exist an arguably applicable second definition, which asserts that a career is "a field for or pursuit of consecutive progressive achievement."

In civilian life we have a general expectation that over the course of our lives we can improve our lot and enhance our standing in the world. We expect to increase our knowledge and perfect our skills, and to demonstrate enhanced competence in our chosen endeavors. We expect to be promoted at work, at minimum because we have put in time and accumulated seniority.

Short-term incarceration may be regarded as a time-out period from a civilian career. At worst, it is dead time or wasted time, though it can be used by the inmate for self-improvement. Long-term incarceration is life. It is a counterpart of the civilian life foreclosed to the prisoners. The long-term inmate lives in prison as opposed to spending time in the prison. Prison is the substitute for the free-world career the prisoner is unable to pursue.

By law, imprisonment is deprivation of freedom. But there is no open-ended invitation to deprive the prisoner of every attribute of normal life, and this includes "consecutive progressive achievement," which is the hallmark of a normal career. Nor is the deprivation of career-attributes a matter of correctional policy. Rather, it is a by-product of the way prisons have traditionally approached programming, one step – or education module – at a time. As Flanagan (1995) has pointed out:

> "The correctional "experience" in most state prison systems was designed with rapid turnover of short-term inmates in mind. For example, vocational and educational programs in prisons are designed to cycle inmates through in periods of 12 to 36 months. Except for sequential secondary and postsecondary educational programs, few efforts are planned to involve inmates in a sustained effort of learning and growth over many years. Hypothetically, a long-term inmate could select from these training programs cafeteria-style, and emerge from the sentence an odd sort of 'Renaissance Man' with certificates in plumbing, computer programming, small engine repairs, and an A.S. degree in sociology." (p. 235).

Where prisoners have access to educational opportunities, I can conceive of no reason why such opportunities cannot involve progressive attainments for bright or talented prisoners. There is also no reason why vocational training cannot continue to enhance the competence of prisoners who have the requisite skills and interests. The remaining question is whether one can provide long-term prisoners with increasing opportunity to apply knowledge and exercise skills, to expand the range of contributions they can make, and to receive commensurate increments in status, responsibility and recognition.

This question has been eloquently examined in a report released in 1998 by the Task Force on Long-Term Offenders of the Correctional Service of Canada. Grant and Johnson (2000) note that "the Report ... points out that offenders with long sentences could serve as a resource for institutions. Given their long period of confinement, they can be trained to provide services within the prison to make their periods of incarceration more meaningful and productive" (p. 25). The report in fact proposed the development and training of long-term offenders as "in-reach workers" to do reintegrative social service work, and envisaged such workers as becoming involved in "correctional careers." A summary of the Report (Task Force, 2000) points out that

> "The Task Force looked at ways to achieve better sentence planning and make more constructive use of time for all incarcerated long-term offenders. The concept of long-term

> *offenders participating in correctional careers offered a constructive alternative to allowing offenders to possibly drift within the system for ten or fifteen years before they become the focus of real attention immediately prior to their release. These offenders could support and assist staff in the conduct of their correctional work while at the same time contribute significantly to their own personal growth. They should have the opportunity to acquire and practice the skills to contribute to society while incarcerated."* (p. 5).

The model is not revolutionary nor difficult to implement. At issue is the sort of case management or classification process that would sequence learning opportunities and jobs for the prisoners. Career ladders for the prisoners could be created to provide for individualized stages of development and progressive attainment. Such stages could be congruent with a more or less rapid maturation process as it unfolds over time, would facilitate this process and capitalize on it.

The model bears on the notion of prison adjustment as it was gauged by Wolfgang in his study. Prison adjustment could be seen as an ongoing, dynamic process. Aging is part of that process, and it is the individual's contribution to the person-environment (or prisoner-prison) transaction.

Wolfgang Revisited

As I have noted, Marvin Wolfgang wrote in his paper that "more concentrated attention should be given to an analysis of the components that make up [the aging] variable." Others—including Hirschi and Gottfredson (1989)—have expressed similar sentiments. I would have myself rephrased the assertion as reading "more concentrated attention should be given to an analysis of the components of the maturation-in-relation-to-environmental opportunities variable." Nothing less comprehensive would be fair when applied to prisoners of the kind studied by Wolfgang—men who had spent at least nine long years in a somewhat benign but immensely stultifying environment. In this setting, the men had arguably matured, but they had hardly had a chance to blossom. Most of the group had occupied prison assignments for hefty periods of time; others had not. Some of the prisoners were favorably described by correctional officers; others less favorably. Some of the inmates had lost prison jobs, and others had retained them.

Such entries categorized by Wolfgang portray limited achievements, given limited opportunities. The results of the study could probably have been more encouraging in a more progressive prison, under more decent and more enriched conditions. Results would be less encouraging under conditions such as those that tend to prevail in American corrections today.

The picture of prison adjustment generally is a picture of wasted opportunity. Prisons are total or total-control environments. This means that one can arrange many environmental conditions in prison. One could in theory create conditions under which younger prisoners are more apt to mature and mature out of crime. Instead, prisons reliably reinforce youthful immaturity by playing cop-and-robber games that challenge the prisoners to defy prison rules so that security measures can be escalated. As for older inmates, prisons are hypothetically in a position to reinforce incipient maturation instead of consistently promoting stultification. Prisons could create varied opportunities for mature long-term inmates to contribute to the world, and to reach as much of their potential as is possible in confinement.

An index of a prisoner's adjustment in the best of possible prisons could be his level of creativity, productivity, and efficacy. A measure of the inmate's adjustment in the worst of possible prisons (such as our supermaximum prisons) could be his resilience under stressful circumstances. In each case, the best measures of behavior would depend on the type of challenges and opportunities afforded by the setting in which the prisoners were imprisoned.

The most prevalent measure of adjustment in prison research is the rate of disciplinary infractions. This is the measure of most interest to the prison, and the most easily available to researchers. Indices of positive adjustment are by contrast hard to come by. Such measures were also hard to come by in Wolfgang's day, though he did his ingenious best.

Rates of prison infraction are irrelevant in studying the lives of most lifers, who commit few, if any infractions. We would have to exercise ingenuity to find meaningful and relevant indexes of positive achievement. Today, we might unfortunately have to settle for measures of make-dos and get-bys that make up a compromise existence. For another set of measures, we could nowadays gauge evolving levels of suspiciousness and self-insulation and the frequency of situational depression. To make sense of these data we would need to describe then the custodial regimes to which the prisoners were subjected. We would need to reconstruct the prison settings as the prisoners experienced them, so as to define the context for their adjustment behaviors.

The enterprise might yield numbers, I suppose, as research projects do. It might even qualify as a "quantitative analysis of adjustment." (It might do so, for example, by comparing what different inmates achieve—or fail to achieve—in comparable settings). But what is unlikely to emerge is an all-purpose prison adjustment scoring system of the kind envisaged by Wolfgang—and I guess that is what we mean by progress, or prison adjustment of researchers.

REFERENCES

Bergner, D. (1988). *God of the Rodeo: The Quest for Redemption in Louisiana's Angola Prison*. New York: Ballantine Books.

Berne, E. (1967). *Games People Play*. New York: Grove Press.

Conover, T. (2000). "Guarding Sing Sing." *The New Yorker*, April 3.

Finckenauer, J.O. and Gavin, P.W. (1999). *Scared Straight: The Panacea Phenomenon Revisited*. Prospect Heights, IL: Waveland Press.

Flanagan, T.J. (1995). "Sentence planning for long-term inmates." In Flanagan, T.J. (ed.) *Long-term Imprisonment: Policy, Science and Correction Practice*. Thousand Oaks, CA: Sage Publications.

Glueck, S. and Glueck, E.T. (1937). *Later Criminal Careers*. New York: Commonwealth Fund.

Goord, G. S. (2000). *Commissioner's Policy Paper on Prison Safety and Inmate Programming*. Albany, NY: Department of Correctional Services (November).

Grant, B. A. and Johnson, S. L. (2000). "Women offenders serving long sentences in custody." *Forum on Correctional Research*, 12(3), 25-27.

Grassian, S. (1983). "Psychopathological effects of solitary confinement." *American Journal of Psychiatry*, *140*(11), 1450-1455.

Healy, B. (1996). "The time of his life." *Prison Writing*, *9*, 16-19.

Hirschi, T. and Gottfredson, M.R. (1983). "Age and explanation of crime." *American Journal of Sociology*, *89*, 552-584.

King, R.D. (1999). "The rise and rise of supermax: An American solution in search of a problem?" *Punishment and Society*, 1, 163-186.

LaRue, M. (2000). Personal communication.

Luciano, F. P. (2000). "Classifying offenders serving life sentences." *Forum on Correctional Research*, 12(3), 21-24.

Martin, D.M. and Sussman, P.Y. (1993). *Committing Journalism: The Prison Writings of Red Hogg*. New York: W.W. Norton & Company.

"Task Force on Long-term Offenders: A Summary" (2000) *Forum on Correctional Research*, 12(3), 3-5.

Toch, H. (1977). "The long-term inmate on a long-term problem" in *Proceedings: International Seminar on the Effects of Long-term Imprisonment*. Montreal: University of Montreal.

Toch, H. (1997). *Corrections: A Humanistic Approach*. Guilderland, NY: Harrow and Heston.

Toch, H. (2000). "Altruistic activity as correctional treatment." *International Journal of Offender Therapy and Comparative Criminology*, 44, 270-278.

Toch, H. and Adams, K. (1989). *Coping: Maladaptation in Prisons*. New Brunswick, NJ: Transaction Publishers.

Vogel, J. (1998). "Behind closed doors." *Seattle Weekly*, *23*, April 23, 7-17.

Wolfgang, M.E. (1961). "Quantitative analysis of adjustment to the prison community." *Journal of Criminal Law, Criminology and Police Science*, *51*, 607-618.

Wormser, R. (1991). *Lifers: Learn the Truth at the Expense of Our Sorrow*. Englewood Cliffs, NJ: Julian Messner.

Zamble, E. (1992). "Behavior and adaptation in long-term prison inmates: Descriptive longitudinal results." *Criminal Justice and Behavior*, *18*(4), 409-525.

TRUTH IN SENTENCING AND PRISON INFRACTIONS

James J. Collins, Donna L. Spencer, George H. Dunteman, Peter H. Siegel
Research Triangle Institute, Research Triangle Park, North Carolina

This chapter is based partially on work supported by the National Institute of Justice under Grant No. 96-CE-VX-0013. Points of view are those of the authors and do not necessarily represent the position of the National Institute of Justice. We would like to thank Kenneth Parker and Thomas Sutton at the North Carolina Department of Correction and Richard Straw at the Research Triangle Institute for their word-processing and editorial support.

Truth in Sentencing and Prison Infractions

Marvin E. Wolfgang was at the cutting edge of the major criminological issues of the day over his entire career. In 1961, he published an article titled "Quantitative Analysis of Adjustment to the Prison Community" (Wolfgang, 1961). The research reported in the article followed a sample of the homicide offenders he studied in his seminal *Patterns in Criminal Homicide* during their imprisonment (Wolfgang, 1958). During the period from the mid-1950s to the mid-1960s, the study of prison organization and culture, and the responses of inmates to prison, were major foci for criminologists. Major criminological thinkers of the time, such as Richard Cloward, Donald Cressey, Lloyd McCorkle, Lloyd Ohlin, Gresham Sykes, and Stanton Wheeler, were studying American prisons and inmates' responses to prison. Characteristically, Marvin Wolfgang focused his attention on the topic as well and brought a quantitative research perspective to bear on it. His 1961 article is a quantitative study of the correlates of adjustment to prison that broke new conceptual and empirical ground in its development of a multidimensional prison adjustment index. Specific findings are discussed below.

Criminological interest in prisons waned after the 1960s. From the late 1960s to the new millennium, the study of prisons as social organizations, and the impact of prisons on their inhabitants, has been infrequent. But at the close of the 20th century, after years of increasing incarceration rates, and with the number of individuals incarcerated in the United States having exceeded 2 million, the topic deserves a more prominent place on the criminological agenda. Important questions about the use and effects of incarceration need to be addressed. Millions of lives are affected by U.S. correctional policies and practices, and billions of dollars are spent each year to build, maintain, and operate prisons.

The study reported in this chapter examined an important aspect of incarceration—the impact of sentencing policies on inmates' prison adjustment as reflected by their violation of prison rules. The study used a quantitative methodology to generate findings and insights in the spirit of Marvin Wolfgang. The research was supported by a grant from the National Institute of Justice (NIJ) and examined the impact of North Carolina's 1994 structured sentencing law on the adjudication of cases and on the involvement of inmates in prison rule violations. This chapter describes the findings for the rule violations aspect of the study. Full study results are reported in a final report to the NIJ (Collins et al., 1999).

Background

Major sentencing reforms have occurred in the United States since the mid-1970s. The Federal system has changed, and virtually every State has modified its sentencing laws and practices. The reforms are grounded in a number of factors that were a source of dissatisfaction with the largely indeterminate form of sentencing that had characterized U.S. sentencing practices after World War II (Blumstein et al., 1983; Wicharaya, 1995). Many thought that judicial sentencing discretion was excessive under the indeterminate sentencing model, and the wide discretion resulted in substantial sentencing disparities for individuals convicted of similar offenses. A change in correctional philosophy from an emphasis on rehabilitation (which is consistent with an indeterminate sentencing approach) to one emphasizing punishment and "just deserts" also helped to push sentencing reforms in the direction of determinate sentencing.

The idea of "truth in sentencing" also became an influential idea in the development of sentencing reforms. Typically, individuals sentenced to prison would serve less than half of their sentence due to credits they received for adhering to prison rules, for participating in educational or other programs, and as a result of parole decisions. Truth in sentencing legislative and policy changes attempted to make the sentence given to individuals and the time they actually served more commensurate with each other. Specific changes to accomplish this goal were sharp reductions in the sentencing reduction credits that inmates can earn and the elimination of parole. North Carolina's new sentencing law included the major sentencing features discussed above: (a) reduced sentencing discretion reflected in a more determinate model, (b) the elimination of "good" and "gain" time that prison inmates could earn to reduce the length of time served, and (c) the elimination of parole (North Carolina Sentencing and Policy Advisory Commission, 1996a). The law had the desired effect of bringing incarceration sentences and actual time served into much closer alignment (North Carolina Sentencing and Policy Advisory Commission, 1996b).

There has been concern that the elimination or reduction of inmates' opportunities to reduce the amount of time they remain incarcerated through good and gain time and parole might also reduce incentives for them to abide by institutional rules while incarcerated and to participate in educational and treatment programs. This expectation is logical, and there is anecdotal and quantitative empirical evidence from North Carolina's correctional officials and correctional records that structured sentencing may be having these negative effects (Memory et al., 1998). Managing the behavior of prison inmates is a challenge under the best of conditions, so any reduction in incentives for inmates to follow the rules could result in the deterioration of institutional order and safety. To the extent that additional infractions involve attacks against correctional personnel and other inmates, the dangerousness of the prison environment is increased. And even nonviolent infractions have the potential to diminish the stability and orderliness of the prison environment, raise levels of stress for staff and inmates, and increase the costs of operating prisons. Wooldredge (1991) noted that institutional disorder also could hinder the success of treatment programs.

Wolfgang's and Others' Findings

Wolfgang (1961) examined the prison adjustment of 44 homicide offenders serving life sentences in Eastern State Penitentiary in Philadelphia in the 1950s. The inmates were first identified as offenders who committed homicide in Philadelphia between 1948 and 1952 in Wolfgang's (1958) *Patterns in Criminal Homicide* study. Wolfgang used prison records to create an index of adjustment to prison that included the following factors:

- the number of prison jobs held, and the length of time the jobs were held;
- the number of times discharged from a prison job for misconduct; and
- the number of "bad" statements recorded against inmates by cell block guards.

Wolfgang found that the following factors were related to positive adjustment: being aged 35 or older, being currently or previously married, having been incarcerated previously, and having been convicted of non-felony murder. Inmates who were younger, never married, convicted of felony murder, and had no previous penal experience were less well adjusted on the scale. No relationship was found between race, intelligence, and length of time incarcerated.

The modest body of empirical literature on inmate involvement in infractions is largely consistent with Wolfgang's age finding; younger inmates are more likely to violate prison rules (Brown and Spevacek, 1971; Craddock, 1996; Ekland-Olson, Barrick, and Cohen, 1983; Ellis, 1984; Flanagan, 1983; Goetting and Howsen, 1986; Mackenzie, 1987). Wolfgang's finding for race was also consistent in that race is sometimes found to be related to infractions and sometimes not (Craddock, 1996; Ellis, Grasmick, and Gilman, 1974; Wright, 1989). Poole and Regoli (1980) reported that whites and blacks did not differ in their self-reported involvement in infractions, but blacks were more likely to be charged when they committed an infraction. Inconsistent relationships have also been found between education, marital status, a record of previous incarceration, and length of time served (Craddock, 1996; Ellis et al., 1974; Goetting and Howsen, 1986; Wooldredge, 1991).

Structured Sentencing and Prison Infractions in North Carolina

For the study, we selected inmates who entered North Carolina prisons between June 1, 1995, and January 31, 1998. Those entering prison during this period were sentenced under both fair sentencing (the old law) and under structured sentencing (the new law). North Carolina's Department of Correction extracted information from their records for inmates meeting selection criteria and provided these records in electronic format for analysis.

Method

The major purpose of the study described here was to determine whether there were differences in the commission of institutional infractions between inmates sentenced to North Carolina prisons under the fair and structured sentencing laws. We used statistical techniques to compare inmates sentenced under the two laws and included in the analysis a number of variables known or thought to be relevant to the commission of institutional infractions to control for possible differences between the fair- and structured-sentenced inmates.

Some categories of inmates were excluded from the analyses:

- those serving "mixed" sentences (i.e., those whose sentences were subject to both structured and fair sentencing provisions);

- inmates serving life sentences (because we thought that the very long length of sentence might affect inmate's propensity to commit infractions);
- inmates serving time for driving while impaired (DWI), which was not covered by the new law; and
- inmates serving sentences with special conditions that might affect their incentive to follow institutional rules.

These categories of inmates were excluded from the analyses because their inclusion would have compromised our capacity to draw inferences about the impact of structured sentencing.

Analytic Techniques

Besides the total number of infractions that occurred during the time an inmate was incarcerated, there were five specific infraction categories for which counts were available: assault, drug/alcohol, profanity/disobedience, work absence, and money/property offenses. Models were estimated separately for males and females. Because counts (i.e., the number of times an event occurred in a given time interval) would be expected to have a Poisson distribution, we used Poisson regression to conduct the analysis.

Inmate infractions were observed for varying lengths of time, so we controlled for this by using an *offset* variable on the right-hand side of the regression equation. The offset variable was the natural logarithm of the number of years that an inmate was observed. In Poisson regression, the log of the expected number of infractions or mean number of infractions is modeled as a linear function of the independent variables plus the offset. Thus, the Poisson regression model is $\log \mu_i = \log (\text{time observed}) + \Sigma\beta_i X_i$. In terms of the mean, this model is expressed as $\mu = (\text{time observed})e^{\Sigma\beta_i X_i}$. Consequently, the effect of ith variable on the mean is e^{β_i}.

A key characteristic of the Poisson distribution is that the mean is equal to the variance. For real data, sometimes the variance is larger or smaller than the mean. These conditions are known as overdispersion and underdispersion, respectively. The Statistical Analysis System (SAS) GENMOD procedure (Stokes, Davis, and Koch, 1995) allowed us to adjust for these conditions in the estimation of the standard errors of the estimated regression parameters.

The independent variables were a mixture of continuous variables (e.g., age) and categorical variables (e.g., three levels of crime seriousness: high, medium, and low). The exponentiated estimated regression parameter associated with a continuous variable is interpreted as the increase (decrease) in the mean infraction or infraction rate as a result of a one unit increase in the corresponding independent variable. For categorical variables, the exponentiated parameter is interpreted as the increase (decrease) of the infraction rate for a particular level of the categorical variable (high serious level of crime) when compared to a reference level (low serious level of crime) for that categorical variable.

The sentence-type variable is the variable of primary interest in the study. Because we compared infractions between structured- and fair-sentenced inmates, the independent variable was sentence type, which is defined as structured (1) or fair (0).

The offset variable, which is described above, is the natural log of years confined for the current period of incarceration.

Control Variables

In the models using Poisson regression, we statistically controlled for variables that may affect the infraction rate. For example, we expected that younger inmates would have a higher infraction rate than older inmates. Therefore, if the structured-sentenced inmates were mostly younger and fair-sentenced inmates were mostly older, then a higher infraction rate for the structured-sentenced inmates may be the result of overrepresentation of younger inmates. Based on the research literature, discussion with North Carolina's Department of Correction, and the Memory et al. (1998) study, we identified control variables to include in the models. Therefore, the models determine if there is a difference in inmate infractions between structured- and fair-sentenced inmates, holding constant the effects of the control variables.

Below is a brief description of the control variables we used:

- *Crime class* – Under structured sentencing, North Carolina classifies felonies into 10 classes (A, B1, B2, C, D, E, F, G, H, and I) depending on the seriousness of the crime. Crime class A felonies that result in death or life in prison were not included in our study.
- *Prior time served (in years)* – Time served on prior incarcerations (in days) in North Carolina prisons divided by 365.25.
- *Jail credit (in years)* – Jail credit days divided by 365.25.
- *Race* – White, black, and other.
- *Age* – Age at admission (continuous).
- *Probation revokee* – Yes or no.
- *Prior infractions* – No prior incarcerations; prior incarceration, no infractions; prior incarceration, infraction(s).

- *Expected time served* – Expected time served (in years) estimated based on actual sentences served for the years 1995, 1996, and 1997.[1]
- *Chemical dependency* – Low risk: screening score less than 3; high risk: screening score 3 or higher.
- *Alcohol dependency* – Low risk: screening score less than 3; high risk: screening score 3 or higher.

Dependent Variables

We used total infraction counts and infraction counts for offense groups as the dependent variables. The following lists the groupings and the infractions included in each:

- *Total* – All infractions.
- *Assault* – Assault staff with weapon; assault person with weapon; provoke assault; fighting; verbal threat; fight involving weapons.
- *Drug/alcohol* – Substance possession; inhale substance; refuse drug/breath test; misuse medicine.
- *Profanity/disobedience* – Profane language; disobey order; interfere with staff; negligently perform duties.
- *Work absence* – Unauthorized leave; unauthorized location; escape.
- *Money/property* – Theft of property; barter/trade/loan money; forgery; property tampering; unauthorized funds; possession of money; misuse of supplies.

Findings

Table 1 compares the inmates in our samples sentenced under structured and fair sentencing. The gender distribution and means of ages were similar, but a larger proportion of inmates incarcerated under structured sentencing were younger than 20 years of age. Inmates incarcerated under structured sentencing were more likely to be classified as high risk on the alcohol and chemical dependency scales. A larger proportion of the structured-sentenced inmates had been incarcerated for more serious crimes. Inmates currently incarcerated under structured sentencing were more likely to have been incarcerated previously, and a higher proportion of structured-sentenced inmates had three or more prior incarcerations (17% vs. 8%). Structured-sentenced inmates who had been incarcerated previously were more likely to have had infractions during those incarcerations. Fair-sentenced inmates were more likely to have had their probation revoked.

The amount of time already served on the current sentence was higher for fair-sentenced inmates, but the expected time to be served was similar for the two inmate groups (1.30 vs. 1.34 years). Structured-sentenced inmates had been previously incarcerated for a longer period (0.91 vs. 0.50 year).

Based on the inmate profiles, the structured-sentenced inmates appear to be at higher risk of committing infractions. Thus, the inclusion of infraction risk variables in the analyses is important to our major analysis goal of accessing the impact of structured sentencing on involvement in institutional infractions.

Table 2 breaks down the infraction frequencies for structured- and fair-sentenced inmates. The general pattern was for inmates sentenced under structured sentencing to have a higher likelihood than fair-sentenced inmates of committing at least one infraction, as well as having a comparatively high likelihood of committing multiple infractions. Approximately 30% of structured-sentenced inmates had one or more infractions compared to 29% of fair-sentenced inmates. Approximately 9% of structured-sentenced inmates had assault infractions compared to 6% of fair-sentenced inmates. This relationship, however, did not hold in the drug/alcohol, work absence, and money/property offense categories. In the drug/alcohol and money/property categories fair-sentenced inmates were more likely to have infractions. Infraction rates were approximately equal for the two sentencing groups in the work absence category.

The estimates in the cells of Table 3 are the exponentiated Poisson regression coefficients and indicate the contribution of each variable to the likelihood of involvement in infractions. Values greater than 1.00 indicate an elevated likelihood of involvement in infractions, and values less than 1.00 indicate a decreased likelihood of involvement. Values close to 1.00 indicate no significant relationship between the variable and involvement in infractions.

Table 3 shows that the total infraction rate was significantly higher for structured-sentenced inmates than for fair-sentenced inmates for both males and females. For males, the average number of infractions was 25% higher for structured-sentenced than for fair-sentenced inmates. The corresponding percentage increase for females was 55%. For males, assault and profanity/disobedience infraction rates were 37% and 41% higher, respectively, for structured-sentenced inmates. The corresponding increases for females were 39% and 57%, respectively.

For males, there were no significant differences in the work absence and money/property infraction rates between the two sentence types. The drug/alcohol infraction rate was 17% lower for males sentenced under structured sentencing than for males sentenced under fair sentencing. In contrast to males, structured-sentenced females had significantly higher work absence and money/property infraction rates than fair-sentenced females. These infraction rates were 28% and 85% higher, respectively, for

Table 1: **Characteristics of Structured- and Fair-Sentenced Inmates**

Characteristic	Structured-Sentenced Inmates (N=11,339)	Fair-Sentenced Inmates (N=4,310)
GENDER (%)		
Male	88.8	86.1
Female	11.2	13.9
AGE[a] (MEAN)	29.4	30.5
AGE[a] (%)		
20 or younger	20.4	11.1
21-24	16.4	20.4
25-35	37.8	41.6
36 or older	25.4	27.0
HIGH RISK FOR ALCOHOL DEPENDENCY[a] (%)	35.3	31.6
HIGH RISK FOR CHEMICAL DEPENDENCY[a] (%)	47.6	41.1
JAIL CREDIT (MEAN)	0.20	0.17
CRIME CLASS[a] (%)		
B1-G	25.4	20.8
H	50.5	46.3
I	24.1	32.9
CRIME GROUP (%)		
Violent	23.4	20.0
Property	34.1	34.4
Drug offenses	39.7	43.9
Other offenses	2.9	1.7
PRIOR INCARCERATIONS (%)		
0	52.3	61.2
1	19.8	22.1
2	10.9	8.9
3 or more	17.0	7.8
PRIOR INFRACTIONS[a] (%)		
No prior prison	52.3	61.1

Table 1: Characteristics of Structured- and Fair-Sentenced Inmates

Characteristic	Structured-Sentenced Inmates (*N*=11,339)	Fair-Sentenced Inmates (*N*=4,310)
Prior prison, no infractions	26.3	25.8
Prior prison, infractions	21.4	13.0
PROBATION REVOKEE (%)		
Yes	52.9	80.8
YEARS CONFINED (MEAN), CURRENT SENTENCE	0.57	0.77
EXPECTED TIME SERVED (MEAN),[a] CURRENT SENTENCE	1.30	1.34
PRIOR TIME SERVED[b] (MEAN)	0.91	0.50
RACE/ETHNICITY (%)		
White	25.2	29.7
Black	71.6	66.9
Other	3.2	03.5

Note: Percentages may not sum to 100 due to rounding error.

[a]Characteristic is unknown for at least one inmate.

[b]Includes all inmates in the study, including those who had not previously been incarcerated.

Table 2: **Percentages of Infraction Counts**

Infraction Category	Structured-Sentenced Inmates	Fair-Sentenced Inmates	All Inmates
TOTAL			
0 infractions	70.2	71.5	70.5
1 infraction	12.1	12.7	12.3
2 or more infractions	17.7	15.9	17.2
ASSAULT			
0 infractions	92.3	94.3	92.9
1 infraction	5.6	4.3	5.3
2 or more infractions	2.0	1.5	1.9
DRUG/ALCOHOL			
0 infractions	94.9	93.1	94.4
1 infraction	4.3	5.4	4.6
2 or more infractions	0.8	1.5	1.0
PROFANITY/DISOBEDIENCE			
0 infractions	80.5	83.8	81.4
1 infraction	9.7	8.7	9.4
2 or more infractions	9.8	7.5	9.2
WORK ABSENCE			
0 infractions	94.0	94.0	94.0
1 infraction	4.4	4.2	4.3
2 or more infractions	1.6	1.7	1.7
MONEY/PROPERTY			
0 infractions	94.0	92.5	93.6
1 infraction	5.0	6.6	5.5
2 or more infractions	0.9	0.9	0.9

Note: Percentages may not sum to 100 due to rounding error.

Table 3: **Poisson Regression Findings, by Gender and Infraction Category**

Parameter	Total	Assault	Drug/ Alcohol	Profanity/ Disobedience	Work Absence	Money/ Property
				MALES		
Structured Sentence vs. Fair Sentence	1.25***	1.37***	0.83***	1.41***	1.07	1.00
Crime Class B1-G vs. Crime Class I	1.41***	1.85***	0.99	1.44***	1.36***	1.07
Crime Class H vs. Crime Class I	1.30***	1.36***	1.13**	1.34***	1.37***	1.15**
Prior Time Served	1.05***	1.11***	1.02	1.06***	1.04***	0.98
Jail Credit	1.37***	1.40***	0.83**	1.53***	1.26***	0.93
Black vs. White	1.04	1.63***	0.59***	1.26***	1.25***	0.64***
Other race vs. White	0.99	1.17	0.73***	1.15	0.88	1.15
Age	0.92***	0.89***	0.96***	0.90***	0.93***	0.96***
Probation Revokee vs. not Probation Revokee	1.10***	1.17***	0.87***	1.14***	0.95	1.00
Expected time served	0.96***	0.98***	0.94***	0.95***	0.94***	0.94***
Alcohol Dependence: High Risk vs. Low Risk	1.00	1.15***	0.84***	1.03	0.83***	0.91**
Chemical Dependence: High Risk vs. Low Risk	1.02	1.16***	1.15***	1.02	0.98	0.93*
Prior Prison vs. No Prior Prison	1.67***	1.39***	1.68***	1.68***	2.17***	1.56***
Prior Prison/ No Infraction vs. No Prior Prison	0.97	0.98	1.21***	0.94	0.99	0.86***

*p ≤ .05.
**p ≤ .01.
***p ≤ .001.

Table 3 (cont.): Poisson Regression Findings, by Gender and Infraction Category

Parameter	FEMALES					
	Total	Assault	Drug/ Alcohol	Profanity/ Disobedience	Work Absence	Money/ Property
Structured Sentence vs. Fair Sentence	1.55***	1.39***	1.06	1.57***	1.28*	1.85***
Crime Class B1-G vs. Crime Class I	1.12	1.69***	1.09	1.15	0.80	1.24
Crime Class H vs. Crime Class I	1.00	0.90	0.88	1.18	0.95	0.82
Prior Time Served	1.07**	1.09**	1.12*	1.11***	0.65***	1.11**
Jail Credit	2.10***	2.26***	0.40**	2.63***	1.37	1.31
Black vs. White	1.29***	1.89***	0.32***	1.44***	1.54***	0.74***
Other race vs. White	0.86	0.94	0.00	0.85	2.41***	0.00
Age	0.92***	0.92***	0.92***	0.97***	0.89***	0.95***
Probation Revokee vs. not Probation Revokee	1.12	1.30**	0.99	1.17	0.77**	1.00
Expected time served	0.93*	0.83***	1.09***	0.91**	0.98	0.96
Alcohol Dependence: High Risk vs. Low Risk	0.98	0.85	0.67***	0.98	1.37**	1.12
Chemical Dependence: High Risk vs. Low Risk	0.87*	1.04	1.38**	0.80**	0.76**	1.07
Prior Prison vs. No Prior Prison	2.49***	3.24***	1.26	2.35***	5.20***	1.12
Prior Prison/ No Infraction vs. No Prior Prison	1.46***	1.69***	1.08	1.51***	2.18***	0.86

*p ≤ .05.
**p ≤ .01.
***p ≤ .001.

structured-sentenced females. There was no significant difference in drug/alcohol infractions between the two sentence types for females.

In general, structured sentencing seemed to have had a somewhat larger effect on females than for males. However, for both genders, the assault infraction rate was over one third higher for structured-sentenced inmates than for fair-sentenced inmates. This is a relatively large increase in a serious infraction rate, especially when one considers that well over one half of the inmates are incarcerated under structured sentencing, and the proportion of inmates incarcerated under structured sentencing will continue to grow.

Although structured sentencing had a relatively large direct effect on infractions for both genders, other inmate background characteristics had even a larger direct impact on infractions. Male inmates in the most serious crime category had a total infraction rate that was 41% higher than the rate for inmates in the least serious crime category. For assault infractions, the infraction rate was 85% higher for those in the most serious crime category than for those in the least serious crime category. The infraction rates for profanity/disobedience and work absence were 44% and 36% higher, respectively. For females, the assault infraction rate was 69% higher for those in the most serious crime category compared to those in the least serious crime category.

Other factors associated with infractions include the following:

- For both males and females, prior time served had a significant and positive impact on total, assault, and profanity/disobedience infraction rates.
- The number of years of jail credit had a significant and positive effect on most infraction rates for both males and females.
- There was no significant difference in the total infraction rates between black and white men, but the infraction rates of black men were higher than white men for assault (63% higher), profanity/disobedience (26% higher), and work absence infractions (25% higher). However, black men's infraction rates for drug/alcohol and money/property infractions were 41% and 36% lower, respectively.
- For females, the total infraction rate was 29% higher for blacks than for whites. However, the drug/alcohol and money/property infraction rates for black females were 68% and 26% lower, respectively, than for white females.

- As age increased, there was a significant decline in infractions for all infraction categories for both males and females.
- For males, an increase in expected time served decreased all six infraction rates. For females, there was a 7% decline in the total infraction rate for each additional year of expected time served (52% decline for 10 years).
- For males, the total infraction rate was 67% higher for those who had one or more infractions while serving a prior prison sentence than for those who had no prior prison record. For females, the effect of a prior prison record with infractions was even stronger. The total infraction rate for them was 149% higher than those with no prior prison record.

Summary of Results

Both male and female inmates sentenced under structured sentencing laws had higher total infraction rates than those sentenced under fair sentencing laws. Both genders also had higher assault infraction rates. Most of the other risk factors that were used as covariates or independent variables in the Poisson regression models to adjust the effects of structured versus fair sentencing for differences in background characteristics between the two sentence groups also had substantial relationships to both total infractions and various specific infractions. In fact, some of the covariates (e.g., infractions during prior incarcerations vs. no prior incarcerations) had a stronger effect on infraction rates than the effect of structured versus fair sentencing.

For males, those with high infraction rates could be characterized as being sentenced under structured sentencing; being sentenced for the most serious crimes; having served more time for prior incarcerations; having had more jail credit time; being young; being a probation violator; having a shorter expected sentence; and having one or more infractions during prior incarcerations. Male inmates with these characteristics would be expected to have an extremely high infraction rate compared to inmates who did not have those characteristics.

For females, the profile of those with high infraction rates was similar to that described above for males. However, in general, structured versus fair sentencing and the other covariates had a stronger relationship with the total infraction rate and various infraction categories for females than for males. For example, the total infraction rate for males who had one or more infractions in prior incarcerations compared to those with no prior prison was 67% higher, whereas for females the corresponding infraction rate was 149% higher. For assault infractions, the differential effect of this variables was even stronger—39% for males and 224% for females.

Considerable confidence is justified in our findings regarding the impact of structured sentencing on prison infractions. The current study largely replicates an earlier one (Memory et al., 1998), and improvements in methodology also were made. But other factors may have influenced the recent increases in inmate infractions. During the period of the study, the prison system was undergoing changes along with the sentencing law change. Prison capacity and staffing were increasing so that the physical and environmental features of the system were changing and the characteristics of the correctional officer staff were modified. Although these changes may have impacted the overall likelihood of occurrence and mix of infraction types, we know of no reason to think that structured- and fair-sentenced inmates would have been affected differentially by the changes.

Implications

This analysis of the effects of structured sentencing on the involvement of inmates in infractions demonstrates how legislative initiatives that modify behavioral incentives can have an impact on inmate behavior. The structured sentencing law implemented in North Carolina made the management of the State's prisons more difficult and more costly. The results of our analysis provided some information that, when used in combination with prison management and housing practices, might have a positive impact on the safety and orderliness of the State's correctional institutions.

Another important implication of the infractions analysis is that as the proportion of inmates sentenced under structured sentencing increases over time, which will occur inexorably unless the law is changed, the behavior management problems of the system will likely grow. Of course, it is possible that the system can adapt successfully by modifying its practices to manage inmate behavior more effectively. But barring more effective methods of dealing with infractions, North Carolina's prisons face major challenges when a larger proportion of its charges are incarcerated under structured sentencing.

Certain classes of inmates were much more likely to be involved in infractions, indicating that risk profiling can provide direction to inmate management approaches. Inmates with a risk factor profile indicating a relatively strong likelihood of committing infractions could be monitored more closely than those without such a profile. They also could be housed together in order to make the monitoring more efficient. Because the risk factors are more predictive of infractions for females than for males, monitoring females with a high infraction rate risk factor profile more closely could pay even higher dividends. Prison management practices might also be used to attempt to modify the prevalence of infractions, such as by refining inmate classification and security assignment approaches and promising more favorable housing and job assignments for inmates who avoid infractions.

It is clear from the findings in this chapter that modifications in sentencing can have far-reaching implications for prisons. It has been demonstrated by other research that sentencing policies and practices have major impacts on the size of correctional populations. But the features of sentencing can also affect inmates' behavior while incarcerated, making the management of prisons more difficult and more costly. Future legislation should consider these effects, as well as those impacting the need for bed space. The orderliness and safety of the prison environment can have negative consequences that may be every bit as serious as overcrowding.

Almost 40 years ago, Marvin Wolfgang conducted a study that was very similar in form and intent to the one we have described here. He was attempting to understand what factors were related to individuals' adjustment to prison life. His work helped to illuminate this question, and the work reported here has advanced understanding a little further. It is appropriate that the criminological enterprise that Marvin was such an important part of for so many years thus goes on in this way, and it is fitting that his work will continue to enrich the process as it advances into the future.

REFERENCES

Blumstein, Alfred, Jacqueline Cohen, Susan E. Martin, and Michael H. Tonry (eds.). (1983). *Research on Sentencing: The Search for Reform.* Washington, DC: National Academy Press.

Brown, Barry S. and John D. Spevacek. (1971). "Disciplinary Offenses and Offenders at Two Differing Correctional Institutions." *Correctional Psychiatry and Journal of Social Therapy* 17:48-56.

Collins, James J., Donna L. Spencer, George H. Dunteman, Harlene C. Gogan, Peter H. Siegel, Brad A. Lessler, Kenneth Parker, and Thomas Sutton. (1999). *Evaluation of North Carolina's Structured Sentencing Law: Final Report.* National Institute of Justice Grant No. 96-CE-VX-0013; RTI/6780-006. Research Triangle Park, NC: Research Triangle Institute.

Craddock, Amy. (1996). "A Comparative Study of Male and Female Prison Misconduct Careers." *The Prison Journal* 76(1):60-80.

Ekland-Olson, Sheldon, Dennis M. Barrick, and Lawrence E. Cohen. (1983). "Prison Overcrowding and Disciplinary Problems: An Analysis of the Texas Prison System." *Journal of Applied Behavioral Science* 19:163-176.

Ellis, Desmond. (1984). "Crowding and Prison Violence: Integration of Research and Theory." *Criminal Justice and Behavior* 11:277-308.

Ellis, Desmond, Harold G. Grasmick, and Bernard Gilman. (1974). "Violence in Prisons: A Sociological Analysis." *American Journal of Sociology* 80(1):16-43.

Flanagan, Timothy J. (1983). "Correlates of Institutional Misconduct among State Prisoners: A Research Note." *Criminology* 21(1):29-39.

Goetting, Ann and Roy M. Howsen. (1986). "Correlations of Prisoner Misconduct" *Journal of Quantitative Criminology* 2(1):49-67.

MacKenzie, Doris L. (1987). "Age and Adjustment to Prison: Interactions with Attitudes and Anxiety." *Criminal Justice and Behavior* 14:427-447.

Memory, J.M., G. Guo, Kenneth Parker, Thomas Sutton, D. Thompson, J. Klapovic, and K. Herrin. (1998). *Comparing Disciplinary Infraction Rates of North Carolina Fair Sentencing and Structured Sentencing Inmates: A Natural Experiment.* Raleigh, NC: North Carolina Department of Crime Control and Public Safety, Division of the Governor's Crime Commission.

North Carolina Sentencing and Policy Advisory Commission. (1996a). *A Citizen's Guide to Structured Sentencing* (rev. ed.). Raleigh, NC: North Carolina Sentencing and Policy Advisory Commission.

North Carolina Sentencing and Policy Advisory Commission. (1996b). *Progress Report on Structured Sentencing.* Raleigh, NC: North Carolina Sentencing and Policy Advisory Commission.

Poole, Eric D. and Robert M. Regoli. (1980). "Race, Institutional Rule Breaking, and Disciplinary Response: A Study of Discretionary Decision Making in Prison." *Law and Society Review* 14:931-946.

Stokes, M.E., C.S. Davis, and G.G. Koch. (1995). Categorical Data Analysis Using the SAS System. Cary, NC: SAS Institute, Inc.

Wicharaya, Tamasak. (1995). *Simple Theory, Hard Reality: The Impact of Sentencing Reforms on Courts, Prisons, and Crime.* New York: State University of New York Press.

Wolfgang, Marvin E. (1958). *Patterns in Criminal Homicide.* Philadelphia: University of Pennsylvania Press.

Wolfgang, Marvin E. (1961). "Quantitative Analysis of Adjustment to the Prison Community." *Journal of Criminal Law, Criminology, and Police Science* 51:607-618.

Wooldredge, J.D. (1991). "Correlates of Deviant Behavior among Inmates of U.S. Correctional Facilities." *Journal of Crime & Justice* 14(1):1-25.

Collins, Spencer, Dunteman, Siegel 277

Wright, Kevin N. (1989). "Race and Economic Marginality in Explaining Prison Adjustment." *Journal of Research in Crime and Delinquency* 26(1):67-8

NOTES

[1] For fair-sentenced inmates, the Department of Correction provided us with the average percentage of the maximum sentence length served for the years 1995, 1996, and 1997. For fair-sentenced inmates, we took the average of the 3 years (27.0667%) and multiplied it by each inmate's maximum sentence length (in years). Then we subtracted jail credit (in years) from this product. For structured-sentenced inmates, the Department provided us with the average percentage of minimum sentence length served for the years 1995, 1996, and 1997. We took the average of the 3 years (113.0333%) and multiplied it by each inmate's minimum sentence length (in years). Then we subtracted jail credit years) from this product. However, we first had to compute minimum sentence length by reversing the method to compute maximum sentence length. For Class B1 through E felonies, the minimum sentence length is the maximum length (in months) minus 9 months and then divided by 120%. Then this quotient is rounded down to the next lowest month and divided by 12 to get it in terms of years. For Class F through I felonies, the minimum sentence length is the maximum length (in months) divided by 120%. Then this quotient is rounded down to the next lowest month and divided by 12 to get it in terms of years.

IN HIS OWN VOICE

Barry Krisberg
National Council on Crime and Delinquency

That voice, it was so distinctive, so confident, so calming. Most students of Marvin Wolfgang still remember the private conversations and public lectures that formed a crucial part of their educational development. It is fitting that this book honoring his contributions to Criminology includes a selection of Wolfgang's most insightful writings. The essays that follow span nearly half a century of American Criminology, and yet they seem to pass the test of time.

A common theme that Wolfgang pursued was that "things are seldom what they seem." For example, his classic doctoral dissertation *Patterns in Criminal Homicide* illustrated that there were sociological regularities in the deeply individual act of murder. Indeed, Wolfgang raised the radical notion that there were some homicides that were precipitated by the victim.

Wolfgang's ideas on race and crime (co-authored by Bernard Cohen) were well ahead of the thinking of his time. In fact, some of his contemporaries like James Q. Wilson, never understood Wolfgang's sophisticated level of social analysis in the topic. My very favorite essay in this group *Violence USA* remains a profound statement about how to improve race relations in this nation. That essay was delivered at a national meeting of the National Council on Crime and Delinquency (NCCD) in the turbulent days following the assassinations of Martin Luther King and Robert F. Kennedy. As always, Wolfgang offered a historical and sociological context through which his readers could interpret and transcend the enormous tragedy of the moment. He reached back to the European Renaissance (his favorite historical period) to remind us that violence is part of every social order, even those that we later come to idealize. Wolfgang's message was both calming and encouraging. He urged his audience to rededicate themselves to the principles of democracy and freedom that he believed would sustain the best of our nation's values in a period of intense racial conflict.

Ironically, Wolfgang epitomized the Gandhian Ideal in American Criminology. Although his research was so focused on violence, he was the consummate advocate for peaceful social change. He had experienced the horror of war first-hand and wished to promote intergroup harmony and cooperation. This sometimes meant taking personal risks such as traveling to totalitarian countries like Brazil or China, and yet preaching the values of democracy. Wolfgang, like his mentor Thorsten Sellin, struggled continuously to bring an end to capital punishment. His last published writings focused on how the death penalty corrupted the very concept of justice.

Wolfgang was a prolific author, who often collaborated with his students in some of his most important writings. He left no single book that summarized his major theories on crime and justice. Instead, he gifted us with a broad range of observations on crucial topics in Criminology. World leaders, justice system professionals, and thousands of students were enlightened and energized by his voice. This chapter is just a small sampling of Wolfgang's vast intellectual and humanitarian legacy.

VICTIM-PRECIPITATED CRIMINAL HOMICIDE

Marvin E. Wolfgang

In many crimes, especially in criminal homicide, the victim is often a major contributor to the criminal act. Except in cases in which the victim is an innocent bystander and is killed in lieu of an intended victim, or in cases in which a pure accident is involved, the victim may be one of the major precipitating causes of his own demise.

Various theories of social interaction, particularly in social psychology, have established the framework for the present discussion. In criminological literature, however, probably von Hentig in *The Criminal and His Victim,* has provided the most useful theoretical basis for analysis of the victim-offender relationship. In Chapter XII, entitled "The Contribution of the Victim to the Genesis of Crime," the author discusses this "duet frame of crime" and suggests that homicide is particularly amenable to analysis.[1] In *Penal Philosophy,* Tarde [2] frequently attacks the "legislative mistake" of concentrating too much on premeditation and paying too little attention to motives, which indicate an important interrelationship between victim and offender. And in one of his satirical essays, "On Murder Considered as One of the Fine Arts," Thomas DeQuincey[3] shows cognizance of the idea that sometimes the victim is a would-be murderer. Garofalo,[4] too, noted that the victim may provoke another individual into attack, and though the provocation be slight, if perceived by an egoistic attacker it may be sufficient to result in homicide.

Besides these theoretical concepts, the law of homicide has long recognized provocation by the victim as a possible reason for mitigation of the offense from murder to manslaughter, or from criminal to excusable homicide. In order that such reductions occur, there are four prerequisites.[5]

1) There must have been adequate provocation.
2) The killing must have been in the heat of passion.
3) The killing must have followed the provocation before there had been a reasonable opportunity for the passion to cool.
4) A causal connection must exist between provocation, the heat of passion, and the homicidal act. Such, for example, are: adultery, seduction of the offender's

juvenile daughter, rape of the offender's wife or close relative, etc.

Finally 4), a causal connection must exist between provocation, the heat of passion, and the homicidal act. Perkins claims that "the adequate provocation must have engendered the heat of passion, and the heat of passion must have been the cause of the act which resulted in death."[6]

Definition and Illustration

The term victim-precipitated is applied to those criminal homicides in which the victim is a direct, positive precipitator in the crime. The role of the victim is characterized by his having been the first in the homicide drama to use physical force directed against his subsequent slayer. The victim-precipitated cases are those in which the victim was the first to show and use a deadly weapon, to strike a blow in an altercation - in short, the first to commence the interplay or resort to physical violence.

In seeking to identify the victim-precipitated cases recorded in police files it has not been possible always to determine whether the homicides strictly parallel legal interpretations. In general, there appears to be much similarity. In a few cases included under the present definition, the nature of the provocation is such that it would not legally serve to mitigate the offender's responsibility. In these cases the victim was threatened in a robbery, and either attempted to prevent the robbery, failed to take the robber seriously, or in some other fashion irritated, frightened, or alarmed the felon by physical force so that the robber, either by accident or compulsion, killed the victim. Infidelity of a mate or lover, failure to pay a debt, use of vile names by the victim, obviously means that he played an important role in inciting the offender to overt action in order to seek revenge, to win an argument, or to defend himself. However, mutual quarrels and wordy altercations do not constitute sufficient provocation under law, and they are not included in the meaning of victim-precipitated homicide.

Below are sketched several typical cases to illustrate the pattern of these homicides. Primary demonstration of physical force by the victim, supplemented by scurrilous language, characterizes the most common victim-precipitated homicides. All of these slayings were listed by the Philadelphia Police as criminal homicides, none of the offenders was exonerated by a coroner's inquest, and all the offenders were tried in criminal court.

A husband accused his wife of giving money to another man, and while she was making breakfast, he attacked her with a milk bottle, then a brick, and finally a piece of concrete block. Having had a butcher knife in hand, she stabbed him during the fight.

A husband threatened to kill his wife on several occasions. In this instance, he attacked her with a pair of scissors, dropped them, and grabbed a butcher knife from the kitchen. In the ensuing struggle that ended on their bed, he fell on the knife.

In an argument over a business transaction, the victim first fired several shots at his adversary, who in turn fatally returned the fire.

The victim was the aggressor in a fight, having struck his enemy several times. Friends tried to interfere, but the victim persisted. Finally, the offender retaliated with blows, causing the victim to fall and hit his head on the sidewalk, as a result of which he died.

A husband had beaten his wife on several previous occasions. In the present instance, she insisted that he take her to the hospital. He refused, and a violent quarrel followed, during which he slapped her several times, and she concluded by stabbing him.

During a lover's quarrel, the male (victim) hit his mistress and threw a can of kerosene at her. She retaliated by throwing the liquid on him, and then tossed a lighted match in his direction. He died from the burns.

A drunken husband, beating his wife in their kitchen, gave her a butcher knife and dared her to use it on him. She claimed that if he should strike her once more, she would use the knife, whereupon he slapped her in the face and she fatally stabbed him.

A victim became incensed when his eventual slayer asked for money which the victim owed him. The victim grabbed a hatchet and started in the direction of his creditor, who pulled out a knife and stabbed him.

A victim attempted to commit sodomy with his girlfriend, who refused his overtures. He struck her several times on the side of her head with his fists before she grabbed a butcher knife and cut him fatally.

A drunken victim with knife in hand approached his slayer during a quarrel. The slayer showed a gun, and the victim dared him to shoot. He did.

During an argument in which a male called a female many vile names, she tried to telephone the police. But he grabbed the phone from her hands, knocked her down, kicked her, and hit her with a tire gauge. She ran to the kitchen, grabbed a butcher knife, and stabbed him in the stomach.

The Philadelphia Study

Empirical data for analysis of victim-precipitated homicides were collected from the files of the Homicide Squad of the Philadelphia Police Department, and include 588 consecutive cases of criminal homicide which occurred between January 1, 1948 and December 31, 1952. Because more than one person was sometimes involved in the slaying of a single victim, there was a total of 621 offenders responsible for the killing of 588 victims. The present study is part of a much larger work that analyzes criminal homicide in greater detail. Such material that is relevant to victim-precipitation is included in the present analysis. The 588 criminal homicides provide sufficient background information to establish much about the nature of the victim-offender relationship. Of these cases, 150, or 26 percent, have been designated, on the basis of the previously stated definition, as VP cases.[7] The remaining 438, therefore, have been designated as non-VP cases.

Thorough study of police files, theoretical discussions of the victim's contribution, and previous analysis of criminal homicide suggest that there may be important differences between VP and non-VP cases. The chi-square test has been used to test the significance in proportions between VP and non-VP homicides and a series of variables. Hence, any spurious association which is just due to chance has been reduced to a minimum by application of this test, and significant differences of distributions are revealed. Where any expected class frequency of less than five existed, the test was not applied; and in each tested association, a correction for continuity was used, although the difference resulting without it was only slight. In this study a value of P less than .05, or the 5 percent level of significance, is used as the minimal level of significant association. Throughout the subsequent discussion, the term *significant* in italics is used to indicate that a chi-square test of significance of association has been made and that the value of P less than .05 has been found. The discussion that follows (with respect to race, sex, age, etc.) reveals some interesting differences and similarities between the two. (Table I)

Table I

Victim-Precipitated and Non-Victim-Precipitated Criminal Homicide by Selected Variables, Philadelphia, 1948-1952

	Total Victims		Victim-Precipitated		Non-Victim-Precipitated	
	Number	Percent of Total	Number	Percent of Total	Number	Percent of Total
Race and Sex of Victim						
Both Races	588	100.0	150	100.0	438	100.0
Male	449	76.4	141	94.0	308	70.3
Female	139	23.6	9	6.0	130	29.7
Negro	427	72.6	119	79.3	308	70.3
Male	331	56.3	111	74.0	220	50.2
Female	96	16.3	8	5.3	88	20.1
White	161	27.4	31	20.7	130	29.7
Male	118	20.1	30	20.0	88	20.1
Female	43	7.3	1	0.7	42	9.6

Table I (cont.)

Victim-Precipitated and Non-Victim-Precipitated Criminal Homicide by Selected Variables, Philadelphia, 1948-1952

	Total Victims		Victim-Precipitated		Non-Victim-Precipitated	
	Number	Percent of Total	Number	Percent of Total	Number	Percent of Total
Age of Victim						
Under 15	28	4.8	0	-	28	6.4
15-19	25	4.3	7	4.7	18	4.1
20-24	59	10.0	18	12.0	41	9.4
25-29	93	15.8	17	11.3	76	17.3
30-34	88	15.0	20	13.3	68	15.5
35-39	75	12.8	25	16.7	50	11.4
Race and Sex of Victim						
40-44	57	9.7	23	15.3	34	7.8
45-49	43	7.3	13	8.7	30	6.8
50-54	48	8.2	11	7.3	37	8.5
55-59	26	4.4	6	4.0	20	4.6
60-64	18	3.1	7	4.7	11	2.5
65 and over	28	4.7	3	2.0	25	5.7
Total	**588**	**100.0**	**150**	**100.0**	**438**	**100.0**
Method						
Stabbing	228	38.8	81	54.0	147	33.6
Shooting	194	33.0	39	26.0	155	35.4
Beating	128	21.8	26	17.3	102	23.3
Other	38	6.4	4	2.7	34	7.7
Total	**588**	**100.0**	**150**	**100.0**	**438**	**100.0**
Place						
Home	301	51.2	80	53.3	221	50.5
Not Home	287	48.8	70	46.7	217	49.5
Total	**588**	**100.0**	**150**	**100.0**	**438**	**100.0**
Interpersonal Relationship						
Relatively close friend	155	28.2	46	30.7	109	27.3
Family relationship	136	24.7	38	25.3	98	24.5
(Spouse)	(100)	(73.5)	(33)	(86.8)	(67)	(68.4)
(Other)	(36)	(26.5)	(5)	(13.2)	(31)	(31.6)
Acquaintance	74	13.5	20	13.3	54	13.5
Stranger	67	12.2	16	10.7	51	12.8
Paramour, Mistress, Prostitute	54	9.8	15	10.0	39	9.8
Sex rival	22	4.0	6	4.0	16	4.0
Enemy	16	2.9	6	4.0	10	2.5
Paramour of Offender's mate	11	2.0	1	.7	10	2.5
Felon or police officer	6	1.1	1	.7	5	1.3
Innocent bystander	6	1.1	-	-	6	1.5
Homosexual partner	3	.6	1	.7	2	.5
Total	**550**	**100.0**	**150**	**100.0**	**400**	**100.0**
Presence of alcohol during Defense						
Present	374	63.6	111	74.0	263	60.0
Not Present	214	36.4	39	26.0	175	40.0
Total	**588**	**100.0**	**150**	**100.0**	**438**	**100.0**

Table I (cont.)

Victim-Precipitated and Non-Victim-Precipitated Criminal Homicide by Selected Variables, Philadelphia, 1948-1952

| | Total Victims | | Victim-Precipitated | | Non-Victim-Precipitated | |
	Number	Percent of Total	Number	Percent of Total	Number	Percent of Total
Presence of alcohol in the victim						
Present	310	52.7	104	69.3	206	47.0
Not Present	278	47.3	46	30.7	232	53.0
Total	**588**	**100.0**	**150**	**100.0**	**438**	**100.0**
Previous Arrest record of victim						
Previous arrest record	277	47.3	93	62.0	184	42.0
Offenses against the person	150	25.5 (54.2)	56	37.3 (60.2)	94	21.4 (50.1)
Other offenses only	127	21.6 (45.8)	37	24.7 (39.8)	90	20.5 (49.9)
No previous arrest record	311	52.7	57	38.0	254	58.0
Total	**588**	**100.0**	**150**	**100.0**	**438**	**100.0**
Previous arrest record of Offender						
Previous arrest record	400	64.4	81	54.0	319	67.7
Offenses against the person	264	42.5 (66.0)	49	32.7 (60.5)	215	45.6 (67.4)
Other offenses only	136	21.8 (34.0)	32	21.3 (39.5)	104	22.1 (32.6)
No previous arrest record	221	35.6	69	(46.0)	152	32.3
Total	**621**	**100.0**	**150**	**100.0**	**471**	**100.0**

Race

Because Negroes and males have been shown by their high rates of homicide, assaults against the person, etc., to be more criminally aggressive than whites and females, it may be inferred that there are more Negroes and males among VP victims than among non-VP victims. The data confirm this inference. Nearly 80 percent of VP cases compared to 70 percent of non-VP cases involve Negroes, a proportional difference that results in a *significant* association between race and VP homicide.

Sex

As victims, males comprise *94* percent of VP homicides, but only 72 percent of non-VP homicides, showing a *significant* association between sex of the victim and VP homicide.

Since females have been shown by their low rates of homicide, assaults against the person, etc., to be less criminally aggressive than males, and since females are less likely to precipitate their own victimization than males, we should expect more female *offenders* among VP homicides than among non-VP homicides. Such is the case, for the comparative data reveal that females are twice as frequently offenders in VP slayings (29 percent) as they are in non-VP slayings (14 percent)-a proportional difference which is also highly *significant.*

The number of white female offenders (16) in this study is too small to permit statistical analysis, but the tendency among both Negro and white females as separate groups is toward a much higher proportion among VP than among non-VP offenders. As noted above, analysis of Negro and white females as a combined group does result in the finding of a *significant* association between female offenders and VP homicide.

Age

The age distributions of victims and offenders in VP and non-VP homicides are strikingly similar; study of the data suggests that age has no apparent effect on VP homicide. The median age of VP victims is 33.3 years, while that of non-VP victims is 31.2 years.

Methods

In general, there is a *significant* association between method used to inflict death and VP homicide. Because Negroes and females comprise a larger proportion of offenders in VP cases, and because previous analysis has shown that stabbings occurred more often than any of the other methods of inflicting death,[8] it is implied that the frequency of homicides by stabbing is greater among VP than among non-VP cases. The data support such an implication and reveal that homicides by stabbing account for 54 percent of the VP cases but only 34 percent of non-VP cases, a difference which is *significant.* The distribution of shootings, beatings, and "other" methods of inflicting death among the VP and non-VP cases shows no significant differences. The high frequency of stabbings among VP homicides appears to result from an almost equal reduction in each of the remaining methods; yet the lower proportions in each of these three other categories among VP cases are not separately very different from the proportions among non-VP cases.

Place and Motive

There is no important difference between VP and non-VP homicides with respect to a home/not-home dichotomy, nor with respect to motives listed by the police. Slightly over half of both VP and non-VP slayings occurred in the home. General altercations (43 percent) and domestic quarrels (20 percent) rank highest among VP cases, as they do among non-VP cases (32 and 12 percent), although with lower frequency. Combined, these two motives account for a slightly larger share of the VP cases (3 out of 5) than of the non-VP cases (2 out of 5).

Victim-Offender Relationships[9]

Intra-racial slayings predominate in both groups, but inter-racial homicides comprise a larger share of VP cases (8 percent) than they do of non-VP cases (5 percent). Although VP cases make up one-fourth of all criminal homicides, they account for over one-third (35 percent) of all inter-racial slayings. Thus it appears that a homicide which crosses race lines is often likely to be one in which the slayer was provoked to assault by the victim. The association between inter-racial slayings and VP homicides, however, is not statistically significant.

Homicides involving victims and offenders of opposite sex (regardless of which sex is the victim or which is the offender) occur with about the same frequency among VP cases (34 percent) as among non-VP cases (37 percent). But a *significant* difference between VP and non-VP cases does emerge when determination of the sex of the victim, relative to the sex of his specific slayer, is taken into account. Of all criminal homicides for which the sex of both victim and offender is known, 88 involve a male victim and a female offender; and of these 88 cases, 43 are VP homicides. Thus, it may be said that 43, or 29 percent, of the 150 VP homicides, compared to 45, or only 11 percent, of the 400 non-VP homicides, are males slain by females.

It seems highly desirable, in view of these findings, that the police thoroughly investigate every possibility of strong provocation by the male victim when he is slain by a female - and particularly, as noted below, if the female is his wife, which is also a strong possibility. It is, of course, the further responsibility of defense counsel, prosecuting attorney, and subsequently the court, to determine whether such provocation was sufficient either to reduce or to eliminate culpability altogether.

The proportion that Negro male/Negro male[10] and white male/white male homicides constitute among VP cases (45 and 13 percent) is similar to the proportion these same relationships constitute among non-VP cases (41 and 14 percent). The important contribution of the Negro male as a victim-precipitator is indicated by the fact that Negro male/Negro female homicides are, proportionately, nearly three times as frequent among VP cases (25 percent) as they are among non-VP cases (9 percent). It is apparent, therefore, that Negroes and males not only are the groups most likely to make positive and direct contributions to the genesis of their own victimization, but that, in particular, Negro males more frequently provoke females of their own race to slay them than they do members of their own sex and race.

For both VP and non-VP groups, close friends, relatives, and acquaintances are the major types of specific relationships between victims and offenders. Combined, these three relationships constitute 69 percent of the VP homicides and 65 percent of the non-VP cases. Victims are relatives of their slayers in one-fourth of both types of homicide. But of 38 family slayings among VP cases, 33 are husband-wife killings; while of 98 family slayings among non-VP cases, only 67 are husband-wife killings. This proportional difference results in a *significant* association between mate slayings and VP homicide.

Finally, of VP mate slayings, 28 victims are husbands and only 5 are wives; but of non-VP mate slayings, only 19 victims are husbands while 48 are wives. Thus there is a *significant* association between husbands who are victims in mate slayings and VP homicide. This fact, namely, that *significantly* more husbands than wives are victims in VP mate slayings-means that (1) husbands actually may provoke their wives more often than wives provoke their husbands to assault their respective mates; or, (2) assuming that provocation by wives is as intense and equally as frequent, or even more frequent, than provocation by husbands, then husbands may not receive and define provocation stimuli with as great or as violent a reaction as do wives; or (3) husbands may have a greater felt sense of guilt in a marital conflict for one reason or another, and receive verbal insults and overt physical assaults without retaliation as a form of compensatory punishment; or, (4) husbands may withdraw more often than wives from the scene of marital conflict, and thus eliminate, for the time being, a violent overt reaction to their wives' provocation. Clearly, this is only a suggestive, not an exhaustive, list of probable explanations. In any case, we are left with the undeniable fact that husbands more often than wives are major, precipitating factors in their own homicidal deaths.

Alcohol

In the larger work of which this study is a part, the previous discovery of an association between the presence of alcohol in the homicide situation and Negro male offenders, combined with knowledge of the important contribution Negro males make to their own victimization, suggests an association (by transitivity) between VP homicide and the presence of alcohol. Moreover, whether alcohol is present in the victim or offender, lowered inhibitions due to ingestion of alcohol may cause an individual to give vent more freely to pent up frustrations, tensions, and emotional conflicts that have either built up over a prolonged period of time or that arise within an immediate emotional crisis. The data do in fact confirm the suggested hypothesis above and reveal a *significant* association between VP homicide and alcohol in the homicide situation. Comparison of VP to non-VP cases with respect to the presence of alcohol in the homicide situation (alcohol present in either the victim, offender, or both), reveals that alcohol was present in 74 percent of the VP cases and in 60 per cent of the non-VP cases. The proportional difference results in a *significant* association between alcohol and VP homicide. It should be noted that the association is not necessarily a causal one, or that a causal relationship is not proved by the association.

Because the present analysis is concerned primarily with the contribution of the victim to the homicide, it is necessary to determine whether an association exists between VP homicide and presence of alcohol in the victim. No association was found to exist between VP homicide and alcohol in the offender. But victims had been drinking immediately prior to their death in more VP cases *(69* percent) than in non-VP cases (47 percent). A positive and *significant* relationship is, therefore, clearly established between victims who had been drinking and who precipitated their own death. In many of these cases the victim was intoxicated, or nearly so, and lost control of his own defensive powers. He frequently was a victim with no intent to harm anyone maliciously, but who, nonetheless, struck his friend, acquaintance, or wife, who later became his assailant. Impulsive, aggressive, and often dangerously violent, the victim was the first to slap, punch, stab, or in some other manner commit an assault. Perhaps the presence of alcohol in this kind of homicide victim played no small part in his taking this first and major physical step toward victimization. Perhaps if he had not been drinking he would have been less violent, less ready to plunge into an assaultive stage of interaction. Or, if the presence of alcohol had no causal relation to his being the first to assault, perhaps it reduced his facility to combat successfully, to defend himself from retaliatory assault and, hence, contributed in this way to his death.

Previous Arrest Record

The victim-precipitator is the first actor in the homicide drama to display and to use a deadly weapon; and the description of him thus far infers that he is in some respects an offender in reverse. Because he is the first to assume an aggressive role, he probably has engaged previously in similar but less serious physical assaults. On the basis of these assumptions several meaningful hypotheses were established and tested. Each hypothesis is supported by empirical data, which in some cases reach the level of statistical significance accepted by this study; and in other cases indicate strong associations in directions suggested by the hypotheses. A summary of each hypothesis with its collated data follows:

(1) In VP cases, the victim is more likely than the offender to have a previous arrest, or police, record. The data show that 62 percent of the victims and 54 percent of the offenders in VP cases have a previous record.

(2) A higher proportion of VP victims than non-VP victims have a previous police record. Comparison reveals that 62 percent of VP victims but only 42 percent of non-VP victims have a previous record. The association between VP victims and previous arrest record is a *significant* one.

(3) With respect to the percentage having a previous arrest record, VP victims are more similar to non-VP offenders than to non-VP victims. Examination of the data reveals no significant difference between VP victims and non-VP offenders with a previous record. This lack of a significant difference is very meaningful and confirms the validity of the proposition above. While 62 percent of VP victims have a police record, 68 percent of non-VP offenders have such a record, and we have already noted in (2) above that only 42 percent of non-VP victims have a record. Thus, the existence of a statistically *significant* difference between VP victims and non-VP victims and the *lack* of a statistically significant difference between VP victims and non-VP offenders indicate that the victim of VP homicide is quite similar to the offender in non-VP homicide--and that the VP victim more closely resembles the non-VP offender than the non-VP victim.

(4) A higher proportion of VP victims than of non-VP victims have a record of offenses against the person. The data show a *significant* association between VP victims and a previous record of offenses against the person, for 37 percent of VP victims and only 21 percent of non-VP Victims have a record of such offenses.

(5) Also with respect to the percentage having a previous arrest record of offenses against the person, VP victims are more similar to non-VP offenders than non-VP victims. Analysis of the data indicates support for this assumption, for we have observed that the difference between VP victims (37 percent) and non-VP victims (21 percent) is *significant;* this difference is almost twice as great as the difference between VP victims (27 percent) and non-VP offenders (46 percent), and this latter difference is not significant. The general tendency again is for victims in VP homicides to resemble offenders in non-VP homicides.

(6) A lower proportion of VP offenders have a previous arrest record than do non-VP offenders. The data also tend to support this hypothesis, for 54 percent of offenders in VP cases, compared to 68 percent of offenders in non-VP cases have a previous police record.

In general, the rank order of recidivism - defined in terms of having a previous arrest record and of having a previous record of assaults for victims and offenders involved in the two types of homicide is as follows:

Table 2
**Percent with Previous Percent with Previous Arrest Record ~
Record of Assault**

(1) Offenders in non-VP Homicide	68	46
(2) Victims in VP Homicide	62	37
(3) Offenders in VP Homicide	54	33
(4) Victims in non-VP Homicide	42	21

Because he is the initial aggressor and has provoked his subsequent slayer into killing him, this particular type of victim (VP) is likely to have engaged previously in physical assaults which were either less provoking than the present situation, or which afforded him greater opportunity to defer attacks made upon him. It is known officially that over one-third of them assaulted others previously. It is not known how many formerly provoked others to assault them. In any case, the circumstances leading up to the present crime in which he plays the role of victim are probably not foreign to him since he has, in many cases, participated in similar encounters before this, his last episode.

Summary

Criminal homicide usually involves intense personal interaction in which the victim's behavior is often an important factor. As Porterfield has recently pointed out, "the intensity of interaction between the murderer and his victim may vary from complete non-participation on the part of the victim to almost perfect cooperation with the killer in the process of getting killed .... It is amazing to note the large number of would-be murderers who become the victim."[11] By defining a VP homicide in terms of the victim's direct, immediate, and positive contribution to his own death, manifested by his being the first to make a physical assault, it has been possible to identify 150 VP cases.

Comparison of this VP group with non-VP cases reveals significantly higher proportions of the following characteristics among VP homicide:

1) Negro victims;
2) Negro offenders;
3) male victims;
4) female offenders;
5) stabbings;
6) victim-offender relationship involving male victims of female offenders;

7) mate slayings;
8) husbands who are victims in mate slayings;
9) alcohol in the homicide situation;
10) alcohol in the victim;
11) victims with a previous arrest record;
12) victims with a previous arrest record of assault.

In addition, VP homicides have slightly higher proportions than non-VP homicides of altercations and domestic quarrels; inter-racial slayings, victims who are close friends, relatives, or acquaintances of their slayers.

Empirical evidence analyzed in the present study lends support to, and measurement of, von Hentig's theoretical contention that "there are cases in which they (victim and offender) are reversed and in the long chain of causative forces the victim assumes the role of a determinant."[12]

In many cases the victim has most of the major characteristics of an offender; in some cases two potential offenders come together in a homicide situation and it is probably often only chance which results in one becoming a victim and the other an offender. At any rate, connotations of a victim as a weak and passive individual, seeking to withdraw from an assaultive situation, and of an offender as a brutal, strong, and overly aggressive person seeking out his victim, are not always correct. Societal attitudes are generally positive toward the victim and negative toward the offender, who is often feared as a violent and dangerous threat to others when not exonerated. However, data in the present study – especially that of previous arrest record – mitigate, destroy, or reverse these connotations of victim-offender roles in one out of every four criminal homicides.

NOTES

[1] Von Hentig, Hans, *The Criminal and His Victim*, New Haven: Yale University Press, *1948, pp. 383-385.*

[2] Tarde, Gabriel, *Penal Philosophy*, Boston: Little, Brown, and Company, *1912, p. 466.*

[3] De Quincey, T *On Murder Considered as One of the Fine Arts, The Arts of Cheating, Swindling and Murder,* Edward Bulwer-Lytton and Douglas Jerrold, and Thomas De Quincey, New *York:* The Arnold *Co., 1925, p. 153.*

[4] Garofolo, Baron Rafaaele, *Criminology* Boston: Little, Brown, and Company, *1914, p. 373.*

[5] For an excellent discussion of the rule of provocation, from which these four requirements are taken, see: Rollin M. Perkins, The Law of Homicide, *Jour. of Crim. Law and Criminol.,* (March-April, 1946), 36: 412-427; and Herbert Wechsler and Jerome Michael, *A Rationale of the Law of Homocide*, pp. 1280-1282. A general review of the rule of provocation, both in this country and abroad, may be found in *The Royal Commission on Captial Punishment*, 1949-1952 Report, Appendix *II*, pp. *453-458.*

[6] Ibid., *p. 425*. The term "cause" is here used in a legal and not a psychological sense.

[7] In order to facilitate reading of the following sections, the victim-precipitated cases are referred to simply as VP cases or VP homicides. Those homicides in which the victim was not a direct precipitator are referred to as non-VP cases.

[8] Of 588 victims, 228, or *39* percent, were stabbed; *194,* or *33* percent, were shot; 128, or 22 percent were beaten; and *38,* or 6 percent, were killed by other methods.

[9] Only *550* victim-offender relationships are identified since *38* of the *588* criminal homicides are classified as unsolved, or those in which the perpetrator is unknown.

[10] The diagonal line represents "killed by". Thus, Negro male/Negro male means a Negro male killed by a Negro male; the victim precedes the offender.

[11] Porterfield, Austin L. and Talbert, Robert H., *Mid-Century Crime in our Culture Personality and Crime in the Cultural Patterns of American States*, Fort Worth: Leo Potishman Foundation, *1954, pp. 47-48.*

[12] Von Hentig, 0p. *cit., p. 383.*

RACE AND CRIME:
SEEKING AN EXPLANATION

Marvin E. Wolfgang
Bernard E. Cohen

Our society has witnessed remarkable scientific growth and change since the beginning of the century. Nearly half of us now marveling at landings on the moon were living before the first airplane was flown across the Atlantic. Yet social change is sluggish. The Supreme Court decision on school desegregation did not come about until nearly a hundred years after the Civil War and its intent is yet to be realized. And a little more than 40 years ago Thorsten Sellin concluded a statistical note on Negro criminality that is still a valid commentary on the need to accelerate social change:

> Nothing ... points to a conclusion that the Negro's real criminality is lower or as low as the white's. The American Negro lacks education and earthly goods. He has had very little political experience and industrial training. His contact with city life has been unfortunate, for it has forced him into the most dilapidated and vicious areas of our great cities. Like a shadow over his whole existence lies the oppressive race prejudice of his white neighbor, restricting his activities and thwarting his ambitions. It would be extraordinary, indeed, if this group were to prove more law-abiding than the white, which enjoys more fully the advantages of a civilization the Negro has helped to create.
> The assumption that the Negro presents the higher rate of real criminality is therefore, no indictment of the Negro race. The responsibility lies where power, authority, and discrimination has its source, the dominant white group. To that group the existence of a high rate of crime among Negroes is a challenge which cannot be brushed aside by platitudes about "race inferiority," "inherited depravity," or similar generalizations. The only way to meet it is by a conscientious and determined search for the causes of crime in general and among Negroes in particular.[1]

The search for causes goes on, but while men of good science and good will have long abandoned the concept of the "born criminal" and of a "genetic" theory of crime, there are still voices in the wilderness of ignorance or prejudice who contend that the non-white, by reason of his biology alone, is a predisposed criminal. A statement made by one group arguing this "genetic" position in 1963 reads as follows: "The enormously greater incidence of criminality on the part of Negroes is largely attributable to genetically determined racial differences in personality and behavioral traits."[2]

The recently published article by Arthur Jensen[3] referred to in an earlier chapter, which suggests a genetic racial difference in I.Q., has added new fuel to this controversy. One Congressman inserted the entire article into the Congressional *Record,* and segregationists are citing it in court cases. [4]

Jensen and others holding similar positions gloss over almost entirely the large body of evidence documenting the strong environmental influences on intelligence. As Professor Jerome S. Kagan of Harvard University points out:

> The essential error in Jensen's argument is the conclusion that if a trait is under genetic control, differences between two populations on that trait must be due to genetic factors. This is the heart of Jensen's position and it is not persuasive.[5]

And James Crow, the respected author of *Genetic Notes,* adds:

> It is clear, I think, that a high heritability of intelligence in the white population would not, even if there were similar evidence in the black population, tell that the differences between the groups are genetic. No matter how high the heritability (unless it is 1), there is no assurance that a sufficiently great environmental difference does not account for the difference in the two means, especially when one considers that the environmental factors may differ qualitatively in the two groups. So, I think. evidence regarding the importance of heredity in determining group mean differences must come from other kinds of studies ....
> It can be argued that being white or being black in our society changes one or more aspects of the environment so importantly as to account for the difference.[6]

Other psychologists and sociologists who disagree sharply with Jensen[7] point out that intelligence - like criminal behavior - is determined by so many factors, that unless all the relevant variables are controlled except race, definitive conclusions cannot be made. There are many factors besides separate gene pools that can account for differences in I.Q. or crime rates – brain damage resulting from malnutrition and impoverishment, lack of preschool training, father's absence from the household, hostile teachers, subservience by blacks, racism and self-fulfilling prophecy, among others.[8]

In a highly significant experiment designed to test the relationship between teacher expectation and child performance, Rosenthal and Jacobsen demonstrated that when teachers anticipated great intellectual growth in certain children, the youngsters actually showed unusual intellectual gains. In one classroom, teachers were told at the beginning of the school year that certain children whom the authors had selected at random for the purpose of the study were intellectually gifted "late bloomers." Their I.Q. rating rose by 41 points during the year. In another classroom: youngsters similarly designated scored 22.5 points higher at the end of the year than at the beginning.[9]

Another study, comparing 38 pairs of identical twins reared in different environments, revealed I.Q. differences averaging 14 points, despite their identical genes.[10] In more than one quarter of the identical pairs tested, the difference was larger than 16 points - a greater difference than the average I.Q. difference between blacks and whites in the United States today. Thus, concludes behavioral geneticist Irving I. Gottesman, who conducted this experiment: "The difference observed so far between whites and Negroes can hardly be accepted as sufficient evidence that with respect to intelligence the Negro-American is genetically less endowed." [11]

A third relevant study, involving 13 babies aged 7 to 36 months, who were transferred from an orphanage where they received little individual care and stimulation to a home where they enjoyed much more attention, noted remarkable gains in I.Q. after two years in the enriched environment. While the babies remaining in the institution showed a decrease of 26 points during this period, the babies transferred to more enriching and congenial environments gained an average of 27 points. [12]

The evidence of these and other studies clearly demonstrates that significant changes in I.Q. scores occur with changes in environment. "If you compare the I.Q. of different racial groups or economic classes, the environments are no longer uniform and any observed differences in I.Q. are bound to be much more strongly influenced by the environmental differences," explains the noted geneticist, Theodosius Dobzhansky. [13]

Rates of criminality, as has been shown, are also strongly influenced by environmental differences. What we know about genetically determined traits suggests that they are specific; that is, we inherit hair and eyes of specific color and perhaps certain specific psychological potentialities. But criminal behavior is not specific, for there are almost as many kinds of crime as differences in behavior. According to Mendel's rule of inheritance of specific traits, if criminality were genetically determined, we should inherit specific tendencies for embezzlement, burglary, forgery, etc. And if we inherited specific criminal forms of behavior, and some of us were genetically destined to be burglars or stock embezzlers, rapists or check forgers, we would also have to inherit specific non-criminal occupations, which means some of us would be as genetically destined to become police officers or truck drivers or schoolteachers, as to have red hair.

Nor can it be argued that Negroes or whites or any group of people have personality and behavioral traits that genetically predetermine them toward general criminality. This position not only ignores the fact that the definition of crime is not stable in time or place, it also fails to recognize that most criminals obey most laws - indeed, are extremely careful to do so in order to avoid drawing police attention. A valid genetic theory would have to explain why criminals observe most laws and only break some laws some times.

For a short while, during the past year or two, there seemed to be some support for genetic theories of criminality in statistics indicating a high incidence of individuals with XYY chromosomes in prison populations. (Most of these statistics dealt with white prisoners in British prisons; thus there was no racial issue involved; indeed, it seems that very few blacks are carriers of the XYY chromosome.) But as more information came to light it became clear that the earlier assumptions had been based on insufficient data, because the exact distribution of XYY chromosomes in the criminal and non-criminal population was not known. Some studies of XYY incidence in the general population indicate that this chromosome makeup is present with about the same frequency among stable, law-abiding males as it is among men in prison.[14] Thus it would appear that the large majority of people with XYY makeup are not law violators. Clearly, any further speculation about causal links between criminal behavior and the XYY chromosome must await additional research, both as to the incidence of the XYY anomaly in law-abiding and law-violating populations and as to the reasons some XYY males violate the law while others do not.

The false genetic theory of crime is sometimes reduced to a contention that certain minority groups are by heredity impulsive, lazy, irresponsible, and that these traits lead to criminality. If so, we might ask, do not whites also inherit these traits? And how do we account for the fact that these traits sometimes lead to criminal conduct and other times to non-criminal lives? How do we account for the increasing appearance of non-whites in outstanding positions of social service. science, business and industry? Or for the fact that some white crime rates in certain parts of the country are three or four times higher than the white crime rates in other parts?

Thus, as we observed at the start. no genetic theory of crime is given credence by the community of scholars concerned with either crime or genetics. Everything we know about criminal behavior indicates that it is learned and what is learned comes from experience with our surrounding environment. It is to that environment we must turn our attention.

Crime and Environment

When queried, most people who are not students of criminology will say that a person becomes a delinquent or criminal because of adverse conditions, such as poverty, poor education, unemployment, lack of parental supervision, deterioration of moral values. The more sophisticated theories of criminologists also take cognizance of these factors, weaving them into a logical array of influences and ideas that seek to explain typical forms of crime and delinquency. An important point to keep in mind, therefore, is that instead of asking why a Negro becomes delinquent or criminal, we should ask why anyone does.

Among some of the most compelling writings on delinquency today are those of Albert K. Cohen, Richard Cloward and Lloyd Ohlin, and Walter B. Miller, who base many of their ideas on the early researches of Frederick M. Thrasher, Clifford R. Shaw and Henry D. McKay in Chicago and the sociological theory of Talcott Parsons and Robert K. Merton.[15] Although there are important differences among these writers, their dominant themes are similar: There are values in American society which emphasize the goals of (mostly material) success. Because the means to achieve these goals are not available to all in equal measure, many people fall prey to feelings of anxiety and despair which may be expressed in forms of deviance and delinquency.

In one sense, delinquency and crime are conceived as normal responses to conditions of life that close the doors of opportunity. Delinquency becomes both a protest against the social system that blocks the path to success and a way, albeit illegitimate, to acquire recognition and status among equal sharers in the same subjected group. Difficult to find are the legitimate opportunities for success (education, good job, proper contacts); far more accessible are the illegitimate opportunities (theft, gambling, drugs), to obtain the symbols of success (car, property, power).

This approach to understanding crime means concerning ourselves with the physical and social conditions - low income, unskilled occupation and unemployment family disruption, poor education - which prevent some groups even the minimal promises of the American Dream. Psychological aspects of this relative deprivation may involve frustration, serious damage to self-conception, and other personality disorders, for these social conditions engender not only delinquency, but also disqualification and despair. The catalogue of crises in the life style of the culturally deprived has been abundantly described in scientific studies, essays and popular fiction. We need not review them here. It is clear, however, that while many whites suffer social disabilities, the visibility of the Negro, Puerto Rican, and Mexican American, along with the weight of a history of prejudice, renders these groups more vulnerable to isolation and a diminished share in the economic, political and social life of the larger democratic community. [16]

In the large-scale efforts of the New York City Youth Board to predict delinquency, using the Glueck Social Prediction Table, the results thus far suggest that the same set of factors - the type of supervision and discipline by mother, the degree of family cohesiveness-are useful for predicting delinquency among white, Negro or Puerto Rican youth.[17] With greater exposure to deleterious conditions, it would not be surprising if Negroes displayed a higher crime rate. When white delinquents and non-delinquents are compared, differences in their backgrounds are similar to those observed when Negro delinquents are compared with Negro non-delinquents.

We cannot say with conclusiveness why some children in life's poorer circumstances become delinquent while others do not, for certainly not all homes in rundown neighborhoods, with missing parents, low incomes and crime in the streets produce delinquent juveniles. But these conditions are more likely to yield failure than success, to encourage children to drop out of school and into crime. Convinced that neither the child nor the adult freely chooses to become a criminal, we recognize that a society which does not provide sufficient acceptable alternatives to successful adjustment will encourage unacceptable ones.

The amounts of mobility and family disorganization common to many of the conditions noted above have also been associated with delinquency. Once again non-whites experience more of both. Many studies repeatedly find the same conclusion. One of these by Sidney Axelrod pointed out that among institutionalized children, only 18 per cent of the Negroes lived with both parents, compared with 46 per cent of the whites; and 85 per cent of the Negroes came from broken homes, compared with 50 per cent of the whites.[18] It was also disclosed that Negro children committed by the courts were younger, had committed less serious offenses, and had fewer previous court appearances than white children.

There are certain occupational groups which are virtually free of recorded crime. These include professionals, managers and technicians who constitute about 25 per cent of the white labor force but only 9 per cent of the non-white. The highest proportion of offenders, both white and non-white, comes from unskilled laboring groups or the unemployed. There are three times as many non-whites as whites in the unskilled category, and at least twice as many unemployed.

As of 1967, the average (median) family income of whites ($8,274) was more than one and a half that of non-whites ($5,141), with the regional difference greatest in the South ($7,408 for whites; $3,994 for non-whites).[19] Furthermore, while the income; gap was closing between 1940 and 1950, no progress seems to have been made between 1950 and 1960. In 1940, the average non-white male's wages were 41 per cent of the average white male's; by 1950, this had risen to 61 per cent, but the improvement stopped there. By 1960, the figure was only 60 per cent, and by 1966 it had regressed further to 58 per cent.[20]

Again, in a Philadelphia report, about one-third of whites, but less than one-fourth of the non-whites, had finished high school. As a matter of fact, about the same percentage of non-whites finished high school in 1960 as had whites in 1940, showing a 20-year lag in educational attainment. Fewer non-whites in that city had finished college in 1960 (3 per cent) than had .whites in 1960 (6 per cent) or even in 1940 (4 per cent). Certainly this disparity is due to the greater difficulties of entering college than of staying in once admitted, for the dropout rate of Negroes is low. In a national study, fewer than 10 per cent of Negro students failed to complete college while approximately 40 per cent of white students did not graduate.[21]   As recently as 1965 the Census Bureau reported that twice the percentage of whites (14 per cent) as of blacks (7 per cent) had completed four years of college or more. [22]

When all of these conditions are linked with segregation, particularly in highly deteriorated neighborhoods, they assume even greater weight as contributions to delinquency. Yet we have good reason to believe that it is not merely the concentration of Negroes that produces high rates of delinquency; as Lander has shown in his Baltimore study, neighborhoods with highest concentration had rates as low as or lower than rates for whites throughout the city. And even in the highly congested, relatively segregated areas housing Puerto Ricans in New York City, the amount of delinquency is not high, as we have noted.[23] The overwhelming majority obey the law.

Mozell Hill has summarized our thesis well: "Negroes who live in blighted areas suffer deeply from discrimination, rejection and lack of integration into the society. juvenile delinquency among them is generated by this lack of integration rather than by processes of social disorganization. An increase in juvenile delinquency is likely to occur most frequently when and where aspirations of youth persist under conditions of limited and prescribed opportunities. Under such circumstances access to success goals by legitimate means is seldom available to Negro youth in cities. They do not have opportunities for internalization of acceptable and respectable norms of conduct."[24]

NOTES

---

[1] Thorsten Sellin. "The Negro Criminal. A Statistical Note," *The Annals of the American Academy of Political and Social Science* (1928), 140:52-64, p. 64 cited.

[2] H. C. Sanborn, "Dr. W. C. George's *The Biology of the Race Problem*: A Review," New York: National Putnam Letters Committee, n.d.

[3] Arthur R. Jensen, "How Much Can We Boost I.Q. and Scholastic Achievement," *Harvard Educational Review*, 39:1 Winter 1969, pp. 1-123.

[4] As cited in Lee Edson, "jensenism . . . ," *The New York Times Magazine*, op. cit., p. 46.

[5] Jerome S. Kagan, *Harvard Educational Review*, Spring 1969, op. cit., p. 275.

[6] Ibid., p. 308.

[7] Statement of George W. Albee et al., Council of the Society for the Psychological Study of Social Issues, May 2, 1969.

[8] See Martin Deutsch, Irwin Katz, and Arthur R. Jensen (eds.) *Social Class, Race and Psychological Development*, New York: Holt, Rinehart, and Winston, Inc., 1968, p. 345 and *Harvard Educational Review*, Spring 1969, op. cit., p. 355.

[9] Robert Rosenthal and Lenore Jacobson, "Self-Fulfilling Prophecies in the Classroom: Teacher's Expectations as Unintended Determinants of Pupil's Intellectual Competence." In Deutsch et al., op. cit., pp. 219-253, especially 234-35.

[10] I. I. Gottesman, "Biogenetics of Race and Class." In Deutsch et al., op. cit., pp. 11-51. See especially pp. 27-28.

[11] *Harvard Educational Review*, Spring 1969, op. cit., p. 275.

[12] H. M. Skeels and H. B. Dye, "A Study of the Effects of Differential Stimulation on Mentally Retarded Children," *Proceedings of the American Association on Mental Deficiency*, 1939, 44, pp. 114-136., Cited by Celia Stendler-LaVatelli, "Environmental Intervention in Infancy and Early Childhood." In Deutsch et al., op. cit., p. 353.

[13] Theodosius Dobzhansky, "Genetic Differences Between People," *Scientific Research*, July 22, 1968, p. 33.

[14] "A Kind Word Said for XYY Men," *The New York Times*, May 6, 1969, p. 93.

[15] For the main themes of these authors, see the following works: Albert K. Cohen, *Delinquent Boys*, Glencoe, Ill.: The Free Press, 1955; Richard Cloward and Lloyd Ohlin, *Delinquency and Opportunity*, Glencoe, Ill.: The Free Press. 1960; Walter B. Miller. "Lower Class Culture as a Generating Milieu of Gang Delinquency," *Journal of Social Issues* (1959), 14:5-19; Frederic M. Thrasher, *The Gang*, Chicago: University of Chicago Press, 1936; Shaw and McKay, loc. cit., Talcott Parsons, *The Social System*, Glencoe. Ill.: The Free Press, 1951, especially Ch. VII; Robert K. Merton, *Social Theory and Social Structure*, Glencoe, Ill.: The Free Press. 1957.

[16] For discussions of many problems of delinquency among Negroes, see the entire issue of the *Journal of Negro Education*, (Summer 1959), vol. 28. Also see: Nathan Wright, Jr., *Let's Work Together*, New York: Hawthorn Books, Inc., 1968.

[17] Maude M. Craig and Selma J. Glick, "Ten Years' Experience With the Glueck Social Prediction Table," *Crime and Delinquency*, (1963), 9:249-261.

[18] *Philadelphia's Non-White Population 1960*, Report No. 3, Socioeconomic Data, Philadelphia: Commission on Human Relations, December 1962.

[19] These data may be found in reports issued by the Bureau of the Census. See: "Social and Economic Conditions of Negroes in the U.S.," October 1967, BLS Report #332, *Current Population Reports*, Series P-23, No. 24, Washington D.C.: U.S. Government Printing Office, pp. 12, 39, 41 and 47; "Consumer Income: Income in 1967 of Families in the United States," *Current Population Reports*, Series P-60, No. 59, April 18, 1969, Washington, D.C.: U.S. Government Printing Office, p. 51. We are drawing also from the concise article by

Philip M. Hauser, "More from the Census of 1960," *Scientific American*, October 1962, pp. 30-37.

[20] Herman P. Miller, "Is the Income Gap Closed? 'No!'" *The New York Times Magazine*, November 11, 1962. "Social and Economic Conditions of Negroes in the United States," op. cit., p. 15.

[21] Kenneth B. Clark and Lawrence Plotkin, *The Negro Student at Integrated Colleges*, National Scholarship Service and Fund for Negro Students, 1963.

[22] "Social and Economic Conditions of Negroes in the U.S." op. cit., p.47.

[23] Lander, op. cit.

[24] Mozell Hill, "The Metropolis and Juvenile Delinquency Among Negroes," *Journal of Negro Education* (1959), 28:277-285, p. 284 cited.

VIOLENCE, U.S.A.: RIOTS AND CRIME

Marvin E. Wolfgang

*Keynote address, 15th National Institute on Crime and Delinquency, Dallas, June 16, 1968.
Reprinted in Crime and Delinquency, (National Council on Crime and Delinquency).
14:4:289-305. (Oct. 1968).*

Violence in America today is more than the society wishes to tolerate, but should be considered historically and cross-culturally. Labor and other riots in the nineteenth and twentieth centuries were probably more destructive than current disturbances. America is not a "sick" society but does have violence within an essentially nonviolent culture. The fear of being victimized from crimes of violence is real but greater than statistics on victimization indicate. To riot is a violation of the law and partially a reflection of inadequate response from government and other agencies to legitimate grievance and dissent. To resort to violence is a sign of despair and a failure to have alternative avenues of expression. A subculture of violence exists in many cities and is generated from the value system associated with the poor, the deprived, the residents of segregation. Dispersal of the Population from this subculture is the major solution for its elimination. The task of a democracy is to guarantee the right to dissent, to respond to protest, and to fortify freedom while maintaining social control.

The vanguard of the Renaissance of western civilization was Florence, Italy. Scholars and tourists alike glowingly describe the rebirth of our classical heritage, the humanistic philosophy, new perspectives in art, the political structure and processes of the Florentine Commune, the new architecture and legal system. Yet, with this renascent spirit there was still mob violence, riots, and bloodshed in the streets.

When the dictatorial Duke of Athens was compelled by an angry mob to flee the city in 1343, some of his political assistants were grabbed on the street, tortured, and murdered. The apex of the mob fury was reached in the scene described as follows:

> Those who could not wound them while alive, wounded them after they were dead; and not satisfied with tearing them to pieces, they hewed their bodies with swords, tore them with their hands, and even with their teeth. And that every sense might be satiated with vengeance, having first heard their moans, seen their wounds, and touched their

lacerated bodies, they wished even the stomach to be satisfied, that having glutted the external sense, the one within might also have its share.[1]

The poor boy, only eighteen years of age, dressed with sorrowful significance in black, was thrust through the heavy portal of the palace by the Burgundian soldiers, and torn limb from limb in the sight of his father, on whom the same fate descended immediately afterwards. The limbs of these victims were paraded on sticks through the town, and some boasted that they had eaten the raw flesh.[2]

This mob action helped to sustain Machiavelli's insistence that "the rage of men is certainly always found greater, and their revenge more furious upon the recovery of liberty, than when it has only been defended."[3]

By 1378 a vicious circle of popular lawlessness and governmental retaliation had been formed. One chronicler described conditions this way:

> The populace perpetually penetrated into the palace, and interfered with the Priors in the discharge of their functions, ordering any name which they did not like to be torn up; and as the ranks of the malcontents were increased by those whom the government had ejected as too democratic, it may be imagined how the restless suspicions of the people were utilized for personal ends. The town was honeycombed with conspiracy, the banished of all classes keeping up communications with their friends and adherents inside the walls. Torture was freely applied, and numerous people decapitated in consequence of "confessions" thus obtained. Every man went about with invisible eyes fixed upon him, and names of "suspects" were found written up at the corners of the streets.[4]

A century later, in 1478, at the time of the Pazzi conspiracy against the life of Lorenzo de' Medici, we read:

> The streets of Florence were polluted with the dead bodies and mangled limbs of the slaughtered. The palace was recovered from its assailants, whose carcasses were thrown into the street, and dragged about for the amusement of the people. The name of the Medici echoed everywhere; and portions of the bodies of the slain were borne about the streets on lances by mobs, who incessantly raised the cry "Palle! Palle!" Perish the traitors. As to the Pazzi, they became at once objects of universal detestation.[5]

My reason for referring to these scenes is patent: to draw upon examples of riot and violence from a beautiful city at the most glorious time in its history, to show the brutal side of man's behavior in the midst of another period's affluence, political enlightenment, and highly humanistic culture.

Violence Then and Now, Here and There

We are faced today with the questions of whether American society is more violent than earlier and whether we are more violent than other societies.

I should preface these remarks with caution. Most of my own research experience is concerned with collecting and carefully examining empirical data, using appropriate statistical tools for computation, and analyzing computer printouts with supported interpretations. My penchant for speculation and leaping into sweeping generalizations about "national character," the American society, and our "culture style" is probably as great as the next fellow's. But I have been reared in the constraints of logic, the scientific method, and the language of critical analysis, and it is therefore with a sense of hypothesis-formation, tentative assumptions, and heuristic suggestion that I venture into the game of pontificating about the stance of our society with respect to violence.

Man is not innately criminal, violent, or aggressive. He responds to people, events, or other kinds of stimuli that precipitate violative, violent, or aggressive behavior. But he learns what is fearful or frustrating so that the things to which he reacts are interpreted by him as such, and the resolution of events which he defines as problems is also learned. Cats, dogs, monkeys do not shoot their adversaries because they cannot or have not learned to use guns. Only man has the capacity, to make and to use such artificial weapons designed to destroy himself and others.

I am enough of a behaviorist to believe that the normal human being is born amoral, with plasticity to his personality, capable of being molded not only by his genes but by the generations before him and beside him. I am sufficiently a collectivist to realize the power that groups have over me, from large-scale political and economic organizations to crowds, the amorphous public, neighborhoods, and professional peers. I am enough of an individualist to enjoy privacy, to want the right to be different, to believe that I have the capacity to use reason. I have been reared in values, learned from family and friends, that oppose violence and crime. Like most others I refrain from crime not because of the negative fear of detection or punishment but because of the positive commitment to a moral system that views crime as socially dysfunctional and individually reprehensible. But I am also enough of a realist to know that these propositions contain inconsistencies and contradictions. At the extremes of social life and in the crises of history, the logic of love can change to hatred and sweet reason turn sour.

When colonies collected themselves in the eighteenth century to sever their maternal ties, we called the action revolution and good despite the violence it engendered. When some states in the nineteenth century sought to bifurcate the nation, we called the action civil war and bad and lamented the bloodshed. The Nazis gave justice to our bombs and enlisted the world's generation of youth to react violently to violence. Violence becomes viewed as a rapid collective problem-solver, from the three and twenty stabs in Caesar, according to Suetonius, to riots in city streets. Riots, rebellion, and revolution - the words we use to describe the stages provide more than alliterative language of the process; the rapid transition from one action to the other now causes our restless and anxious point in history, and commands our attention for response.

When men perceive oppression as their lot and know of others not oppressed, when ordered avenues of change are blocked by kings or legis- lators or some vague variety of any social system, the oppressed will either resign themselves to fate or rise up to taste the fruit of freedom, and having tasted will want the feast.

Like whites, Negroes are men who have learned of their oppression. By forced migration they became slaves. The politics of war redefined their citizenry but little their status. Slaves became servants in the economics of change. The quiet process of elevation has been too slow for all but a trickle of black humanity to enjoy white privilege, and today color is a description not of the skin but of one's status in society. That status is a depressed, deprived, and now frustrating one.

There are those who argue that American society is "sick" with vio- lence and worse today than ever. The argument includes the following items, some of which are real, others exaggerated or false: crime rates are rising; there are more killings and rapes than ever before; students are going wild with violence on campuses across the country; assassinations are upon us from President Kennedy to Martin Luther King to Senator Kennedy, with Medgar Evers, Viola Liuzzo, Michael Schwerner, James Chaney, Andrew Goodman, and Malcolm X in between; race riots are changing our cities into battlefields.

The explanations for current violence often become each observer's special scapegoat theory: the frontier mores; machismo; our permissive so- ciety; poverty amidst affluence; rising expectations with angry disenchant- ment; violence on television and in comics; working mothers and broken homes; recent Supreme Court decisions; black power; the Vietnam war; mail-order guns.

I am not prepared with evidence to deny the validity of these assertions singly or in combination. What I suggest, however, is that there is evidence in rebuttal to the general interpretation of our society's being newly, excessively, distinctively violent. In contrast to an ideal of nonviolence, we obviously have violence. But it is in the comparative mode, over our own history and other nations that the assertion is made and the rebuttal is offered.

Recall some of our own history that suggests violence as severe as or worse than now. We might discount the Revolution and the War between the States, the latter of which took approximately a half million lives. But we cannot neglect the Shay and Whiskey Rebellions over debts and taxes; the slaughter and subjugation of American Indians; the Know-Nothings who fought rising Irish political power, who had a 48-hour orgy of mob violence in St. Louis in 1854 in which a dozen persons were killed and fifty homes of Irish Catholics wrecked and looted, who killed twenty persons in a two-day riot in Louisville the next year and burned two churches and two parochial schools in Philadelphia; and the Irish antidraft riot in New York in 1863 that killed nearly 2,000 and injured 8,000 in four days.

There were the bloody railroad strikes in 1877 that killed 150; the Rocky Mountain mining wars that took the lives of 198, including a governor, at the turn of the century; the brutal Molly Maguires, a secret band of Irish miners in Pennsylvania; the Wobblies, or Industrial Workers of the World; the industrial and railroad police who brutally beat laborers from Pennsylvania to California; the garment workers' strike in Chicago in 1910 that resulted in seven deaths, an unknown number seriously injured, and 874 arrests; the twenty lives lost in the Illinois Central Railroad strikes in 1911; the 1919 steel strike in which twenty persons perished; the national cotton textile labor dispute of 1934 that spread from Georgia and South Carolina to Alabama, even to Rhode Island and Connecticut, with twenty-one deaths and 10,000 soldiers on strike duty.[6]

By 1871 the invisible empire of the Ku Klux Klan "had a membership of over half a million, and a Congressional investigation that year uncovered hangings, shootings, whippings, and mutilations in the thousands. In Louisiana alone, two thousand persons had been killed, wounded, or injured in a short few weeks before the election of 1868. The commanding general of federal forces in Texas reported: 'Murders of Negroes are so common as to render it impossible to keep accurate accounts of them.'"[7]

That violence is not unique to the United States is an assertion that needs no more than a few illustrations. The aftermath of the French Revolution had a kind of terror and bloodshed never witnessed in this country; the 1845 student riots in France spread throughout Europe; assassinations occurred from Austrian Archduke Francis Ferdinand in 1914 to Prime Minister Vervoerd recently in South Africa. The Nazis need not even be mentioned. There is still fresh in history the tortures in French Algeria; the Stalinist terrors of a generation; the mob violence and riots off and on for another generation involving Pakistanis and Indians; the current Nigerian civil war; the student and union violence in France today; the *violencia* of Colombia for nearly twenty years that resulted in the assassination of Dr. Jorge Gaitan in 1948 and an estimated 200,000 deaths up to 1967; the confused "cultural revolution" in mainland China; and the horrendous, little-publicized massacre of 400,000 persons in recent years in Indonesia.

The homicide rate in the United States today is steadily around 4 or 5 per 100,000, with only slight variations from year to year. In 1933 it was over twice as high, or around 11. The murder rate for Colombia is 34; for Mexico, 30; Nicaragua, 29; Guatemala, 12; Ecuador, 6 - even with poorly collected statistics. Of course the United States stands high in comparison with England and most of northern Europe. Our homicide rate is four times as high as Canada's and Australia's. These two countries also had "frontier mores"; in fact, Australia was first colonized by convicts.

Today we have more police, more bookkeepers of crime statistics, more definitions of delinquency - like truancy, running away from home, being incorrigible - that include one-third of our delinquents, who are not defined as such in other countries. Most large cities have large Juvenile Aid Divisions or Bureaus with the opportunity to apprehend juveniles under the label of "nonarrest," "remedial," or "warned" who nonetheless are counted in the police delinquency statistics. In Philadelphia this category comprises two-thirds of those under eighteen years who are taken into custody. Recent studies of Boston and Buffalo, using police and court data that reach back to the eighteenth century, indicate that rates of serious crimes were higher in the nineteenth century than they are today.

Supreme Court decisions regarding appearance of suspects for hearings within forty-eight hours were also viewed as "tying the hands of the police" and blamed for crime waves that never existed, Technical means and institutional modes of adjusting to the requirement slowly quieted earlier opposition until the rule is now taken for granted. Violence on television is distasteful to many, but the link to violent behavior is deemed unproved. And although I would prefer all guns in private hands to be turned in to public authorities and believe that many lives would be saved by very restrictive gun legislation, I am also aware that there are probably twice as many guns around the country today as in the 1930's, and I note a steady decline in criminal homicides since then. The inverse correlation is not causative, but neither is a reverse interpretation.

Violence in our own past, in 'the past and present of other nations, does not diminish it in our current scene. But its present dimensions and our instant explanations should be viewed with these perspectives.

The Fear of Being Victimized

There appears to be a widespread fear in the United States, especially in central cities, of being assaulted, robbed, and raped on the streets. Most social analysts agree that the fear is present and real, although there is only meager evidence and much conjecture about the validity of facts to justify the fear. As the mass media present more information (news) more rapidly about a phenomenon (crime) to more consumers over wider areas, these consumers tend to assume that the frequency of the phenomenon is increasing. This kind of "instant" news may be partially responsible for the increased fear of being victimized.

Official rates of crimes of violence are, among some offenses, moderately increasing. We do not know the extent to which the crime rate may be affected by improved methods of recording, higher proportions of civilian employees to tabulate and correctly calculate crime statistics in the city police departments, the increase in citizens' willingness to report crimes, and other such factors, but they may be contributing to some of the official rate increases.

Surveys conducted for the President's Commission on Law Enforcement and Administration of justice interestingly reveal that most people are not victimized sufficiently often for crime to make a major impact on their lives. Nonetheless, if the actual experience of victimization is not a major determinant of attitudes about crime, there is a sense in which vulnerability influences fear. The greater concern of Negroes is consistent with the risks of victimization suggested by police statistics. Negroes are far more likely to be victims of a serious offense against the person than are white persons. The greater anxiety of women than men, however, is not consistent with what is known of the victimization risks. When citizens in Washington, D.C., were asked what steps they took to protect themselves against crime, they commonly spoke of avoiding danger in the streets and indicated that they sometimes stayed home at night or used taxis, or that they avoided talking to strangers. Some spoke of measures to protect themselves and their property at home, such as keeping firearms or watchdogs or putting stronger locks on the doors and windows. The crimes which the public seems to fear most crimes of violence - are those which occur least frequently. People appear to be more tolerant of crimes against property. They fear most being attacked by strangers, although the probabilities of being assaulted by strangers, especially in the streets, are very low. From abundant research we know that crimes of violence are commonly committed in the intimacy of the home; they are intra-ethnic and generally intra-group offenses. For example, only about 5 or 6 per cent of all rapes in the United States involve strangers and victim-offender relationships that are at the same time interracial.

Urban Space and Victimization Probabilities

Although the rates of increase of crime in the city have not been alarming, especially when computed as age-specific rates that take into account the increase in the teen-age and young adult population due to the high postwar birth rate, the probability of being victimized may have considerably increased over the past fifteen years.

Even if *rates* of violent crime have changed little over time, the *volume* of violent crimes has increased simply because of the increase in population. From the perspective of the potential victim, what is critical is not the crime rate of offenders or even the rate at which persons become victims of crime but rather the probability of an individual's being victimized in a given dimension of space, like a city street corner, a given block, or the center of the city. While the crude rate of violent crime or even the rate of juvenile crime may have remained fairly steady, the population of the neighborhood and the number of youths of crime-prone age may indeed have increased over fifteen years. Yet, the spatial dimension of the neighborhood has not increased; a street intersection remains the same. The result is that the chances of a given citizen's being assaulted at that intersection have increased.

It has also been observed that one of the historical methods of urban crime control has been to cluster the lower classes in densely populated and residentially restricted areas. This style of ghetto crime control, common from Greco-Roman times, medieval Paris, industrial London, and modern America, is declining as social policy mounts an increasing attack against poverty and ghetto-living. As barriers of streets and prejudice break down, the lower socioeconomic classes are spreading throughout the city and slowly beginning to spill out of the city boundaries.

The long-range effects of this geographic dispersion should have widespread social benefits, but the immediate, transitory effect of a lower class dispersing and still harboring some of the deleterious markings of slum living and social values - often including those connected with the ready resort to violence - may be to increase the amount of crime in old sections of cities that previously were accustomed to low crime rates. Thus, the older residents of formerly low crime-rate areas begin to note that the old familiar streets are "not as safe as they used to be." And, their perception may indeed be correct.

If, however, a democratic society opts for increased opportunities for all citizens, including freedom of residential choice, the transition stage to which we referred must be faced and accelerated so that a change in life style and value orientations toward property and the dignity of persons accompanies the change of residence.

Crime and Riots

Criminogenic Forces of the City

The forces that generate conditions conducive to crime and riots are stronger in an urban community than in rural areas. Urban living is more anonymous living. It releases the individual from community restraints more common in tradition-oriented societies. But more freedom from constraints and controls also provides greater freedom to deviate. And living in the more impersonalized, formally controlled urban society means that regulatory orders of conduct are often directed by distant bureaucrats. The police are strangers executing these prescriptions on, at worst, an alien subcommunity and, at best, an anonymous set of subjects. Minor offenses in a small town or village are often handled without resort to official police action. As eufunctional as such action may seem to be, it nonetheless results in fewer recorded violations of the law compared to the city. Although perhaps causing some decision difficulties for the police in small towns, formal and objective law enforcement is not acceptable to the villagers.

Urban areas with mass populations, greater wealth, more commercial establishments, and more products of our technology also provide more frequent opportunities for theft. Victims are impersonalized, property is insured, consumer goods in more abundance are vividly displayed and are more portable.

Urban life is commonly characterized by population density, spatial mobility, ethnic and class heterogeneity, reduced family functions, and, as we have said, greater anonymity. All of these traits are expressed in comparison to nonurban life, or varying degrees of urbanism and urbanization. When, on a scale, these traits are found in high degree, and when they are combined with poverty, physical deterioration, low education, residence in industrial and commercial centers, unemployment or unskilled labor, economic dependency, marital instability or breaks, poor or absent male models for young boys, overcrowding, lack of legitimate opportunities to make a better life, the absence of positive anticriminal behavior patterns, higher frequency of organic diseases, and a cultural minority status of inferiority, it is generally assumed that social-psychological mechanisms leading to deviance are more likely to emerge. These include frustration, lack of motivation to obey external demands, internalized cultural strains of inconsistency between means available and ends desired, conflicting norms, anomie, and so forth. The link between these two conditions-physical features of subparts of a city and the social-psychological aspects-has not been fully researched to the point where the latter can be safely said to be invariable or highly probable consequences of the former. Thus, to move onto a third level - namely, a tradition of lawlessness, of delinquent or criminal behavior, as a further consequence of the physical and social-- psychological conditions of much urban life - is an even more tenuous scientific position. Nonetheless, these are the assumptions under which the community of scholars and public administrators operate today. The assumptions are the most justified and logically adequate we can make unless or until successfully refuted.

It has often been suggested that high crime areas of a city (meaning both residence of offenders and place of crime occurrence) contain, in high numbers, new migrants, the residue of earlier residential groups that have - mostly moved out, and competitive failures from better districts who were forced to move back to the cheaper rent areas. This "selective migration" thesis may have some validity, but it has also been noted that most of the criminals in the high crime areas had been reared in delinquency areas of other cities.

It is abundantly clear even to the most casual observer that Negroes in American society are the current carriers of a ghetto tradition. More than any other socially defined group, they are the recipients of urban deterioration and the social-psychological forces leading to legal deviance. And for this reason, concern with crime in the city is commonly a concern with Negro crime. Although there are good reasons for raising serious questions about criminal statistics that report race of the offender and the fact that Negro crime rates are in general three or four times higher than white rates, and although Negroes probably suffer more injustices than whites in the law enforcement process from arrest to imprisonment, it is no surprise that the most valid efforts to measure crime still find Negro crime rates high. When the untoward aspects of urban life are found among Italians, Germans, Poles, or almost any other group, their crime rates are similarly high. Relative deprivation and social disqualification are thus dramatically chained to despair and delinquency.

All of this is not meant to obscure the fact that poverty also exists in small towns and rural areas. But when multiplied by congested thousands and transmitted over generations, poverty becomes a culture. The expectations of social intercourse change and irritable, frustrated parents often become neglectful and aggressive. Their children inherit a sub-*culture of violence* where physically aggressive responses are either expected or required by all members sharing not only the tenement's plumbing but also its system of values. Ready access and resort to weapons in this milieu may be essential to protection against others who respond in similarly violent ways in certain situations. Carrying a knife or some other protective device becomes a common symbol of willingness to participate in violence, to expect violence, and to be ready for its retaliation.

A subculture of violence is not the product of cities alone. The Thugs of India, the *vendetta barbaricina* in Sardinia, the *mafioso* in Sicily have existed for a long time. But the contemporary American city has the accoutrements not only for the genesis but also for the highly accelerated development of this subculture, and it is from this subculture that most violent crimes come.

The Crime of Riot

Crimes do not cause riots, but riots cause and are themselves crimes. Studies of riots by the Brandeis University Lemberg Center for the Study of Violence and studies of the Watts and Detroit riots tell us that "high levels of discontent" about job opportunities, housing, school integration, police behavior, and the efforts of federal and local governments to encourage integration characterized the feelings of the Negro population in six riot cities. Inflammatory incidents, usually perceived as police brutality, are the common precipitating, triggering factors. Although rioters are usually from the "under-class," the Watts study indicated that Negro readiness to participate in violence is not confined to this group.

A Howard University study of the early days of Negro nonviolent sit-ins and demonstrations tells us that, during the period when these incidents occurred, the rate of delinquency went down, and it explains this reduction in part by the fact that adolescent boys who might otherwise have been engaged in malicious mischief, corner lounging, disorderly conduct, and other similar acts had their attention and energies diverted to the demonstrations. The participation of juvenile gangs in riot control in Chicago after the assassination of Martin Luther King has been recorded as somewhat successful.

But it is also recorded that a high proportion of persons arrested during riots have previous arrest and criminal records. Many of these persons were looters, and looters are the parasitical wave in the riot and its aftermath who take advantage of the anomic situation. In one sense, carrying off color television sets, guns, and even pianos is a collective symbolic gesture of stealing a piece of the rewards of privilege requested by but denied to the Negro poor.

While not having a firm political ideology any more than students who riot on campus, the "young militants" responsible for the fire-bombing and the sniping - the bitter and alienated activists - surely perceive the bureaucrats and the broader social order as distant impersonal targets for distaste and disruption. Having seen that it is possible to get attention and dethrone the complacency of the white establishment, and having gained hope that their lot can be improved, they regard their present deprivation as unendurable. In referring to the French Revolution, De Tocqueville said: "A people which has supported without complaint, as if they were not felt, the most oppressive laws, violently throws them off as soon as their weight is lightened. The social order destroyed by a revolution is always better than that which immediately preceded it. The end which was suffered patiently as inevitable seems unendurable as soon as the idea of escaping from it is conceived."[8]

To riot is a crime in any state penal code definition. To incite to riot, to loot, burglarize, set on fire, destroy property, rob, assault, shoot, carry deadly weapons - each of these is a crime. Surely the unrecorded number of crimes and of unapprehended offenders is enormous. Deaths that occur from retaliation by the police are, in strictly legalistic terms in some states, felony murders because they occurred as a consequence of other felonious acts committed by the rioters.

In still another sense, not compatible with a legalistic proximate cause notion, the white society, as the Kerner Commission noted, is responsible for inciting to riot. While displaying before the Negro poor the democratic idealism of opportunity, it has inflicted on them the prejudice, the economic blockage of opportunities, the subjugation, and the alienation from power and participation in democracy that have produced among Negroes the power to respond, exploding now in attacks to express their feelings. The urban riots thus far are a mixed bag of some confusing revolutionary ideology among a few, gnomic acts expressive of social malaise among many, and almost adventuresome play among still others. Should there be another round of riot, it will be either moderate skirmishes in more muted tones, reflecting a skewness toward dissipation of the ghetto thrust, or more violent guerilla warfare that can result only in more stringent repressive force by the state. If riots this summer are few or more moderate, we might conclude that the massively diffused efforts for better police-community relations, coalitions of white business with the Negro community, and all our other strategies of solution that reject tokenism and gradualism are beginning to pay off.

I am inclined to link the causes of urban riots and those of urban crime. Where riots have begun, crime rates have been highest, especially crimes of violence. The social forces that have generated crime overlay the forces that erupt into riot. The players in both dramas are the same or similar. The parallelism is too strong to ignore or deny. Correct the conditions causing the one phenomenon and you change the other concomitantly.

Citizen Response

Dispersion of the Subculture of Violence [9]

I have spoken of the subculture of violence, mostly with reference to high rates of crimes of violence, outside the domain of concern with riots. My personal theoretical proclivity is to disperse the subculture's members, thus eliminating that subcultural set of values attached to the use of violence. The form of this dispersal is subsidized relocation and redistribution of the population:

To intervene socially means taking some kind of action designed to break into the information loop that links the subcultural representatives in a constant chain of reinforcement of the use of violence. Political, economic, and other forms of social action sometimes buttress the subculture by forcing it to seek strength and solace within itself as a defense against the larger culture and thereby more strongly establish the subcultural value system. Social inaction probably does the same in lesser degree, for inaction is not generally indifference and thereby does not produce zero response.

The residential propinquity of the actors in a subculture of violence has been noted. Breaking up this propinquity, dispersing the members who share intense commitment to the violence value, could also cause a break in the inter- and intra-generational communication of this value system. Dispersion can be done in many ways and does not necessarily imply massive population shifts, although urban renewal, slum clearance, and housing projects suggest feasible ways. Renewal programs that simply shift the location of the subculture from one part of the city to another do not destroy the subculture. For the subculture to be distributed so that it dissipates, the scattered units should be small. Housing projects and neighborhood areas should be microcosms of the social hierarchy and value system of the central dominant culture. It is in homogeneity that the subculture has strength and durability.

For all its apparent, but still questionable, virtues and victories, the detached-worker programs of handling juvenile and delinquent gangs must still be viewed as a kind of holding action, or containment policy, until a more or less "spontaneous remission" of gang members occurs through aging, marrying, or moving away. The occasionally reported solidifying of formerly diffused activities is an untoward turn of events in the detached-worker programs. The point is, however, that detached-worker action, like any program that moves into a subculture from the outside, even with the language and dress associated with it, is designed to introduce values from the dominant culture by subtly and slowly bending the subculture values to parallel the former. (Where deviant values are not delinquent, it is probably more propitious for the dominant culture to become more flexible and permit the deviancy to function freely.) But such purposeful action by the larger society has been only piecemeal, outnumbered and outmaneuvered by the subculture, which, to the invading team, itself becomes the dominant culture within this setting.

In a sense, then, the larger culture sets up its own outposts within a subculture and seeks by subversive action to undermine the subcultural values. The police in these neighborhoods are like enemy troops in alien territory; they are the most blatant large-culture bearers. The detached workers, while still not undercover agents, are the most subtle subversives. With neither form of control, however, has society been able to record much success; and certainly no, or at best few, claims can be made for destroying the subculture of violence by these means.

While operating within the subculture that uses nonlegal methods, the legal nonviolent methods of the invaders often appear to have little or no utility. In many cases, the larger culture invaders who seek to control the subculture of violence ultimately resort to violence themselves and hence use the very methods of the subculture to subdue it. This usage reinforces and provides new subcultural justification for violence.

Before one set of values can replace another, before the subculture of violence can be substituted by the establishment of nonviolence, the former must be disrupted, dispersed, disorganized. The resocialization, relearning process best takes place when the old socialization and old learning are forgotten or denied their validity. Once the subculture is disintegrated by dispersion of its members, aggressive attitudes are not supported by like companions, and violent behavior is not regularly on display to encourage initiation and repetition.

To be most immediately effective beyond this point, however, the normative system of the larger culture must be presented as a reasonably clear, if not codified statement. But neither national goals nor the middleclass value system in a democratic society constitutes a dogma. One virtue of a more doctrinal system is its clarification of principles. To remain fluid and flexible is another kind and perhaps a more enduring quality of strength. To reconvert, retrain, reform may require some exaggeration of the elements of the value system; i.e., a presentation of an ideal and idealized type. Most cultures can array a stronger consensus against violence, especially criminal homicide, than against anything else, and can be more explicit about it. Except for a somewhat schizoid attitude toward war, the larger culture values contain strong prescriptions for nonviolence. Thus, if the dominant middle-class ethic is clearly opposed to the use of violence in interpersonal relationships, the clarity of its opposition should be a useful element in its efforts to resocialize the dispersed members of a former subculture of violence.

The dominant culture value of nonviolence would be transmitted by new patterns of residential propinquity to families, schools, and peer groups that contain very few and muted expressions of violence in child rearing, marital life, playground activities, and other episodes in the dramas of personal interaction; the resocialization process would take place in the subtleties of daily social life, without the vast network of a previous subcultural communication system that reported events of violence as commonplace. Community service centers, less locked in the zones of poverty and deviance and more widely distributed throughout the city, could buttress the otherwise slow shift in attitudes and values.

Recreational facilities, child guidance clinics, boy and girl scout clubs, hobby clubs, Police Athletic League centers, Little League baseball, and neighborhood associations could function as demonstrably effective vehicles for conversion to nonviolent activities. There is no solid empirical evidence that the catalogue of clubs and playgrounds in American cities has been effective in preventing delinquency or reducing violent crime. A common criticism is that they do not reach the delinquent or highly potential delinquent population. Even when they are located in congested neighborhoods with high crime rates, they are often viewed as unwanted invaders of the territory and are consequently unattended except by the bad area's "good boys."

When the families from the subculture of violence have been distributed and increasingly absorbed by the surrounding middle-class milieu, they will become conditioned to the behavior expectations around them. Instead of the old and consistent role models from generations before them and peers beside them, the territorially transplanted families could see, not inadequate images of middle-class conformity and life style from mass media projections, but nearby neighbors with whom they could interact. The nearly compulsive adoption of middle-class roles by Negro families in integrated communities is well known. We are drawing attention here to the general social-psychological processes of norm learning, empathy, projection, identification, internalization, ego-ideals, primary reference groups, and differential association theory.

There may be some concern that the middle-class value system too often requires overconformity, is "bourgeois" in a pejorative sense, produces neurotics, and is overly supplied with mediocrity and banality. One might well ask what are the alternatives to the middle-class ethic to which our policy decision-makers would have criminal deviants resocialized. The range of alternative forms of behavior and attitude within the broad spectrum of the middle class is wide enough to avoid the stultifying and stagnant homogenization feared by some observers.

Under the suggestions of dispersion and newly found attachments to the middle-class milieu, community treatment of delinquents and placement of offenders on probation or returned to the community on parole should facilitate the retraining process. Instead of returning to the old criminal subculture or subculture of violence, the offender would be placed in an environment predominantly nonviolent.

Response to Riot

Citizens respond to riots in ways that reflect their backgrounds and the status they occupy in society. With our cultural pluralism, ethnic heterogeneity, and class clusters, not to mention personality variations, it is dangerous to generalize. Young and poor Negro males living in ghettoes would be expected to have a response different from middle-aged, middle-class whites. In addressing myself to all men I hope to be saying something to at least some.

Crash programs of coalition groups are necessary all over the land. Bankers and bomb-carriers must sit at the same table to explore grievances and devise ways for the former to provide money and the latter to provide people to do what reason and reality can suggest. Business leaders, community organization workers, fellowship commissions, local government, and other civic leaders must do more than talk to themselves about the problems and prospects of others. The colonialism of help is no longer an acceptable mode among those who are frustrated and historical victims of social injustice. Beneath and beyond the former riots there is an intense morality and a demand for clear commitments, coming from middle-class students as well as the Negro poor. Impatience, discontent, and dissatisfaction with the state of American society should be viewed as healthy reflections of a desire for change and for participation in directing the change. Those deprived or dethroned are seeking self-respect and the dignity of being listened to, of being taken seriously. The dialogue between haves and have-nots has begun, and if the former do not pay attention to and seek out the latter, violence that can end only in violent repression will be the outcome.

To say that the police need support is a truism, as it is to suggest that they should always approach all persons with courtesy. Pejorative remarks breed pejoratives, as does violence itself. When the police move to curtail a disorder and function with propriety, citizens in the area should be supportive of them. Those who enter a riot are forsaking all other alternatives of resolution. If a city government or university administration offers no procedural alternatives, it has itself contributed to its own victimization. If the white middle class turns its homes into armed fortresses, it is also contributing more to the climate of challenge and fear than to the dissolution of violence.

Citizens must continue to impress their representatives at all levels of government to enact effective laws against the absurd sale of firearms. They should urge the formal and structured teaching of nonviolence as a virtue in the school's educational value system, and they should encourage their children to have enormous enthusiasm for any humane cause. War games and toys of violence can hardly be deemed a healthy environment, even as an outlet for hostility. The marketing of violence in toys or in media simply desensitizes generations to the display of and exposure to violence even if it teaches no techniques. Every citizen should become a part of one or more organizations seeking to talk to those who harbor hate and hostility. If social contacts do not always promote love, they should at least reduce fear and hatred and increase understanding.

Lest We Forget

The capacity for violence lies in all normal men. But aggression is learned behavior, not innate or instinctive and not unalterable. The stimuli that arouse to anger or to fear are learned from our environment. The "climate of a culture," the "mood of a generation," the "drift of sentiment" are phrases that represent a collectivity; they are also clichés formulated by the articulate, educated classes making pop sociology, pop psychology, and pop history. The grammar of violence and its physical manifestation in riots may in part be a reflection of the self-fulfilling rhetoric of the analysts. The quiet, tree-lined main street of America, the daily routines of breakfast, dish-washing, parent-child play and learning are not dramatic incidents of a society, but they form the life style of most of us. Garbage collection attracts no public interest until the garbage is uncollected.

The diffusion of many good acts, or even of bad ones, over time, space, and people rarely receives wide display and hence has muted drama. But compressed courage, congealed catastrophe, and focal violence on culture heroes receive immediate and wide display. Instant explanations abound and the depths of our collective despair are matched only by our confusion and inability to explain the complexities of causation.

Ten thousand acts of police service, of courtesy and assistance, are little more than IBM holes on computer cards that tally the troubles of the citizenry from domestic cats in trees or quarrels in the home to providing the fastest service to transport wounded and heart-attacked victims to hospitals. But one observed act of brutality - or excessive force - wipes out the nine rows and eighty columns on 10,000 IBM cards of service.

Fifty thousand automobile deaths a year are regularly recorded without fanfare; the catastrophe of one jet plane carrying 120 passengers is a more dramatic headline because the disaster is a single stroke. Ten thousand homicides a year are hard for the public to contemplate; even worse is the execution of six million Jews. The ingredients of one dramatic death make all the difference. Several major attempts were made on President Roosevelt's life, as on President Truman's. In one case, the bullet missed FDR by inches. The news was reported, but there was no flurry of pop psychiatric analysis of mass violence. Yet, this was the Depression, a time of labor violence, of hordes of unemployed, of poverty at its height, of the first major Harlem race riot when there were not "rising expectations" but declining ones. The press and radio gave no ready explanations for a "sick" society. Would three inches' difference in the flight of a bullet have produced editorials denouncing American society, indicting a hundred million people for generating a climate of violence?

In short, I am not persuaded that our society is morally decayed, that kids are worse today than they used to be, that there is anything particularly distinctive about the way we destroy one another, that the United States has any special gift for violence. The idiosyncrasies of disturbed minds and dreadful, dramatic tragedies do not make a pattern of culture.

That there is violence in America cannot be denied. Few would deny that our society would be better with less display of violence on television, no racial prejudice, no or fewer guns in private possession, the removal of ghettoes, education for nonviolence, and more efficacious treatment of criminal offenders.

But the case can be made with equal vigor and evidence that ours is a gentle society, that our culture has helped to elevate man to the dignity he deserves, that the rule of law has rarely enjoyed such a high stance in history, that a greater number of good things have come to a greater number of people, that the number of alternatives available to a people with more freedom of expression has never been greater.

In historical moments of calm and conformity we need to remind ourselves of our deficiencies, our faulty democracy, our fallacies of justice and decisions. In moments of tragedy and violence we need to remind ourselves and others of our continued determination to protect the harmony history has carved for us from chaos.

Mind over Muscle – the Rule of Law

Violence is not power. It is a means of seeking power and may be defined as an act of despair committed when the door is closed to alternative resolutions of repression, depression, and conflict. It comes from the failure to have a more abundant repertoire of means to gain a goal. The existence of a society is dependent on the repression of violence within its borders.

Sporadic, limited acts of violence on the authority of a society are like pin pricks on the political corpus. Watts, Detroit, and Newark are like suicidal wrist slashes of a patient who wants the doctor to save him from total destruction. The convergence of family, friends, and physicians on the attempted suicide promotes the protection and attention the patient wanted. Law and order must always prevail if a society is to endure; hence, violent jabs against it can be tolerated only to a finite point before societal retaliation becomes imperative and itself often excessively repressive.

The lessons to be learned from current collective riot conduct seem clear: as Columbia University officials remarked recently, acts wherein muscles usurp the role of minds are alien to a university. I suggest the same dictum for the larger society. Where reason is ruined and collective violence is viable, the social system has failed to provide the kind of participatory democracy we basically extol.

In the abstract there can be no side of violence with virtue. The course of the dominant society built on law and intrinsically the inheritor of the value of nonviolence must be to maintain itself. The black militant who would burn cities in this land harbors no better way of life than the Ku Klux

Klaner who would burn crosses or bomb Sunday schools. But the responsibility of that dominant society is to offer alternatives for expression, provide reasonable access to the thrones of power, permit grievances to be known, and execute the provisions of our Constitution with dispatch.

Our national goals and culture values are clearer than we realize because we take them much for granted and have failed to formulate them into the kind of belief system or ideology more tightly knitted in its own logic and represented, for example, by communism. Some of our political and social norms have stability, but the flexibility of others has probably prevented our establishing an ideological set of rubrics for our civilization. Yet, the values are there and should be announced with as much clarity and precision as we can muster. And in the light of those values we can judge the violence that defends injustice because we will better know our definitions of justice.

Change occurs in all societies, albeit the change in some may be slow or, even if rapid, unplanned. It is when those persons opposed to change become intransigent and those who wish consciously to promote change are willing to resort to violence that order becomes disorder. When protest moves to riot and riot to rebellion, dissent is transformed into disruption. The right to exercise dissent peaceably is our basic constitutional guarantee. When physical harm to persons and things occurs, another guarantee is called into focus and used to force assaulters to retreat. This kind of balance is a fundamental which the police and the courts are designed to protect and maintain.

Lincoln asked the question succinctly: "Must a government of necessity be too strong for the liberties of its own people, or too weak to maintain its own existence?" I trust that our nation is sufficiently sensitive to the liberties of all to listen and to act, and strong enough to maintain them under the rule of law.

NOTES

---

[1] Niccolo Machiavelli, *History of Florence and of the Affairs of Italy* (London: M. Walter Dunne, 1901), Book II, p. 100.

[2] Bella Duffy, *The Tuscan Republic* (New York: G. P. Putnam's Sons, 1893) , p. 159.

[3] Machiavelli, *op. cit. supra* note 1.

[4] Duffy, *op. cit. supra* note 2, p. 194.

[5] W. C. Stafford and Charles Ball, Italy Illustrated (London: The London Printing and Publishing Company), p. 278.

[6] Most of this history of labor violence has been abstracted from Philip Taft, "Violence in American Labor Disputes," Annals *of* the American Academy *of* Political and .Social Science, March 1966, pp. 127-40.

[7] Arnold Forster, "Violence on the Fanatical Left and Right," Annals *of* the American Academy *of* Political and Social Science, March 1966, p. 143.

[8] Alexis de Tocqueville, *L'Ancien Regime,* M. W. Patterson, translator (Oxford, Eng.: Basic Blackwell, 1949) , p. 186. Cited and brought to my attention by Judd Marmor, "Some Psychological Aspects of Contemporary Urban Violence" n.d. (mimeo.).

[9] In this section I am drawing upon some notions similarly expressed in Marvin E. Wolfgang and Franco Ferracuti, *The Subculture* of Violence (London: Tavistock; New York: Barnes and Noble, 1967).

THE SOCIAL SCIENTIST IN COURT

Marvin E. Wolfgang

From: "Marvin E. Wolfgang, "The Social Scientist in Court", Journal of Criminal Law and Criminology, 65: 2:239-247, 1974.

Every profession has its own conflicts of interests, ethical issues and relativities. As a sociologist and, more particularly, as a criminologist, I have encountered a few. Although they were not excessively troublesome and may not even have bothered some of my colleagues, they nevertheless did cause me to be cautious. Among such encounters were those related to my role as a social scientist testifying as an "expert witness" for civil rights causes.

My experiences began in 1965 with the NAACP Legal Defense and Educational Fund, Inc. I gave my first testimony in Federal District Court in Little Rock, Arkansas, in connection with the famous case of *Maxwell v. Bishop*,[1] which was later pursued through the United States Supreme Court. Long and elaborate depositions in Louisiana, Florida, South Carolina, Alabama and Georgia followed, all dealing with blacks who, like Maxwell, had been convicted of rape and sentenced to death. My last major court experience was as a witness in *Gregory v. Litton Systems*, Inc.[2] in Los Angeles in 1970, a case involving denial of a job because of a "substantial" arrest record. The case was handled through the Equal Employment Opportunity Commission.

I am a sociologist and criminologist, opposed to the death penalty, in favor of equality of opportunities and opposed to discrimination, whether on the street, in the factory, or in the courts. As a citizen and as a professor with a social conscience, I should, on the surface, experience no conflict serving as an expert witness on behalf of defendants or organizations representing such defendants. These individuals are, after all, in a posture of disadvantage. They are products of socially disgraceful ways of being treated as minority members of society.

Nevertheless, problems did arise from the very fact that these were worthy causes to which I had long been devoted and about which I did feel keenly. Had they not been issues that attracted my social senses, the problems of personal versus professional perspectives, and of internal scientific data analysis, would not have arisen. For example, I was once requested by the National Rifle Association to undertake research on their behalf; I had no difficulty rejecting what amounted to a very lucrative offer. Being opposed to civilian gun ownership and in favor of very restrictive gun control legislation, I encountered no difficulty rejecting research with an organization that represented the most powerful lobby in favor of private possession of firearms.

The problems I faced as a social scientist working within the framework of social causes that I supported were connected with the following: (a) science versus advocacy, (b) research design, (c) display and suppression of empirical data, (d) style of testimony, (e) interpretation of findings, and (f) vulnerability of scientific inquiry. None of these was a new or esoteric issue, but when the social scientist steps into the arena of adversary games, confronts role conflicts, and subjects the presentation of research to the cross-examination of his mind, he faces problems in the drama that are different from those described in textbooks. He meets challenges different from those presented by his own colleagues and students in professional articles and university seminars. A description of the research issues, designs and analyses in which I participated will illustrate some of the problems to which I refer.

During the summer of 1965, I embarked upon research to examine in detail the relationship between race and sentencing for rape in eleven Southern and border states in which rape was a capital offense. The study was requested and sponsored by the NAACP Legal Defense Fund, and conducted by the Center for Studies in Criminology and Criminal Law at the University of Pennsylvania. Professor Anthony Amsterdam and I were co-directors of the study.

At each step in the development and implementation of the research design, from the selection of the sample to the analysis of the data, emphasis was on the use of research criteria that would increase the reliability and objectivity of the data while minimizing sources of bias and subjectivity. These are, after all, basic principles of scientific research methodology. The purpose of the research was to examine the extent to which race discrimination functions in the judicial system, at least with respect to sentencing decisions, and to provide source data for possible subsequent litigation.

The research findings were presented as evidence in six states to support petitioners' claims of racial discrimination in the administration of the death penalty. They were, in part, included in testimony in *Maxwell* before the Federal District Court in 1966, and later offered to the United States Supreme Court. They were also part of the testimony offered in 1972 before the Subcommittee of the United States House of Representatives, which was considering bills both to suspend the death penalty for two years, and to abolish it completely.

Because most executions for rape during the past thirty years had occurred in twelve states, we decided that the study could be profitably confined to them, even though six other states allowed the imposition of the death penalty for rape. In order to provide an empirical basis for conclusions about the effect of racial and nonracial factors on capital sentencing for rape, it was necessary to gather data relating to a substantial number of rape cases in each state. Moreover, a sufficiently long period of time covered by the research was necessary in order to satisfy the notion of "custom," i.e., an institutionalized, systematic, judicial norm of sentencing behavior. This is the reason that a twenty-year period, 1945 to 1965, was used.

It was nearly impossible to collect data on every case that occurred. The demands of proper statistical analysis required that cases be examined in a proper sampling procedure. Standard statistical sampling techniques were therefore employed. For each of the states, a random, stratified sample of counties was chosen to represent the urban-rural and black-white demographic distributions. The counties chosen comprised more than 50 per cent of the total population of the twelve states. Every case of conviction for rape, from January 1, 1945 to the summer of 1965, was recorded. Data were gathered for a twenty-year period for over 3000 rape convictions in 230 counties in eleven states. (Maryland was not covered because of time limits.) These states were those that most often executed persons for rape, and which also displayed an apparent racial disparity, in that blacks were more frequently executed than whites. In order to explore the meaning of this apparent racial disparity in capital sentencing, only rape convictions were considered.

It might be asserted that blacks commit rape more frequently than whites, are more frequently arrested, or are more frequently prosecuted. Whether these or any combinations of these-assertions are true was not questioned in this study, mainly because data were not readily available to test such assertions. Instead, the focus was on the reliable and objectively ascertainable fact that defendants had been convicted for the crime of rape. Using this focal point meant that the effect of racial factors on the criminal process prior to conviction could not be explored. Thus, even if blacks were disproportionately sentenced to death for rape, there was no way of knowing whether the pattern could be accounted for by a disproportionate frequency in the commission of rape by blacks, or by a disproportionate frequency in the conviction of blacks for rape. However, among convicted defendants, it was possible to determine whether black defendants were disproportionately frequently sentenced to death, and, if so, whether the disproportion could be explained by nonracial variables.

This research, therefore, concentrated on convictions rather than on an earlier stage in the processing of suspects or defendants, partly because of the need to conduct the research with dispatch for litigation purposes (after all, people were sitting in death rows all across the country awaiting execution), and partly because good empirical data prior to conviction were not readily available. We decided to refrain from trying to make assertions about discriminatory behavior of the police or prosecutors in arresting or prosecuting more blacks than whites. Feelings, sentiments, intuition and anecdotes are not the kernel of scientific research. They may stimulate research inquiry and produce heuristic insights to guide hypothesis formation, but they cannot provide empirical quantitative evidence that can boldly and rigorously withstand cross-examination. Hence, no effort was made to determine whether there was discrimination in the processing of suspects and defendants prior to the determination of guilt. To maintain the capacity to provide statistical material in the traditions of scientific inquiry, we accepted the adjudication of guilt for defendants who had been charged with forcible rape. In no way were we prepared to question the adjudication of guilt, however strong may have been our suspicions about the adjudication process. The base line, then, of data collection was all convictions for rape in the eleven Southern states.

In order to explore the effect of racial as well as nonracial variables on the imposition of the death penalty; we sought to determine which variables could be obtained from the county records of rape convictions. In addition to collecting information on the race of both the defendant and the victim, and on the type of sentence, we gathered information about many nonracial variables that could be construed as mitigating or aggravating circumstances. If standards were sought for sentencing in capital cases, some nonracial variables might have had a telling effect. The following variables were included in the study: (1) offender characteristics: age, marital status, prior criminal record, previous employment and, employment status; (2) victim characteristics: age, marital status, dependent children, prior criminal record and reputation for chastity; (3) nature of relations between the victim and the offender: whether the offender was known to victim and whether there had been prior sexual relations; (4) circumstances of the offense: whether it was a contemporaneous offense, the type of entry (authorized or unauthorized), the location of offense (indoor or outdoor), whether there was a display of a weapon, whether a weapon was carried, the amount of injury to the victim, whether there was a threat made to the victim, the degree of force employed, whether the victim was made pregnant by the offense, whether the offender was acting alone or in concert and the date of offense; (5) the circumstances of the trial: the plea, whether there was a defense of insanity, whether counsel was appointed or retained, the length of time of the trial, whether there was a defense of consent and whether the defendant testified.

A twenty-eight page research schedule was constructed to obtain uniform data from records of widely varying quality and geographically dispersed locations. To reduce the amount of subjective or judgmental variation recorded by field investigators, each variable was described in a manner that focused the investigator's attention on objective facts or quantities that could be recorded on a check list.

Some information, including that about race and type of plea, was unambiguous and offered little difficulty in establishing accuracy. More difficulty occurred in trying to obtain reliable, objective data for items such as "injuries sustained by victim." To make reliable comparisons from case to case, a check-list of categories of predescribed injuries was developed, using brief phrases that focused the recorder's attention on specific, significant, objective details, and upon the consequences of injuries. For example, categories for the latter item included recording whether the victim suffered "minor injury requiring no medical treatment;" suffered "physical injuries requiring medical treatment, but not requiring hospitalization;" or suffered "physical injuries requiring hospitalization."

Thirty law students were recruited from across the country to serve as field investigators. This is a critical point. The social science researcher has a fear of his being captured subtly and; perhaps even unconsciously, by the desire to prove his case, to show the kinds of evidence he believes and wants to believe exist. Therefore, it was extremely important that the field investigators be carefully prepared to recognize their own potential biases. As a supervisor, my task was to exercise as much quality control over the collection and recording of data as was possible. Before going into the field the students were given a two-day orientation by Professor Amsterdam and myself. The instruction process outlined in detail the research design and the legal components of the task. Emphasis was placed on the importance of providing reliable data, founded upon uniformity in observing and recording data. We emphasized particularly that the investigators should not let their personal assumptions about the probable results of the study influence the manner in which they recorded the data. The field investigators were instructed to call central personnel for advice if instances arose in which they had trouble classifying their observations while in the field. After completion of the field work, schedules were forwarded to the Center for Studies in Criminology and Criminal Law for coding and statistical analysis.

To determine whether the death penalty was given with disproportionate frequency to blacks, we employed the null hypothesis and the chi-square (χ^2) statistical test, for which P less than 0.05 was chosen as the level of significance. Two major null hypotheses were proposed. The first was as follows: Among all defendants convicted of rape, there is no significant association between the race of the defendant and the type of sentence. The second was stated thusly: Among all defendants convicted of rape, there are no significant differences between the proportions of black defendants with white victims, and all other classes of rape defendants sentenced to death. Both of these hypotheses were rejected in each state analyzed.

The data were compiled from seven states - Alabama, Arkansas, Florida, Georgia, Louisiana, South Carolina and Tennessee - in order to prepare testimony for use in litigation being conducted by the Legal Defense Fund. Each state was separately reviewed. However, the findings and conclusions were uniform in all states. No attempt will be made here to review the statistical data. Such analyses have been presented elsewhere.[3]

Suffice it to say that black defendants whose victims were white were sentenced to death approximately eighteen times more frequently than defendants in any other racial combination of defendant and victim. The probability of such a relationship between the sentence of death and black defendants with white victims was, by chance alone, less than one out of a thousand. The statistical probabilities were not as high in Arkansas, but nonetheless were compelling and significant in the language of the statisticians. As Michael Meltsner reported in his recent book; *Cruel and Unusual*,[4] about my testimony in the *Maxwell* case in Arkansas:

> [. . .the disparity between the number of death sentences imposed on Negroes with white victims and all other racial combinations of convicted defendants and victims was such that it could have occurred less than twice in 100 times by chance.] Put another way, if race were not related to capital sentencing in Arkansas, the results observed in the twenty-year period study could have occurred fortuitously in two (or less) twenty-year periods since the birth of Christ. He believed that the study documented racial discrimination that previously available data - not collected systematically or in a form permitting rigorous analysis - could only suggest. With a qualification that "information is always limited;" Wolfgang concluded that the study had made definite what before had been merely suspected.[5]

My scientific orientation and training confronted my social consciousness as I performed the research and offered testimony in Little Rock. I had to be cautious in my choice of language in order to imbue my conclusions with precision, accuracy and validity. I drew particular attention to the distinction between "differential" sentencing, "disproportionate" sentencing and "discriminatory" sentencing. My friends at the Legal Defense Fund who are attorneys, and who schooled me in the process of direct and cross-examination, had to be schooled themselves in the reluctance of a researcher to leap too quickly to a conclusion of discrimination, which was the conclusion desired by the adversaries in seeking to obtain a judicial decision favorable to their cause. Meltsner described this process:

> [H]e had no experience in testifying about sociological matters in court. Indeed, this was one of the many reasons that the lawyers thought that he would be an extremely effective witness - here was no "expert" witness for hire .... Although his testimony should not appear canned, Wolfgang did have to know precisely how the lawyer questioning him intended to bring out the purpose and results of the rape

study. He also had to learn what he might expect on cross-examination.... Long before Maxwell's second habeas petition was filed, Wolfgang's schooling as a witness had been attended to, for [Norman] Amaker and I had travelled to Philadelphia to help him prepare. We wrote out long lists of questions, and posed them to Wolfgang. After he responded, we discussed his answer - had a word of jargon crept in? would the judge understand a particular scientific concept? - and then moved on. It was tedious work for all concerned, but we knew that the best stories told in court had generally been told in lawyers' offices first.[6]

One of these stories had to do with the distinctions between "differential," "disproportionate" and "discriminatory." I vividly remember the long discussions that Amaker, Meltsner, Amsterdam and I had on several occasions as we were preparing my testimony. Amaker, a black lawyer working full-time with the Legal Defense Fund, and one of the brilliant minds that engineered the entrance of my testimony, was particularly intent on using, as early as possible, the word "discrimination" in the testimony. Amsterdam, who was a bit more patient, a patience perhaps partly borne from big deep involvement in construction of the twenty-eight page schedule for interview purposes and research design, appreciated my reluctance to leap from a priori intuitive assumption of discrimination to the conclusion of discrimination. As I laboriously indicated to all of the lawyers, despite the elaborate nature of the information we had concerning the victim, the offender, the character of the offense and the judicial proceedings, we had no direct evidence of discrimination.

"Discrimination" refers to behavior that resides in the mind of the actor which is expressed overtly for observation by others. I tried to impress upon the lawyers that I was uncomfortable using the term "discrimination" until all of the evidence was documented, that even if the findings were in accord with their adversary position, I could not use the term in the null hypothesis, nor in the description of the research, until the final statement. The final statement asserted that there was a disproportionate sentencing of blacks to the death penalty in comparison with whites. This meant a differential sentencing pattern over the twenty-year period. "Differential" meant a degree of statistical difference that was significant according to traditional probability statistics. Professor John de Cani has carefully and clearly described what those probability statistics mean in the language of statisticians.[7] Differential sentencing, i.e., disproportionate frequency of blacks sentenced to death in comparison to whites, could mean only inferentially that there was a pattern of discrimination. I felt secure as a social scientist in asserting in court and in depositions that so clearly differential and disproportionate had been the sentencing that there was historically a pattern of discrimination in the imposition of the death penalty.

It was my belief then, and it is my continued belief, that by exercising scientific caution in the style of expressing research findings, the social scientist retains his integrity as a scientist, and, at the same time, can produce compelling, persuasive, convincing and rigorous testimony as an expert witness.

I often wondered what would have been my stance if the research data over a twenty-year period of sentencing in the eleven Southern states had yielded results opposite those that we found. That is, suppose most of the nonracial factors we had examined in the conviction of rape and the imposition of the death penalty had shown that blacks had committed more aggravated rape; had, in greater frequency than whites, prior criminal records; had inflicted greater injury; had committed more corollary offenses such as burglary and robbery; had more frequently impregnated the victim, etc. As I indicated earlier, none of these nonracial variables was in any way related to race, and the differential sentencing pattern we observed, with more blacks sentenced to death than whites, occurred only when the defendant was black and the victim was white. If the nonracial factors had been related to black defendants, I suppose the lawyers from the Legal Defense Fund would have used some other tactic and not presented our studies. Under those circumstances, I probably would not have been an expert witness.

I was aware of this situation before the data had been collected and analyzed, and was prepared for the possibility that I might not testify. However, had I not testified, I would still have published the results of these studies in social science journals, even though the findings, had they been the reverse of those we found, could have been used by prosecutors in the Southern states as evidence contrary to the proposition advocated by the Legal Defense Fund lawyers.

The basic question was this: Does the social scientist have an obligation to publish or to refrain from publishing material which might be damaging to the political-social position he feels as a citizen? I was fortunate in not having to face this dilemma because all of the evidence we collected fell within the domain of our social sentiments. The question of suppression of evidence, therefore, never arose. The dilemma would have been further compounded by the fact that the NAACP Legal Defense Fund provided funds for the research. But the social scientist should never feel subjugated to the source of funds when engaging in scientific research. The right to release, to publish, and to display results is a basic academic freedom and a research freedom that should not, be relinquished.

Vulnerability and the limitations of scientific research are features well-recognized within the scientific community. There are no scientific laws in social science. The best and most rigorous empirical research rests upon statements of probability. Other scholars who examine the results, the findings, descriptions, interpretations and explanations of a body of research respond to these limitations and vulnerabilities in ways that may be muted by their own understanding of them. They are faced with similar limitations in their own research. However, under the conditions of testifying in court, these vulnerabilities and limitations may be subject to hypothetical questioning and the sometimes abrasive interrogation of a lawyer whose primary task is not to appreciate the problems of science and treat them gently, but to deny the strength of the assertions and to destroy the assumption of scientificity.

After years of experience presenting evidence before various courts, I am now prepared for cross-examination which does not address itself specifically to the same issues that I, as a scientist, examined in my research. In my first exposure in the Federal District Court in Little Rock, I was not fully prepared for the style in which the Assistant Attorney General of Arkansas examined me. I had been prepared for the possibility of another statistician being placed on the witness stand by the Attorney General, but as John de Cani has indicated, no statistical expert witness was ever offered to contradict this evidence. Nor has any statistician, social scientist, or criminologist ever been offered by opposing advocates to contradict or reinterpret my research data. Thus, instead of being asked questions directly related to the scientific limitations of the research, I was asked a series of questions that, from my scientific perspective, lead no relationship to the thrust of the inquiry, or to the reliability or validity of the findings.

I was asked under cross-examination if I had ever been in Arkansas before my appearance as an expert witness for the Legal Defense Fund. I responded in the negative. The Assistant Attorney General used this response to imply that I did not fully understand the social conditions or the litigation processes in Arkansas. It was further brought out under cross-examination that Garland County, in which Maxwell had been tried, was not included in the survey sampling of Arkansas counties. The state argued that failure to include Garland County was a fatal error that the generalized conclusions drawn from the Arkansas rape-death penalty study could not apply to the *Maxwell* case.

Based upon my own research, this conclusion was absurd. We had taken a carefully drawn random sample of counties in Arkansas, as well as in the other ten Southern states, without attention to the counties in which specific cases for litigation may finally occur. Our primary interest had been to determine whether there had been a customary, institutionalized, systematic process of differential sentencing to the death penalty based on race; hence, the specific litigated cases were of no consequence to our random selection. If we had drawn our sample counties purposefully to pick counties in which cases like *Maxwell* had occurred, we would have destroyed the statistical randomness of the selection of counties and would have also distorted the character of the scientific inquiry. Yet, this fact and this kind of reasoning had little impact on either Assistant Attorney General Fletcher Jackson or Judge J. Smith Henley.

The social scientist who becomes involved in testifying and displaying research evidence must also be prepared for opinions that contravene the traditional scientific canons of response. For example, Judge Henley accepted my conclusion that sentencing patterns of Arkansas Negroes convicted of raping white victims "could not be due to the operation of the laws of chance." He accepted the conclusion that a black convicted of raping a white woman had about a 50 per cent chance of receiving a death sentence, and that any man convicted of raping a woman of his own race stood only a 14 per cent chance. But Judge Henley thought the difference could be explained on grounds other than race, and contended that the imposition of the death sentence might be due to some factor for which statistical analysis had not been possible or presentable. He announced in his decision that the "variables which Dr. Wolfgang considered are objective . . . broad in instances ... imprecise.... Discrimination moreover is a highly subjective matter [and might not] be detected by a statistical analysis .... Statistics are elusive things at best, and it is a truism that almost anything can be proven by them."[8] These are common assertions made by persons who are not social scientists trained in statistics. Yet, the social scientist who becomes involved in testifying in this area must be prepared for arguments and decisions that are political or that reside in legal vicissitudes outside the framework of social science inquiry and evidence.[9]

With respect to my experience on the witness stand in the *Maxwell* trial, I can honestly say that I never felt frustrated. I was well directed under direct examination, and well prepared beforehand by the very capable lawyers of the Legal Defense Fund. Nor have I ever felt abused or treated offensively in court by unfriendly crossexaminers. Unlike psychiatrists who testify as expert witnesses in insanity cases, I have always felt that both the opposing lawyers and the judges were civil, and afforded me appropriate opportunities for expansion of my answers. I never had to respond in a simple yes-or-no style. Moreover, because of the appreciation and understanding of the role of the social scientist by the Legal Defense Fund lawyers, I never felt that I had to suppress, mute, or otherwise distort any of my findings or any of the scientific inquiry that led to the evidence I ultimately presented. In short, the role conflicts that I felt initially and the dilemmas that I anticipated were all smoothly resolved because the legal staff accepted the caution of language and the style of the scientist. This fact is perhaps one of the most important historical lessons that can be of utility both to social scientists and to their companion lawyers with whom they work in future civil rights litigation.

The research design of social scientists who are involved in litigation and as expert witnesses should conform, as always, to the rules of scientific methodology, without being prejudiced by the underlying litigation purpose. That purpose may be the original or basic reason for becoming involved, and in that sense clearly reveals a value judgment. Failure to abide by the known rules of scientific inquiry can only damage the evidence, as well as the presenter. The statistical techniques of analysis, the methods of research, and the emphasis upon the traditional canons of reliability, validity and objectivity should be observed if the thrust of the scientificity of the testimony is to be maintained with integrity. The null hypothesis or other theoretical guides for the selection of variables and data analysis are equally important for maintaining a posture of a scientist and not of an advocate. The acuity of the companion lawyers should be sufficient for the social scientist as a linguistic and institutionalized vehicle for the transportation of his findings.

The social scientist should not try to convert his design, his data, or his conclusions to conform to the litigation process. There is no reason for him to use statistical measures of significance and techniques different from those used in any other level of scientific inquiry. The language employed to present evidence should be as precise and clear and as devoid of jargon as the scientist is capable of providing. The inductive process, including serendipity, of obtaining insights from a review of data should be described in testimony in the same way it is communicated to the scientific community. Conditional clauses should be employed despite the fact that they are more vulnerable to cross-examination. Such words and phrases as "may," "probable," "other things being equal," "holding constant certain variables," and "associated" rather than "cause" are important verbal accouterments of the probabilistic language of science, and should not be neglected when presenting evidence in court.

There may be some apprehension associated with the fact that a court stenographer is recording every word. There is a considerable difference between speaking under those circumstances and expounding sometimes unsure evidence before a group of students in a seminar where cross-examination is not employed. Speculations, interpretations beyond secure data, and attempts to get reactions to a new idea can be exciting features of a seminar, but such forays are not meant for a record upon which cross-examination is based. Nevertheless, the scientist who does testify, and who is confident of his own research and the integrity of his findings, need not fear the attack. Like the candidate in defense of his doctoral thesis, the expert witness should be more fully informed and more erudite about his material than an attorney who is questioning him critically.

The lawyer is informed about his case and the legal issues at stake. He is not particularly interested in being in command of the scientific material. The expert and the lawyer use different skills and languages. Their dialogue has oblique contact, with the one using verbal assaults in an effort to pierce the linguistic mail of the other. Unless the social scientist is prepared to understand these perspectives and to be assured of his own rule, unperturbed by the drama of the court and the critical capacities of his cross-examiner, he should not participate in this kind of episode. Lawyers should beware of those social scientists who are only too willing to be expert witnesses on the basis of their fervent feelings for the cause at issue. Unless such scientists have empirical evidentiary material to buttress an argument, they will be more of a burden than a blessing.

Gregory v. Litton Systems, Inc. represented other kinds of problems. Gregory was a black sheetmetal worker who sought a job with Litton Systems, Inc. in Los Angeles in 1968. He filled out the usual application forms. When he returned a week later to begin work, he was informed that he should fill out another form. The new form demanded information about whether the applicant had ever been arrested, how often, and for what reasons. Gregory filled out the form frankly, indicating that he had been arrested fourteen times. There had been no convictions, and most of the arrests had been for trivial offenses, including failure to carry his registration for selective service. Yet, because his record reflected fourteen arrests, Gregory was deemed ineligible for hire. He contacted the Equal Employment Opportunity Commission, which turned the case over to the law firm of Simon, Sheridan, Murphy, Thornton and Medvene for litigation.

I was asked by Edward Medvene to testify in July, 1970, as a criminologist on behalf of Gregory's claim. After learning the particulars of the case, I agreed. I contended that, as a black, Gregory had a higher probability of being inappropriately arrested than a white, and that therefore the notion of "substantial" arrest record as a basis for deciding to employ or not employ was discriminatory. In this case, I did not collect new empirical research. Time permitted only co-ordination of existing material, some of which was anecdotal, but most of which was previously collected empirical and statistical data. This was the basis for my testimony that the use of arrest records was improper because of the discriminatory character of official arrest records. I argued that blacks are more likely to be entrapped in the network of the criminal justice system than are whites, this despite the sufficiency of evidence in individual cases. I referred to what is known as "self-reporting" studies of "hidden delinquency and crime." These studies, from the United States, England and Scandinavia, show that in anonymous questionnaires or interviews there are no statistically significant social class differences among persons who admit having committed a variety of criminal offenses. Ethnic and racial differences that are traditionally recorded in official police arrest records, showing that blacks in America are disproportionately represented four times beyond their "share" in the general population, are reduced to insignificance in the hidden delinquency, self-reported studies. Fortified by these findings, I testified, with various documentation, that whites admit having committed about as many offenses as blacks, and that variations by social class, recognizing that blacks are mostly represented in the lower social class in the official police statistics, virtually disappear in the self-reported studies. The study by Chambliss and Nagasawa[10] was particularly useful because it referred to whites, blacks, and Japanese and offered these same conclusions.

The major dilemma I faced as a social scientist in *Gregory* arose from my request for special computer runs in Philadelphia and in St. Louis on the attrition of cases, by race, from police arrest to the preliminary hearing and presentation for trial. My student assistants at the Center for Studies in Criminology and Criminal Law quickly undertook a special study of the Philadelphia cases to determine whether a greater number of blacks than whites were arrested, and whether a greater number of blacks had their cases dismissed by the magistrate at the preliminary hearing. I also asked Nelson Heller, who was a researcher in the St. Louis Police Department, where quick computer analysis was available, to do a special run of the same kinds of analysis.

The conclusion in both cities was that proportionately no more blacks than whites had cases dismissed at the preliminary hearing, and that there was no statistical evidence to show that the grounds of probable cause for arrest were different for blacks and whites.

Not being able to present clear evidence of disproportion from which inferences of discrimination could be made, I tried to determine whether these materials could be used in testimony. It was clear to the lawyers that this small and inconclusive research effort was of no benefit to them and should not be presented. Evidence unsupportive of one's case, however complete or segmental it may be, has no function in the adversary game. Such evidence may be useful in a scientific article, but if one piece of evidence is contravened by other evidence, it has no proper place in argument before a court. Evidence from a scientific perspective may be neutral or negative, and should be presented in an essay that examines a given phenomenon, even if that evidence is relatively weak, in order to show the contrary position of more firm evidence. But in court, evidence negative to one's position is omitted. There is selectivity unlike that which exists in science. If history were written with such selectivity, if psychological, sociological and other kinds of research were performed in an adversary style, science would rush too quickly to conclusions or be aborted in its efforts.

These differences must be recognized by scientists who coalesce with trial and appellate lawyers. This recognition should not be viewed as a capitulation by the rules of science, but instead as a filtering of the scientific rules through a set of values that may be different, but which are equally powerful, useful and absolutely necessary in the defense or prosecution of a position. The litigation process has a different set of operating procedures than does scientific inquiry. Scientific evidence is judged within the context of legal rules of evidence, especially doctrines of constitutionality that do not always coincide with the rubrics of science in the manner in which they order knowledge of empiric reality. Moreover, there is as wide a range from soft to hard data, and of rigor and sophistication of analysis in science as well as in law. The preceptors of science must be alerted to their own fallibilities and be prepared to accept challenges outside their disciplines by others trained in the parameters of law, the adequacy of logic and the rigors of reasoning: It is in these attributes that the scientist and the lawyer can find firm meeting ground for their minds, and for the exciting display of their separate talents and training.

As the findings from social and behavioral science become increasingly relevant to the resolution of critical legal issues,[11] as trial and constitutional lawyers recognize the relevance of behavioral science, and as statements of probability and inferential statistics become more acceptable to judicial decision making processes, the number of cases employing this disciplinary mix should increase. Legal education should reflect these changes by introducing more behavioral science courses and materials in law schools, and by appointing social scientists to law school faculties. I also urge social scientists, to become involved in the exciting and dramatic work of litigation with lawyers.

Theories, assumptions, hypotheses, reliability and validity are concepts that can be readily transferred, without distortion of meaning, from the scientific treatise to the courtroom. To satisfy the scientist, the vehicle of that transference must be through the capable articulation of competent companion lawyers: Judges should be urged to understand the testimony of scientists, not as a language of faith nor of heresy, but as a discourse of reason whose rules are sometimes as firm; sometimes as flexible, as those of criminal precedence and procedure.

NOTES

[1] 257 F. Supp. 710 (E.D. Ark. 1966).

[2] 316 F. Supp. 401 (S.D. Cal. 1970).

[3] See Wolfgang & Riedel, Race, Judicial Discretion, and the Death Penalty, in *Blacks and the Law* (J. Greenberg ed. 1973).

[4] M. Meltsner, Cruel and Unusual, *The Supreme Court and Capital Punishment* (1973).

[5] Id. at 100-01.

[6] Id. at 98.

[7] See, de Cani, *The Role of the Statistician in Jury Discrimination Cases* 65 J. CRIM. L. & C. 234 (1974).

[8] 257 F. Supp. 710 (E. D. Ark. 1966), cited by Meltsner supra note 4, at 322.

[9] For a history of the use of the research data, see Meltsner supra note 4, at 73-105.

[10] See Chambliss and Nagasawa, On the Validity of Official Statistics-A Comparative Study of White, Black, and. Japanese High School Boys, 6 J. Res. *Crime & Delinquency* 111 (1969).

[11] See Furman v. Georgia, 408 U.S. 238 (1972); G. Myrdal, The Negro Problem and Modern Democracy (1962). Myrdal's *An American Dilemma* (1944) is one of the important sociological studies referred to in Brown v. Board of Education, 347 U. S. 483, 495 n.11 (1954).

YOUTH CRIME: SUMER AND LATER

Marvin E. Wolfgang

Reprinted from "Youth and Crime: Sumer and Later", Center for Youth Policy at the University of Michigan

Introduction

We all know that crime is predominantly a male, youth problem, particularly between the ages of 15 and 24. Every historical period, every culture experiences the same age period of crime proclivity. To help us realize more than we generally do that the unrest of youth and the disparities between generations are not new phenomena, I am happy to quote from a tablet written in Sumer around 2000 B.C. Professor Samuel Kramer, the renowned Sumerian scholar from the University of Pennsylvania, translated this tablet and called it the first recorded case of delinquency in Western civilization. His successor, Professor Ake Sjöberg, has graciously translated additional lines of this tablet expressly for my use here. The drama begins as a dialogue between a father and his son:

"Where did you go?"
"I did not go anywhere."
"If you did not go anywhere, why do you idle about? Go to school, stand before your 'school-father' [professor], recite your assignment, open your schoolbag, write your tablet, let your 'big brother' write your new tablet for you. After you have finished your assignment and reported to your monitor, come to me, and do not wander about in the street. Come now, do you know what I said?
"Come now, be a man. Don't stand about in the public square or wander about the boulevard. When walking in the street, don't look all around. Be humble and show fear before your monitor. When you show terror, the monitor will like you.
"You who wander about in the public square, would you achieve success? Then seek out the first generations. Go to school, it will be of benefit to you. My son, seek out the first generations, inquire of them.
"I, never in all my life, did I make you carry reeds to the canebrake. The reed rushes which the young and the little carry, you, never in your life did you carry them. I never said

to you 'Follow my caravans,' I never sent you to work, to plow my field. I never sent you to work, to dig up my field. I never sent you to work as a laborer. 'Go, work and support me,' I never in my life said to you.

"I, night and day am tortured because of you. Night and day you waste in pleasures. You have accumulated much wealth, have expanded far and wide, have become fat, big, broad, powerful and puffed. But your kin waits expectantly for your misfortune and will rejoice at it because you looked not to your humanity."

He is beaten by a god, criminal...., criminal, robber, he breaks into houses, He is a slanderer, he stinks, He is a fool, a wild man, He is a driveling person, he neglects everything, . . . , he is a weak person, He smells bad, stinking very badly, He is [like] ill-smelling oil, he is a stinking person, He is crazy, he is wild, he eats stinking food, His body is marked by . . . disease, every one points him out, He says evil things, he is an informer.

I think we do well to recall the message which this Sumerian tablet gives us, lest we become too enamored of or too disturbed by our own rebellious youth. On October 25, 1829 Charles Williams, a youth from Delaware County, Pennsylvania became the first prisoner admitted to the new Eastern State Penitentiary at Twenty-First Street and Fairmount Avenue in Philadelphia, Pennsylvania. According to the records, he was a "farmer, light black, black eyes; curly black hair; 5'7"; foot 11"; flat nose, scar on bridge of nose; broad mouth, scar from dirk in thigh; can read." He had been sentenced to imprisonment for two years for having broken into the house of Nathan Lukens in Upper Darby, where he stole "1 silver watch, value $20; 1 gold seal, value $3; 1 gold key, value $2." Thus began the corporeal implementation of the most significant philosophy of prison reform of the late 18th and early 19th centuries in the United States, England and the entire European continent.

Charles Williams was only 18 years old in 1829.

I spent the month of June 1986 in the People's Republic of China. Their chief concern is with the youth, their hooliganism, their failure to conform to the norms of society. China has some of the same problems Sumer and, I am sure, China had four millenia ago.

Difficulties in Evaluating Youth Crime Statistics

There are traditional, contemporary statistics that should be presented about youth crime in the United States. I shall concentrate on violent crimes, that is, homicide, rape, robbery and aggravated assault. The nationwide crime statistics upon which I draw are from the annual *Uniform*

Crime Reports (UCR) collated by the FBI from approximately 15,000 police jurisdictions. The nationwide crime victimization data are from the National Crime Survey (NCS) conducted since 1973 by the Bureau of Justice Statistics, Department of Justice. Both series have methodological deficits that have been thoroughly discussed in the criminological literature. Comparisons between the two series are fraught with difficulties, but still they remain as our chief sources of information on a national basis. (I have left to Delbert Elliott discussion of the National Youth Survey.)

Anyone who seeks to examine crime statistics based on age of offenders will be struck by the difficulties in making comparisons among different authors. Part of the problem in writing about youth crime and trying to determine its extent, volume, character and trends lies in the definition of youth. Some sources describe changes in violent crime among persons under age 18; some use age groups such as under 15, 15 to 17, 18 to 20; others use 12 to 17, or 11 to 25, or 15 to 24. The FBI commonly uses under age 18, but also gives data for persons under age 25. From 11 to 25, the FBI can provide single age-specific statistics. The NCS refers to victims 12 years of age and over. Neil Weiner and I, in our updating of the Eisenhower National Violence Commission report in "Violent Crimes in America, 1969-1982" refer to young adults (aged 18 to 24) and older juveniles (aged 15 to 17). Patrick Langan and Christopher Innes, in a special report of the Bureau of Justice Statistics on "The Risk of Violent Crime" (May 1985), use ages 16 to 24 in one place and ages 16 to 19 in another. Paul Strasburg, in his comprehensive review entitled "Recent National Trends in Serious Juvenile Crime"; uses different age groupings. He gives arrest figures for persons aged 7 to 17, but mostly uses juveniles (13-17), young adults (18-20) and adults (21+).

I mention these differences not to extol one scheme over another; one is not more precious, virtuous or useful than another. I mention them because different inferences and conclusions about the volume and trends of youth crime can be made, depending on which age grouping is used. Calculating a rate of juvenile delinquency by using in the numerator all persons arrested under age 18 and the total population under age 18, or even those aged 12 to 18, in the denominator can yield something quite different from an age-specific rate calculated for persons aged 15 to 17. When these rates are then compared over a decade, considerable variations may occur because of the changes in the composition of given ages, that is, changes in proportions in the total population. As Strasburg points out, "The nation's juvenile population (ages 7 through 17) declined by 11% between 1970 and 1981: in 1970 juveniles constituted 22% of the population, in 1981, only 17.4%" (p. 9).

For these reasons, the consumer of juvenile statistics must exercise caution and avoid alarmist remarks that may unintentionally inflate the statistics on increases in juvenile crime. Again, as Strasburg reminds us,

"The baby boom of the post World War II years generated an unprecedented 50% increase in the American adolescent [?] population during the 1960s, five times the average increase of the previous seven decades" (p. 27). That the size of given birth cohorts may have a significant impact on the juvenile crime rate has been discussed by Richard Easterlin, by M.D. Smith and, most recently and comprehensively, by Daniel Klepinger and Joseph Weis.

Another complicating factor in analyzing juvenile crime, and the share of juveniles in various kinds of crime, is the considerable group offending character of juvenile crime. At least since the writings of Shaw and McKay in the late 1930s and early 1940s, we know that a high proportion of juvenile delinquency is committed in groups of two, three or more. The 1979 victim survey, for example, shows that groups composed of juveniles only were responsible for 43 percent of all multiple-offender crimes that year, or more than any other age or mixed-age group (U.S. Department of Justice 1981, p. 9). The younger the offender, the higher the proportion of offenses will be committed in groups. Robbery probably is the highest multiple-offender crime, and 34 percent of robbery offenses attributed to juveniles is committed in groups of three or more (Strasburg, p. 22).

The difference between "offenses cleared" and "persons arrested" is an important one when the proportionate involvement of juveniles or young people is discussed - for any given year or for analyses over several years. An offense reported to the police is "cleared" when one or more suspects are taken into custody and made available for prosecution. Hence, one offense may be cleared by arresting four persons. The total number of juveniles arrested for robbery is invariably higher than the number of single events of robbery committed by juveniles. For example, in 1985 "persons under the age of 18 were the offenders in 12 percent of all 1985 robbery clearances" (UCR 1985, p. 19). The UCR does not tell us for 1985 how may persons under 18 were arrested for robbery, but in 1982 over 26 percent of robbery arrests were under age 18, and in 1985, 65 percent of all robbery arrests were under 25 years of age.

"The impact of group offending by juveniles on official statistics is not trivial," rightly says Paul Strasburg. As he points out:

> . . . juveniles appear in violence arrest statistics at nearly twice the rate they appear in statistics on violent crimes cleared. Since robbery is the most common juvenile crime of violence, and also the crime in which group offending occurs most frequently, robbery arrests contribute most to an exaggerated perception of the amount of crime being committed by juveniles. It is also worth recalling that juvenile robbery is predominantly an offense of black youths. Consequently, the number of crimes committed by black youths in particular is likely to be overstated if measured only by arrests (Strasburg, p. 22).

Professor Albert Reiss has just completed a thorough analysis of group offending for the National Academy of Sciences' panel on Criminal Careers and "Career Criminals": His study has just appeared in Volume II of that report.

How Old Are the Juveniles Who Commit Most of Our Serious Crime?

Having admonished caution in examining juvenile or youth crime, I shall now properly produce confusion by referring to statistics from several sources. I am drawing heavily upon the work that Neil Weiner and I did in order to bring up to date the early analyses by the National Commission on the Causes and Prevention of Violence. The 13 volumes produced by that Commission were published in 1968-69. Our current review includes some data on juveniles and youth between 1969 and 1982. Accompanying these remarks are two laboriously - but affectionately - calculated tables that show (1) the percentage distribution of arrests for violent index crimes by age groups (under 15, 15-17, 18-24, 25 and over), specific violent crimes for each year from 1969 through 1982; and (2) rates per 100,000 by each of the four age categories, each specific violent crime, from 1970 through 1981.

UCR data show that young adults (aged 18 to 24) and older juveniles (aged 15 to 17) have been responsible disproportionately for acts of criminal violence. Although young adults have constituted about 13 percent of the population of the United States, according to *UCR* statistics they have accounted generally for more than 30 percent of those arrested for criminal homicide and aggravated assault and for about 40 to 45 percent of those arrested for forcible rape and robbery (Table I). Older juveniles, who have constituted just under six percent of the population, have accumulated approximately 10 to 15 percent of the arrests for forcible rape and between 20 and 25 percent of the arrests for robbery. This age group was also responsible for a disproportionately greater share of the arrests for criminal homicide (about eight percent) and aggravated assault (about 11 percent); but clearly the magnitude of the disproportionality is less for those offenses than for forcible rape and robbery.

Table 1: Percentage Distribution of Arrests for Violent Index Crimes by Age: United States, 1969-1982

	Total Violent Index Crimes				Murder and Nonnegligent Manslaughter				Forcible Rape	
	Under Age 15	Ages 15 to 17	Ages 18 to 24	Age 25 and Over	Under Age 15	Ages 15 to 17	Ages 18 to 24	Age 25 and Over	Under Age 15	Ages 15 to 17
	%	%	%	%	%	%	%	%	%	%
Year	(N)	(N)	(N)	(N)	(N)	(N)	(N)	(N)	(N)	(N)
1969	7.3	15.1	36.2	41.5	0.1	6.0	32.7	57.9	3.8	16.4
	(15,739)	(32,457)	(76,285)	(89,699)	(157)	(926)	(3,767)	(6,654)	(541)	(2,391)
1970	7.1	15.4	36.0	41.5	1.5	9.0	33.0	56.5	4.1	16.7
	(17,263)	(37,313)	(86,939)	(100,319)	(187)	(1,169)	(4,229)	(7,265)	(634)	(2,571)
1971	7.2	15.6	36.5	40.7	1.3	6.9	33.9	55.9	4.0	16.6
	(19,539)	(42,763)	(99,642)	(111,205)	(190)	(1,300)	(4,927)	(8,132)	(667)	(2,757)
1972	7.2	15.4	36.0	41.4	1.5	9.4	32.8	56.5	4.2	15.5
	(21,520)	(46,035)	(107,627)	(123,660)	(221)	(1,413)	(4,944)	(8,461)	(818)	(3,024)
1973	7.0	15.7	35.7	41.6	1.5	8.9	34.2	55.4	4.2	15.4
	(20,244)	(45,669)	(103,643)	(120,613)	(216)	(1,281)	(4,929)	(7,973)	(813)	(2,959)
1974	6.4	16.2	37.1	40.2	1.5	8.6	34.9	55.0	4.3	15.1
	(18,904)	(47,595)	(109,316)	(118,566)	(205)	(1,193)	(4,826)	(7,584)	(771)	(2,684)
1975	6.5	16.5	36.4	40.4	1.1	8.4	35.3	55.2	4.0	13.6
	(24,186)	(61,252)	(134,956)	(149,854)	(184)	(1,389)	(5,823)	(9,082)	(867)	(2,996)
1976	6.1	15.9	35.8	42.2	1.4	7.9	33.4	57.4	4.2	13.0
	(20,813)	(53,902)	(121,036)	(142,913)	(190)	(1,112)	(4,711)	(8,055)	(915)	(2,830)
1977	5.7	15.4	35.4	44.1	1.2	8.5	33.8	56.5	4.2	12.3
	(21,997)	(59,371)	(140,328)	(164,953)	(215)	(1,455)	(5,792)	(9,652)	(1,081)	(3,176)
1978	5.6	15.6	36.1	42.5	1.3	8.0	34.1	56.7	3.9	12.1
	(25,940)	(69,653)	(180,952)	(189,357)	(244)	(1,491)	(6,401)	(10,609)	(1,102)	(3,415)
1979	5.2	14.9	37.3	42.5	1.1	8.2	34.9	55.7	3.7	12.2
	(22,597)	(64,778)	(162,246)	(184,817)	(205)	(1,501)	(6,356)	(8,053)	(1,081)	(3,570)
1980	4.8	14.6	37.3	43.4	1.1	8.2	35.4	44.7	3.6	11.2
	(21,181)	(65,039)	(186,595)	(193,557)	(200)	(1,542)	(6,636)	(10,376)	(1,052)	(3,294)
1981	4.6	13.7	36.3	45.2	1.0	8.1	34.1	56.8	4.0	10.8
	(22,106)	(63,747)	(168,726)	(210,245)	(205)	(1,653)	(6,971)	(11,603)	(1,193)	(3,256)
1982	4.5	12.7	36.2	46.6	1.0	7.5	34.4	57.1	4.0	10.7
	(19,894)	(56,469)	(160,777)	(206,720)	(183)	(1,396)	(6,370)	(10,562)	(1,134)	(3,025)

Source: Adapted from U.S. Department of Justice, Federal Bureau of Investigation, *Uniform Crime Reports for the United States, 1969-1982: 1969*, table 27, pp. 113-14; *1970*, table 28, pp. 126-27; *1971*, table 29, pp. 122-23; *1972*, table 32, pp. 126-27; *1973*; table 30, pp. 128-29; *1974*, table 34, pp. 185-87; *1975*, table 36, pp. 188-89; *1976*, table 32, pp, 181-82; *1977*, table 32, pp. 180-81; *1978*, table 32, pp. 194-95; *1979*, table 32, pp. 196-97; *1980*, table 32, pp. 200-201; *1981*, table 31, pp. 171-72; *1982*, table 31, pp. 176-77.
Reprinted from Weiner and Wolfgang, "Violent Crime in America, 1969-1982," Table 15

Table 1 (cont.): Percentage Distribution of Arrests for Violent Index Crimes by Age: United States, 1969-1982

Forcible Rape		Robbery				Aggravated Assault			
Ages 18 to 24	Age 25 and Over	Under Age 15	Ages 15 to 17	Ages 18 to 24	Age 25 and Over	Under Age15	Ages 15 to 17	Ages 18 to 24	Age 25 and Over
%	%	%	%	%	%	%	%	%	%
(N)	(N)	(N)	(N)	(N)	(N)	(N)	(N)	(N)	(N)
45.0	34.9	11.8	21.6	43.3	23.2	5.3	11.1	30.6	53.0
(6,489)	(5,034)	(9,022)	(16,577)	(33,175)	(17,757)	(6,019)	(12,593)	(34,854)	(60,254)
43.7	35.5	11.1	22.4	43.6	23.0	5.4	11.1	30.0	53.5
(6,735)	(5,471)	(9,695)	(19,594)	(36,221)	(20,177)	(6,767)	(13,989)	(37,754)	(67,461)
43.4	36	10.4	21.8	44.7	23.1	5.8	11.8	30.0	52.4
(7,209)	(5,945)	(10,534)	(22,221)	(45,443)	(23,500)	(8,148)	(16,485)	(42,063)	(73,628)
42.8	37.4	10.4	21.5	44.0	24.1	5.6	11.7	29.8	52.6
(6,293)	(7,231)	(11,367)	(23,436)	(46,077)	(26,279)	(9,094)	(18,162)	(46,313)	(81,888)
41.0	39.4	10.8	22.9	42.6	23.7	5.3	11.7	30.6	52.4
(7,661)	(7,549)	(11,015)	(23,359)	(43,399)	(24,077)	(6,200)	(18,070)	(47,454)	(61,014)
40.7	39.9	9.2	23.4	44.3	23.1	5.1	11.9	31.8	51.2
(7,250)	(7,055)	(9,984)	(25,361)	(48,074)	(25,002)	(7,943)	(16,357)	(49,166)	(78,894)
40.4	42.0	9.6	24.6	42.8	22.9	5.2	12.3	32.0	50.3
(8,880)	(9,213)	(12,515)	(31,955)	(65,483)	(29,768)	(10,600)	(24,912)	(64,770)	(101,791)
39.9	42.8	9.2	24.3	42.5	24.0	5.0	12.0	31.5	51.5
(8,858)	(9,275)	(10,156)	(26,834)	(45,866)	(26,395)	(9,552)	(23,125)	(60,803)	(94,830)
39.8	43.7	8.4	23.6	42.4	25.6	4.7	11.6	32.7	50.9
(10,278)	(11,253)	(10,309)	(26,950)	(51,890)	(31,324)	(10,392)	(25,790)	(72,366)	(112,684)
37.8	46.2	9.2	24.7	41.4	24.6	4.5	11.6	33.1	50.9
(10,694)	(13,034)	(13,066)	(35,002)	(58,605)	(34,747)	(11,508)	(29,745)	(85,232)	(130,987)
39.8	43.4	6.1	23.4	42.9	25.8	4.2	11.4	34.4	49.9
(11,619)	(12,876)	(10,622)	(30,535)	(56,091)	(33,446)	(10,655)	(29,172)	(68,350)	(128,132)
39.2	46.0	7.1	23.0	42.9	27.8	3.9	10.9	34.2	51.1
(11,529)	(13,556)	(9,941)	(32,056)	(59,873)	(37,605)	(9,968)	(28,147)	(86,558)	(132,028)
37.1	48.1	7.0	21.7	42.5	28.9	3.9	10.1	33.0	53.0
(11,144)	(14,457)	(10,250)	(31,964)	(62,593)	(42,589)	(10,458)	(26,874)	(88,020)	(141,596)
37.4	48.0	6.5	19.8	42.9	30.7	3.7	9.5	32.7	54.2
(10,581)	(13,592)	(9,114)	(27,366)	(59,273)	(42,965)	(9,483)	(24,662)	(84,553)	(140,201)

Source: Adapted from U.S. Department of Justice, Federal Bureau of Investigation, *Uniform Crime Reports for the United States, 1969-1982*: *1969*, table 27, pp. 113-14; *1970*, table 28, pp. 126-27; *1971*, table 29, pp. 122-23; *1972*, table 32, pp. 126-27; *1973*; table 30, pp. 128-29; *1974*, table 34, pp. 185-87; *1975*, table 36, pp. 188-89; *1976*, table 32, pp, 181-82; *1977*, table 32, pp. 180-81; *1978*, table 32, pp. 194-95; *1979*, table 32, pp. 196-97; *1980*, table 32, pp. 200-201; *1981*, table 31, pp. 171-72; *1982*, table 31, pp. 176-77.
Reprinted from Weiner and Wolfgang, "Violent Crime in America, 1969-1982," Table 15

Striking results appear when arrest *rates* for the different age groups are computed from UCR data. Examination of the rates for violent index crimes combined indicates that young adults (aged 18 to 24) had the highest overall rates, followed fairly closely by older juveniles (aged 15 to 17) and then, far behind, by older adults (aged 25 and over) and, still further behind, by younger juveniles and children (below age 15) (Table II). Furthermore, young adults and older juveniles registered the highest rates regardless of the type of violent crime. When these two age groups were compared, young adults recorded higher arrest rates for three of the four violent offenses: criminal homicide by a factor of two, forcible rape by a factor of about one and one-third, and aggravated assault by a factor of about one and one-quarter. Robbery, however, was committed more often by older juveniles, especially since the middle of the past decade, when their arrest rates began to exceed those of young adults by about one and one-third. Older juveniles also incurred a higher rate increase than young adults for robbery and a fairly similar rate increases for criminal homicide and aggravated assault. Neither older juveniles nor young adults experienced much of a rate increase for forcible rape, however.

After World War 11, the country entered a period of about a decade (1946 to 1956) in which the birthrate soared. The first of these large baby-boom cohorts entered its peak arrest ages (15 to 25) for violent crimes about 1963, the time at which the violent crime rate began to rise sharply in the nation. The last of these cohorts entered its peak arrest ages in the early 1970s and matured out of this highrisk period in about 1980. The high and increasing levels of violent crime witnessed in the 1960s and the 1970s are attributable in part to these birth cohorts. As the last of these cohorts has passed out of the high-risk ages, we might expect a decline in the level of violent crime during the latter part of the 1980s. The decline is likely to be modest, however, for those demographic groups that exhibit the highest arrest rates for violent crimes tend also to have the highest birthrates. As a result, even after the baby-boom cohorts have moved out of their high-risk ages, these age groups will nevertheless in forthcoming years still have a high proportion of persons most likely to engage in violent crimes.

Table 2: Arrest for Violent Crimes by Age: United States, 1970 – 1981 (Rates per 100,000 Age-Specific Population)*

Year	Total Violent Index Crimes				Murder and Nonnegligent Manslaughter				Forcible Rape	
	Under Age 15	Ages 15 to 17	Ages 18 to 24	Age 25 and Over	Under Age 15	Ages 15 to 17	Ages 18 to 24	Age 25 and Over	Under Age 15	Ages 15 to 17
1970	40.1	424.3	456.0	121.7	0.4	13.2	23.6	8.8	1.5	29.2
1971	45.0	474.3	525.4	132.5	0.4	14.4	26.0	9.7	1.5	30.6
1972	49.1	466.4	545.5	141.9	0.5	14.9	25.0	9.7	1.9	32.0
1973	49.1	491.1	539.3	141.5	0.5	13.8	25.6	9.4	2.0	31.8
1974	54.4	591.6	647.0	159.3	0.6	14.8	28.6	10.2	2.2	33.4
1975	53.5	579.4	583.8	149.6	0.4	13.1	25.2	9.1	1.9	26.3
1976	48.4	520.6	530.5	144.1	0.4	10.7	20.6	8.1	2.1	27.3
1977	46.3	515.9	535.8	145.9	0.4	12.6	22.1	8.6	2.3	27.6
1978	53.5	580.0	589.0	158.8	0.5	12.4	23.4	8.9	2.3	28.4
1979	48.2	565.3	596.2	155.2	0.4	13.1	23.4	6.6	2.3	31.2
1980	45.0	578.5	606.2	158.4	0.4	13.7	24.1	8.5	2.2	29.3
1981	46.2	571.9	593.3	165.4	0.4	14.8	24.6	9.1	2.5	29.2
% Change 1970 to 1981	(+15.2)	(+34.8)	(+22.7)	(+35.9)	(0.0)	(+12.1)	(+5.6)	(+3.4)	(+66.7)	(0.00)

*The computations presented in this table were derived as follows: (1) The percentage of the population in each age group in each year was calculated from estimates of the resident population of the United States. See U.S. Bureau of the Census, Current Population Reports, Estimates of the United States by Age, Race and Sex: July 1, 1969 (Washington, D.C.: U.S. Government Printing Office, 1969), table 2, p. 2; Preliminary Estimates of the Population of the United States by Age, Race and Sex: 1970 to 1981 (Washington, D.C.: U.S. Government Printing Office, 1982), table 2, pp. 26-43. (2) The percentage of the resident population in each age group in a given year was multiplied by the "estimated population" covered by the UCR reporting agencies for the corresponding year as listed at the head of the UCR table, "Total Arrests, Distribution by Age," producing the number of persons in each age group in the "estimated population." This computation assumes that the distribution by age in the resident population of the United States in a given year is the same as that in the "estimated population" covered by the UCR reporting agencies for that same year.

The UCR data on "estimated population" were obtained from U.S. Department of Justice, Federal Bureau of Investigation, Uniform Crime Reports for the United States, 1969-1981 (Washington, D.C.: U.S. Government Printing Office, 1979-82): 1969, pp. 113-14; 1970, pp. 126-27; 1971, pp. 122-23; 1972, pp. 126-27; 1973, pp. 128-29; 1974, pp. 186-87; 1975, pp. 188-89; 1976, pp. 181-82; 1977, pp. 180-81; 1978, pp. 194-95; 1979, pp. 196-97; 1980, pp. 200-201; 1981, pp. 171-72. (3) The number of arrests in each age group for a given year was divided by the number of persons in that age group as calculated from the "estimated population" for that year (see step 2), producing the age-specific arrest rate. The number of arrests within each age group in a given year was obtained from the same table that provided the data on the "estimated population" covered by the UCR reporting agencies (see step 2). (4) The age-specific arrest rates calculated in step 3 were multiplied by 100,000 for purposes of standardization.

It should also be noted that census data were not available for 1969 in age groupings that allowed us to compute rates for this table.

Reprinted form Weiner and Wolfgang, "Violent Crime in America, 1969-1982," Table 16.

Table 2 (cont.): **Arrest for Violent Crimes by Age: United States, 1970 – 1981 (Rates per 100,000 Age-Specific Population)***

Year	Forcible Rape		Robbery				Aggravated Assault			
	Ages 18 to 24	Age 25 and Over	Under Age 15	Ages 15 to 17	Ages 18 to 24	Age 25 and Over	Under Age15	Ages 15 to 17	Ages 18 to 24	Age 25 and Over
1970	37.6	6.6	22.5	222.8	213.6	24.5	15.7	159.1	211.0	61.6
1971	38.0	7.1	24.3	245.5	239.6	28.0	18.8	182.8	221.6	87.7
1972	42.0	8.3	26.0	247.5	243.7	30.1	20.6	191.9	234.7	93.8
1973	40.9	8.9	26.7	251.2	224.6	28.3	19.9	194.3	245.9	95.0
1974	42.9	9.5	26.7	315.2	284.6	33.7	22.9	228.2	291.0	106.0
1975	36.4	9.2	27.7	302.2	240.0	29.7	23.5	235.6	280.2	101.6
1976	37.9	9.4	23.6	259.2	205.4	26.6	22.2	223.3	265.5	95.6
1977	39.2	10.0	21.7	251.6	196.1	27.7	21.9	224.1	276.3	99.6
1978	39.1	10.9	27.0	291.4	214.4	29.2	23.8	247.7	311.6	109.8
1979	42.7	10.5	22.7	266.5	206.1	26.1	22.8	254.6	324.6	107.6
1980	42.0	11.1	21.1	285.1	217.9	30.8	21.2	250.4	322.2	108.0
1981	39.4	11.4	21.4	266.7	221.2	33.5	21.9	241.1	311.1	111.4
% Change 1970 to 1981	(+4.8)	(+72.7)	(-4.9)	(+28.7)	(+3.6)	(+36.7)	(+39.5)	(+51.5)	(+47.4)	(+38.2)

*The computations presented in this table were derived as follows: (1) The percentage of the population in each age group in each year was calculated from estimates of the resident population of the United States. See U.S. Bureau of the Census, Current Population Reports, Estimates of the United States by Age, Race and Sex: July 1, 1969 (Washington, D.C.: U.S. Government Printing Office, 1969), table 2, p. 2; Preliminary Estimates of the Population of the United States by Age, Race and Sex: 1970 to 1981 (Washington, D.C.: U.S. Government Printing Office, 1982), table 2, pp. 26-43. (2) The percentage of the resident population in each age group in a given year was multiplied by the "estimated population" covered by the UCR reporting agencies for the corresponding year as listed at the head of the UCR table, "Total Arrests, Distribution by Age," producing the number of persons in each age group in the "estimated population." This computation assumes that the distribution by age in the resident population of the United States in a given year is the same as that in the "estimated population" covered by the UCR reporting agencies for that same year.

The UCR data on "estimated population" were obtained from U.S. Department of Justice, Federal Bureau of Investigation, Uniform Crime Reports for the United States, 1969-1981 (Washington, D.C.: U.S. Government Printing Office, 1979-82): 1969, pp. 113-14; 1970, pp. 126-27; 1971, pp. 122-23; 1972, pp. 126-27; 1973, pp. 128-29; 1974, pp. 186-87; 1975, pp. 188-89; 1976, pp. 181-82; 1977, pp. 180-81; 1978, pp. 194-95; 1979, pp. 196-97; 1980, pp. 200-201; 1981, pp. 171-72. (3) The number of arrests in each age group for a given year was divided by the number of persons in that age group as calculated from the "estimated population" for that year (see step 2), producing the age-specific arrest rate. The number of arrests within each age group in a given year was obtained from the same table that provided the data on the "estimated population" covered by the UCR reporting agencies (see step 2). (4) The age-specific arrest rates calculated in step 3 were multiplied by 100,000 for purposes of standardization.

It should also be noted that census data were not available for 1969 in age groupings that allowed us to compute rates for this table.

Reprinted form Weiner and Wolfgang, "Violent Crime in America, 1969-1982," Table 16.

As the table with rates per 100,000 age-specific groups shows, violent crimes rose in each age category save one between 1970 and 1981. (The exception is a 4.9 decrease in robbery arrests for persons under 15 years of age.) Combining all violent crime arrests (murder and non-negligent manslaughter, forcible rape, robbery, aggravated assault), the increase was greatest for persons aged 25 and over (35.9), about the same for those aged 15 to 17 (34.8), but less for ages 18 to 24 (22.7) and least for those under age 15 (15.2). Although there were huge increases in juvenile crime between 1960 and 1975 increases of 200 to over 300 percent - the increases from 1970 to 1981 are much more modest and are now relatively stabilized.

We also examined victimizations. Older juveniles (aged 16 to 19) and young adults (aged 20 to 24) have been found to be disproportionately the targets of violent crimes. NCS data firmly support the currency of this finding. Persons in these age groups experienced the highest and roughly comparable chances of being raped, which were approximately two times as high as those of other age groups. Older juveniles and young adults also suffered the highest and roughly comparable risks of being assaulted seriously. They were about twice as likely to be assaulted as their two closes rivals, the 12-to 15-year-olds and the 25- to 34-year-olds. Robbery victims also fell, for the most part, into the younger age brackets: 12to 15-year-olds, 16- to 19-year-olds and 20- to 24-year-olds all shared a similarly high risk of being robbed, which was two to three times higher than that of older age groups.

In a Bureau of Justice Statistics study of violent crime victimization for 1982, persons aged 16 to 19 had the highest risk (6.51%), followed by ages 20 to 24 (6.22%), then 12 to 15 years (4.83%) and 25 to 34 (4.03%). The 65 and older group had the lowest, which was less than one percent (.60%).

Predicting crime is hazardous, but Klepinger and Weis have recently provided a methodologically careful and comprehensive projection, taking into account significant variables. I quote from some of their concluding remarks about the age structure and distribution of crime:

> In 1978 about 56% of all property crimes were committed by persons under the age of 20. By 1990 this figure is expected to drop to about 46%. In effect, [during] the 1980s and early 1990s property crime will no longer be primarily a youth phenomenon. In general, the average age of offenders for all crimes will rise . . . the age pattern for violent crimes rises sharply to a double peak at ages 18 and 21 and then declines rather gradually throughout the remaining years .... The proportion of violent crimes due to 15- to 19-year-olds declines until the late 1990s, when the new larger cohorts

enter. For ages 20-24 the percentage of the total peaks in 1982. The peaks for ages 25-29 and 30-34, respectively, are 1987 and about 1992. The aging effect is most pronounced for violent crimes because the age pattern of violent crimes maintains the influence of older cohorts (pp. 411-413).

Predictive Knowledge Of Juvenile Behavior Has Its Limits

I shall now shift attention to a different dimension of research on juvenile delinquency. I refer to work we have done at the Sellin Center for Studies in Criminology and Criminal Law. For over 25 years we have been doing longitudinal research on birth cohorts (Wolfgang, Figlio, Sellin). A birth cohort is a demographic term that refers to all persons born in the same year and who are followed through their biographies, in our case, at least from age 10 to age 18. We have also followed them into their adult years.

Birth Cohort I comprised 9975 boys born in 1945 who lived in Philadelphia at least from ages 10 to 18. Birth Cohort II comprised 13,160 males born in 1958 and who met the same criteria. We included 14,000 females in Cohort II, but cohort comparisons can only be made for males.

The prevalence rates - that is, the probability of being arrested at least once before age 18 - was the same for both birth cohorts born 13 years apart: 35 percent of the 1945 cohort had at least one arrest, and 33 percent of the 1958 cohort had the same. Moreover, six percent of Cohort I were identified as chronic offenders - those who had five or more arrests before reaching age 18. These 627 boys out of the nearly 10,000 birth cohort were responsible for 53 percent of all the offenses committed by cohort and nearly two-thirds of the serious index offenses. We noted that 627 chronic offenders committed 5300 offenses *before* age 18.

We found the same situation for the later Cohort II: 982 male chronic delinquents, representing only 7.5 percent of the cohort and 23 percent of the delinquents accounted for 9240 offenses, or 61 percent of all offenses. They were responsible for 68 percent of all index offenses - 61 percent of homicides, 75 percent of rapes, 73 percent of robberies, 65 percent of aggravated assaults, 66 percent involving personal injury. Moreover, the *incidence* rate for Cohort 11 was three times that of Cohort I. That is, Cohort 11 males committed three times the amount of violent crime.

What are the implications of this longitudinal research? First, we recognize that about two-thirds of a birth cohort of males are never seen in the criminal, juvenile, justice system. Moreover, between 42 and 47 percent are only one-time offenders; they are never seen again and their offenses are usually trivial. By the third offense, this small cadre should be given focus and the attention of our resources of time, talent and funds to try to prevent future delinquency and crime.

Can we identify the chronic, serious, violent offender early in his career? We cannot do so very well except in the aggregate. If he begins his offending behavior early, say at age 13 or 14, if his delinquency involves a violent offense, and if his continued delinquency is rapid - meaning little time between offenses - then he is a highly predictable future offender.

What shall we do with that knowledge?

What are the social implications of predictive knowledge? I consider them dangerous; they raise ethical issues that have not been resolved and that need to be discussed.

In a recent issue .of *Daedalus* ("Art and Science", Summer 1986) Susan P. Gill writes most cogently about "The Paradox of Prediction" and warns us as follows:

> Prediction is linked with emergence precisely because of the *paradox of prediction:* the uncertainty inherent in observation means that any prediction (which the observer attempts to verify) will influence the observation. So the *paradox of prediction* warns us: a theory may predict, but the experiment that would confirm or refute that prediction may also be influenced by the prediction itself (pp. 27-28).

Prediction, as part of scientific studies of human behavior, should surely be made and continue. Science is cumulative, and knowledge will increase about past, present and future behavior. We need not know causes of phenomena in order to predict changes or stability in phenomena.

In criminal justice utility, however, prediction should not be used to lengthen the sentence. Only *past behavior* of offending, by the type of that offensive behavior, should govern the length of sentence.

All citizens should know in advance, through specified penal codes, what acts are criminal and what the presumptive sentence is, *a la* Cesare Beccaria, 1764. Extending a sentence based on research models that change fails to give the citizen adequate knowledge of his future.

Models can be used to predict assaultive, violent behavior *in prison,* for classification purposes, both initial classification *and* reclassification during later periods.

Prediction may be used as a basis for planning intervention or treatment programs. A more focal concern, more intensive work with high-risk convicted offenders might be viewed as appropriate. Prediction should never be used to make any program more harsh, more punitive, more onerous in any way.

Prediction should be used for *benevolent purposes,* that is, benign or benevolent for the offender, which in turn could have a further effect of protecting the public, society.

Invasion of the purity of the just desserts model, which claims that one should be punished only for what one has done in the instant case, occurs when prior offenses, for which punishment was inflicted, are taken into account when there is augmentation of the instant sanction.

But at least that invasion of purity of the just desserts model is based on information clearly known - 100 percent known - both by the defendant and the criminal justice system, the defendant and the judge.

However, using predictive probabilities regarding relatively unknown behavior to increase the defendant's sentence I view as unfair, perhaps unethical. Neither the judge nor the defendant knows for sure what the future will hold.

Moreover, if incarceration is "criminogenic", as more than a few of my colleagues assert, augmentation of the length of imprisonment biases the dice game in favor of the predictors and reduces the future protection of society. The augmented period of imprisonment, based on the prediction model, may incapacitate the offender during that time, but his future criminality, after the augmented time may be accelerated in velocity and gravity.

The defendant is given no right to invoke his prediction of his own future conduct, nor to predict the failure of the criminal justice system to provide him with sufficient treatment programs to help him alter his behavior, nor to predict the deleterious or beneficial conditions in the community when he returns.

We arrest on suspicion that says there is probable cause to arrest (meaning about 50 percent reason to suspect this particular suspect).

We convict with the traditional phrase "beyond reasonable doubt" (which I interpret as the 95 percentile).

What probability level wold be used by those who would use prediciton to augment sanctions? The extra two years, say, added to a defendant's incarceration because he is a high-risk person, could be as long as the entire sentence for a low-risk person, when both have committed the same offense.

Surely "beyond reasonable doubt" about the assertation of future crime should be the minimal standard - that is, if criminal justice policy invoked prediction.

I am not prepared to make a cozy peace with the advocates of prediction use for increasing penalties. I do not wish to put into the hands of those who have the means to define and manufacture "normal," the additional power to control people by the manufacturing of future expectations.

It is not a contradiction to argue that juvenile court records should selectively be available to the sentencing judge in adult criminal court. A major article on "Juvenile Court Records: Confidentiality vs. the Public's Right to Know" appeared in the Winter 1986 issue of American Criminal Law Review (Vol. 23, No. 3). I shall not attempt to summarize the issues or recommendations. The panel of the National Academy of Sciences on Criminal Careers and "Career Criminals" recommends that, upon conviction of a felony in criminal court, the defendant's juvenile record should be available to the sentencing judge. The dual system of juvenile and criminal justice that prevents the sharing of information and permits a serious, chronic, violent juvenile to become a virgin or first offender after his eighteenth birthday is a strange cultural invention.

But let me hasten to add that even highly selective sharing of a juvenile record should be used only to inform the criminal court judge that the convicted felon is not a first offender and thereby should not enjoy any statutory or judicial benefit of a first-offender status. So long as prior record is taken into account in either system, prior record should be taken into account across systems. Once again, however, the sharing of information should not be used to augment the sanction because of the likelihood of future recidivism. That the sanction may be heavier because first-offender status might be denied is recognized but, under that condition, the sanction is still past-oriented and thereby less tarnishing to the just desserts or retributive model. This model, in any case, should always be tempered with non-coercive rehabilitation and efforts by the justice system to intervene benevolently.

REFERENCES

American Criminal Law Review, "Juvenile Court Records: Confidentiality vs. the Public's Right to Know," Vol. 23, No. 3, Winter 1986, 379-401.

Gill, Susan P, "The Paradox of Prediction," in Arts and Science, Daedalus, Summer 1986.

Klepinger, Daniel H. and Weis, Joseph G., "Projecting Crime Rates: An Age, Period and Cohort Model Using ARIMA Techniques," Journal of Quantitative Criminology, Vol. 1, No. 4, 1985.

Langan, Patrick A. and Innes, Christopher A., "The Risk of Violent Crime," Special Report of the Bureau of Justice Statistics, Washington, D.C., May 1985.

Strasburg, Paul A., "Recent National Trends in Serious Juvenile Crime," in Mathias, R.S., DeMuro, Paul and Allinson, Richard S. (eds.), Violent Juvenile Offenders: An Anthology, San Francisco, CA: National Council on Crime and Delinquency, 1984.

Tracy Paul E., Wolfgang, M.E. and Figlio, R.M., *Delinquency in Two Birth Cohorts: Executive Summary*, Washington, D.C.: U.S. Department of Justice, Office of Juvenile Justice and Delinquency Prevention, September 1985.

Uniform Crime Reports, Federal Bureau of Investigation, U.S. Department of Justice, Washington, D.C., 1985.

Weiner, Neil A. and Wolfgang, Marvin E., "Violent Crime in America, 1969-1982," in Curtis, Lynn (ed.), *American Violence and Public Policy*, New Haven, CT: Yale University Press, 1983.

Wolfgang, Marvin E., Figlio, R.M. and Sellin, Thorsten. (1972). *Delinquency in a Birth Cohort*, Chicago, Illinois: University of Chicago Press.

CRIME AND PUNISHMENT IN
RENAISSANCE FLORENCE

Marvin E. Wolfgang*

* *Professor of Criminology and of Law, University of Pennsylvania. This study was supported by two Fellowships from the John Simon Guggenheim Foundation and a Fulbright Research Grant from the United States Government. This paper was delivered at the 41st annual meeting of the American Society of Criminology in Reno, Nevada, in November, 1989, for the Edwin Sutherland Award.*

This paper centers attention on available records that best reflect the sentiments and behavioral manifestations of those sentiments concerned with the treatment of criminal offenders in Florence, Italy, during the fourteenth and fifteenth centuries. Florence is regarded as the birthplace of the Renaissance spirit, and the history of punishment there in this period has basic relevance to the development of methods dealing with persons who committed crimes. Many of the historical details which this study contains are reasonably well known, others are new or newly uncovered. The sociological implications of these details are less widely recognized. The view that crime and punishment of any period are not divorced from their social and cultural context is commonplace, but there are few empirical studies of this relationship. In general terms, this paper is an empirical examination of the genesis and development of some of the cultural values which underlie the social reaction to crime during the Early Renaissance in Florence.[1]

The temporal setting for the larger study of which this analysis is a part reaches from 1293, the year of the enactment of the famous Ordinances of Justice, to 1530 and the fall of the Florentine Republic. Historians generally agree that this was the period of greatest glory for Florence, where the Rinascita, or the rebirth of classical humanism, first and with most vigor occurred.

John Gillin defined crime as "an act that has been shown to be actually harmful to society, or that is believed to be harmful by a group of people that has the power to enforce its beliefs, and that places such act under the ban of positive penalties." [2] We shall adopt this widely applicable definition and the interrogative formulation of hypothesis in order to ask: What form did positive criminal penalties take in Florence during the period of its highest cultural prominence? What relationships existed between cultural values and the social sanctions employed by the group that had the power to enforce its beliefs? More positively stated, we might hypothesize [3] that, because Florence was the early home of the Renaissance and gave rise to a variety of new cultural traits, institutional patterns, artistic and scientific advances, and modes of thought, it correspondingly would have developed new patterns of social action for both the penal codes and the general treatment of offenders.

Examination of historical data relevant to this hypothesis has been made within a sociological orientation. The sociologist entering into this kind of interdisciplinary research is faced with the dual problem of obtaining historical detail and accuracy, and of synthesizing social, economic, and other institutional history with a variety of sociological conceptualisms. Most of the present paper is concerned with the latter problem, although brief reference to the former reveals some of the methodological problems of this research.

SOURCES OF DATA

Our analysis of crime and punishment in Renaissance Florence centers on an old prison known as *Le Stinche*. The prison was the focal point of the social reactions to law violation throughout the whole period of Florentine preeminence; it was constructed in 1301 and endured until 1835 when it was unceremoniously demolished. *Le Stinche is* not a common Italian name, and the etymology of the term offers interesting historical insight [4]

The singular nouns *stinco* (m.) and, archaically, *stinca* (f.) are derived from Longobardian roots, and refer to the front edge of the tibia, the shin, or shinbone. [5] In Old High German, this same part of the anatomy is called the *scina;* in German, *schiene;* in Anglo-Saxon, *scinn;* in Middle *English, shine* and schine; and in Dutch, *scheen.* [6] This anthropomorphic meaning was logically projected to a topographically similar phenomenon. Thus, in Italian, the word also denoted the top of a hill, the highest ridge of a mountain, and the apex of a knoll. There is a close relationship between the archaic *stinca* and *cima* in Italian, for both words refer to the ridge or crest of a hill. The English word *chine* illustrates the same duality, meaning both backbone, or spine, and ridge or crest *(echine* in French and *eschine* in Old French), and has the same Teutonic origin as *scina.*

The first prisoners in the newly opened communal prison were political prisoners taken from the Ghibelline stronghold in Val di Greve, a castle belonging to the Cavalcanti family. The castle, named *Castello delle Stinche,* was located on the ridge of a hill. Through popular references to the *Carceri di Comune* as *Le Stinche,* official manuscripts and legal documents soon adopted the nomenclature that persisted for over five centuries. [7]

Renaissance and even Florentine historians rarely mention the prison, or, if reference is made, it is usually peripheral to some political event. However, there are few court dispositions of criminal cases or few legal documents that fail to refer repeatedly to *Le Stinche.*

Prominent Florentines were imprisoned in *Le Stinche* at a time when the prison was used principally for debtors and for offenders against the common law. Francesco Berni, the satirical poet, was imprisoned there for debt during the fifteenth century, and he incorporated the name of the prison into one of his poems, entitled *"In lode del debito."*

Giovanni Villani, one of the best-known chroniclers of the city, also spent some time in *Le Stinche.* In volume IV of one of the Sansoni editions of Villani's *Cronica,*[8] a section, written by Pietro Massa and entitled *"Elogio di Giovanni villani,"* includes a full reference to the imprisonment of Villani in *Le Stinche.* [9]

In the records of people condemned by the *Otto di Guardia e Balia* for the years 1555 to 1560, there is a reference to an order of February *28,* 1556, indicating that Benventuo Cellini; the well-known goldsmith, was convicted of having engaged in the act of sodomy, and was sentenced to confinement for four years in *Le Carceri delle Stinche.*

Finally, there is good evidence that in 1513, Niccolo Machiavelli was temporarily incarcerated in *Le Stinche* while he was subjected to questioning regarding his role in a local conspiracy. The questioning occurred as a result of a document found by the authorities that contained a list of names of some eighteen people, of whom Machiavelli was one.[10] Pietro Paolo Boscoli, one of the two youthful fanatics who resolved to assassinate Giuliano and Lorenzo de'Medici, had accidentally dropped the paper. Although Boscoli and his associate, Agostino Capponi, confessed on the rack, they contended that none of the people on the list knew of their tyrannicidal designs. Nonetheless, Machiavelli was tortured under questioning; he confessed nothing and was subsequently released.[11] During those arduous days, he wrote three poems dedicated, presumably, to Giuliano. Two of these were composed in his prison cell for the purpose of obtaining a pardon. In one, he describes the prison after having suffered six turns on the rack. He complains of the stench and the fact that the walls were crawling with vermin so big and swollen that they seemed like moths. One prisoner was being chained, another loosened, and a third crying that the ropes were hoisting him too far from the ground.

Although there appears to be no etymological association between *stench* and *stink* in English and *stinche* in Italian, the word *stinche* was used occasionally as a metaphor for bad conditions of life, and even for a bad odor. In a sonnet by Jacopo Paganelli, sent to his cousin, Antonio Paganelli in 1468, the poet writes: *"E son in una stufa, onde un odore surge, che quel delle Stinche . . . ."* (*"And* I am in an oven whence a stench arises, that of *Le Stinche.")*.[12] In time, the word became a generic term for prisons even outside Florence, but the principal reference after the fourteenth century remained that of the Florence prison.

Although many source materials have been employed to ascertain the conditions of crime and punishment in Florence, the 500 volumes in the Archivio di Stato, Florence, that relate directly to the prison constitute the most direct evidence of the type of treatment accorded criminal offenders. These volumes, which have remained virtually untouched by historians, are known as the *Archivio delle Stinche:* they are part of the state archives and are housed below the Uffizi Gallery in Florence. The manuscripts, both in Latin and Italian, supply information regarding commitments and discharges of prisoners, the types of offenses, length of stay in the institution, and how inmates were discharged *(i.e.,* payment of debt, sentence served, amnesty, and pardon). The rules and regulations of the prison administration, the treatment to be given various offenders, and the relationship between crime and punishment are clearly detailed in these manuscripts. [13]

A basic problem for contemporary sociologists engaging in this kind of archival research is their naivete regarding historical documents and detail. They must become aware not only of the fundamental historical facts related to the period in question, but they also must determine which documents and manuscripts are important, which have been accepted as authentic, and how to read them. There is a variety of auxiliary experts, such as Latin philologists, epigraphers, paleographers, numismatists, heraldists, genealogists, chartists, bibliographers, and chronologists, who can aid them in this process. At the very least, sociologists must become acquainted with the works of these experts, if not with all their techniques of textual criticism. As Max Weber has eloquently said,

> He who is not in daily contact with source materials . . . is never safe from error in details, and it is therefore quite evident that the final verdict concerning these problems is a matter for historians, archaeologists, and philologists, to whom on our part we merely offer for testing the heuristic aids and suggestive questions that derive from our experience as sociological specialists. [14]

It would be inappropriate in this paper to discuss problems of historiography or the rules of validity and reliability of historical documents, but reference to Louis Gottschalk's outline in abbreviated form will serve to illustrate the kinds of source materials employed in this research.[15]

(a) Records contemporary to the times included bills, appropriations for prison construction, payment of salaries to guards and administrators, reception of fines and taxes, and commitments and discharges from prison. The *Archivio delle Stinche* falls into this classification. Training in problems of paleography was necessary in this case in order to read the more difficult passages. Handwriting was consistent for long periods of time, which was fortunate, but during a long period, such as that from *1301* to *1530,* many different hand writing styles inevitably appeared. It was necessary to learn an abundant number of Latin and Italian abbreviations common to amanuenses of the period. Many writing shortcuts do not appear in current dictionaries of medieval and Renaissance abbreviations, and it became necessary to rely upon an expert paleographer for assistance.[16] A sociologist cannot hope to master all the techniques, but repetition of terms and similarity of materials often results in sufficient delimitation of these problems so that he or she can overcome most of them.

(b) Confidential reports included journals, diaries, and personal letters. The diary of Landucci during the fifteenth century, for example, was immensely valuable. [17] Although the diary was used by chroniclers throughout the history of Florence for a variety of.selective purposes, it has not been fully exploited for its references to the crimes and punishments that Landucci knew, heard about, or saw himself. Other diaries, some of which were anonymous, appear to reflect accurately the social conditions of the times during which they were written. Several letters written by prisoners in *Le Stinche* to people outside were especially useful for descriptions of their crimes and the forms of treatment they received while in prison.

(c) Public reports, such as memoirs of important political figures, were useful, and some of the histories of Florence were in many respects autobiographical. Such is the case with Villani, [18] the famous chronicler, and Giovanni Cavalcanti,[19] who wrote much of his history of Florence while in the prison in 1427. In the Sala Tuscana of the Biblioteca Nazionale Centrale in Florence, there is a section devoted exclusively to official and unofficial histories of Florence and Tuscany. A considerable amount of time was spent going through 450 books in this section because most of these did not have indexes, and the books required careful reading in order to determine whether anything of value may have been mentioned relative to legislation, governmental structure, public and private morals, crimes and punishments, and prisons. Books on Florentine historiography were regularly consulted to determine which histories were no longer considered accurate and valid. Unfortunately, few books are devoted to the examination of crime and punishment as such in Florence. The works of Dorini,[20] Fiorelli,[21] and Beltrani-Scalia,[22] however, are extremely useful historical accounts.

(d) Governmental documents included proceedings of official bodies, laws, regulations, and municipal ordinances, administrative orders found in the records of the Podesta, the Capitano del Popolo, the Priors, Councils of the Signory, and in the *Consulti, Provvisioni,* and *Statuti.*

(e) Fiction, song, and poetry provided some insights, especially the satirical works of Berni[23] and Machiavelli,[24] both of whom wrote poems briefly describing their surroundings in *Le Stinche* while imprisoned there.

Sacchetti's novella, his short stories of public morals and punishments meted out for a variety of offenses, offered delightful descriptions of the times.[25]

THE CULTURAL SETTING[26]

There is no need to elaborate here the details of the rise of Florence to a position of political, economic, and artistic dominance. The facts are well known and documented, but some generalizations particularly pertinent to our main interests may be useful.

As Crane Brinton has graphically pointed out, the Early Renaissance and the Late Middle Ages are fused like a trainwreck in time. The Renaissance was less a time period than a mode of life and thought. Florence was the Athens of the continent, and during this period had reached a capitalistic stage of large investment, central provision of materials and machinery, a systematic division of labor, and control of production by the suppliers of capital. Almost all life was organized into guilds - the bankers, merchants, manufacturers, professional men and skilled workers. The seven guilds were known as *arti maggiori,* or greater guilds, whereas the minor trades were known as *arti minori.* Every voter had to be a member of one or another of these guilds; the nobles who had been disenfranchised in *1282* by a bourgeoisie revolution also joined the guilds to regain the vote. Members of the greater guilds constituted in politics the popolo grasso, the fat or well-fed people; the rest of the population composed the *popolo minuto,* or the little people.

The political history of Florence, like that of modern states, consisted of the victory of the business class over the land-owning aristocracy *(1293)* followed by the struggle of the working class to acquire political power. This struggle for power involved two social classes. The Ghibellines were a group associated with nobles and imperial rulers in Europe; the Guelfs were associated with the Comune, the People of Florence, and had loose but favorable ties with the papacy. The *Bianchi* (Whites) and *Neri* (Blacks) were divisions that occurred within the Guelf party, the former having become identified with the Ghibellines and the latter with the Guelfs. As the Guelfs struggled with the Ghibellines, exile, banishment, confiscation of property, mob violence, and public hangings became part of the political intrigues and machinations throughout the Renaissance.

But this was also the period of great artistic advancement: Ghiberti worked on the great bronze doors of the Baptistry; Masaccio gave new life and realism to painting with his frescoes in the Carmine church; and Brunelleschi raised the vast dome that surprised the architects of his day. Similarly, interest in antiquity flourished: two wealthy families-the Strozzi and the Medici-vied with each other in the collection of Greek manuscripts from the East, and the Strozzi brought from Byzantium the learned Manuel Chrysolaras to teach at the University of Florence. Finally, it was in 1434 that Cosimo de' Medici inaugurated that subtle, indirect personal rule that lasted for over a century and during which *"vivano le palle"* ("long live the balls")[27] was often heard.

In the Middle Ages, political power with religious sanction had prevailed; then came the era of an intellectually supported economic power. The spirit of capitalism began to rule and to replace the former divine element. For the sociologist, says Alfred von Martin, interest in the period lies in the fact that it presents him or her with the complete rhythmic progression of the ideal type of cultural epoch dominated by the bourgeoisie.[28] Because the mercantile and industrial capitalist elements asserted power over the master craftsmen and all others, Florence became an aristocracy of commerce. Social values came to be dominated by a money economy, and it was the power of money that lead Aeneas Sylvius in the early Renaissance to say, "Italy, always delighting in a new thing, has lost all stability . . . a servant may easily become a king."[29] The state itself became a capitalist entrepreneur, for business methods served political ends and political means served economic ends. Criminal and other types of legislation were dictated by bourgeoisie aims and interests; merchants and politicians began to calculate and plan, and politics took on the spirit of reason, which had been alien to the medieval state at a time when the church was the only guiding institution. The new governing class of the Florentine Commune, regardless of specific family or party changes, was built upon the foundation of the new money economy, the free development of individual forces, and the centralization of power. Almost all spheres of life were subjected to conscious and rational regulation, and the unifying factor, using Durkheim's dichotomy, was no longer an organic and communal one but a mechanical social organization.[30]

THE IDEA OF IMPRISONMENT AS PUNISHMENT

Although judicial torture, corporal punishments, and many executions occurred during this period, the idea of imprisonment as punishment *per se* and without corporal punishment was born and cultivated within the culture context of Renaissance Florence. Dungeons, prisons, and cells have always existed, of course, but generally not until the nineteenth century were prisons used for anything but detention of prisoners awaiting trial or execution after conviction. The Justinian *Digest* states: *"Carcer enin ad continendos homines non ad puniendos haberi debet"* ("Prisons exist only in order to keep men, not to punish them"). This was the dominant principle throughout the Middle Ages and until recent modern times in most countries.[31] There are probably isolated antecedent examples of imprisonment as a form of punishment, but the earliest known general usage

appeared in the Houses of Correction in Amsterdam beginning in 1596, and
in the Elizabethan Houses of Correction.[32]

The major evolutionary line of historical continuity of the
penitentiary idea and of the use of imprisonment as a form of punishment or
treatment of the offender can be traced through the charitable work and
institution of Filippo Franci [33] and the monastic cells described by Dom Jean
Mabillon in the seventeenth century;[34] the Hospice of San Michele in Rome
erected by Pope Clement XI; the *maison de force* developed by Vilain at
Ghent during the eighteenth century;[35] and the Pennsylvania, or separate
system, in the Eastern State Penitentiary in Philadelphia, along with the
Auburn, or silent system, in New York during the nineteenth century.

Evidence from the records of *Le Stinche* pushes back the use of
imprisonment as a form of punishment to the early fourteenth century. In the
Archivio delle Stinche may be found references to commitments of people
convicted of theft, homicide, gambling, robbery, rape, sodomy, and so forth,
for specific periods of time. Life imprisonment *("confinato a perpetuo
carcere")* was used frequently. Generally, judges in Florence, unlike those
elsewhere on the Continent, were given little or no latitude in the choice of
sentence because the type of punishment for particular crimes existed in the
penal statute books.[36] The rise of the Classical School of Criminology,
stemming from Cesare Beccaria's *Dei delitti a delle pene* (1764), it should be
remembered, occurred primarily because of opposition to the arbitrary
dispositions and sentences of judges-common pre-Classical phenomena that
returned to Florence only after the fall of the last Republic in 1530.

During the fourteenth and fifteenth centuries, however; crimes in
Florence were defined by and punishment came to be mitigated by
substitution of deprivation of liberty alone. Children and other relatives on
demand of parents, guardians, or the Comune could be imprisoned *"pro
amendare"* or *"pro correctione"* -an indication that imprisonment was
viewed both as a punitive and rehabilitative measure. In prison, the men were
separated from the women, the children from the adults, and the sane from
the insane, as indicated by the *provvisioni* (1296), which set up and
appropriated funds for the new prison. Prisoners were enclosed in separate
cells, with serious felons segregated from minor offenders, and heretics from
common-law violators. Imprisonment replaced corporal punishment for
bankruptcy and default on public or private debts. Unlike other parts of
Europe where people awaiting trial spent years under detention, the amount
of time in Florence was usually less than thirty days, and limited to thirty
days by statute. Release procedures were fully established by law, furloughs
and conditional releases were permitted, and commutation of death sentences
to five to ten years in prison was not uncommon. It is also of interest to note
that the scattered private buildings rented by the Comune as prisons to detain
the untried and those sentenced to death (the Bellanda, Burella, Paliazze and
Volognano) disappeared with the construction of *Le Stinche, the* municipal

prison in 1301 ordered built by the newly solidified, centralized political power.

Thus, the untapped *Archivio delle Stinche* has opened a new and earlier chapter in the evolution of punishment and provided the historical sociologist and penologist with abundant and fresh historical details regarding definite periods of imprisonment, the use of deterrence and even of reformation as a rationale for punishment. Deprivation of liberty, with many additional new concomitants, instead of deprivation of limb, was a Renaissance Florentine innovation. Only continuing historical research will determine whether Florence was positively the first place, and the fourteenth century the first time, that imprisonment was used as a social form of punishment *per se*. Research at present takes us back no further and to no other locale. In any case, the association between restriction of freedom as a means of punishing criminal offenders and the socio-cultural environment of a rising capitalist society appears undeniable.

THE SOCIOLOGICAL SYNTHESIS

Although culture case study is ideographic, the goal of historical analysis for the sociologist is, as Becker says,[37] toward the nomothetic pole, to try to generalize, to produce some kind of *Gesetzwissenschaften* ("legal science"). If it is true that punishment is used by society to the extent that it is acceptable to that society, then the introduction of sentences for definite periods of time, which occurred during the fourteenth century and markedly increased in the fifteenth century, are symptoms of the changing temper of the time.[38]

Social institutions generally do not move or change in a phalanx;[39] one or more basic institutions move into a position of cultural dominance for a period, but not without effecting change in other institutional structures and functions. Fundamental changes in the original structure of capitalism took place in the thirteenth and fourteenth centuries in Florence, and were felt in politics, religion, art, and in the social reaction to the criminal. The money economy of the *haute bourgeoisie* encompassed the idea of expediency, calculation, and planning, and the rationalism which was a more or less dominant feature of profit economy from the outset became absolute. As Arnold Hauser has suggested, the new element in the economic life of the Renaissance was "the consistency with which tradition was sacrificed to rationality and the ruthlessness with which all the resources of economic life were put into practical use and turned into an item in the ledger."[40] There was a new materialistic approach that estimated a person according to his or her achievement and his or her output according to its value in money.

The attitude of the merchant toward God was a reflection of the money economy. God was something like a business partner; and Giannozzo

Manetti could speak of God as the *"maestro d'uno trafico"* ("master of commerce"), for the world became analogous to a big firm [41] The religious emphasis on good works in Roman Catholic Florence implied that one could open an account with God. Villani regarded the giving of alms as a means of securing divine help almost by contract; the honoring of the contract was of the highest virtue in the code of the honest merchant. Similarly, the Comune opened a kind of contract with the criminal offender, who paid for his failure to abide by legal norms through punishment by fine or by time in prison.

The relationship between money, time, and punishment provides a meaningful "understanding" (in Weber's terms) of the Florentine innovation of imprisonment as a form of punishment for crime. Money, capital, and mobile property were linked together and, seen from this perspective, time was money. The power of space -the immobile soil- had been considered a conservative power, while time was now viewed as the great liberal power. In the Middle Ages, power belonged to the person who owned the soil, the feudal lord; but, in the Renaissance, Alberti in Florence could rightfully say that he who knew how to exploit time and money fully could make himself the master of all things.[42] In Simmel's framework, money and time imply motion; as he said:

> There is no more apt symbol than money to show the dynamic character of this world: as soon as it lies idle it ceases to be money in the specific sense of the word... the function of money is to facilitate motion.[43]

Money, because it circulates as landed property cannot, produced a new mobility in Florence.

Typical corporal punishments of the Middle Ages were static in nature. When a man's hands were cut off for forgery or stealing, his tongue removed for blasphemy, or his eyes gouged out for spying, there was an irrevocable "poetic" or symbolic punishment inflicted on the offender -a punishment that was static and constant both in the form it took on the person and in its meaningful nexus to the crime. However, beginning with the fourteenth century, punishment in Florence took on a more mobile, dynamic tenor. A period of time in prison is of this character. Punishment for failure to pay a debt was not uncommon throughout Europe, but the form it took was static and amounted in most cases to corporal punishment of some sort -the pillory, the carcan and so forth. In Florence, however, where time and money were closely allied, imprisonment for a determinate, calculated amount of time was a conceptually natural concomitant to one's failure to pay a civic or public debt. Thus, the more dynamic nature of time spent in prison replaced the staid quality of a corporal punishment, such as branding or a loss of a hand, that had permanently stigmatized an offender in the Middle Ages. Under social conditions that permitted greater mobility, an individual could overcome the past experience of imprisonment and still rise to a position of wealth and prominence without the scars of infamy.

Not only was time equated with money, but the tempo of life was likewise increased. Only then was there formulated a new interpretation of time as a value, as something of utility. Time seemed continuously to be slipping away, and it is interesting to note that only after the fourteen century did clocks in Italian cities of Tuscany strike all twenty-four hours of the day.[44] This changed conception of time viewed it as short and valuable, and one had to use it economically if one wanted to become the "master of all things." We are told that Antonius of Florence recognized time as "res pretiosissima et irrecuperabilis" ("a thing most precious and irrecoverable").[45] Such an attitude had been unknown in the Middle Ages when time was plentiful and there was no need to look upon it as something precious. It became so only when regarded from the viewpoint of the individual who could think in terms of the time measured out personally to him. It was scarce simply because of natural limitations, and thus everything had to move more quickly. The merchant or banker wanted his villa built quickly; whereas, in the Middle Ages, it had been possible to spend hundreds of years on the completion of a castle, town hall, or cathedral. Man was part of the all embracing unity during the Middle Ages, and life transcended its natural span. In the naturalism, individualism, and rationalism of the Renaissance, life and time began to move rapidly.

When time is so conceived as a major value, when time even in value terms is correlated with money, then the bourgeoisie that writes the laws and determines the punishments might naturally view a time of imprisonment as a just and sufficient punishment. Months or years out of a man's life rob him of a period of vitality, of social mobility, of opportunities for accumulating wealth. A man's labor is his time; a man's time is his money; and a punishment that takes both from him is consistent with the value system. Not all punishments were in the form of a prison term; however, corporal punishments still occurred, but less frequently. The most flagrant examples of earlier forms of corporal punishments came largely through the extra-legal methods used during riots, mob violence, and rapid changes in which political leaders punished their enemies.[46]

In the commitment records of Le Stinche there are many references to a quantum of time considered as equivalent to money. In the provvisioni, in the statuti, in the Reforma delle Stinche (1514) and elsewhere, repeated mention is made of the fact that a certain number of days is equal to a certain portion of money. If a man did not pay his debt in England or Germany, he usually suffered corporal forms of punishment. In Florence, he was sent to prison for a definite period of time and ways were found to help him pay his debt. The use of a determinate sentence also was employed for robbers, thieves, prostitutes, and other kinds of common-law offenders. So far as it is known, such careful calculations as those made by the councils and courts of Florence were among the first to be found in Europe.

In one sense then, each individual was a kind of temporal entrepreneur, a concept which truly coincided with the new capitalist attitude in economic affairs. Simmel discerns a causal relationship to the money economy when he says that "it is a money economy which for the first time created the idea of exact numerical calculation," and when he suggests that the "mathematically exact interpretation of the cosmos" is the "theoretical counterpart of a money economy."[47] As von Martin suggests, this method of interpreting the world by a number of mathematical equations, this way of regarding the world as a big arithmetical problem with absolutely impersonal, abstract, interchangeable, and measurable qualities presents a complete contrast to the more spontaneous and emotional attitude of the Middle Ages.[48] The "spontaneous and emotional attitude" is also descriptive of the earlier arbitrary sentences given by medieval judges. In a way that Beccaria was to suggest much later, Florentine criminal statutes expressed the sentiments, and prison commitment documents recorded the behavioral manifestations of these sentiments, regarding a calculated, impersonal, measurable amount of time or money as punishment for specific criminal offenses.

A feeling of liberty was part of the *Zeitgeist* ("spirit of the time") of early Renaissance Florence. In his description of this period, Jacob Burckhardt combines the idea of individualism with that of sensualism, the idea of self-determination of personality with emphasis on the protest against medieval asceticism, the gospel of the joy of life and "emancipation of the flesh."[49] Thus, restriction of liberty could now be considered a punishment commensurate with legal norm violation. We are contending, therefore, that a significant interrelationship existed between increasing individualism, the greater freedom- of movement in an urban democracy, the increasing sense of liberty (despite the presence of some slaves and occasional restrictions placed on Jews) and the birth of the concept of deprivation of liberty as a socially sanctioned and sufficiently severe punishment that began to replace corporal penalties.

Changes in the plastic arts and in architecture have been correlated with socioeconomic changes, and artistic innovations in the Early Florentine Renaissance were not unrelated to the cultural conception of crime and punishment. In his *Philosophy of Art* History, Arnold Hauser makes a trenchant comment directly related to our theoretical position:

> If one allows that some social preconditions of criminality can be found, it seems incomprehensible that one should not admit similar conditions of artistic production. The spiritual world of the artist may be incomparably more complex than that of the criminal, but as far as the relation between

individual freedom and social causation goes, there seems to
be no difference of principle between the creation of a work
of art and the commission of a crime.[50]

To approach Weber's *Verstehen* in an analysis of crime and
punishment during this period of Florentine history, the sociologist, it seems,
can turn with profit to art history. Florentine art was characterized, we are
told, by "limitation and order," "monumental forms and firm structures," and
the basic element in this conception of art was the principle of uniformity.[51]
With this line of reasoning, we are suggesting that penalties according to
statute instead of by judicial caprice symbolized an approach to penal
uniformity. Moreover, Hauser claims:

> The principles of unity which now become authoritative in
> art- the unification of space and the unified standards of
> proportions, the restriction of the artistic representation to
> one single theme, and the concentration of the composition
> into one immediately intelligible form-are also in accordance
> with this new rationalism. They express the same dislike for
> the incalculable and the uncontrollable as the economy of the
> same period with its emphasis on planning, expediency and
> calculability.... The things that are now felt as 'beautiful' are
> the logical conformity of the individual parts of a whole, the
> arithmetically definable harmony of the relationships and the
> calculable rhythm of a composition.[52]

In the new theory of punishment implicit in criminal codes, judicial
precedents, and prison records, Florence expressed these same sentiments of
calculability and an "arithmetically definable harmony." A calculated,
definite period of time spent in prison, when time was equated with money
and personal value, reflected the ethos as well as did the new art forms. The
conveying of an impression of depth by means of perspective in painting also
became something of a mathematical problem. That perspective remained
linear in Florentine art is related to the linear perspective toward punishment
for crime. Time is a continuum, and a specific term of imprisonment is a
legal linear perspective the Florentines embraced in their penalties.

Among the common factors that Simmel mentions in his analogy of
money and intellectualism are a "lack of tangible substance," "independence
of matter," and "a degree of impersonal objectivity that may be released in a
purely formal way and applied to any end."[53] Using this framework, we are
led to suggest that, whereas corporal punishment was dependent on matter,
and quite obviously, was manifestly personal and had a very tangle substance
implied in its use, the serving of time in prison possessed the characteristics

of impersonal objectivity, independence of matter, lack of tangible substance, and could be applied to any particular offender regardless of the offense.

FURTHER RESEARCH AND CONCLUSIONS

Further research is required to determine whether it is possible to project the generalizations contained in this analysis of Florence to any other time or locus. Sellin's study of the Amsterdam Houses of Correction, Rusche and Kirchheimer's analysis of punishment and the social structure, and the development of prisons in the United States in the nineteenth century suggest that historically, social structures dominated by emerging capitalism were associated with the use of imprisonment as a new form of punishment.[54]

The history of *Le Stinche* from this point on, the innovations introduced in the administration and treatment of prisoners, the poisition of the prison in the history of penology, an analysis of the records of commitment and discharge of offenders, changes in the criminal statutes, and an interpretive theoretical discussion of the relationship of these phenomena of crime and punishment to the culture milieu of the *Rinascimento* in Florence -all of these topics constitute significant areas for further examination. I shall conclude with a brief reference to the fact of the structure itself and what is remembered of it today.

For over 500 years *Le Stinche* occupied a large block of real estate -a quadrilateral area isolated from the rest of the city by a street on each side. Before the buildings inside the surrounding walls were torn down, the streets that bordered the prison were: Via *del Luvio* (east), *Via del Palagio* (north), *Via del Mercantino,* also called *San Simone* (west), and *Via del Lavatoi* (south).[55] On August *15, 1833,* Leopold II approved the sale of the prison, and the buildings were demolished. The Accademia Filarmonica and later the Teatro Verdi, which still stands, were architectural euphemisms that replaced the prison. The street names have changed over the course of time. After the destruction of the prison, *Via del Mercantino* was changed to *Via dell' Isola delle Stinche* as a reminder of the site of the former prison. Only *Via del Lavatoi* on the south retained its name when the other streets were changed to *Via Verdi* (east), *Via Ghibellina* (north), and *Via dell' Isola delle Stinche* (west).

From *Via Torta,* past the small square in front of the Chiesa di San Simone, toward *Via Ghibellina,* the name of *Stinche* has become a short street reminiscent of a long history, a small stretch of land instead of a large building, and an open area that recalls a former enclosure. From a Ghibelline fortress on the summit of a hill in Val di Greve to a prison of significance during the Early Renaissance, and finally to a contemporary street in Florence, the name *Le Stinche* has evolved and survived.

NOTES

---

[1] In this introductory statement, adapted to the topic under discussion, we have made use of Robert K. Merton's carefully stated qualifications, found in his study, "*Science, Technology and Society in Seventeenth Century England*" See Merton, *Science Technology and Society in Seventeenth Century England, IV* OSIRIS 360 (1938).

[2] Some specific details of the present topic may be found in Wolfgang, Political Crimes and Punishments in Renaissance Florence, 44 J. Grim. L., *Criminology & Police* SCI. 555 (1954), and Wolfgang, Socio-Economic Factors Related to Crime and Punishment in Renaissance Florence, 47 J. Grim. L., *Criminology & Police* SCI. 311 (1956).

[3] The idea that thought patterns are relative conditions arising out of the cultural and historical climate of a given area and time has been eloquently expressed by Louis Gottschalk. *See* Gottschalk, The Historian and the Historical Document, in *The Use of Personal Documents in History, Anthropology and Sociology 3* (Soc. Sci. Res. Council Bull. No. 53, 1945). Historicism, he suggests, "insists upon the relation of ideas to historical circumstances (including other ideas); it maintains that ideas are only 'reflex functions of the sociological conditions under which they arose." Id. at 25.

[4] J. Gillin, *Criminology and Penology* 9(1945).

[5] For a succinct discussion of the problems of historical analysis, especially problems of constructing hypotheses in a sociological study of history, see *The Social Sciences in Historical Study: A Report of the Committee on Histography* 66105 (Soc. Sci. Res. Council Bull. No. 64, 1954); Mandelbaum, History and the Social Sciences: Social Facts, in *Theories of History* 476-88 (P. Gardiner ed. 1959).

[4] Wolfgang, A Florentine Prison: Le Carceri delle Stinche, in *VII Studies in the Renaissance* 161-62 (1960).

[5] Niccolo Tommaseo and Bernardo Bellini suggest: "ltri forse dal ted. Stengel, gambale, peddle, tronco, o dal celt. gall. Stang, stecco brocco." ("Others, perhaps from the German, Stengel: leggings, pedals, trunk; or from the Celtic Gallic, Stang: dry twig.") *IV* N. Tommaseo, SC B. Bellini, *Dizionario Dellla Lingua Italiana* 1216 (1872). Nicola Zingarelli gives the root as a fusion of the Longobardian *skinko* and of *stecco*. N. Zingarelli, *Vocabolario Della Lingua Italiana* 1587 (1957). It should be recalled that the Lombards were one of the Teutonic tribes that invaded and settled in the Po Valley between 568 and 774.

[6] IV N. Tammaseo EC B. Bellini, *Dizionario Della Lingua Italiana* 1216 (1872).

[7] The name *Le Stinche* was applied first to the castle of the noble Cavalcanti family, then to the city prison, and presently only to a small Florentine street. Pareto's reference to non-logical action represented in "residues of aggregates," or, combinations once made tend to persist regardless of changes in time and space dimensions, provides an interesting theoretical framework for analysis of the etymology of *Le Stinche. See V.* Pareto, *Mind and Society* 11, 64-65 (A. Livingston trans. 1935).

[8] IV G. Villani, *Cronica* 187-207 (Firenze 1845) [hereinafter G. Villani].

[9] There is no treatise on penology in English that mentions Le Stinche, except a brief reference by John Howard, the English penal reformer, who visited the prison in the eighteenth century. See J. Howard, *The State of the Prisons in England and Wales* 108 (1792).

[10] For a careful description of this episode, see, e.g., P. Villani, *The Life and Times of Niccolo Machiavelli* 11, 32-33 (1878).

[11] A brief composite of documentary references to the torture of Machiavelli may be found in Wolfgang, Political Crimes and Punishments in Renaissance Florence, 44 J. *Crim. L., Criminology & Police Sci.* 555, 566-67 (1954).

[12] F. Flamini, *La Lirica Toscana Del Rinascimento* 546 (1891).

[13] Although the state archives of Florence contain reference to a provision passed by the Consiglio de' Cento for construction of the prison on March 12, 1297 *(Provvisioni, Archivo di Stato di Firenze,* 8, c. 51), the earliest records of the prison itself unfortunately were destroyed in the siege of the institution in 1343 during the popular overthrow of the government of the Duke of Athens. Consequently, there are no documents of commitments to the prison in 1304 when the first prisoners were housed there. The earliest date found among the commitment records of the *Archivio Belle Stinche is* for October 16, 1343 *("Inventario dei Magistrato dei Soprastanti alle Stinche").*

[14] Becker, *Culture Case Study and Greek History: Comparison Viewed Sociologically, 23* AM. Soc. REV. 489, 490 (1958) (citing M. Weber, Gesammelte Aufsatze Zur Sozial und Wirtschaftsgeschichte 280 (1924)).

[15] Gottschalk, The Historian and the Historical Document, in *The Use of Personal Documents in History, Anthropology and Sociology* 15-27 (Soc. Sci. Res. Council Bull. *No. 53,* 1945).

[16] A debt of gratitude is due Professor Gino Corti, Florentine archivist, for his paleographic assistance. Professor Corti is as known as the chief paleographer contributing to 1. Origo, *The Merchant of Prato* (1957).

[17] L. Landucci, *Diario Fiorentino* Dal 1450 AL 1516 (1883).

[18] G. Villani, supra note 8.

[19] G. Cavalcanti, *Istorie Fiorentine* (Firenze 1845).

[20] U. Dorini, *Il Diritto Penale e La Delinquenza in Firenze nel Secolo* XIV (1916) [hereinafter U. Dorini].

[21] P. Fiorelli. *La Tortura Giudiziaria Nel Diritto Comune* (1953).

[22] M. Beltrani-Scaliai, *Sul Governo e Sulla Riforma Delle Carceri* ;Torino 1867) [hereinafter M. Beltrani-Scaliai

[23] Opere di Francesco Berni 148-49 (1887).

[24] N, Machiavelli, *Opere 1076* (Milano n.d.).

[25] F, Sacchetti, *Il Trecentonovelle* (1956).

[26] It would be impossible to list here the histories of Florence that present in detail substantially the summary material used in this section. Any standard social history of the city is recommended; of particular value is F. Schevill, *A History of Florence From the Founding of the City through the Renaissance* (1936). Perhaps one of the most authoritive histories is R. Davidsohn, Forschungen Zur Geschichte von Florenz (1908).

[27] Three balls symbolized the Medici family.

[28] A. Von Martin, *Soziologie der Renaissance* (1992); A. Von Martin, *Sociology of the Renaissance* (w. Luetkens trans. 1944) [hereinafter A. Von Martin, *Sociology*].

[29] A. Von Martin, *Sociology,* supra note 28, at 5.

[30] E. Durkheim, *Division of Labor in Society* (G. Simpson trans. 1964).

[31] G. RuscHE & O. Kirchheimer, *Punishment and Social Structure* 62-71 (1939).

[32] For the Amsterdam Houses of Correction, see T. Sellin, *Pioneering in Penology* (1944); for those in England, see Van der Slice, Elizabethan Houses of Correction, 27 J. *Crim. L. & Criminology* 45 (1936).

[33] Sellin, Filippo Franci A Precursor of Modern Penology, 17 J. . *Crim. L. & Criminology* 104, 107-09 (1926).

[34] Sellin, Dom Jean Mabillon-A Reformer of the Seventeenth Century, 17 J. *Crim. L. & Criminology* 581 (1927).

[35] Sellin, The House of Correction for Boys in the Hospice of St. Michael in Rome, 20 J. . *Crim. L. & Criminology* 533 (1950).

[36] See, e.g., U. Dorini, supra note 20; M. Beltrani-Scalia, supra note 22, at 24.

[37] Becker, *Culture Case Study and Greek History: Comparison Vowed Sociologically, 23 Am.* Soc. REV. *489 (1958).*

[38] This statement is an adaptation of an earlier assertion in a different context found in Merton, *Science Technology and Society in Seventeenth Century England,* IV OSIRIS *360, 414 (1938).*

[39] P. Schrecker, *Work and History (1948)*. See especially Schrecker's Chapter XIII, "On Patterns, and the Influence of Knowledge on Their Function." Id. at *151*.

[40] A. Hauser, *The Social History of Art* 11, *24 (1957)*.

[41] A. Von Martin, *Sociology*, supra note 28, at 17.

[42] Id at 15 (citing A. Alberti, Della Familglia 137 (Mancini ed. n.d.)).

[43] Id. at 15 (citing G. Simmel, *Philosophie des Geldes* (n.d.)). General use is made of von Martin's sociological approach in this section.

[44] Cf. C. Cipolla, *Clocks and Culture*, 1300-1700 (1967.

[45] A. Von Martin, *Sociology*, supra note 28, at 86.

[46] Wolfgang, *Political Crimes and Punishments in Renaissance Florence, 44 J. Crim. L. & Criminology & Police Scf. 555 (1954)*.

[47] A. Von Martin, *Sociology*, *supra* note 28, at 21 (citing G. Simmel, *Philosophie des Geldes* (n.d.)).

[48] A. Von Martin, *Sociology*, *supra* note 28, at 21-22.

[49] J. Burckhardt, *The Civilization of the Renaissance in Italy* (1954).

[50] A. Hauser, *The Philosophy of Art History* 275-76 (1959).

[51] A. Hauser, *The Social History of Art* 10 (1957).

[52] Id. at 15.

[53] As summarized by A. Von Martin, *Sociology*, supra note 28, at 37-38.

[54] See supra notes 35 and 31, respectively.

[55] D. Guccerelli, *Stradario Storico Della Citta di Firenze* 258-59 (1928)

WE DO NOT DESERVE TO KILL

Marvin E. Wolfgang

This article was part of the 1996 Death Penalty Symposium and is reprinted with the permission of the Thomas M. Cooley Law Review. Parts 2 and 3 are adapted with permission from Marvin E. Wolfgang, "The Death Penalty: Social Philosophy and Social Science Research," Crim L Bull. 14 (18):18-25

Punishment that is Deserved

The major purposes of punishment historically have been retribution, expiation, deterrence, reformation, and social defense. Throughout history, an eye for an eye, the payment of one's debt to society by expiation, general deterrence of crime by exemplary punishment and specific or special deterrence of an individual offender, reformation of the individual so that he or she will not commit further crime, and protection of society against criminality by detaining or imprisoning offenders have been the principal rationales for the disposition of criminal offenders.

These rationales have not moved through history like a Roman army phalanx but have moved instead, as the historian Crane Brinton has said, "like a train-wreck in time, a telescoping of historical thought." Periods in history gave dominant position to each of these penal purposes. The Hammurabi Code was a brilliant civilization advance in 1700 B.C., with its emphasis on retribution, the call for talion, partly because it represented an attempt to keep cruelty within bounds.

But Hammurabi's code, we should remember, was not always the strict proportionality often attributed to it, that is, approximating the punishment to the crime. Professor James B. Pritchard (1955) from the University of Pennsylvania reminds us that if a noble destroyed the eye of another noble, his eye shall be destroyed; if he has broken the bone of another noble, "they shall break his bone"; and if he has knocked out the teeth of a noble "of his own rank, they shall knock out his tooth." But if the victim is not a noble, the punishment is a fine, as was the case of a commoner striking the cheek of a commoner. If a noble struck the cheek of a noble of higher rank, he received 60 lashes with an oxtail whip. Striking a noble of equal rank resulted in a fine. But if a slave struck a noble, off came his ear; if a son struck his father, they cut off his hand (Pritchard 1955, pp. 163-80).

The Law of Moses is usually claimed to be retributive, based on the principle of an eye for an eye, but as Princeton's Professor Walter Kaufman

(1973) points out, careful reading of Exodus, Leviticus, Numbers, and Deuteronomy may show that the phrase appears three times, but that the utilitarian notion of deterrence is also present, as in Deuteronomy: "The rest shall hear and fear, and shall never again commit any such evil in your midst" (Deuteronomy 19:20).

Moreover, it has been asserted that even with the rationale of retribution, with an effort to produce a kind of equilibrium or homeostasis, the meaning of an eye *under* an eye refers to the letters of the Hebrew alphabet, and the letters preceding the "eye," *ayian tachat ayian,* spell money, which is interpreted as monetary compensation or restitution to the victim by the offender.[1] The Talmud makes a clear effort to avoid the literal translation. Now this interpretation is, from my viewpoint, extremely important because it raises the issue of retributive equivalences. The claim is, therefore, that corresponding and proportional sanctions-that is, the punishment proportionate to the crime-even with precision are possible without requiring exactly the same pain. Similarity, not sameness, becomes the consequence of equivalences. This principle becomes more important with respect to the death penalty.

Although Socrates, through Plato and Aristotle, are more future oriented than past oriented relative to punishment, Plato, in particular, also refers to retribution as just desserts. Deterrence is future minded, meant to cause others or the same offender from committing crimes in the future. To punish an offender for what he or she has done and not what he or she might do in the future is, of course, past oriented. To punish one based on what he or she deserves to receive is retributive. Plato (427-347 B.C.) said, "Let the penalty be according to his deserts" (Hutchins 1952, Book 1X, pp. 743, 744).

Plato sounds quite modern:

> When a man does another any injury by theft or violence, for the greater injury let him pay greater damages to the injured man, and less for the smaller injury; but in all cases, whatever the injury may have been, as much as will compensate the loss. And besides the compensation of the wrong, let a man pay a further penalty for the chastisement of his offence: he who has done the wrong instigated by the folly of another, through the lightheartedness of youth or the like, shall pay a lighter penalty; but he who has injured another through his own folly, when overcome by pleasure or pain, in cowardly fear, or lust, or envy, or implacable anger, shall endure a heavier punishment.... The law, like a good archer, should aim at the *right measure* of *punishment,* and in all cases at the *deserved punishment.* (Hutchins 1952, Book IX, pp. 743, 744, emphasis added)

I should like to put the death penalty into this analysis.

Neither the absolute determinist nor the partial determinist should favor the death penalty for any reason. On examining Pythagorean, Epicurean, Stoic, Aristotelian, and Platonic views of determinism, one can see that only Plato fails the test of consistency. In Aristotelian terms, even a just man can act unjustly or be treated unjustly.[2] But Aristotle seems to skirt the issue of the penalty of death. He is a partial determinist when he speaks of voluntarism and involuntarism relative to passion connected to a man's sleeping with his neighbor's wife or striking the neighbor or his father:

> For a man might even lie with a woman knowing who she was, but the origin of his act might be not deliberate choice but passion. He acts unjustly, then, but is not unjust; e.g. a man is not a thief, yet he stole, nor an adulterer, yet he committed adultery; and similarly in all other cases. (Hutchins 1952, p. 339)

The inference to be drawn is that even when committing a crime - an unjust act - the person may nonetheless be just, and therefore punishment should be tempered.

Plato, I admit, is different. He is at once retributive in calling for punishment that is deserved and nods noticeably toward reformation. Hear him in Book IX of Laws:

> Such are the preludes which we sing to all who have thoughts of unholy and treasonable actions, and to him who hearkens to them the law has nothing to say. But to him who is disobedient when the prelude is over, cry with a loud voice - He who is taken in the act of robbing temples, if he be a slave or a stranger, shall have his evil deed engraven on his face and hands, and shall be beaten with as many stripes as may seem good to the judges, and be cast naked beyond the borders of the land. And if he suffers this punishment he will probably return to his right mind and be improved; for no penalty which the law inflicts is designed for evil, but always makes him who suffers either better or not so much worse as he would have been. (Hutchins 1952, p. 743)

However, he favors the death penalty for the "greatest of crimes," as the following passage from Book IX of Laws shows:

> But if any citizen be found guilty of any great or unmentionable wrong, either in relation to the gods, or his parents, or the state, let the judge deem him to be incurable,

remembering that after receiving such an excellent education and training from youth upward, he has not abstained from the greatest of crimes. His punishment shall be death, which to him will be the least of evils; and his example will benefit others, if he perish ingloriously, and be cast beyond the borders of the land. (Hutchins 1952, p. 743)

Hence, Plato claims cognitive, rational free will in committing an "unmentionable wrong." However, in the dialogues between Cleinias and an Athenian Stranger, beginning in Book IX of Laws, Plato recognizes, in the words of the Athenian Stranger, ignorance as a cause of crime.

A man may truly say that ignorance is a third cause of crimes. Ignorance, however, may be conveniently divided by the legislator into two sorts: there is simple ignorance, which is the source of lighter offenses, and double ignorance, which is accompanied by a conceit of wisdom; and he who is under the influence of the latter fancies that he knows all about matters of which he knows nothing. This second kind of ignorance, when possessed of power and strength, will be held by the legislator to be the source of great and monstrous crimes, but when attended with weakness, will only result in the errors of children and old men; and these he will treat as errors, and will make laws accordingly for those who commit them, which will be the mildest and most merciful of all laws. (Hutchins 1952, p. 748)

Plato's sense of retributive justice is very clear in a fuller passage from Book IX of Laws (Athenian Stranger speaking):

But if any one seems to deserve a greater penalty, let him undergo a long and public imprisonment and be dishonoured, unless some of his friends are willing to be surety for him, and liberate him by assisting him to pay the fine. No criminal shall go unpunished, not even for a single offence, nor if he have fled the country; but let the penalty be according to his deserts-death, or bonds, or blows, or degrading places of sitting or standing, or removal to some temple on the borders of the land; or let him pay fines, as we said before. (Hutchins 1952, p. 744)

Death and Retribution

There is no rationale of punishment or disposition of a convicted offender that requires the death penalty. No logic of any rationale leads ineluctably to the death penalty. What are these rationales? Retribution, expiation, the utilitarian notion of deterrence, rehabilitation, social protection, or defense. We know they are not mutually exclusive except in abstract analysis, perhaps not even in that.

Several of these I should like to dispense with quickly because either the argument of the rationale clearly does not lead to the death penalty, or the evidence required to support the argument for the death penalty is weak, inadequate, or inconclusive. Death is not expiatory for the offender, for expiation implies that the offender has atoned for his guilt and is now cleansed in this life so he is free to accept the grace of God or a God - surrogate in the name of the state. Rehabilitation also requires life to continue so the former offending person can be restored to a life of social conformity. Deterrence is an unproven case. The Committee on Deterrent and Incapacitative Effects, of the National Research Council, National Academy of Science, concluded, after extensive research on crime in general and the death penalty in particular, that "in summary, the flaws . . . lead the Panel to conclude that the results of the analyses on capital punishment provide no useful evidence on the deterrent effect of capital punishment" (Blumstein et al., 1978, p. 62). What is left? Social protection and retribution. But social protection is so closely linked to deterrence and the utilitarian position that we need not pursue it further. Moreover, the social protection argument can lead to the undesirable consequences of executing potentially "dangerous" violent offenders and those who, as in the case of the Soviet penal code of the late 1920 and early 1930s, are "socially dangerous" to the state, even though they may not have committed any other specifically designated capital crime.

Retribution would appear to contain the most reasonable logic leading to the death penalty. Part of the reasoning in retribution theory includes Hobbes's notion of establishing an equilibrium, of restoring the state of being to what it had been before the offensive behavior had been committed. Strict homeostasis cannot be achieved with the death penalty for, as we all know, the victim of a killing cannot be restored. Nor is the abstract sense of equilibrium satisfied by execution, that is, the lex talionis, eye for an eye, tooth for a tooth (see Pritchard 1955). For retribution requires pain equal to that inflicted on the victim, plus an additional pain for committing the crime, crossing the threshold from law-abiding to law-violative behavior (see Hutchins 1952, Book IX, p. 782).

The state's killing of a convicted offender, especially under the medically protective circumstances now used, is not likely to cause him as much pain as he inflicted on his victim. Even if the pain to each were the same, the second requirement of retribution is not met-namely, the pain to be inflicted for the crime per se. What then would meet the requirement? A torturous execution? Perhaps, but that solution conflicts with other attitudes in our society, particularly those concerned with physical assaults by or in the name of the state. Apparently, Western society considers corporal punishment an anathema of civilization. We permit the police to shoot at fleeing felons under certain circumstances, but even this act is discouraged unless life is endangered.[3] Physical force may be used to arrest a suspect. But once a suspect is arrested, we mount glorious attacks against any physical abuse of arrestees, detainees, and defendants. We decry inadequate diets and urge good medical care for prisoners. The philosophy of our health delivery system is such that we must present our sacrifice to the rationalization for death in good physical condition. The state has made efforts to reduce the suffering of death in most exquisite ways.

Thus, there is a strong cultural opposition to corporal punishment. Western society today would not tolerate, I am sure, cutting off limbs, gouging out eyes, or splitting the tongue. Even for murder, there would be opposition to "partial execution" (i.e., cutting off legs, cutting of the penis, etc.). If we cringe at the thought of eliminating part of the corporal substance, is it logical to eliminate the total corpus?

A principal part of the rationale of retribution is proportional sentencing. Beccaria, Bentham, and other rationalists recognized the principle. The "just deserts" or "commensurate deserts" model amply anticipates it. Beccaria's scales of seriousness of crime and severity of sanction were meant to be proportional. Equal punishment for equal crime does not mean that the punishment should be exactly like the crime but that the ratios of sanction severity should have a corresponding set of ratios of crime seriousness.

Moreover, punishment can or should be expressed in equivalences rather than in the same physical form of the crime. For example, we do not prescribe state-inflicted injuries for offenders who have injured but not killed their victims. It is not banal to argue this point because it is critical to the logic of capital punishment. If the victim has been assaulted and then treated by a physician and discharged or is hospitalized, the state does not exact the same penalty for the offender. We do not in the name of the state stab, shoot, throw acid, maim, or mug persons convicted of such aggravated assaults. Where, then, is the rational logic for retention of the death penalty for inflicting death?

Instead, equivalences in pain are sought in kind, not in physical exactitude. The common commodity of pain in our democratic society is deprivation of liberty over time, measured in days, months, and years. Other forms of deprivation are subsumed under this deprivation. It is but a reasonable extension of the equivalences between deprivation of liberty for crimes less than murder and the same deprivation for longer periods of time for the crime of homicide.

In the Beccarian mode, more can be said about the "pains of imprisonment." Death eliminates all. It does away with guilt, frustration, aspiration, achievement disparities, desires for unattained and unattainable things, anxieties, and fears. By execution, the state deprives itself of the functioning of these self-inflicted punishments and of those punishments derived from the deprivation of liberty. Death ends all pain, and the offender is punished no more.

By "slavery," Beccaria means the restraints that accompany imprisonment when he says,

> Were one to say that slavery for life is as sinful as death and therefore equally cruel, I would reply that, adding all the unhappy moments of slavery together, the former would be even worse, but these moments are spread over a lifetime, while the death penalty expends its total influence in a single moment . . . . Therefore the intensity of the punishment of penal slavery, as substitute for the death penalty, possesses that which suffices to deter any determined soul. I say that it has more. Many look on death with a firm and calm regard-some from fanaticism, some from vanity which always accompanies men beyond the tomb, some in a last desperate attempt either to live no longer or to escape misery-but neither fanaticism nor vanity dwells among fetters and chains, under the rod, under the yoke or in an iron cage, when the evildoer begins his sufferings instead of terminating them.[4]

The historical consequence of implementing a penalty "worse than death" has recently been described by Sellin, who said that Beccaria's "advocacy of penal slavery encouraged [in Austria, Hungary and elsewhere] the invention of horrid forms of imprisonment believed to be more deterrent than death" (Sellin 1977, p. 8). But the point I wish to emphasize is the psychological one made by Beccaria about pain that ends quickly with execution but lingers on with imprisonment. The issue is empirical, and the evidence today is little more than the 18th century could offer.

Beccaria also speaks of a punishment more deterrent than death that he thought he found in penal slavery, which in its very duration would be a constant reminder of the consequences of crime: "In the case of an execution a crime can furnish only one example to the nation, but in the case of lifelong penal slavery a single crime can provide numerous and lasting warnings"

(Sellin 1977, p. 4). In short, the speed and for us now the secrecy of death and the socially intended meaning of execution are of little moment in the minds of the survivors. We can identify only momentarily with death. But the lingering reminder of deprived liberty is more of a sustained constant. It is easier to identify with a living example than with a dead and past example of suffering.

There is one other comment I should like to make at this point about deterrence without reference to the social science literature on the topic. Relative to the death penalty, there seems to be a greater willingness by the U.S. Supreme Court to listen to and be affected by arguments about deterrence than by arguments about racial, social class, or sex discrimination. Deterrence may be related to protection of society and legally is a state interest issue, but it is not rooted to any article or amendment in the Constitution. Discrimination is tied to due process in the 5th and 14th Amendments, to impartial juries in the 6th Amendment, and to equal protection also in the 14th Amendment. Further claims of cruelty are linked with the 8th Amendment, as it is claimed that the death penalty is inflicted disproportionately on the poor and on Blacks. But, to repeat, deterrence has no immediately recognizable legal isomorphism in the Constitution. It is related to legislative intent but not to specific constitutional issues to be decided by judicial review.[5]

Failure Systems: A Socratic Dialogue

I should like now to introduce the notion of system failures as a sociophilosophical argument against the death penalty. The first is social system failure; the second is criminal justice system failure.

To some extent, this position is similar to Gabriel Tarde's reference that society has the criminals it deserves. The point is that the social system that has crime has failed to educate, to form, to socialize its citizens to conform to the pre- and proscriptions. Such failure may be nearly inevitable, may vary by degree, but nonetheless exists. Individuals may share some portion of failure, some responsibility for the crime, but a social system that is not totally just-in the sense expressed from Plato to Rawls, or in Marx and Engels-has also failed. Such failure denudes the state's right to take away the lives of its failures. The philosophy does not apply to crimes less serious than murder.

"But why not?" Socrates' pupil, Adeimantus, might ask.[6]

"Because," Socrates would say, "we still imply with punishment, even with retribution, a restoration to an earlier state and, simultaneously, or hoped for, reformation. Death precludes both the restorative and the rehabilitative functions of punishment. By execution the state has dramatically and clearly proclaimed its failure and shut off any chance of rectifying it. Moreover, execution is an unjust finality to the failure the state itself has caused."

The criminal justice system also fails, and this failure should prevent the punishment of death.

"But what about the premeditated murderer, or the hired killer?" questions Adeimantus. "Surely he knows what he is doing, and although society may have failed to educate him in the virtues, he does not respond properly to the fear of punishment and when he is caught should be used as an example to others. Execution will function in an exemplary way and serves the interest of education."

"Not so," says Socrates. "It is an unjust punishment because it is an unequal punishment. The premeditated murder is planned not out of fear of being arrested, but on the perceived or real probability of not being caught, convicted, and punished. The criminal justice system is not totally efficient. It fails to arrest, convict, and punish most criminal offenders and many murderers. The failure, the inefficiency of the criminal justice system to capture and convict *all* murderers, promotes the cognitive stance of the offender's willingness to risk the probabilities."

Adeimantus rises to the reasoning and responds with enthusiastic cogency: "Should not this selective efficiency then be used to justify the execution of the few who are caught?"

"But again I remind you of equal protection and due process," says his mentor. "For if the criminal justice system were totally efficient, all murderers would be caught and the certainty of punishment principle could be invoked to deter without having to resort to greater severity of punishment. If we view this drama as a probability game instead of a battle of right against wrong, of the mammoth power of the state, with law enforcement and the prosecutorial armamentaria, against the individual, the state should be expected to win, to capture its attackers. The capacity to capture only some offenders produces reduced risk in the game of the individual against the state. Hence, the more the system fails (low 'clearance' rates, low conviction rates), the more the burden of the death penalty falls on the few who are captured. Execution of the few is thus an inequity on all, the total universe, because of the failure of pursuit by the state."

"Again, this logic does not apply to less severe sanctions for less serious offenses because the punished offender, not executed, can be restored and permitted to play the game again."

Proportionality and Deprivation of Liberty

In 1764, Beccaria, in his classic book *Dei delitti a della pena,* wrote that there should be a scale of the seriousness of crime with a corresponding scale of the severity of sanctions (Beccaria 1963). In the Age of Reason in the 18th century, with an emphasis on the rationality of man, deterrence was the principal purpose of punishment. And Beccaria wrote poignantly about this rationale. One of his major statements - which surely has contemporary value - was that it is not the severity but the certainty of punishment that deters.

Despite Beccaria's focus on deterrence as the main purpose of punishment, the principle of proportionality between the gravity of the crime and the severity of the sanction, was an integral part of his philosophy and can be applied to the just deserts model. The principle of proportionality, equivalences, and punishment based on what is deserved all are now linked in a way that permits construction of a logical sequencing of scaling of sanctions. We need not agree with Professor Kaufman's (1977) assertion that there is no proportional punishment for raping a child or for treason or genocide, although admittedly these present difficult solutions.

Thomas Jefferson knew of Beccaria's essay and in his first inaugural address proposed what he called "Equal and exact justice to all men" (cited in Kaufman 1977, p. 223). In 1779, he drafted "A Bill for Proportioning Crimes and Punishments" (Padover 1943). For example, "Whosoever shall be guilty of rape, polygamy, or sodomy with man or woman, shall be punished, if a man, by castration, if a woman, by cutting through the cartilage of her nose a hole of one half inch in diameter at the least" (Padover 1943, pp. 95-96). He also wrote,

> Whosoever on purpose, and of malice forethought, shall maim another, or shall disfigure him, by cutting out or disabling the tongue, slitting or cutting of a nose, lip, or ear, branding, or otherwise, shall be maimed, or disfigured in *like sort:* or if that cannot be, for want of the same part, then *as nearly as may be,* in some other part of at least equal value and estimation, in the opinion of the jury, and moreover, shall forfeit one half of his lands and goods to the sufferer. (Padover 1943, 96)

Although some of what Jefferson says here may sound bizarre, he nonetheless nods in the direction of equivalences and proportionality.

I have tried to show elsewhere that sanctioning equivalences took an important step forward when, in 14th-century Florence, imprisonment became a form of punishment per se and essentially was meant to replace corporal punishments (Wolfgang 1960). Previously, prisons were used to detain defendants awaiting trial or awaiting flogging, branding, mutilation, exile, and banishment, but not as a punishment. In 1300, Florence opened its new prison, Le Stinche, and under the Ordinances of Justice of 1298 for the first time sentenced convicted offenders to the cells for definite, flat periods of time-without corporal punishment: 2 years for simple theft, 4 years for robbery, 4 years for sodomy (as I have found in the archives of the Uffizi for

Benvenuto Cellini, although he never served the term), and so forth (Wolfgang 1960, p. 150).

I have no time to develop this thesis here a la Jacob Burkhardt, or Georg Simmel with his theory of money, or Arnold Hauser on Renaissance art, but the thesis claims that moving from the other worldliness and timelessness of the Middle Ages to the this-worldly orientation, to an economy based on mercantile capitalism, to building the Pitti Palace during the lifetime of the Patriarch of the Pitti family, to the chiming of clocks in the city piazzas, to new concise perspective in art, to Petrarch's climbing of Mt. Vesuvius just for the view, all converged to make equivalences of man's labor, his time and his money. Moreover, there was an effort to promote new political freedom. When time, labor, and money can be equated, when liberty becomes a precious commodity, then deprivation of liberty for given and specific amounts of time can become a disutility and a proper and just punishment.

In 1790, the Walnut Street Jail in Philadelphia opened a wing that was designated as the state prison. On October 29, 1829, the famous Eastern State Penitentiary was opened for prisoners and the term *penitentiary* came into use, a place for prisoners to do penance. Here was born the so-called Pennsylvania System of punishment that, like its Florentine counterpart, used imprisonment for specific periods of time as punishment sufficient unto itself. No more whippings, no more brandings, ducking stools, or corporal tortures. Specific periods of time in prison became equivalences for the gravity of crime.

Conclusion

I have mentioned proportionality, equivalence, retribution, capital punishment, and deprivation of liberty because I have tried to show their linkages and that death is not a punishment required by any logically consistent philosophy.

I have drawn on ancient Greek scholars for ideas concerning punishment, including the death penalty, because early on they thoroughly explored these issues, long before society became involved in the complexities of the costs of capital punishment versus life imprisonment, before racial discrimination was an issue, before Bedau and Radelet (1987) gave us studies of innocents executed or sentenced to death, and before Sellin's studies of the lack of deterrence appeared before the Royal Commission on Capital Punishment (Her Majesty's Stationery Office 1953).

As we all know, the United States is alone among Western industrialized countries that retain the death penalty. And South Africa last year became the 42nd nation since World War II to abolish capital punishment and declare it unconstitutional. If we can pull the thinking of ancient scholars of more than 2,000 years ago into our century of the unjust administration of justice of laws that still permit our government to kill people with premeditation, we might be more humble, more respectful of the dignity of human life, however horrible the acts of the offender.

As Sister Helen Prejean (1993) has observed, "You could say, 'They deserve to die,' but the key moral question is, 'Do we deserve to kill them?'"

The philosophy of logic, ethics, and morality is surely the bulwark of opposition to the death penalty. But so are our emotions. Some time ago, the governor of Pennsylvania asked me to be a state witness to an execution. I hesitated at first. I had seen men next to me die in combat during the war. I was not a stranger to seeing death before me. I accepted the offer because I wondered if my cool, intellectual, and philosophical opposition to the death penalty was shared by my emotions.

I shall not describe the horribleness of an electrical execution. There are descriptions better than I could write. I wish only to report that death in wartime combat, as ugly as it is, has no parallel to the state's premeditated, highly organized, calculated death of a human being, however heinous his crimes. I was moved to a new emotional height of opposition to capital punishment upon witnessing a clearly violent, ugly, truly premeditated state killing.

The state of Michigan must be applauded for having abolished the death penalty a century and a half ago, the first political jurisdiction in the English-speaking world to do so (see Bedau and Radelet 1987) and for maintaining abolition despite political rhetoric for the penalty. Michigan was there even before Western Europe (Bedau and Radelet 1987). I salute you, Michigan, for your original stance and for your proper perseverance against the death penalty.

REFERENCES

Beccaria, Cesare. (1963). *On Crimes and Punishments.* Trans. Henry Paolucci. NY: Botts-Merrill. (Original publication, *Dei delitti a della pena,* in 1764)

Bedau, Hugo Adam and Michael L. Radelet. (1987). "Miscarriages of Justice in Potentially Capital Cases." *Stanford Law Review* 40 (21).

Blumstein, Alfred, et al. (1978). *Estimating the Effects of Criminal Sanctions on Crime Rates.* Washington, DC: Panel on Research on Deterrent and Incapacitation Effects, National Academy of Science, Deterrence and Incapacitation.

Her Majesty's Stationery Office. (1953). *Royal Commission on Capital Punishment, 1949-1953 Report.* London: Her Majesty's Stationery Office.

Hutchins, Robert Maynard. (1952.9) *Great Books of the Western World.* Trans. Benjamin Jowett. Chicago: Encyclopedia Britannica.

Kaufman, Walter. (1975). *Without Guilt and Justice.* NY: Dell.

Padover, Saul K., ed. (1943). *The Complete Jefferson.*

Prejean, H. (1993). *Dead Man Walking: An Eyewitness Account of the Death Penalty in the United States.*

Pritchard, James B. (1955). *Ancient Near Eastern Texts Relating to the Old Testament.* 2d ed. Princeton, NJ: Princeton University Press.

Pritchard, James B. (1977). "Retribution and the Ethics of Punishment." In *Assessing the Criminal: Restitution, Retribution, and the Legal Process,* edited by Randy E. Barnett and John Hagel III.

Sellin, Thorsten. (1977). "Beccaria's Substitute for the Death Penalty." In *Criminology in Perspective,* edited by Simha F. Landau and Leslie Sebba.

Tennessee v. Garner. (1985). 471 U.S. 1.

Wolfgang, Marvin E. (1960). "A Florentine Prison: Le Carceri delle Stinche." *Studies in the Renaissance,* 148-66. NY: Renaissance Society of America.

NOTES

[1] I am grateful to Edna Erez for bringing this use of the Hebrew alphabet and the interpretation by the Gaon Mevilna (the genius of Vilna) to my attention.

[2] See Aristotle, Nichomachean Ethics, in Hutchins (1952).

[3] See, for example, *Tennessee v Garner* (1985) (holding that deadly force may not be used to prevent the escape of a criminal suspect unless a significant threat of harm exists).

[4] This translation appears in Sellin (1977). A similar phrasing in English appears in Cesare Beccaria (1963), *Dei delitti a delta pena* which was originally published in 1764.

[5] The assertion that I have made here is buttressed by my dialogue with Louis H. Pollack, Dean of the Law School, University of Pennsylvania, and one of the leading constitutional lawyers in the United States.

[6] I have used Adeimantus here in the hypothetical dialogue with Socrates because Adeimantus was one of the delightful questioners in Plato's *Republic.*

OF CRIMES AND PUNISHMENTS*

Marvin E. Wolfgang

* *Introduction to Cesare Beccaria, Of Crimes and Punishments, New York, Marsilio Publishers, 1996. Reprinted with permission.*

Synopsis of the Work and Its Influence

I shall not elaborately summarize Beccaria's famous essay in this Introduction, though I hope the readers will absorb carefully every word of this, the most significant essay on crime and punishment in Western civilization.

Beccaria was an undistinguished economist and student of philosophy before he became involved in the Milanese salon of intellectuals in the seventh decade of the eighteenth century. He was born in Milan in 1738 and died in 1794. He was only 25 years old when he began writing *Dei delitti a delle pene*, which was published in Italian in 1764. Voltaire and Montesquieu were his predecessors in the philosophy of justice, and Beccaria acknowledged his indebtedness, especially to Montesquieu, when writing his simple, clear, enormously important essay.

His essay was read by Thomas Jefferson, Benjamin Franklin, and other Founding Fathers of the American Constitution. His essay was importantly involved in the Constitution and in several major Articles of the Amendments. Voltaire in his *Commentary* to the French edition of Beccaria's essay recommended it to his friends, many of whom held high office. Among his admirers were Pope Clement XIV, Emperor Joseph II of Austria, King Frederick the Great of Prussia, Empress Catherine II of Russia, King Gustaf III of Sweden, King Christian VII of Denmark, and King Stanislaus of Poland. Thomas Jefferson's *Commonplace Book* (1776) contains 26 extracts from Beccaria's essay, most quoted in the original Italian. When John Adams rose in Boston to deliver his famous speech in defense of Corporal William Wemms and five other British soldiers - accused of murder in the event that became known as the Boston Massacre - whom he defended successfully, his opening words were:

> May it please your honors, and you, gentlemen of the jury: I am for the prisoners at the bar, and shall apologize for it only in the words of the Marquis Beccaria: "If I can but be the instrument of preserving one life; his blessing and tears of

transport, shall be sufficient compensation to me for the contempt of all mankind."[1]

In France, Pastoret set up a list of 120 capital offenses and proposed a reorganization of the French laws following Beccaria's principles, favoring non-capital penalties.[2] Other French writers such as De la Madeleine, Marat and, later, Condorcet proposed similar arguments. Von Sonnenfels, a professor at Vienna, argued against torture and the death penalty, based on Beccaria's writings.[3]

Lord Mansfield, William Blackstone, and other leading eighteenth-century legal scholars praised Beccaria, but none more so than Jeremy Bentham, who wrote on Beccaria as follows:

> My master, first evangelist of reason who has raised thy Italy so much above England and also France... thou who speaketh reason on laws whilst in France they speak only jargon (which, however, is reason itself compared with the English jargon), thou who hast made such frequent and useful excursions in the paths of utility.[4]

In Russia Empress Catherine II tried unsuccessfully to have Beccaria visit her court. In 1766 she convened a commission and directed it to compile an all new criminal code, the *Instructions*, for which she wrote personally, in her own hand, clearly influenced by Beccaria. She said "every punishment which is not inflicted through necessity is tyrannical ...it is unjust to punish a thief who robs on the highway in the same manner as another who not only robs, but commits murder. Every One sees clearly that some difference ought to be made in their punishment, for the sake of the general safety "[5]

Catherine II became even more specific regarding the kinds of punishment and the method of its infliction, again drawing almost entirely from Beccaria:

All punishments, by which the human body might be maimed, ought to be abolished... the use of Torture is contrary to all Dictates of Nature or Reason; even mankind itself cries out against it, and demands loudly the total Abolition of it.

The Swedish parliament approved criminal law reforms on January 20, 1779 which were inspired by King Gustaf III, who admired Beccaria. Sweden abolished torture formally in 1786, having abandoned that practice years earlier.

On October 8-9, 1789 the constituent assembly in Paris approved the principles contained in the Declaration of the Rights of Man dated August 26, 1789, which originated from Beccaria's essay almost verbatim: "The law has the right to prohibit any actions harmful to society and the law shall inflict only punishments that are dearly necessary, and no one shall be punished, except in virtue of a law enacted before the offense and legally applied."[6]

Based upon Beccaria's essay, King Louis XVI abolished "preparatory" torture in 1780 and "preliminary" torture in 1788.

In 1785, Thomas Jefferson introduced a Bill of Proportion in Crimes and Punishments in Cases heretofore before the Virginia House of Delegates. He drafted the Bill in 1778 but even in 1785 it failed to pass the first time it was introduced, which Jefferson explained in his autobiography:

> Beccaria and other writers on crimes and punishments had satisfied the reasonable world of the unrightfulness and inefficiency of the punishment of crimes by death; and hard labor on roads, canals and other public works had been suggested as a proper substitute. The Revisors had adopted these opinions; but the general idea of our country had not yet advanced to that point. The Bill, therefore, was lost in the House of Delegates by a majority of a single vote. Meanwhile, the public opinion was ripening, by time, reflection, and by the example of Pennsylvania . . . in 1796 [the Virginia] legislature resumed the subject and passed the law for amending the penals of the commonwealth.[7]

In short, the influence of Beccaria's *Dei delitti a delle pene* was enormous in Europe, in Asia, and in the United States. The French rationalists, welcomed by Voltaire, proclaimed that his essay would assure the author immortality and would work a revolution in the moral world. Eminent writers in law and criminal reform, such as von Sonnenfels in Austria, Filangieri and Renzzi in Italy, and Blackstone, Bentham, and Romilly in England were very profoundly influenced by Beccaria's doctrines and freely acknowledged their indebtedness to him.

A Brief Biography

Let us now examine briefly the biography of this famous essayist. He was born Cesare Bonesana, Marquis of Beccaria, on March is, 1738. He died on November 28, 1794. According to Elio Monachesi, Beccaria became partially interested in mathematics but then dropped it and was unenthusiastic about scholarship in general. When his formal education was completed he returned to Milan, after which he developed an interest in philosophical works. He was inspired by Montesquieu's *Lettres Persanes* and in this satire on the political and religious institutions of Montesquieu's world he found something which he had so sorely missed before. This interest aroused him to read and digest the philosophical writings of others, especially those of the French Encyclopedists. He began to read extensively in the philosophical literature. His interest in penology and crime, however, was aroused by his friendly association with two stimulating and intellectually keen brothers in Milan, Pietro, and Alessandro Verri. Beccaria knew practically nothing about crime and punishment until he was selected by the intellectual salon to devote time to the topic. These two men, Pietro who was a well-known Italian economist, and Alessandro, who was a creative writer, enormously influenced Beccaria.

Beccaria's first published work appeared in 1762 and was entitled *Del disordine a de' rimedi delle monete nello stato di Milano nell' anno 1762*. This monograph dealt with the plight and remedies for the monetary system in the State of Milan. It was original but did not demonstrate that Beccaria possessed the ability to write clearly and forcefully.

With the assignment given to him by Pietro Verri in the intellectual salon of Milan, Beccaria, who knew nothing of penology, learned a great deal from Alessandro Verri, who held the office of Protector of Prisoners and was able to give Beccaria the help and the suggestions he needed. He began working on the essay in March 1763 and completed the manuscript in January 1764. It was first published anonymously in July 1764 when Beccaria was only twenty-six years of age. The essay was immediately acclaimed by almost all who read it. The fact that the essay was first published anonymously indicated that its contents were designed to undermine many, if not all, of the cherished beliefs of those in position to determine the fate of those accused and convicted of crime. His essay was a tightly reasoned and devastating attack on the prevailing systems for the administration of criminal justice. His essay aroused hostility and resistance from those who stood to gain by the perpetuation of what Beccaria considered to be the barbaric and archaic penological institutions of the day.

With the publication of *Dei delitti a delle pene*, Beccaria's literary ability came to an end. He visited Paris in 1766 at the request of Voltaire and others, and was appointed Professor of Political Economy in the Palantine School of Milan in 1768. He held this post for only two years. He delivered lectures on political economy that were collected and published in 1804, ten years after his death, and represent his only other major published creative work.[8]

His Treatise

His advocacy is clear. The essentials of the system which Beccaria recommended and which arose as the Classical School of Penology are the following: (1) All social action must be of the Utilitarian conception of the greatest happiness for the greatest number. (2) Crime should be considered as an injury to society and the only rational measurement of crime is the extent of this injury. (3) Prevention of crime is more important than punishment of crimes. Punishment is justifiable only on the supposition that it helps to prevent criminal conduct. (4) Secret accusations and torture should be abolished. There should be speedier trials. The accused should be treated humanely before trial and must have every right and facility to bring forward evidence in his behalf. (5) The purpose of punishment is to deter persons from the commission of crime and not to provide social revenge. It is not severity but the certainty and the expedition of punishment that bests secures this result of deterrence. (6) Punishment should be sure, swift, and penalties should be determined strictly in accordance with the social damage committed by the crime. Crimes against property should be punished solely by fines or imprisonment when the person is not able to pay the fine. (7) There should be no capital punishment. Capital punishment does not eliminate crime. Life imprisonment is a better deterrent. Capital punishment is irreparable and hence makes no provision for possible mistakes and desirability of later rectification. (8) Imprisonment should be more widely employed, but its application should be greatly improved through providing better quarters and by separating and by classifying prisoners by age and by degree of criminality.

Beccaria concluded his essay with considerable clarity and succinctness: "In order that every punishment may not be an act of violence committed by one man or by many against a single individual, it ought to be above all things public, speedy, necessary, and the least possible in the given circumstances, proportioned to its crime, dictated by the laws."

In view of a decade of an increasingly punitive public attitude in the United States toward crime and punishment, Beccaria's prescriptions and prohibitions are particularly pertinent today. His essay is part of Western history, but his words have a highly contemporary ring in the debates about prevention of crime and "getting tough" with criminals.

The recently passed federal crime act authorizing thirty billion dollars has a proportionate distribution of approximately eighty percent for construction of prisons, setting up "boot" camps, adding one hundred thousand new police officers, and making around fifty new crimes punishable by death. Only about twenty percent of the funds are scheduled for prevention programs such as Head Start, drug treatment, and other therapeutic measures. Most professional, research criminologists would reverse these proportions and put eighty percent into prevention.

Beccaria, I believe, would do the same, for he emphasized that prevention is more important than punishment. Moreover, were he with us today, he most likely would be appalled at the number and the types of crime carrying the death penalty because he was opposed to the death penalty altogether. In public opinion polls, a higher percentage than ever of the United States population, nearly eighty percent, are in favor of the death penalty. Those of us who are professionally and morally opposed to capital punishment still refer to Beccaria's arguments. His voice on this topic should be heard today by retentionists and abolitionists.

The criminal justice system should seek to increase the certainty and the celerity of arrest, conviction, and punishment is a continual goal since Beccaria's 1764 essay. His famous statement has engaged increasingly sophisticated empirical research for one hundred years on this complex hypothesis which he so succinctly and simply stated: It is the certainty not the severity of punishment that deters. Research consistently shows he is right. Research also shows across time and space, i.e., historically and cross-nationally, that the death penalty is not a deterrent; hence, from a utilitarian perspective, it is unnecessary and undesirable.

Beccaria thought that imprisonment should be used more widely when he wrote his essay. He meant that imprisonment, not corporal punishment, should be used and should replace both interrogatory and punitive torture. Prisons should be humane, have decent quarters, and not suffer from overcrowding are issues of current prison reform movements that echo the advice of Beccaria. He would, I am sure, oppose the recent re-introduction of the chain gang in Alabama as a "cruel and unusual" punishment, in violation of the Eighth Amendment.

He also called for separating prisoners by age, a juvenile justice reform request we still hear in most of our states today. There is some retrogression of correctional policy in the United States as more and more juveniles under age 18 are being transferred from the juvenile court to the criminal court, and are detained awaiting trial or who, upon conviction, are sentenced to prisons with adults. Here again, Beccaria showed a wisdom that current correctional policy still often fails to implement.

Beccaria's principle of proportionality between the seriousness of the crime and the severity of the sanction has inspired more than a few of us in criminology to engage in elaborate research on establishing a scale of crimes from the most serious to the least serious, based on samples of populations. A random representative sample of households in the United States, involving over fifty thousand interviews, has produced a Beccarian scale of the perceived seriousness of 204 offenses. [9] Other studies with smaller samples have addressed the same research issue, both on a scale of seriousness of crime and on a scale of punishments. Beccaria's request for such scales has most recently inspired the draft of a revision of the penal code of Puerto Rico which has been before the Puerto Rican senate. [10]

It is clear that Beccaria's remarks are not only part of our history, they are part of our present debate and deliberations. Rich in substance and language, his essay is as much with us and has as much influence today as it did in the eighteenth century.

It is a special pleasure for me to be involved in this new publication of Beccaria's essay, for I have been teaching its merits to thousands of students over the years. May this timeless essay renew the interest of those in criminal law, criminology, and the political and social sciences.

Early English-Language References to Beccaria

G. Chinard, ed. (1939). *The Commonplace Book of Thomas Jefferson: A Repertory of His Ideas on Government* 38-39.

"Etas Unis," prepared for the *Encyclopedie Methodique*. See S. Padover, ed. (1943). *The Complete Jefferson* 61.

L.H. Butterfield, ed. (1961). Diary and Autobiography of John Adams 352.

Gordon S. Wood. (1969). *The Creation of the American Republic 1776-1787* 300, 301, 303.

NOTES

[1] David A. Jones. *History of Criminology: A Philosophical Perspective*, Greenwood Press, New York; C. Kidder, History of the Boston Massacre 232 (1968).

[2] Pastoret des Lois Tenales (1790).

[3] J. von Sonnenfels. *Ueber die Abschassung dur Tortur*, Fr. tr. in J. Brissot to Warville (1783).

[4] From manuscript in University College, London, cited in E. Halevy, *La Formation du Radicalisme Philosophique* 30 (1901).

[5] See W. Reddaway, *Documents of Catherine the Great: The Correspondence with Voltaire and the Instructions of 1767*, 215-309, Eng. tr. of 1768. As quoted in David A. Jones, *History of Criminology*, op. cit.

[6] See K. Bar, *A History of Continental Criminal Law* 320 (1968).

[7] Padover, S. ed. *The Complete Jefferson*, 67 (1943).

[8] Elio Monachesi, "Cesare Beccaria" in Hermann Mannheim, ed., *Pioneers in Criminology* p. 49, Quadrangle Books, Inc., Chicago, (1960).

[9] Marvin E. Wolfgang, Robert M. Figlio, Paul E. Tracy, and Simon I. Singer. *The National Survey of Crime Severity*. Washington D.C.: U.S. Department of Justice, Bureau of Justice Statistics, 1985.

[10] See Dora Nevares Muniz. "Informe de Revision Codigo Penal de Puerto Rico." In *Revista Juridica de la Universidad Interamericana de Puerto Rico* Vol. XXVII, Num. 1, Septiembre-Diciembre 1992; Num. 2, Enero-Abril 1993. Santurce, Puerto Rico.